UNDERSTANDING SOCIAL SECURITY

UNDERSTANDING SOCIAL SECURITY

Issues for policy and practice

Second Edition

Edited by Jane Millar

First published in Great Britain in 2009 by

The Policy Press
University of Bristol
Fourth Floor, Beacon House
Queen's Road
Bristol BS8 1QU
UK

Tel +44 (0)117 331 4054
Fax +44 (0)117 331 4093
e-mail tpp-info@bristol.ac.uk
www.policypress.org.uk

North American office:
The Policy Press
c/o International Specialized Books Services (ISBS)
920 NE 58th Avenue, Suite 300
Portland, OR 97213-3786, USA
Tel +1 503 287 3093
Fax +1 503 280 8832
e-mail info@isbs.com

British Library Cataloguing in Publication Data
A catalogue record for this book is available from the British Library

Library of Congress Cataloging-in-Publication Data
A catalog record for this book has been requested

ISBN 978 1 84742 1 869 paperback
ISBN 978 1 84742 1 876 hardcover

Jane Millar is Professor of Social Policy and Pro Vice Chancellor (Research) at the University of Bath.

Cover design by Qube Design Associates, Bristol.
Front cover: photograph kindly supplied by www.alamy.com
Printed and bound in Great Britain by Hobbs the Printers, Southampton.

Contents

Detailed contents vii
List of tables, figures and boxes xiii
Acknowledgements xvi
List of abbreviations xvii
Notes on contributors xix

one Introduction: the role of social security in society 1
Jane Millar

Part One: Foundations and contexts

two Social security: reforms and challenges 11
Fran Bennett and Jane Millar
three Inequalities and social security 31
Tania Burchardt
four Life beyond work? Safety nets and 'security for those who cannot' work 55
Richard Silburn and Saul Becker
five Racism, ethnicity, migration and social security 75
Ian Law
six Governing social security: from protection to markets 93
Emma Carmel and Theodoros Papadopoulos
seven Social security in global context 111
Nicola Yeates

Part Two: Lifecourse and labour markets

eight 'From cradle to grave': social security and the lifecourse 133
Karen Rowlingson
nine Benefiting children? The challenge of social security support for children 151
Tess Ridge
ten Reforming pensions: investing in the future 171
Stephen McKay
eleven Welfare to work 193
Sharon Wright
twelve Sickness, incapacity and disability 213
Roy Sainsbury

thirteen	Tax credits *Jane Millar*	233

Part Three: Users and providers

fourteen	Service delivery and the user *Bruce Stafford*	255
fifteen	The 'welfare market': private sector delivery of *benefits* and employment services *Dan Finn*	275
sixteen	Social security and information technology *John Hudson*	295

Index 313

Detailed contents

one	**Introduction: the role of social security in society**	**1**
Types of benefits/income transfers		2
Expenditure and coverage		4
Reading this book		5
Social security?		6
References		7
two	**Social security: reforms and challenges**	**11**
Summary		11
The 'Fowler' reviews: 'meeting genuine need'		13
The Commission on Social Justice: 'modernising social security'		16
Challenges for the 21st century		20
Overview		24
Questions for discussion		25
Note		25
Website resources		25
References		26
three	**Inequalities and social security**	**31**
Summary		31
Framework for analysing inequality		32
Income inequality as an outcome		35
The impact of the tax–benefit system		39
Inequalities of process and of autonomy		46
Overview		50
Questions for discussion		51
Acknowledgements		51
Notes		51
Website resources		52
References		53
four	**Life beyond work? Safety nets and 'security for those who cannot' work**	**55**
Summary		55
Work and welfare		56
The 'safety net'		56
How did we get into this situation?		58
'Security for those who cannot' work		60
The evidence on 'security' and 'dignity'		62

Improving security and dignity? 63
The Social Fund 66
Assessment and conclusions 67
Overview 69
Questions for discussion 69
Website resources 70
References 70

five Racism, ethnicity, migration and social security 75
Summary 75
Introduction 76
Racism, welfare and human waste in the UK and Europe 76
Immigration policy and social security in the UK 77
Migration, settlement and social security 80
Ethnic diversity, racial discrimination and the delivery of benefits 83
Overview 87
Questions for discussion 87
Acknowledgement 88
Website resources 88
References 88

six Governing social security: from protection to markets 93
Summary 93
Introduction 94
Governance in the 'formal' policy domain of social security 95
Governance in the operational policy domain 99
Governing social security: Britain and the EU 103
Conclusion: the governance of social security 105
Overview 106
Questions for discussion 106
Notes 106
Website resources 107
References 107

seven Social security in global context 111
Summary 111
Social security and social protection 112
Social security around the world 113
Welfare regimes 118
Global social security policy 119
Overview 126

Questions for discussion 127
Notes 127
Website resources 127
References 128

eight 'From cradle to grave': social security and the lifecourse 133
Summary 133
Introduction 134
Changes in the lifecourse 134
Changes in economic risk 137
To what extent has the social security system adapted to these trends? 140
Changes in the risk of poverty from cradle to grave 142
What kinds of reform could provide support 'from cradle to grave'? 144
Overview 146
Questions for discussion 147
Website resources 147
References 147

nine Benefiting children? The challenge of social security support for children 151
Summary 151
Introduction: state support for children 151
Benefits for children: numbers in receipt and expenditure 153
Why does the state provide support for children? 154
The role of social security and tax credits in reducing child poverty 160
Benefiting children? The challenge of social security support for children 165
Overview 165
Questions for discussion 166
Notes 166
Website resources 166
References 167

ten Reforming pensions: investing in the future 171
Summary 171
Introduction 171
Sources of income in older age: an overview 172
The demand for pensions 180

Government policy since 1997	183
Remaining issues, gaps and problems	188
Overview	188
Questions for discussion	188
Notes	189
Website resources	189
References	189
eleven Welfare to work	**193**
Summary	193
Introduction	193
Understanding the context of welfare-to-work policies	194
The development of welfare-to-work policies in the UK	195
Discourse and desert: the social construction of 'benefit dependency'	202
Persistent tensions	205
Conclusion	207
Overview	208
Questions for discussion	208
Website resources	208
References	209
twelve Sickness, incapacity and disability	**213**
Summary	213
Introduction: social security for sickness and disability	214
The landscape of sickness and disability benefits	214
From 'passive' to 'active' welfare	217
Tensions and challenges	220
We are not alone – disability benefits in other countries	224
Future directions	226
Overview	230
Questions for discussion	230
Notes	231
Website resources	231
References	231
thirteen Tax credits	**233**
Summary	233
The start of in-work benefits in the UK: Family Income Supplement	234
'Making work pay': Working Families' Tax Credit	237
Tax credits from 2003: Child Tax Credit and Working Tax Credit	240

Tax credits and welfare reform	247
Overview	247
Questions for discussion	248
Notes	248
Website resources	248
References	249
fourteen Service delivery and the user	**255**
Summary	255
Introduction	255
Users	256
The difficulties that users have encountered	258
Service transformation?	260
Delivery by local authorities	266
Consumers or users?	267
Overview	268
Questions for discussion	269
Website resources	269
References	270
fifteen The 'welfare market': private sector delivery of benefits and employment services	**275**
Summary	275
Introduction	275
Public sector reform and the role of the private sector	277
The New Deals and Jobcentre Plus	279
Contracting with employment programme providers: the transition to job outcome payments	280
The welfare market	283
The risks involved in contracting out employment services	285
Welfare markets in Australia and the US	288
Overview	290
Questions for discussion	290
Website resources	290
References	291
sixteen Social security and information technology	**295**
Summary	295
Introduction	295
Dry and technical?	296
A new development?	297
Back to the future	298

ICTs and social security: the opportunities 300
ICTs and social security: the threats 304
Overview 308
Questions for discussion 308
Web resources 309
References 309

List of tables, figures and boxes

Tables

1.1 Income maintenance in the UK: types of provision 3
3.1 Income inequality between households at various stages from original to post-tax income, 2005/06 41
3.2 Original, gross and disposable incomes by income quintile group and gender 42
3.3 Original, gross and disposable incomes by income quintile group and ethnic group 43
3.4 Original, gross and disposable incomes by income quintile group and age group 45
3.5 Original, gross and disposable incomes by income quintile group and disability status 45
7.1 Selected features of meta-regimes 119
8.1 Trends in marriage in England and Wales, 1961–2005 135
9.1 Number and % of children living in poverty since Labour came to power in 1997 164
10.1 The 'dependency ratio', 1971–2061 181
10.2 Comparative picture of public pension costs: projected spending on public pensions as a percentage of GDP 182
11.1 Welfare to work in Britain: main measures since 1997 196
12.1 Sickness and disability benefits 215
12.2 Classification of sickness and disability benefits based on purpose and eligibility conditions 216
13.1 Family Income Supplement, selected years 1971–79 235
13.2 Family Credit, selected years 1988–96 236
13.3 Working Families' Tax Credit, 1999–2002 240
13.4 Working Tax Credit and Child Tax Credit, provisional awards, 2003–08 242
13.5 Tax credits: in-work families with children, provisional awards, 2008 243

Figures

3.1 Model of the determinants of substantive freedom, highlighting the role of social security 34
3.2 Shares of total income by quintile group: UK households, 2005/06 36
3.3 Distribution of men and of women by income quintile group (adults aged 18 or over in single-adult households only) 37
3.4 Distribution of ethnic groups by income quintile group 38
3.5 Distribution of age groups by income quintile group 38
3.6 Distribution of disabled and non-disabled people by income quintile group 39
3.7 From 'original' to 'post-tax' household income 40
8.1 Births by marital status, 1971–2001 136
10.1 Income distribution of couple pensioners, 1999/2000 179
10.2 Population of the UK, 2008 (thousand people per five-year age group) 180
12.1 A typology of disability policies in OECD countries, c. year 2000 225
12.2 Changes in OECD countries' disability policies, 1985–2000 226

Boxes

2.1 Alongside Fowler: debating social security reform in the 1980s 14
2.2 Alongside the CSJ: debating social security reform in the 1990s 17
2.3 Challenges for social security 21
3.1 Building blocks of the Equality Measurement Framework 32
3.2 Measuring incomes 35
4.1 The social security 'safety net' 57
4.2 The erosion of officer discretion 60
4.3 The meaning of 'security' 61
5.1 Immigration and social security since 1997 79
6.1 Visions of social security 95
7.1 Social security and the 1948 Universal Declaration of Human Rights 114
8.1 Summary of changes in lifecourse patterns since the mid-20th century 137
8.2 Summary of changes in economic risks since the 1970s 139
9.1 State provision for children 152

9.2 Possible aims of social security support for children 154
9.3 Changes to social security and fiscal support for children since 1997 161
10.1 Multi-pillar pension arrangements 174
10.2 Failure of trust in pensions? 177
10.3 Major pension reforms since 1997 184
11.1 Work first versus human capital development 199
11.2 Constructing 'dependency' as the problem and paid work as the solution 203
12.1 Comparing disability policies (OECD, 2003) 224
13.1 Tax credits in the US, Australia and Canada 238
13.2 The administration of tax credits – issues and problems 245
14.1 Size of the user base 257
15.1 Employment Zones 281
15.2 Job outcome and performance targets 282
16.1 The advantages of online information 300

Acknowledgements

This is the second edition of *Understanding social security*. The original book was inspired by the Department of Social Security/Department for Work and Pensions Summer Schools. We remain grateful to the students who have, over the years, helped us to think about the issues involved in the design and delivery of social security support in the UK.

For various reasons, three of the authors from the first edition were unable to contribute to this second edition – Alex Bryson, Karen Kellard and Lucinda Platt. We are grateful to them for their generosity in allowing us to draw on their chapters from the first edition.

Thanks to Karin Silver at the University of Bath for her help in putting this typescript together. Thanks to Alison Shaw at The Policy Press for persuading us to write a second edition and to her colleagues – Jessica Hughes, Kathryn King, Jo Morton and Emily Watt – for their support and efficient work.

Jane Millar
Centre for the Analysis of Social Policy
University of Bath
June 2008

List of abbreviations

ASEAN	Association of South-East Asian Nations
ASW	Allied Steel and Wire
AVCs	Additional Voluntary Contributions
BA	Benefits Agency
CAP	Common Agricultural Policy
CB	Child Benefit
CCTC	Child Care Tax Credit
CPAG	Child Poverty Action Group
CS	Child Support
CSA	Child Support Agency
CSJ	Commission on Social Justice
CTB	Council Tax Benefit
CTC	Child Tax Credit
DLA	Disability Living Allowance
DPTC	Disabled Person's Tax Credit
DSS	Department of Social Security
DWP	Department for Work and Pensions
EEA	European Economic Area
EITC	Earned Income Tax Credit
EMA	Education Maintenance Allowance
ES	Employment Service
ESA	Employment and Support Allowance
EU	European Union
EZ	Employment Zone
FRS	Family Resources Survey
FSA	Financial Services Authority
GDP	Gross Domestic Product
GIS	Geographic Information System
HB	Housing Benefit
HBAI	Households Below Average Income
HMRC	Her Majesty's Revenue & Customs
IB	Incapacity Benefit
ICT	information and communication technology
IGO	international governmental organisation
IIDB	Industrial Injuries Disablement Benefit
ILO	International Labour Office
IMF	International Monetary Fund
IS	Income Support

ISA	Individual Savings Account
ISSA	International Social Security Association
IT	information technology
JSA	Jobseeker's Allowance
LSC	Learning and Skills Council
MDG	Millennium Development Goal
MERCOSUR	Southern Core Common Market
MIG	Minimum Income Guarantee
MIHL	Minimum Income for Healthy Living
MP	Member of Parliament
NA	National Assistance
NAB	National Assistance Board
NACAB	National Association of Citizens Advice Bureaux
NASS	National Asylum Support Service
NDDP	New Deal for Disabled People
NDLP	New Deal for Lone Parents
NDLTU	New Deal for the Long-Term Unemployed
NDYP	New Deal for Young People
NIRS	National Insurance Record System
NMW	National Minimum Wage
OECD	Organisation for Economic Co-operation and Development
OMC	Open Method of Coordination
ONS	Office for National Statistics
PAYG	pay-as-you-go
PPS	Purchasing Power Standards
PSA	Public Service Agreement
PSIC	person subject to immigration control
S2P	State Second Pension
SADC	Southern African Development Community
SB	Supplementary Benefit
SDA	Special Delivery Agreement
SERPS	State Earnings Related Pension Scheme
TEC	Training and Enterprise Council
UAE	United Arab Emirates
UB	Unemployment Benefit
UN	United Nations
USAID	United States Agency for International Development
VAT	Value Added Tax
WFTC	Working Families' Tax Credit
WHO	World Health Organization
WTC	Working Tax Credit

Notes on contributors

Saul Becker is Professor of Social Policy and Social Care, and Director of Research at the School of Sociology and Social Policy, University of Nottingham. He is a former Chair of the Social Policy Association (2004-08). He has researched and published extensively on issues concerned with poverty, social security, informal care and carers. His main research interests now lie in the area of care and caregiving, particularly children who are carers ('young carers'), and he is currently directing a number of research projects in this field. He is the Series Editor for The Policy Press 'Understanding Welfare' book series. www.saulbecker.co.uk

Fran Bennett is Senior Research Fellow at the Department of Social Policy and Social Work, University of Oxford. Her research interests include poverty, social security and gender. She is currently researching (with others) the 'compliance costs' of benefits and tax credits, and within-household inequalities and public policy in the Gender Equality Network. She is also, with Professor Jonathan Bradshaw, an independent expert on social inclusion for the European Commission. www.spsw.ox.ac.uk/staff/academic/profile/details/bennett.html

Tania Burchardt is Senior Research Fellow at the Centre for Analysis of Social Exclusion, London School of Economics and Political Science. Her research interests include theories of social justice, definitions and measurement of inequality and social exclusion, and welfare and employment policy, especially with respect to disabled people. She is Editor of *Benefits: the Journal of Poverty and Social Justice* and Co-editor of the *Journal of Social Policy*. http://sticerd.lse.ac.uk/case/staff/person.asp?UserID=802

Emma Carmel is Lecturer in Social Policy at the University of Bath. She is a member of the executive board of the European Social Policy Analysis Network, and is a former Editor of the *Journal of European Social Policy* (2002-08). Her research interests are in theories of governance and the governance of public and social policy in the UK and the European Union. www.bath.ac.uk/soc-pol/people/profiles/emma-carmel.html

Dan Finn is Professor of Social Inclusion at the University of Portsmouth and Associate Director at the Centre for Economic and Social Inclusion. Dan has written extensively on the reform of public employment services and implementation of welfare-to-work strategies and has a particular interest in 'welfare markets' in the UK, the US, the Netherlands and Australia. He has been a special advisor for parliamentary inquiries and has undertaken many commissioned research projects. www.port.ac.uk/research/ceisr/members/title,62373,en.html

John Hudson is Lecturer in Social Policy at the University of York. He is co-author of *Understanding the policy process: Analysing welfare policy and practice* (second edition, The Policy Press, 2009) and *The short guide to social policy* (The Policy Press, 2008). His current research focuses on the social impacts of the 'information age' and the role political institutions play in shaping social policy reforms. www.york.ac.uk/depts/spsw/staff/hudson.html

Ian Law is Founding Director of the Centre for Ethnicity and Racism Studies (CERS) and Reader in the School of Sociology and Social Policy, University of Leeds. Key works include *Racism, ethnicity and social policy* (Harvester, 1996), *Race in the British news* (Palgrave, 2002), *Institutional racism in higher education* (Trentham Press, 2004, ed with L. Turney and D. Phillips), *Racist futures* (Ethnic and Racial Studies, 2007, ed with S. Sayyid) and *Racism and ethnicity, a global analysis* (Pearson, 2009). www.sociology.leeds.ac.uk/about/staff/law.php

Stephen McKay is Professor of Social Research at the University of Birmingham. He has conducted research on the living standards of families with children, on the effects of the social security (and tax credit) system, and on pensions. Recent works include *Attitudes to pensions* (DWP, 2007), *Debt and older people* (Help the Aged, 2008) and *Levels of financial capability in the UK* (FSA, 2006). www.benefits.org.uk/pubs.htm

Jane Millar is Professor of Social Policy and Pro Vice Chancellor (Research) at the University of Bath. Her research interests include social security policy; poverty, inequality and social exclusion; family policy and the policy implications of family change; gender and social policy; and comparative social policy. www.bath.ac.uk/soc-pol/people/profiles/jane-millar.html

Theodoros Papadopoulos is Director of the European Research Institute and Lecturer in Social Policy at the University of Bath. His research interests include the governance of social security in Britain, cross-national analysis of labour protection policies and the social dimension of EU integration. www.bath.ac.uk/soc-pol/people/profiles/theodoros-papadopoulos.html

Tess Ridge is Senior Lecturer at the University of Bath. Her research interests include childhood poverty and social exclusion, and policies for children and their families. In particular, her research examines how children fare within the policy process, and how best to formulate policies that truly benefit them, including social security policies and Child Support. Her current research (with Jane Millar) explores the lives of children and lone parents in low-income working households. www.bath.ac.uk/soc-pol/people/profiles/tess-ridge.html

Karen Rowlingson is Professor of Social Policy and Director of Research at the School of Social Policy, University of Birmingham. Her research interests include: social security and taxation policy; personal finances; poverty and inequality; wealth and asset-based welfare; and family change. Her teaching interests cover all these fields as well as qualitative and quantitative research methods. www.iass.bham.ac.uk/staff/rowlingson.pdf

Roy Sainsbury is Professor of Social Policy and Assistant Director at the Social Policy Research Unit, University of York, with over 20 years' experience in social research. In recent years he has specialised in the areas of employment, sickness and disability benefits, and mental health. He has a particular interest in the reform of social security and in 2007 acted as a Specialist Advisor to the House of Commons Select Committee on Work and Pensions for their inquiry into benefit simplification. http://php.york.ac.uk/inst/spru/profiles/rs.php

Richard Silburn was Senior Lecturer in Social Policy at the University of Nottingham. His long-standing research interests are with issues of poverty and social security. He is the co-author of *Poverty: The forgotten Englishmen* (Penguin Books, 1970). He and Saul Becker have worked together for nearly 30 years, and (with other colleagues) established the journal *Benefits*, now published by The Policy Press as the *Journal of Poverty and Social Justice*.

Bruce Stafford is Professor of Public Policy at the School of Sociology and Social Policy, University of Nottingham, and Co-convenor of the International Centre for Public and Social Policy. He has undertaken extensive research on social security, including the New Deal for Disabled People, the contributory principle, Housing Benefit administration and the delivery of benefits. His research interests are policy evaluation, the administration and delivery of welfare services, welfare to work, and the links between social security and specific client groups, notably disabled people. www.nottingham.ac.uk/sociology/people/atoz.php?id=ODA2NTgy&page_var=personal

Sharon Wright is Lecturer in Social Policy at the University of Stirling. Her research interests are in the processes of making and implementing social policy, service delivery, unemployment, active labour market policies, social security and poverty. Her teaching specialisms are in understanding social policy; gender, work and welfare; poverty, income and wealth; and qualitative research methods. Sharon is Managing Co-editor of the journal *Social Policy & Society* and Co-convenor of the Scottish Social Policy Network. www.dass.stir.ac.uk/staff/showstaff.php?id=61

Nicola Yeates is Senior Lecturer in Social Policy at the Open University. She has published widely on matters of globalisation, migration and social policy. Among her recent publications are *Globalization and social policy* (Sage Publications, 2001; Italian translation published in 2005), *Understanding global social policy* (The Policy Press, 2008, editor), *Social justice: Welfare, crime and society* (Open University Press, 2008, co-edited with J. Newman), and *Globalising care economies and migrant workers: Explorations in global care chains* (Palgrave, 2009). She is Editor of *Global Social Policy: journal of public policy and social development* (Sage Publications). www.open.ac.uk/socialsciences/staff/people-profile.php?name=Nicola_Yeates

Introduction: the role of social security in society

Jane Millar

Social security policy and provision have a long history and are embedded in our society in many ways. Millions of people are reliant on social security benefits for all or part of their incomes and any changes to social security policy have a very direct effect on their incomes and living standards. Social security forms the largest single component of government expenditure, providing a mechanism for the pursuit of both economic and social goals. The UK is a very unequal society, with high levels of poverty, and the social security system is one of the most important instruments for income redistribution. This redistribution can take different forms, including vertical redistribution (from richer to poorer) and horizontal redistribution (across people in different circumstances, from childless people to those with children, for example). Social security also plays an important role in helping to smooth incomes over the lifecourse, with people making contributions or withdrawals depending on circumstances and need. And social security provisions may have an impact on how people live their lives, in their decisions about jobs, about savings, about retirement, about family formation and about family dissolution.

There are a number of different goals that can be identified for social security policy, both immediate (for example, to replace earnings lost because of unemployment, to meet the additional costs arising from disability, to contribute to the costs of raising children) and ultimate (for example, to eliminate poverty, to create a more equal society, to create a more socially just society). Debates about policy goals are debates about different ideologies of welfare, about the role of the state and the responsibilities of citizens, and about the causes of poverty (Deacon, 2002; Welshman, 2006). These questions are raised and answered by countries in different ways at different times, with social security systems playing an important economic and social role in countries around the world (Clasen, 2002; Walker, 2005).

Reform of the social security and tax systems has been at the heart of the Labour government's aspirations to modernise the welfare state since 1997. The various policy reforms introduced are explored in detail in the chapters in this book and include:

- articulating new principles and setting new goals;
- introducing labour market programmes for wider categories of claimants;
- significant institutional change;
- the introduction of tax credits to replace some social security benefits;
- greater conditionality affecting eligibility for benefits.

Reforms and debates over the nature and impact of social security in society look set to continue, whichever political party is in power in the future. The aim of this book is to provide a critical examination of social security policy and practice, to provide the information and analytical tools to make sense of these policy debates and developments.

Types of benefits/income transfers

Table 1.1 summarises the main features of the UK income transfer system. This shows three main types of benefit, differentiated by the method of funding and the main conditions for receipt.

Universal, or *categorical, benefits* are funded by general taxation, they take no account of income and are paid to those who fit the designated category (for example, Child Benefit [CB] for all children).

Social insurance, or *contributory, benefits* are funded by contributions from workers, employers and the government, and cover interruptions or loss of earnings for specified reasons (retirement, unemployment, sickness and, for women, widowhood).

Social assistance, or *means-tested, benefits* are funded by general taxation and are paid to people with low incomes, taking account of their particular circumstances and family situation. These include benefits for people with no other sources of income as well as various other benefits intended to meet particular needs (for example, housing costs) or circumstances (for example, low wages, large families).

In addition to these three main types of benefit, there are also *tax-based* and *occupational* income transfers. The former use the tax, rather than the benefits, system as the vehicle for making the income transfer. These have become an increasingly important part of the income transfer system in the UK in recent

Table 1.1: *Income maintenance in the UK: types of provision*

Social security				**Tax system**		**Occupational system**		
'Universal'/ contingent or categorical benefits (non-means-tested/non-contributory)	**Social insurance benefits** (contributory)	**Social assistance benefits** (selective/means-tested)			**Fiscal benefits** (tax allowances/ exemptions)	**Employment-related benefits**		
		Regulated schemes	*Discretionary schemes*	*Tax credits*		*Statutory*	*Non-statutory*	*Private (contracted out)*
Child Benefit	Retirement Pension and Second State Pension	Income Support/ Disability and Pensioners' Minimum Income Guarantee/Pension Credit		Working Tax Credit	Personal Allowance	Statutory sick pay	Occupational sick pay/ maternity or paternity pay/ health insurance benefits	Personal pension plans
Disability Living Allowance/ Attendance Allowance	Jobseeker's Allowance				Exemptions on pension contributions	Statutory maternity/ paternity pay	Occupational pensions	Stakeholder pensions
Carer's Allowance	Incapacity Benefit	Social Fund		Child Tax Credit				
Industrial injuries and war pensions schemes	Bereavement benefits	Housing Benefit	Discretionary housing payments					

Source: Adapted from Dean (2002, Table 5.1)

years. Occupational benefits are paid by employers, for example occupational pension schemes, but regulated by government. They also include some schemes that employers are obliged to provide, such as statutory sick pay and statutory maternity pay. The *prime market* also plays a role, particularly in respect of pensions, with membership of private pensions schemes encouraged by state subsidies and regulated by government.

Finally, it should also be noted that the *family* plays a major role in income transfers and that defining family obligations – who should be required to support whom – is an important aspect of social security policy. The assumption that married women would be financially dependent on their husbands was, for example, central to the postwar National Insurance (NI) benefit system. Married women were largely excluded from these benefits on the grounds that they could rely on their husbands for financial support. Married men received allowances for their wives as dependants. This established a particular structure that had wide-reaching and long-term implications for gender divisions. Family means tests, as for Income Support and tax credits, are based on the assumption that families are single economic units, sharing income and needs in common (Bennett, 2002).

Expenditure and coverage

Public expenditure on benefits and tax credits is a significant element in total expenditure. In 2006/07, the government was spending about £119 billion on benefits (DWP, 2008), distributed as follows:

- £4 billion on benefits for children;
- £37 billion on benefits for people of working age;
- £78 billion on benefits for people over working age.

In addition, expenditure via HM Revenue & Customs (HMRC) included about:

- £10 billion on Child Benefit;
- £5.7 billion on tax credits for children in non-working families;
- £14.6 billion on tax credits for working people.

This amounts to about £30 billion, giving a total of about £150 billion on income transfers through the social security and tax systems.

In terms of numbers of recipients, in 2006/07 there were about:

- 7 million families receiving Child Benefit for about 12.9 million children;

- 1.5 million people receiving Incapacity Benefit (IB);
- 2.1 million people receiving Income Support (IS);
- 0.8 million people receiving Jobseeker's Allowance (JSA);
- 2.5 million people receiving Housing Benefit (HB);
- 11.7 million people receiving the basic state pension;
- 2.7 million people receiving Pension Credit;
- 1.4 million non-working people receiving tax credits for children;
- 4.6 million working people receiving tax credits.

These include some of the most vulnerable people in society, but, as noted above, social security is not just about the poor – it affects everyone in society across the whole lifecourse.

Reading this book

The various chapters in this book examine key issues in policy and, in different ways, cover issues of policy goals, programme design and implementation, outcomes and impacts. This is a book about the 'how' of administration as much as it is about the 'why' of policy, not least because elegantly designed policies, tackling important goals, are of no value if they cannot be put into practice. Each chapter is organised in the same way, starting with a brief summary of the contents, and including an overview at the end with questions for discussion and a full list of references for further reading.

The book is divided into three main parts. Part One explores 'Foundations and contexts'. In Chapter Two, Fran Bennett and Jane Millar discuss social security reform and the way that key social security challenges have been defined. In Chapter Three, Tania Burchardt explores different forms of inequality and considers the effectiveness of social security policy at addressing inequality and poverty in society. In Chapter Four, Richard Silburn and Saul Becker focus on the 'safety-net' role of the social security system and specifically the extent to which the system has provided security for people outside the labour market. In Chapter Five, Ian Law discusses issues of racism, ethnicity, migration and social security policy. The final two chapters in Part One place UK policy developments in wider comparative context. In Chapter Six, Emma Carmel and Theodoros Papadopoulos analyse the governance (policy goals and operational structures) of social security in the UK and discuss how this relates to developments in the European Union (EU). In Chapter Seven, Nicola Yeates explores key issues in social security policy in the global context.

Part Two covers 'Lifecourse and labour markets'. In Chapter Eight, Karen Rowlingson examines the aspiration to provide social security 'from cradle to grave' and discusses what this means in the context of changing social and economic risks across the lifecourse. In Chapter Nine, Tess Ridge analyses social security as it affects children and in particular explores the key policy goal of eradicating childhood poverty. In Chapter Ten, Stephen McKay tackles the other end of the lifecourse, outlining policy choices and dilemmas in the provision of pensions, which are the largest single component of social security expenditure. The final three chapters in Part Two focus on support for working-age people. In Chapter Eleven, Sharon Wright examines welfare-to-work policies and provisions. In Chapter Twelve, Roy Sainsbury looks at benefits for sickness, incapacity and disability. And in Chapter Thirteen, Jane Millar discusses tax credits.

The focus of Part Three is on 'Users and providers'. In Chapter Fourteen, Bruce Stafford provides an overview of changing modes of delivery and the impact of these on claimants and staff. In Chapter Fifteen, Dan Finn analyses the increasing role of the private sector in the delivery of benefits and employment services. And in Chapter Sixteen, John Hudson explores social security and information technology.

Social security?

As pointed out in the first edition of this book, the term 'social security' may seem increasingly outdated. There is no longer a government department with this name, and the tax system is increasingly being used to deliver income support measures. Thus, it could be argued that the phrase 'social security' is no longer a good way to encapsulate the institutional arrangements for policy making about, and the delivery of, income transfers. However, we argued then, and still believe now, that the phrase 'social security' captures other important issues, apart from institutional arrangements. The word 'social' indicates that this is a shared system. We are all part of it – as contributors, as recipients, as taxpayers, as citizens – and social security provisions involve various forms of redistribution that are an expression of our values as a society and our commitments to social and economic justice. The word 'security' highlights an important value, which is that people should not be simply at the mercy of the market, but should be enabled to meet needs now and plan for the future. The conditions that create the need for income security, for some assurance that our lives will be protected from the vagaries of economic and social change, take different forms today compared with the 1940s (when Beveridge devised his plan for NI and allied services), or the 1900s (the start of old-age and widows pensions), or the 1830s (the time of the new Poor Law workhouses) or the 1600s (when the Elizabethan Poor Law was classifying different types of 'paupers'). But the need for such security is as strong, if not stronger, than ever.

References

Bennett, F. (2002) 'Gender implications of current social security reforms', *Fiscal Studies*, vol 23, no 4, pp 559-84.

Clasen, J. (2002) *What future for social security? Debates and reforms in national and cross-national perspective*, Bristol: The Policy Press.

Deacon, A. (2002) *Perspectives on welfare ideas, ideologies and policy debates*, Buckingham: Open University Press.

Dean, H. (2002) *Welfare rights and social policy*, London: Pearson Educational.

DWP (Department for Work and Pensions) (2008) *Benefit expenditure tables*, London: DWP, www.dwp.gov.uk/asd/asd4/medium_term.asp

Walker, R. (2005) *Social security and welfare: Concepts and comparisons*, Maidenhead: Open University Press.

Welshman, J. (2006) *Underclass: A history of the excluded, 1880–2000*, London and New York: Continuum.

Part One
Foundations and contexts

Social security: reforms and challenges

Fran Bennett and Jane Millar

Summary

Social security reform has been at the centre of successive Labour governments' policy agendas since 1997 and reform proposals are still being brought forward. This chapter explores the challenges of social security reform, setting the scene for the more detailed discussion of specific issues and groups that follows in later chapters. Social security systems are large and complex and whole system reform is very difficult, if not impossible, to achieve in practice. But the way in which problems are defined is fundamental to the types of solutions that are proposed and adopted. This chapter:

- analyses two previous examples of attempts to define the challenges facing the social security system and to promote particular policy solutions: the Conservative 'Fowler' reviews of the early 1980s and, 10 years later in the early 1990s, the Labour 'Commission on Social Justice' (CSJ); and
- discusses how the key challenges for social security policy are currently being defined.

The purpose of this chapter is to explore some of the different ways in which the challenges facing the UK social security system have been defined, setting the scene for the more detailed discussion of specific issues and groups that follows in later chapters. We do this in two ways: first, by examining two specific

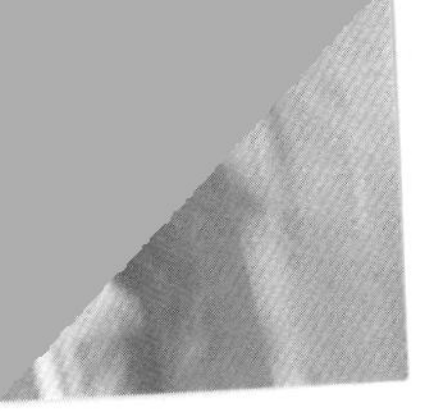

examples of major reform proposals that were put forward, in the 1980s and the 1990s; and, second, by discussing current and emerging challenges for the future. Social security systems are large and complex and whole system reform is very difficult, if not impossible, to achieve in practice. Policy makers very rarely have a clean slate on which to draw their ideal system unrestricted by obligations to current and past claimants and existing administrative structures. The possibilities envisaged for the future also tend to be strongly influenced by the principles and ways of thinking that have shaped what already exists. These sorts of factors can lead to a 'path dependency', which acts as a brake on radical reform. Policy is thus more likely to move forward along a road of incremental change, although there is much debate in the literature about the roles of institutional context and political values in shaping trajectories of both development and retrenchment (Pierson, 2001; Clasen, 2005).

One way that politicians and policy makers can seek to create or accelerate change is through setting up specific reviews, inquiries or commissions, either to examine specific issues or to conduct a wider overall review. The Beveridge Report (1942) was the product of one such fundamental review, which was set up during the Second World War, with the remit to look ahead to the postwar needs for social security (Timmins, 2001). We start this chapter by examining two other substantial attempts to define and articulate the social security 'problem' and on that basis to identify and promote particular policy solutions. In the early 1980s, Margaret Thatcher's Conservative government was adopting an increasingly radical approach to welfare state reform and in the so-called 'Fowler' reviews (named after the then Secretary of State for Social Services) promised the 'most substantial examination of the social security system since the Beveridge report' (House of Commons *Hansard*, 2 April 1984, cols 652-660, cited in Timmins, 2001, p 397). In the early 1990s, the Labour Party was still in opposition and searching for new policies, and the then leader of the party, John Smith, set up the Commission on Social Justice (CSJ) in 1992 with a brief to carry out an 'independent inquiry into social and economic reform in the UK' (CSJ, 1994, p ix).

An editorial in the *Financial Times* (23 July 2008) describes two elements as 'compulsory' in any effort to re-shape Britain's welfare system: 'first, the reforms must be described as radical and far-reaching. Second, there must be an assertion that it fits with the views of William Beveridge.' Both of these reviews in addition were explicit attempts to shift ways of thinking about social security policy and practice. The reviews need to be understood in the context of their time, in respect of not only the economic, social and demographic context but also the political values and ideologies that inspired them. Here we explore how these reviews were set up, and describe their remit and membership; and we discuss the key challenges and problems that they identified. (For a wider history of social policy over this period see Page, 2007.)

The 'Fowler' reviews: 'meeting genuine need'

The Fowler reviews, established by the Conservative government, were initially four separate reviews. The first, announced in November 1983, was into pensions; and the second, announced in February 1984, into Housing Benefit (HB). Then, in April 1984, the reviews of benefits for children and young people and Supplementary Benefit (SB) were announced. Some review teams were chaired by government ministers, and the teams were supported by civil servants who coordinated the responses to the various reviews 'behind the scenes'. The main report was published as a Green Paper in three volumes, the first setting out the case for reform, the second setting out the programme for change and the third providing a set of background papers (DHSS, 1985a, 1985b, 1985c). A report on HB was published separately (DHSS, 1985d). A White Paper, *Reform of social security: Programme for action*, was published by the end of the same year (DHSS, 1985e).

Lister (1989, p 201) has argued that the Fowler reviews cannot be understood without reference to the 'wider political, ideological and economic concerns' that helped to shape them. As the first White Paper on public spending from Margaret Thatcher's 1979 Conservative government stated, 'public expenditure is at the heart of Britain's economic difficulties' (HM Treasury, 1979, p 1). Public spending was seen as crowding out private investment; and social security, as the biggest item of public spending, was a prime target. Margaret Thatcher herself, in an interview in the US in January 1984, talked about the 'time bomb' of social security spending (Sharples, 1985, p 15). The reviews were clearly nil cost, with the Treasury as the principal actor in the process of social security reform (Lister, 1989). There was also concern that benefits that were too high or easy to get could tempt people into 'dependency' rather than self-reliance. The stagflation of the 1970s was still very close; inflation appeared to be a greater threat than unemployment; and governments could not provide full employment, but could only help price people back to work (Deacon, 1991). Murray's (1984) book, *Losing ground*, claimed to show that some benefits could do more harm than good, by incentivising people to behave in ways inimical to their long-term interests. Timmins (2001) describes ministers as 'obsessed' with the 'why work' syndrome, despite the huge increase in unemployment due to economic restructuring and job losses in the manufacturing sector in particular. By the early 1980s, there was also widespread popular imagery of 'scrounging' and abuse in the social security system (Golding and Middleton, 1982) and the number of anti-fraud staff was increased (Lister, 1991).

Thus, there was concern about the supposed negative impact of social security on the economy and on individual behaviour. Various ideas for reform were being promoted from a range of political perspectives (see ***Box 2.1***). Some commentators at the time characterised the social security system as though it was largely unchanged since Beveridge's scheme of 1942. In reality, a number of changes had been made over the 40 years that had elapsed. In particular, in the 1960s, earnings-related contributions and benefits were introduced and the means-tested national assistance scheme became SB (to which claimants had a legal right). In the 1970s, various new benefits were introduced including Child Benefit (CB), a more substantial second-tier pension, disability benefits, HB and in-work benefits for low-waged families. Nevertheless, the Beveridge system remained the touchstone against which the Fowler reviews set the analysis of the problems with the current system.

Box 2.1: Alongside Fowler: debating social security reform in the 1980s

Norman Fowler claimed that 'the debate is not *whether* social security should be reformed but *how* it should be reformed' (DHSS, 1985e, Preface). Certainly, a plethora of publications in the mid-1980s set out principles and plans for tax and/or benefits reform. These included:

- *The structure of personal income taxation and Income Support* (1983), written by the Treasury and Civil Service Select Committee.
- *Of benefit to all: A consumer review of social security* (1984), published by the National Consumer Council for the four UK Consumer Councils.
- *The reform of social security* (1984), written by Dilnot et al (of the Institute for Fiscal Studies).
- *Social security after Beveridge: What next?* (1984), written by Ashby for the National Council for Voluntary Organisations.
- *Omega Project: Social security policy* (1984), written by the Adam Smith Institute.
- Supplement to the journal *Economic Affairs* (1984), edited by Minford.
- *Not just for the poor* (1986), written by the Church of England Board for Social Responsibility.

Alongside discussions about principles and goals, the key issues debated in these publications included the efficient targeting of social security, options for the integration of tax and benefits, how to improve work incentives and reduce benefit 'dependency', how to simplify the system, and the role of private provision (especially for pensions).

The Green Paper *Reform of social security* (DHSS, 1985a, p 1) starts dramatically with the words: 'To be blunt, the British social security system has lost its way'. The achievements of the system are set out in terms that relate almost entirely to the role of social security in relieving poverty (its success in terms of raising the living standards of the poorest, providing a safety net in cases of urgent need and improving the position of the most vulnerable groups), which suggests a narrow view of the objectives of social security (see Chapter One, Millar, this volume). But, it is argued, these achievements are far outweighed by the cumulative disadvantages of rising costs, failure to target those in greatest need, confusion and complexity, and lack of clarity about goals. Thus, in chapter six of the Green Paper, entitled 'Facing up to the future', the challenges that the government needs to address are set out as: ensuring long-term affordability, more effective targeting of need, simplification of the system, modernisation of administration and creating conditions for personal independence. The last of these is described as 'most important of all' and summarised as:

> [T]he Government believe that social security must be designed to reinforce personal independence, rather than extend the power of the state; to widen, not restrict, people's opportunity to make their own choices; to encourage, not discourage, earnings and savings. There is an important role for the state but there is also one for the individual. We want to create a new partnership between the two. (DHSS, 1985a, pp 18-19)

The subsequent White Paper also starts with a flourish: 'The case for reform of social security is overwhelming' (DHSS, 1985e, p 1). It summarises again the 'clear and fundamental defects' in the system: complexity, failure to support needy groups, the trapping of people in poverty and unemployment, the lack of freedom of choice, and doubts about the long-term affordability of the system. The policy proposals that follow focus on three key areas, each concerned with containing costs and with more effective targeting. First, the means-tested system of out-of-work benefits would be reformed, with Income Support (IS) replacing SB, including a much tighter system of controls over extra payments (see Chapter Four, Silburn and Becker, this volume). Second, in order to improve work incentives the system of in-work benefits for low-paid families would be extended in coverage and increased in level, and renamed as Family Credit (see Chapter Thirteen, Millar, this volume). Third, perhaps the most radical proposal was for the abolition of the state second tier pension – the State Earnings Related Pension Scheme (SERPS) – consequently creating a greater role for private provision in pensions, although this proposal was later modified, with the value of SERPS being halved instead (see Chapter Ten, McKay, this volume).

These reforms were introduced in the 1986 Social Security Act and implemented in 1988, just after the most substantial of the tax-cutting budgets of the Thatcher era. As Hills (1988, p 13) argued, 'cuts in direct taxes have been entirely paid for by cuts in the generosity of benefits ... there has ... been a major redistribution from those on low incomes to the better off'. The 1986 Act was, of course, just part of a wider set of changes to social security brought in by the Conservatives in the 1980s and 1990s.[1] Some commentators have argued that both the remit and the specific outcomes of the Fowler reviews were relatively limited and that Norman Fowler's claim that this was the most substantial examination of social security since the Beveridge Report was somewhat overblown. Lister (1989) points out that this was by no means a comprehensive overview of the system as a whole, more of a hotchpotch addressing just some elements. The reviews were also largely silent on a number of important issues, even though these were increasingly apparent as problems for the social security system. They included the issue of women's access to, and support from, social security benefits. Reforms in the 1970s had removed most of the direct discrimination from the system, but outcomes for men and women remained very different (Glendinning and Millar, 1987). Women were less likely than men to have individual entitlement to National Insurance (NI) benefits, including pensions. One particular group of women – lone mothers – was already very visible on the political radar, with an increasingly hostile and negative discourse about their lack of responsibility and benefit 'dependency' (Kiernan et al, 1998). But there was nothing specifically about lone parents in the Fowler reviews, and the key relevant measure of the Conservative government – the 1991 Child Support Act – emerged a few years later.

Both Evans (1996) and Glennerster (2000) conclude that the main impact of the reviews at the time was simply to churn up the incomes of the poorest, with some gaining and some losing. Unemployed and childless people, especially single people under the age of 25 not living with parents or others, lost out and there were only very marginal gains for families with children and pensioners (Dilnot and Webb, 1989; Timmins, 2001). So the direct impact was less than had been intended, or hoped for, by the government. On the other hand, however, the reviews did mark an important development in social security policy by making means-tested benefits the fulcrum of the social security system (Lister, 1991). This marked a significant step in the ongoing shift away from the system based on contributory benefits that Beveridge had designed.

The Commission on Social Justice: 'modernising social security'

Unlike the Fowler reviews, which were set up by the government then in power, the CSJ was established by the Labour Party in opposition. The remit was broad – to carry out an 'independent inquiry into social and economic reform in the UK' (CSJ, 1994, p ix) – and so social security was part of the review, rather than being the sole focus. The Conservative government had implemented a series of benefit reforms in the 1980s and 1990s, including many cuts, and had in 1992 announced a long-term review of state spending. Labour had been defeated again in the 1992 election; this was blamed by many on its shadow Budget, which proposed increases in CB and pensions, paid for by extra NI contributions. This was when the CSJ was set up by the late John Smith, then Labour leader. Timmins (2001, pp 491-2) comments that 'the welfare state and its purposes were in question on both sides of the political divide'. Again, this can be seen in the various reform proposals being put forward at the time (see ***Box 2.2***).

Box 2.2: Alongside the CSJ: debating social security reform in the 1990s

As in the 1980s, there was a flurry of proposals in the mid-1990s about changing the benefits system, either on their own or as part of a broader policy review. These included:

- The report of the Dahrendorf Commission (1995), *Report on wealth creation and social cohesion in a free society*.
- The Inquiry into Income and Wealth, organised by the Joseph Rowntree Foundation and chaired by Sir Peter Barclay (JRF, 1995).
- From Frank Field (Labour MP), *Making welfare work* (1995).
- From Peter Lilley (Conservative government minister), the *Mais* lecture on benefits spending in 1993.
- Proposals for replacing state benefits with private insurance from the No Turning Back group within the Conservative Party (Timmins, 2001).
- Madsen Pirie's *The radical agenda: The privatization of choice* (1993).
- *In place of fear: The future of the welfare state*, produced in 1994 (revised in 1995) by a coalition of trades unions and non-governmental organisations (TWGU, 1995).
- The Citizens' Commission on the Future of the Welfare State, led by service users, which reported a few years later (Beresford and Turner, 1997).

The key issues were not so different from those debated in the mid-1980s, but included more explicit discussion of the problems caused by growing inequality and poverty, and the impact of changing family and employment patterns. There was also more emphasis on how the UK was affected by global economic changes.

The CSJ was chaired by Sir Gordon Borrie, and was independent of the Labour Party; a think tank, the Institute for Public Policy Research, gave secretarial support and issued a series of publications during the Commission's deliberations, including the CSJ's preliminary definition of social justice (CSJ, 1993a, 1993b). Commissioners were unpaid and did not just come from the

Labour Party but also included those from the Centre-Left of the political spectrum and individuals not identified with a political party. They worked in subgroups, and embarked on a series of visits around the country, as well as taking written and oral evidence, before producing a final report in 1994.

The report *Social justice: Strategies for national renewal* (CSJ, 1994) starts by arguing that social justice is not inimical to economic efficiency but essential to it, and thus tackling inequalities has an economic as well as a moral rationale. The challenges facing policy are identified in relation to the recent changes in the economic and social environment. The CSJ placed enormous emphasis on employment, not least because the UK was emerging from a period of deindustrialisation and recession (Pearce and Paxton, 2005). However, it was not just the level of unemployment that was seen as a key issue, but also the distribution of employment and in particular the growing divide between 'work-rich' and 'work-poor' households (Thomas, 1995). This related to another key challenge, which was how to update the social security system to reflect contemporary family patterns, including more women in employment and rising numbers of lone-parent families. National insurance, for example, had been designed around traditional male patterns of employment – sometimes described as more than 40 hours of work a week, over more than 40 years. But increasingly jobs were part time, or even based on zero hours contracts, with many constructed as self-employed (legitimately or not). With so many more women in the labour market, the CSJ also took gender issues on board, rather than ignoring them as the Fowler reviews had. The Commission wrestled with how to provide an independent benefit income for women while not reinforcing the gendered division of labour (Lister, 1995).

The CSJ set up, in order to reject, what they described as the two main existing ways of approaching these challenges. The 'deregulators' emphasised the importance of the private market and so sought to reduce the role of the state. Under Margaret Thatcher and John Major, this had created unjust inequalities. The 'levellers' promoted a redistributive tax–benefits system that would protect people in poverty. But this would not promote economic prosperity and nor would it be likely to find favour with the electorate. Instead, the CSJ argued for a combination of a modern, active welfare state with intelligent regulation – what it called the 'investors' approach.

This analysis led the CSJ to emphasise the importance of 'active' labour market policies, such as welfare-to-work measures, and to argue that the new route to security was not a job for life, or generous benefits, but instead adaptability and skills. This sort of analysis was becoming increasingly influential in many countries at that time (Sinfield, 2001; see also Chapter Eleven, Wright, this volume). There was also an acceptance that many jobs would be low paid, requiring both supplementation in the present and training for people to move on from them in the future. Thus, a key theme in the CSJ approach was the need to shape the social security system around people in work or looking for work. Benefits should be structured to enable people to support themselves through employment and based on a principle of reciprocity, with clear 'rights and responsibilities' (White, 1995).

The CSJ was widely expected to call for a greater role for means testing in the delivery of social security benefits, in the context of the perceived importance of containing, or reducing, public expenditure (Baldwin and Falkingham, 1994). Some Labour politicians were also querying the case for universal benefits (Timmins, 2001). However, the CSJ report argued against using means testing as the main basis for social security benefits. Means testing cannot meet 'modern' needs because of its emphasis on the family rather than the individual and because of its inability to provide a secure floor to the flexible labour market. In addition, Miliband (1994) argued that it was essential not to base benefits solely on poverty – but also that traditional benefits such as CB and pensions were no longer sufficient to bind in the middle class.

The CSJ report proposed a modernised social insurance system, to include all those working eight hours a week or more, and with scope for the better off to pay additional contributions for extra benefits. This was intended to make the system more inclusive and allow scope for more personalisation. A part-time Unemployment Benefit (UB) was proposed, and new insurance benefits would be given for time out of employment for caring responsibilities. The report rejected a citizen's income (paid without conditions to everyone), and the integration of tax and benefits, but instead suggested a small 'participation income', to be paid to all those contributing to society via paid work or in other worthwhile ways, including care and voluntary work. There were detailed proposals for a minimum wage, welfare-to-work measures, and changes to the treatment of earnings and some other means-tested benefit rules (although the CSJ argued that its role was not to suggest short-term reforms).

The CSJ's proposals were not specifically taken up by the Labour government after the 1997 election; but much of its analysis of the issues, problems and challenges was influential (for example, in the first welfare reform Green Paper: DSS, 1998). The Labour government was committed to a freeze on public spending for the first two years, through an election promise to hold to the Conservative government's spending plans, and as part of this same commitment abolished the additional support for lone parents. These measures did not bode well for the CSJ recommendations. Nevertheless, since 1997 many of the CSJ's themes have emerged in various ways:

- the focus on rights and responsibilities and greater conditionality attached to benefit receipt for wider groups of claimants (Chapter Eleven, Wright, and Chapter Twelve, Sainsbury, this volume);

- the commitment to 'active' labour market policies rather than 'passive' benefit provisions (Chapter Eleven, Wright, this volume);
- the introduction of a National Minimum Wage (NMW) and of tax credits for families and low-paid workers (Chapter Thirteen, Millar, this volume).

As noted above, the CSJ argued that tackling inequalities was essential for social justice and compatible with economic growth and development. The importance of investment in children became a key theme of policy. The commitment to early years education and to programmes such as Sure Start, and the pledge to 'end child poverty', reflect this policy agenda (Chapter Nine, Ridge, this volume). The focus on reducing poverty has also been apparent in relation to provisions aimed at reducing pensioner poverty (Chapter Ten, McKay, and Chapter Three, Burchardt, this volume). Hills and Stewart (2005) conclude that the overall impact of Labour's tax and benefit reforms since 1997 has been more progressive than an alternative policy of earnings-linking existing benefits would have achieved. These measures have included increases in levels of support to non-working as well as working people, which is an important element in falling poverty rates. Brewer (2007) argues that there has been some tension in policy between the aims of reducing child poverty (which requires increases in out-of-work benefits) and improving work incentives; and Gregg (2008) notes that the direction of travel compared with the previous regime(s) includes an increase in engagement, support and (disciplinary) required activity functions, alongside increased financial support for children and pensioners and personalised support services. The CSJ's rejection of means testing has not, however, been apparent in the Labour government's approach – and indeed means testing has become more entrenched through the tax credit system, albeit in a form which the government argues distinguishes it from traditional means-tested benefits.

Challenges for the 21st century

Where next for social security policy? As noted in Chapter One, reform of the structure as a whole is difficult, if not impossible, because of the legacy of the system that has built up, and become embedded, over a period of many years. Even the more modest goal of simplifying this complex system is elusive. Social security is inherently complex because it is seeking to address a range of needs and circumstances across the lifecourse and to effect different forms of redistribution (Millar, 2005). The chapters that follow in the rest of this book address a range of issues in UK social security policy and administration. We end this chapter by setting out some of the key questions that we believe will be central to ongoing debates.

Starting with an international perspective, ***Box 2.3*** summarises the views of the challenges for social security in the 21st century from the outgoing Secretary-General of the International Social Security Association (ISSA). These focus on an increased emphasis on individual responsibility; how to make mixed public–private systems work; how to keep employers on board; how to take account of increased longevity; and how to use social security for preventative rather than compensatory purposes.

Box 2.3: Challenges for social security

The ISSA provides a forum for debate between social security institutions throughout the world. Dalmer Hoskins (2007, p 144), outgoing Secretary-General, summarises what he believes are the key 'issues that will be debated almost everywhere but for which the solutions adopted may prove to be very different depending on the history, culture and economic situation of the respective countries'. These are:

- How to take account of an increased focus on individual responsibility. This means shifting risks to individuals but raises concerns about whether people can really make informed choices, especially when these have significant long-term implications.
- How to make multi-tiered systems, made up of a public–private mix, work fairly and efficiently. These create potential problems of targeting, incentives and widening gaps in coverage and levels of support.
- How to 'keep employers in the game'. The social protection model was based on the idea of partnership between employers and workers, but this approach may not be sustainable in the context of the growth of multinational companies, economic globalisation and the weakening of trades unions.
- How to take account of increased longevity, and what this means for the concept of 'retirement' in social security systems.
- How to use social security for prevention rather than compensation, especially in relation to health. Social security systems compensate for accidents and ill health but perhaps governments should try to use social security to motivate and sustain people to live healthier lives.

These are questions that face many countries. Looking to the UK in particular, we can also identify challenges that are specific to its current position. These are not always very different from the international challenges set out above; and they are not necessarily new. In fact, frequently (as we saw in the two examples of recent reviews explored earlier in this chapter) similar topics may be debated when reform is contemplated, albeit from different perspectives and with different outcomes. This is also true today, with competing views and perspectives on how to address these challenges.

One important challenge for the UK is similar to the first issue set out in ***Box 2.3***: how to react to an increasing focus on individual responsibility for self-provision. McKay (2007, p 110) argues that a key principle of very recent UK reforms – in particular in pensions and child support – has been to remove the state from the process of service delivery and to encourage individuals to make their own arrangements. The other area in which this emphasis is evident is the national roll-out of the Saving Gateway, through which the government will encourage people on low incomes to save for the future by matching their savings with a contribution from the public purse. This sort of approach gives rise to concerns about the impact of shifting risks to individuals and whether people are well-informed enough to make the right choices. In addition, however, if public provision is no longer seen as a major mechanism for most people for dealing with risk and saving for the future, with privatised provision via insurance companies or other financial services providers taking over this role instead, there may be a danger that the functions of social security will appear narrower and of relevance only to those at the bottom of the ladder.

However, one policy area in which the functions of benefits seem to have been expanding rather than shrinking in recent years is in relation to care. Family and childcare benefits have been increased considerably, and the government is at the time of writing reviewing financial provision for carers of disabled and older people. But these reforms (together with changes in pensions that increase the recognition of caring roles) do not necessarily signify the existence of a coherent gender perspective on social security. At a time when women's relationship to the state in terms of benefit provision is changing more radically then men's, and joint assessment for couples is increasing because of the growing emphasis on means testing, developing an informed gender perspective on potential social security reforms is a key second challenge for the future. Given the continuing inequality of resources between women and men, this challenge is also related to the first, outlined above, about increasing self-provision.

A third key challenge is how best to deal with social security 'users' (usually called 'claimants' by welfare rights organisations). Debates about choice and user involvement in – or even co-production of – public services tend to bypass benefit claimants in a way that often goes unnoticed. Yet it is benefit claimants who have experienced many of the most unsatisfactory service user experiences of recent years (Chapter Fourteen, Stafford, this volume). These have often been associated with manifest failures of large-scale systems of new technology (child support, tax credits) or the transfer of personal data (CB). Thus, the 'Transformational Government' agenda (Cabinet Office, 2005), in which the business concept of customer relations management is central, and in which channels of communication are seen as key, is a particularly challenging one in relation to social security (Chapter Sixteen, Hudson, this volume). It will be important to ensure that changes to service provision are not driven by an administrative imperative, focused on efficiency savings, with an ideal 'customer' in mind and unrelated to many real claimants' needs, views and preferences. The increased involvement of the private sector in service delivery also raises issues of equity and accountability in the provision of services to claimants (Chapter Fifteen, Finn, this volume).

A further challenge is to identify the best way forward on benefit complexity and proposals for simplification. This policy area has been a focus for government activity in recent years. A 'Benefit Simplification Unit' was set up several years ago within the Department for Work and Pensions (DWP), and began vetting all proposals for changes in social security provision. However, its desire to produce a 'complexity index' seems doomed to failure. In addition, it did not appear to have the power necessary to (for example) query the potential of policy shifts, such as a reduction in the volume of means testing in the UK social security system, to radically simplify benefits. Meanwhile, the varying requirements on claimants in terms of availability for work, and the resulting complexities of moving from one benefit to another, have prompted proposals from both within and outside government for the introduction of a 'single working-age benefit' (Moullin, 2007; Stanley and Sainsbury, 2007; Work and Pensions Select Committee, 2007; Chapter Twelve, Sainsbury, this volume). This benefit would bring together provision for unemployed people, those incapable of work, lone parents and (in some variants) carers as well. The government is proposing instead the abolition of Income Support (DWP, 2008) in the longer term, to achieve a similar goal. Such proposals are likely to be a key focus of debate in the next few years. But they are perhaps also an example of the dominance of employment issues over other concerns – such as the level of benefits and the balance between contributory, universal and means-tested support – which would more traditionally be the central issues preoccupying policy makers working in the social security area.

The issue of conditionality – and in particular the extent to which entitlement to benefits should be dependent on engagement with the labour market – is one that has confounded social security policy for many years. As noted above, extending conditionality to wider groups of claimants, including lone parents and disabled people, has been a key element in the 'work is welfare' approach of the Labour government. The next steps for welfare reform proposed by the government (DWP, 2007, 2008) take this further, as well as introducing a greater role for private sector providers in the delivery of work-focused policies. The government has also commissioned a review of conditionality in the benefit system. The Conservative Party (2008) also proposes a stronger work-based system with more sanctions for failure to comply.

Sometimes, 'welfare reform' appears to be narrowed to welfare-to-work policies only (see, for example, Brewer, 2007). More generally, this dominant focus on the issue of employment within debates about social security is an illustration of the real risk of 'policy closure' that appears prevalent in the current climate. Sinfield (2001, p 223), drawing on Veit-Wilson's (2000) cross-national analysis of poverty and minimum income standards, argues that policy closure happens 'when the very presentation or discussion of an issue excludes some policy alternatives from consideration'. According to Sinfield (2001, p 223), debates about 'active' labour market policies versus so-called 'passive' benefits exemplify this tendency: 'the "active-over-passive" issue is a particularly good example of this policy closure: the change of discourse has set the agenda for subsequent discussion'.

Similarly, Seeleib-Kaiser and Fleckenstein (2007) argue that welfare state changes can be explained by new 'interpretative patterns' among the elite, which emerge and eventually become dominant. Challenges to the welfare state are perceived within a normative framework that interprets them as having specific effects. These interpretative patterns then have the effect of making 'other policy options practically impossible – or at least highly difficult – to enact' (Seeleib-Kaiser and Fleckenstein, 2007, p 437).

The challenges for the future that we have identified above are in part technical questions about how to make the system work in practice. But, as these quotations from Sinfield and Seeleib-Kaiser and Fleckenstein demonstrate, they are not purely technical – social policy never is. They are also based on questions about values, politics and what we as a society want to achieve.

Overview

Social security systems are large and complex, built up over many years, within specific social and economic contexts, and affecting many people. Radical reform is therefore difficult to achieve in practice. But looking at specific attempts at overall reform can highlight the different ways in which values and ideology influence thinking about social security, and show the relationship between the ways in which problems are defined and the kinds of solutions that are proposed.

Social security policy under Labour since 1997 has focused on moving wider groups of people from 'welfare to work' and on reducing poverty for pensioners and in particular for children.

Challenges for the future include the implications of an increasing focus on individual responsibility; how to develop an informed gender analysis of social security changes; how to better take account of claimants' needs and perspectives in the course of administrative reform; how best to simplify benefits; the extent to which benefit entitlement should be conditional on engagement with the labour market; and, perhaps most importantly, how to avoid closing off alternative policy options.

Questions for discussion

(1) What were the key points of similarity and difference in the ways in which the Fowler reviews and the Commission on Social Justice defined the central challenges for social security?
(2) Is 'policy closure' a good way to describe the current focus on employment-based welfare?
(3) What do you think are the key social security challenges for the 21st century?

Note

[1] For example, the 'Restart' programme, implemented in 1986, introduced periodic work-focused interviews on a compulsory basis for some categories of unemployed people, and this was arguably one of the most significant developments of that time, with long-term implications. This was not directly part of the Fowler reviews, although it certainly reflected the same sorts of ideas about unemployment traps and the need to reduce benefit dependency. In addition, benefits for young people were fundamentally changed later in 1988, separately from the implementation of the 1986 Act.

Website resources

www.cpag.org.uk/
Child Poverty Action Group
www.dwp.gov.uk/asd/asd5/
Department for Work and Pensions
www.parliament.uk/parliamentary_publications_and_archives/research_papers.cfm
House of Commons Library Research Papers
www.ippr.org/
Institute for Public Policy Research

www.google.com/search?hl=en&q=International+Social+Security+Association&btnG=Go
International Social Security Association

References

Adam Smith Institute (1984) *Omega Project: Social security policy*, London: Adam Smith Institute.

Ashby, P. (1984) *Social security after Beveridge: What next?*, London: Bedford Square Press/National Council for Voluntary Organisations.

Baldwin, S. and Falkingham, J. (eds) (1994) *Social security and social change: New challenges to the Beveridge model*, Hemel Hempstead: Harvester Wheatsheaf.

Beresford, P. and Turner, M. (1997) *It's our welfare: Report of the Citizens' Commission on the future of the welfare state*, London: National Institute of Social Work.

Beveridge, Sir W. (1942) *Social insurance and allied services*, Cmd 6404, London: HMSO.

Brewer, M. (2007) *Welfare reform in the UK: 1997-2007*, Working Paper 20/07, London: Institute for Fiscal Studies.

Cabinet Office (2005) *Transformational government, enabled by technology*, Cm 6683, London: Cabinet Office.

Church of England Board for Social Responsibility (1986) *Not just for the poor*, London: Church House.

Clasen, J. (2005) *Reforming European welfare states: Germany and the UK compared*, Oxford: Oxford University Press.

Conservative Party (2008) *Work for welfare*, London: Conservative Party.

CSJ (Commission on Social Justice) (1993a) *Social justice in a changing world*, London: Institute for Public Policy Research.

CSJ (1993b) *The justice gap*, London: Institute for Public Policy Research.

CSJ (1994) *Social justice: Strategies for national renewal – The report of the Commission on Social Justice*, London: Vintage.

Dahrendorf, R. (1995) *Report on wealth creation and social cohesion in a free society*, London: Commission on Wealth Creation & Social Cohesion.

Deacon, A. (1991) 'The retreat from state welfare', in S. Becker (ed) *Windows of opportunity: Public policy and the poor*, London: CPAG Ltd, pp 9-19.

DHSS (Department of Health and Social Security) (1985a) *Reform of social security*, Cmnd 9517, Green Paper, Vol 1, London: HMSO.

DHSS (1985b) *Reform of social security: Programme for change*, Cmnd 9518, Green Paper, Vol 2, London: HMSO.

DHSS (1985c) *Reform of social security: Background papers*, Cmnd 9519, Green Paper, Vol 3, London: HMSO.

DHSS (1985d) *Housing Benefit review*, Cmnd 9520, White Paper, London: HMSO.

DHSS (1985e) *Reform of social security: Programme for action*, Cmnd 9691, White Paper, London: HMSO.

Dilnot, A. and Webb, S. (1989) 'The 1988 social security reforms', in A. Dilnot and I. Walker (eds) *The economics of social security*, Oxford: Oxford University Press, pp 239-67.

Dilnot, A. W., Kay, J. A. and Morris, C. N. (1984) *The reform of social security*, Oxford: Clarendon Press.

DSS (Department of Social Security) (1998) *New ambitions for our country: A new contract for welfare*, Cm 3805, Green Paper, London: HMSO.

DWP (Department for Work and Pensions) (2007) *Ready for work: Full employment in our generation*, Cm 7290, London: The Stationery Office.

DWP (2008) *No one written off: Reforming welfare to reward responsibility* (Public Consultation), Cm 7363, London: The Stationery Office.

Evans, M. (1996) 'Fairer or Fowler? The effects of the 1986 Social Security Act on family incomes', in J. Hills (ed) *New inequalities: The changing divide of income and wealth in the UK*, Cambridge: Cambridge University Press, pp 236-61.

Field, F. (1995) *Making welfare work*, London: Institute of Community Studies.

Glendinning, C. and Millar, J. (1987) (eds) *Women and poverty in Britain*, Brighton: Wheatsheaf.

Glennerster, H. (2000) *British social policy since 1945* (second edition), Oxford: Blackwell.

Golding, P. and Middleton, S. (1982) *Images of welfare: Press and public attitudes to welfare*, Oxford: Basil Blackwell and Martin Robertson.

Gregg, P. (2008) 'UK welfare reform 1996 to 2008 and beyond: a personalised and responsive welfare system?', CMPO Working Paper No 08/196, Bristol: Centre for Market and Public Organisation, University of Bristol.

Hills, J. (1987) 'What happened to spending on the welfare state?', in A. Walker and C. Walker (eds) *The growing divide: A social audit 1979-1987*, London: CPAG Ltd, pp 88-100.

Hills, J. (1988) *Changing tax: How the tax system works and how to change it*, London: CPAG Ltd.

Hills, J. and Stewart, K. (2005) *A more equal society? New Labour, poverty, inequality and exclusion*, Bristol: The Policy Press.

HM Treasury (1979) *The government's expenditure plans 1980-81*, Cmnd 7746, White Paper, London: HMSO.

Hoskins, D. (2007) 'Social security: do we need a new social contract?', *International Social Security Review*, vol 60, no 2-3, pp 143-6.

JRF (Joseph Rowntree Foundation) (1995) *Income and wealth: Report of the JRF Inquiry Group*, vols 1 and 2, York: York Publishing Services.

Kiernan, K., Land H. and Lewis, J. (1998) *Lone motherhood in twentieth-century Britain: From footnote to front page*, Oxford: Clarendon Press.

Lilley, P. (1993) *Benefits and costs: Securing the future of the social security*, The *Mais* Lecture, London, 23 June.

Lister, R. (1989) 'The politics of social security: an assessment of the Fowler review', in A. Dilnot and I. Walker (eds) *The economics of social security*, Oxford: Oxford University Press, pp 200-23.

Lister, R. (1991) 'Social security in the 1980s', *Social Policy and Administration*, vol 25, no 2, pp 91-107.

Lister, R. (1995) 'Social justice: radical plan or washout?', *Poverty*, vol 90, pp 10-11.

McKay, S. (2007) 'Laying new foundations: social security reform in 2006', in K. Clarke, T. Maltby and P. Kennett (eds) *Social policy review 19: Analysis and debate in social policy, 2007*, Bristol: The Policy Press, pp 107-24.

Miliband, D. (1994) 'From welfare to wealthfare', *Renewal*, vol 2, no 1, pp 87-90.

Millar, J. (2005) 'Simplification, modernisation and social security', *Benefits*, vol 13, no 1, pp 10-15.

Minford, P. (1984) 'State expenditure: a study in waste', Supplement to *Economic Affairs*, vol 4, no 3, pp i–xix.

Moullin, S. (2007) *Care in a new welfare society: Unpaid care, welfare and employment*, London: Institute for Public Policy Research, www.ippr.org.uk/publicationsandreports/publication.asp?id=580

Murray, C. (1984) *Losing ground*, New York: Basic Books.

National Consumer Council (1984) *Of benefit to all: A consumer review of social security*, London: NCC.

Page, R. M. (2007) *Revisiting the welfare state*, Maidenhead: Open University Press.

Pearce, N. and Paxton, W. (2005) *Social justice: Building a fairer Britain*, London: Politico's.

Pierson, P. (ed) (2001) *The new politics of the welfare state*, Oxford/New York: Oxford University Press.

Pirie, M. (1993) *The radical agenda: The privatisation of choice*, London: Adam Smith Institute.

Seeleib-Kaiser, M. and Fleckenstein, T. (2007) 'Discourse, learning and welfare state change: the case of German labour market reforms', *Social Policy and Administration*, vol 41, no 5, pp 427-48.

Sharples, A. (1985) 'Costs and benefits: the economics of social security', in S. Ward (ed) *DHSS in crisis: Social security – under pressure and under review*, London: Child Poverty Action Group.

Sinfield, A. (2001) 'Benefits and research in the labour market', *European Journal of Social Security*, vol 3, no 3, pp 209-35.

Stanley, K. and Sainsbury, R. (2007) *One for all: Active welfare and the single working-age benefit*, London: Institute for Public Policy Research, www.ippr.org/publicationsandreports/publication.asp?id=552

Thomas, R. (1995) 'Strong welfare and flexible labour? Why Kenneth Clarke is wrong', *Renewal*, vol 3, no 1, pp 37-43.

Timmins, N. (2001) *The five giants: A biography of the welfare state* (second edition), London: HarperCollins.

Treasury and Civil Service Select Committee (1983) *The structure of personal income taxation and Income Support*, HC 386, Session 1982-83, London: HMSO.

TWGU (Transport and General Workers' Union), in association with Child Poverty Action Group, Family Welfare Association and Low Pay Unit (1995) *In place of fear: The future of the welfare state* (revised edition), London: TGWU.

Veit-Wilson, J. (2000) 'Horses for discourses: poverty, purpose and closure in minimum income standards policy', in D. Gordon and P. Townsend (eds) *Breadline Europe: The measurement of poverty*, Bristol: The Policy Press, pp 141-64.

White, S. (1995) 'Rethinking the strategy of equality: an assessment of the report of the Commission on Social Justice', *The Political Quarterly*, vol 66, no 3, pp 205-10.

Work and Pensions Select Committee (2007) *Benefit simplification*, HC 463-I, London: The Stationery Office.

Inequalities and social security

Tania Burchardt

Summary

Social security systems are a feature of all advanced economies. Their shape and size vary greatly, and their objectives are many and various – including contributing to political stability and economic efficiency – but one common element is the reduction of some kinds of inequality.

An equality objective may be adopted instrumentally, as a necessary step to promoting some other objective such as social inclusion, social cohesion or solidarity. Or equality may be considered an end in itself; for example, many liberal egalitarian accounts of social justice include some form of equality as a requirement. Dworkin (1981) provides an account based on equality of resources, and Sen (1985) argues for equality of capability.

This chapter explores the nature of inequality – inequality of what and inequality between whom – in relation to social security policy. It then describes the current state of income inequality in the UK before addressing the key question of the extent to which the tax and benefit system is successful in limiting or redressing various aspects of inequality.

This is not the only possible objective for a social security system, nor is it necessarily the most important, but it is part of the mix.

Framework for analysing inequality

The most direct effect of social security on inequality that we can observe is a narrowing of the gap between the incomes of the rich and poor – so-called 'vertical inequality'. This is critically important, but there are other social divisions that are also significant, such as those characterised by gender, age, disability and ethnicity, sometimes referred to as horizontal inequalities.

In order to make sense of these multiple inequalities, this chapter uses a measurement framework recommended by the UK Equalities Review in 2007 and subsequently adopted by the Equality and Human Rights Commission. As part of the Review, initiated by the government but conducted at arm's length by an independent committee, a steering group on measurement was established, which developed an equality measurement framework informed by Amartya Sen's capability approach (Burchardt and Vizard, 2007; Vizard and Burchardt, 2007).

The basic building blocks of the measurement framework are illustrated in ***Box 3.1***. The concept of equality, in line with the capability approach, is one of substantive freedom, that is, equality in what people are actually able to be and do in central and valuable areas of life. This embodies an idea of positive freedom ('freedom to ...'), recognising that redistribution of resources and other interventions may be necessary to secure real freedom, and is distinct from narrower interpretations of equality of opportunity, which concentrate on formal opportunities, equal treatment and freedom from state interference.

Substantive freedom – what people can actually be and do – cannot be directly observed, but, according to the measurement framework, a reasonably

Box 3.1: Building blocks of the Equality Measurement Framework

Inequality *of* substantive freedom

- Outcomes
- Processes
- Autonomy

Inequality *in* 10 domains

- Life
- Physical security
- Health
- Education
- Standard of living
- Productive and valued activities
- Participation, influence and voice
- Individual, family and social life
- Identity, expression and self-respect
- Legal security

Inequality *by* 6 characteristics

- Gender including transgender
- Ethnicity
- Disability
- Sexual orientation
- Age
- Religion/belief

Source: Based on Burchardt and Vizard (2007) and Vizard and Burchardt (2007)

robust and comprehensive picture can be obtained by examining three aspects of equality: equality of outcome, equality of process and equality of autonomy. Equality of outcome is the most readily measurable, but it is not sufficient by itself because it does not contain information about whether the outcomes are those that the individual would have chosen, given the chance. Equality of outcome is therefore supplemented by information on equality of autonomy – the degree of choice and control individuals themselves have over those outcomes – and on equality of process – about how people are treated, including direct discrimination on the one hand, and being treated with dignity and respect on the other.

The second building block of the measurement framework contains a list of the domains of life in which equality is to be assessed. More details of the method by which the list of domains was derived can be found in Vizard and Burchardt (2007). It draws on the international human rights framework (primarily the International Covenant on Civil and Political Rights, and the International Covenant on Economic, Social and Cultural Rights), and on a process of deliberative consultation in Britain with members of the general public and with individuals and groups at particular risk of discrimination and disadvantage.

The third and final building block of the measurement framework specifies the characteristics by which equality is to be analysed (in response to the question, 'equality between whom?'). For the purposes of the Equalities Review, this was determined by the 'protected grounds' in the 2006 Equality Act – gender, ethnicity, disability, sexual orientation, age and religion/belief.

How might we analyse the impact of the UK tax and benefits system on equality as defined by this framework? Social security is an important determinant of the entitlements members of society have and thus of their outcomes across a range of domains. It can also contribute to autonomy (choice and control) by providing a guarantee of an independent income. Its role in equality of process is more ambiguous; as explored below, the delivery of social security does not always seem to support dignity and respect. The role of social security as a determinant of substantive freedom is illustrated in ***Figure 3.1***.

The rules and operation of the tax–benefit system are part of the institutional context (shown in ***Figure 3.1*** in the middle box on the left-hand-side). This interacts with other formal and informal institutions, such as the labour market, the family, governance structures and so on. The entitlement that an individual can secure in practice (upper box in the middle of ***Figure 3.1***) depends on an interaction between this institutional context, the level of resources available (both public and private) and the individual's own characteristics and circumstances. So, for example, the Income Support (IS) entitlement for a particular individual depends not only on the relevant rules and regulations,

Figure 3.1: Model of the determinants of substantive freedom, highlighting the role of social security

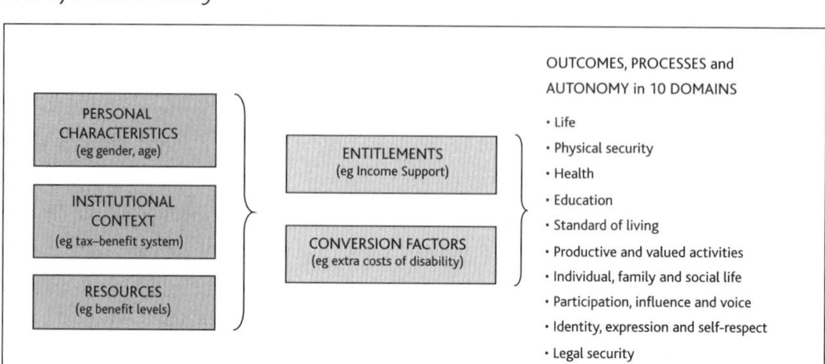

but also on the level at which benefits are set, and on the age, family and disability status of the claimant (among other things). Finally, the standard of living an individual can secure (an outcome in one of the 10 domains listed on the right-hand-side of ***Figure 3.1***) on the basis of their entitlement, depends on a set of conversion factors. For example, if the individual is disabled they may face a higher cost of living, so that a given income will produce a lower standard of living. Or, if an IS entitlement is not in fact claimed, perhaps due to the stigma attached to means-tested benefits, the entitlement is not converted into a contribution to standard of living at all.

Outcomes in other domains will also be affected by the tax–benefit system. Given the close relationship between poverty and ill health, we can expect social security to have an impact on life expectancy and health. Physical security could also be enhanced – for example, by providing a degree of financial independence, social security can be one element of support for women leaving violent relationships. Some aspects of the benefit system support family life, enabling people to spend time caring for children and others.

Tracing all of these possible pathways is too ambitious a task for this chapter. To simplify, inequality of outcome will be examined only in the domain of standard of living, and disposable income will be taken as a proxy for standard of living. Income is an imperfect proxy, of course, because of variations between people in the rate at which it can be converted into standard of living (termed 'conversion factors' in ***Figure 3.1***), but its distribution is nevertheless broadly informative about inequalities in standard of living.

A further simplification is with respect to the characteristics by which inequality will be analysed (see ***Box 3.1***). The 2006 Equality Act includes sexual orientation and religion/belief as relevant characteristics for monitoring equality, but breakdowns of income data by these characteristics are not yet available. The analysis in this chapter will concentrate on overall (vertical) inequality and horizontal inequality by gender, age, disability and ethnicity.

Income inequality as an outcome

Income can be measured in various ways. ***Box 3.2*** sets out the definition of income used in this chapter, which is 'equivalised disposable household income, before housing costs'. We start by examining the distribution of households. A commonly used approach is to look at the shares of total income received by fifths (quintile groups) of households arranged by income. ***Figure 3.2*** groups households in this way and shows the share of total income that each quintile group receives.

Box 3.2: Measuring incomes

The definition of income used in this chapter is 'equivalised disposable household income, before housing costs'.

Equivalised means an adjustment has been made to take account of the fact that the same income goes less far in a larger household than in a smaller household. The equivalence scale is the McClements scale, commonly used by the UK government in official statistics.

Disposable means this is income from all sources (earnings, social security benefits and tax credits, private and occupational pensions, investments and so on) minus direct taxes (Income Tax, National Insurance [NI] contributions and Council Tax); in other words it is the money available to households to spend..

Household means one or more people who live in the same accommodation and share a living/sitting room, meals or housekeeping together. It might include more than one nuclear family. The income of all of these individuals is added together to give household income.,

Before housing costs means that the income is measured before rent or mortgage payments have been made. There is a debate about whether 'before housing costs' or 'after housing costs' measures give a better indication of people's standard of living; see Hills (2004) for further discussion.

Figure 3.2 shows that the bottom fifth, or 20%, of households receive only 8% of total disposable income between them, while the top fifth of households receive more than twice their 'fair' share, at 41% of total disposable income.

Figure 3.2: *Shares of total income by quintile group: UK households, 2005/06*

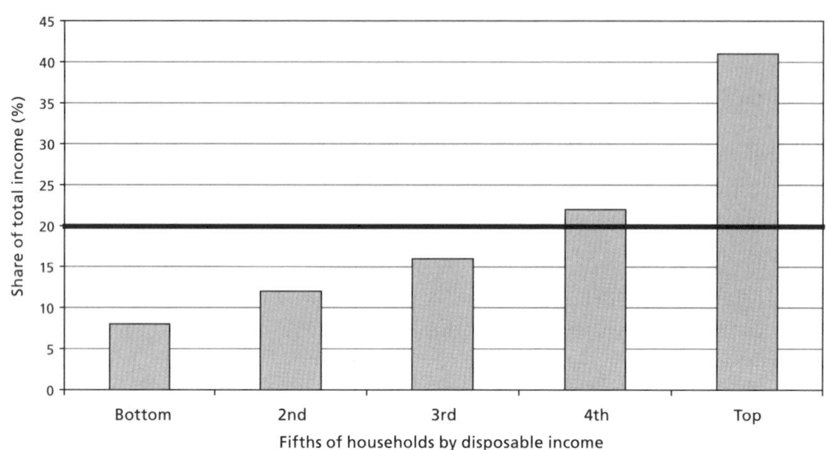

Note: For definitions, see ***Box 3.2***. The thick horizontal line represents perfect equality.
Source: Derived from ONS (2007, Table 2)

Atkinson (2005) shows that the disproportionality between population share and income share becomes even more extreme as one looks at more and more precisely defined groups in the population, for example the top 1% of the distribution received 13 times their 'fair share', and the top 0.1% received 48 times theirs.

What about inequality between men and women, and other so-called horizontal inequalities? Here we switch from households to individuals as the unit of analysis, because characteristics like gender and ethnicity belong to individuals, not to households.[1] The definition of income is the same – equivalised household income – but instead of counting households we are now counting the number of individuals living in these households at various levels of income. The data relate to the year 2004/05. Latest published figures (not yet available for further analysis) suggest that inequality increased in 2005/06 and 2006/07 (DWP, 2008).

The position of men and women in the income distribution is necessarily similar according to this definition because the same level of household income is attributed to men and women living together in a household.[2] Differences can, however, be detected if we restrict our attention to people who live in single-adult households, which represents 8% of men and 16% of women.

Figure 3.3 shows what proportion of men in single-adult households fall into each of the income groups (the pale bars add up to 100%), and compares this with the proportion of women who fall into each income group (the dark bars add up to 100%). Note that this is a different kind of analysis to ***Figure 3.2***, which was concerned with shares of total income. We can see that among the population in single-adult households, a lower proportion of men than of women are in the bottom income groups. Overall, the difference in their position in the income distribution is statistically significant.

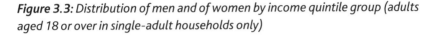

Figure 3.3: *Distribution of men and of women by income quintile group (adults aged 18 or over in single-adult households only)*

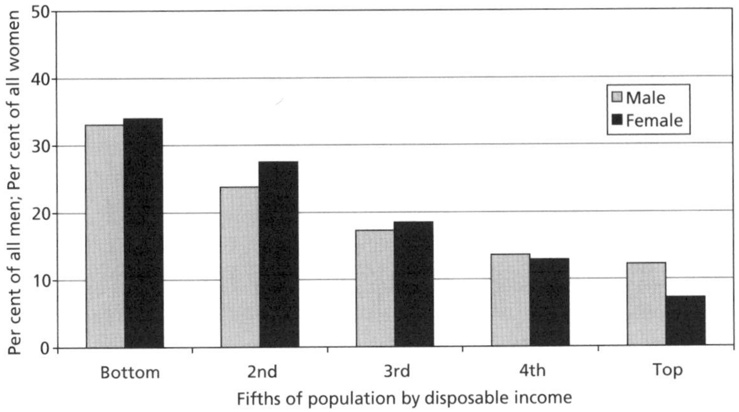

Source: Author's calculation using FRS and HBAI 2004/05

The position of ethnic groups in the income distribution varies widely (***Figure 3.4***). The most striking finding is the position of people from a Pakistani or Bangladeshi background: nearly half (48%) are in the bottom fifth of the income distribution – *three times* the proportion of the majority white population in this income quintile group (16%). Other minority ethnic groups are slightly over-represented in the bottom of the distribution, but not to the same extent (see also Berthoud, 2002).

For Indian and Black Caribbean minority ethnic groups, the distribution is somewhat U-shaped; that is, although the highest proportions are found in the bottom fifth of the income distribution, there is also a small concentration towards the top of the distribution. These are likely to be professionals and businesspeople, the so-called 'new middle class'.

Child poverty and, to a lesser extent, pensioner poverty, have become political priorities over the last decade. ***Figure 3.5*** confirms that while children and pensioners are most likely to be found in the bottom two fifths of the income distribution, adults of working age are most likely to be found towards the top of the distribution.

Finally, ***Figure 3.6*** shows inequality between disabled and non-disabled people. Disabled people are significantly over-represented in the bottom two fifths of the income distribution, and only 10% of disabled people are in the top fifth – less than half the proportion of non-disabled people.

Figure 3.4: Distribution of ethnic groups by income quintile group

White
Black Caribbean
Indian
Pakistani/Bangladeshi
All other

Per cent of each ethnic gorup

Bottom 2nd 3rd 4th Top

Fifths of population by disposable income

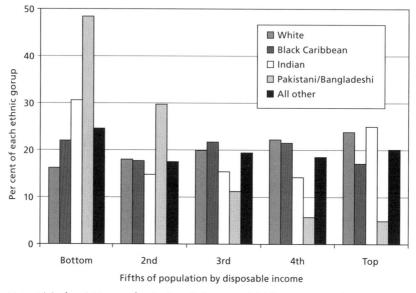

Note: Adults (aged 18 or over) only; the ethnic group of children is not recorded in the dataset.

Source: Author's calculation using FRS and HBAI 2004/05

Figure 3.5: Distribution of age groups by income quintile group

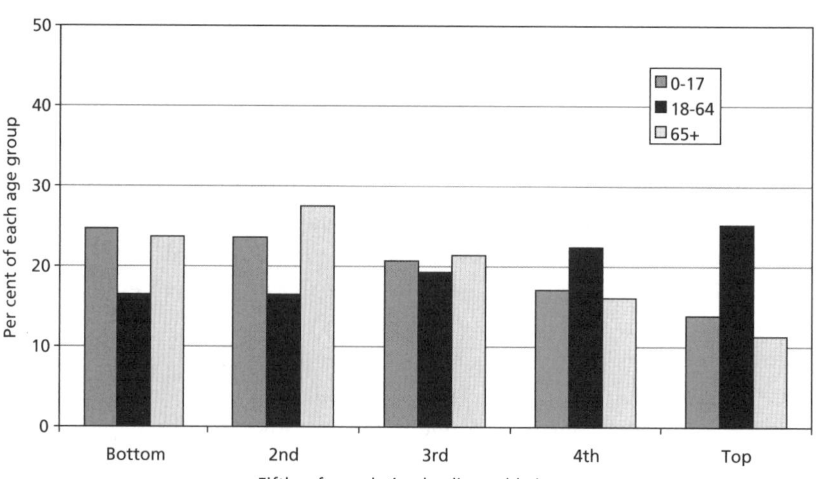

Source: Author's calculation using FRS and HBAI 2004/05

Figure 3.6: *Distribution of disabled and non-disabled people by income quintile group*

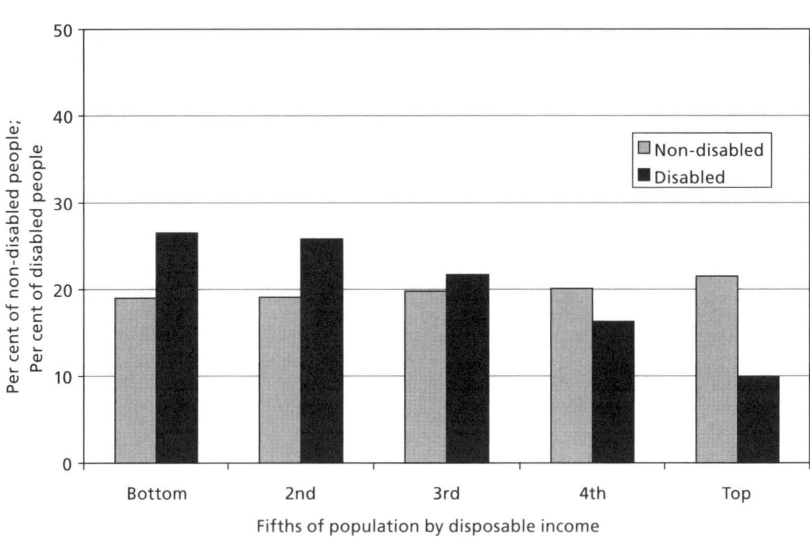

Note: Disability is defined using the 1995 Disability Discrimination Act's definition of disability: a long-standing illness or impairment that significantly limits day-to-day activities.

Source: Author's calculation using FRS and HBAI 2004/05

Of course, any one person has a combination of characteristics and is represented several times over in the preceding figures. Some combinations of characteristics produce a coupling of disadvantage, while others offset one another (Berthoud, 2003). If we compare, for example, disabled people from a Bangladeshi or Pakistani background with non-disabled white people we find that the risk of the former being in the bottom fifth of the income distribution is 57%, more than four times the risk for the advantaged comparison group (14%), and conversely only 6% of the disadvantaged group are in the top fifth of the distribution, compared with 27% of the comparison group.

The impact of the tax–benefit system

Thus far we have concentrated on income as an outcome. But how does social security itself, in combination with taxation, affect these outcomes? To what extent does the tax–benefit system contribute to equalising substantive freedom as far as standards of living are concerned?

First, some definitions. ***Figure 3.7*** shows how original (market) incomes are transformed by social security and taxation. In this chapter we will mainly be concerned with original incomes and disposable incomes, but the intermediary and subsequent steps are also of interest. 'Original income' refers to income

***Figure 3.7:** From 'original' to 'post-tax' household income*

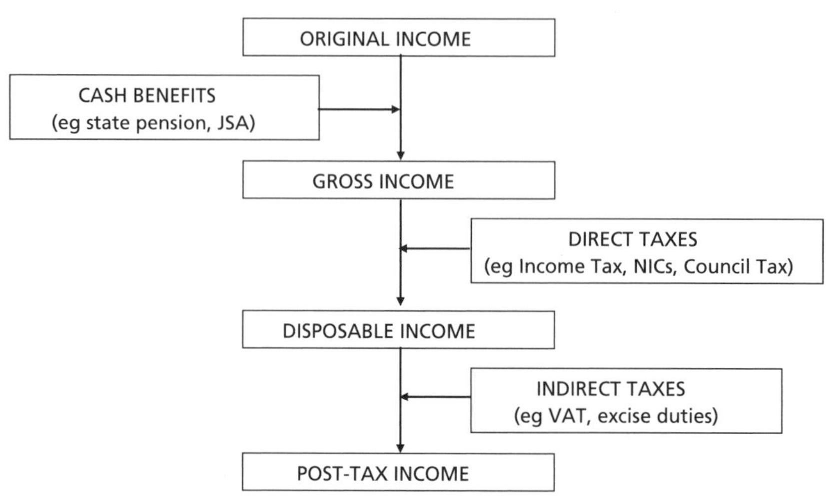

Source: Adapted from ONS (2007)

before any direct government intervention through taxes or benefits, so it includes gross income from employment, self-employment, investments and occupational and private pensions.

Social security benefits, including both contributory and non-contributory benefits, are added to original incomes to give gross incomes. Direct taxes, including Income Tax, NI contributions and Council Tax, are then deducted to give disposable income.

The treatment of tax credits is more complex. In so far as they reduce the amount of Income Tax a household pays, tax credits are treated as negative Income Tax and are included in the direct taxes box. However, for some households, their tax credit entitlement exceeds their Income Tax liability, especially those households that pay little or no Income Tax. In these cases, any amount of tax credits over and above Income Tax liability is treated as a benefit and included in the cash benefits box.

Disposable income measures the total income a household has available to spend. However, to understand the full impact of taxation on households, it is useful to take the next step indicated in ***Figure 3.7*** and subtract indirect (or consumption) taxes, including Value Added Tax (VAT), and duties on alcohol, cigarettes, petrol and so on. This yields post-tax income.[3]

One straightforward way to track the effect of social security and taxation on income inequality is to calculate the Gini coefficient for incomes at each stage indicated in ***Figure 3.7***. The Gini coefficient is a commonly used summary measure of the degree of inequality in a distribution. It ranges between a value of 0, which represents a perfectly equal distribution, in which each 1% of the population receives 1% of total income, and a value of 1, which represents complete inequality. ***Table 3.1*** shows Gini coefficients for the various income measures for the year 2005/06. It indicates that income inequality falls sharply when moving from original incomes to gross incomes, in other words, when social security is taken into account. Direct taxes have a much smaller effect, although they also contribute to a reduction in inequality (moving from gross to disposable income). However, this progressive impact is entirely undone by the incidence of indirect taxes (going from disposable to post-tax incomes).

A similar picture is obtained if we examine the share of total income going to the bottom fifth of the (disposable) income distribution, compared with the share going to the top fifth, as shown in the right-hand column of ***Table 3.1***. The top fifth of the income distribution take over half of *total* income between themselves, and inequality in original, market, incomes is such that the ratio between the total income received by the top quintile group and the income received by the bottom quintile group is 17:1. This would be the status quo in the absence of government intervention. Social security narrows this gap significantly, to just under 6:1, and direct taxes help a little more. Again, however, we can see the regressive impact of indirect taxes, such that the ratio of the top to the bottom quintile groups in post-tax income is back to around 6:1.

Inequality in original incomes has been consistently higher in the 1990s and 2000s than it was in the 1980s. In 1979 the Gini coefficient for original incomes was 0.44, rising to 0.51 in 1987, 0.53 in 1997, and 0.52 today (ONS, 2007, Table 27). This means that social security and taxation would now have to work harder to produce the same outcome in terms of (in)equality in disposable incomes as was achieved in 1979. This is a challenge that has not been met. Inequality in gross incomes (that is, after social security) has risen from 0.30 in 1979 to 0.37 today, and inequality in disposable incomes (that

Table 3.1: *Income inequality between households at various stages from original to post-tax income, 2005/06*

	Gini coefficient	Bottom quintile group share of total income (%)	Top quintile group share of total income (%)	Ratio of top to bottom quintile
Original income	0.52	3	51	17:1
Gross income	0.37	7	44	6:1
Disposable income	0.34	8	41	5:1
Post-tax income	0.37	7	43	6:1

Note: Calculated with households as the unit of analysis and quintile groups based on disposable income distribution.

Source: From ONS (2007, Table 2).

is, after direct taxes) has risen from 0.27 to 0.34. The difference in the Gini coefficients for disposable incomes and original incomes – a rough-and-ready measure of the efficacy of social security and taxation in reducing inequality – stands today at 0.18, almost identical to the gap of 0.17 in 1979.

Thus far in this section we have concentrated on vertical inequality. What impact do social security and taxation have on horizontal inequalities?[4] ***Table 3.2*** provides a breakdown by gender as well as income quintile group. Average household incomes for men are higher than for women, whether we consider original, gross or disposable income. But for women, disposable incomes are a higher proportion of their original incomes, on average, than for men, suggesting that the combination of social security and taxation is doing more to boost women's household incomes than it is to boost men's.

Looking in more detail at the bottom and top income quintile groups for each gender shows this more clearly. While for women in the bottom income quintile, average disposable income is about eight times their average original income, for men the multiple is just about seven. Moreover, the population shares (extreme right-hand column in ***Table 3.2***) indicate that women in the bottom income quintile group make up a higher proportion of the adult population overall (11%) than do men in the bottom income quintile group (8%). So redistribution of household income through the tax and benefit system is both more effective for women than for men and affects a greater number.

This reflects the nature of single-adult households. (Among couples, men's and women's household incomes are the same, according to the definitions used

Table 3.2: *Original, gross and disposable incomes by income quintile group and gender*

Gender and income quintile group		Original £ per week	Gross £ per week	Disposable £ per week	Disposable as proportion of original	Population share (%)
Men – all		532	598	438	0.82	48
Women – all		477	558	416	0.87	52
Quintiles						
Men	– bottom	29	218	200	6.90	8
	– top	1,177	1,194	815	0.69	12
Quintiles						
Women	– bottom	27	229	211	7.81	11
	– top	1,158	1,177	806	0.70	11

Notes: Quintile groups defined on distribution of all individuals' original incomes. This table includes adults (aged 18 or over).

Source: Author's calculations using FRS and HBAI 2004/05

here; see Figari et al, 2007, for analysis of the effect of the tax–benefit system on within-couple income inequality.) Women in single-adult households are more likely to be lone parents or older pensioners, both of whom are likely to benefit from some social security entitlements, while men in single-adult households are more likely to be men of working age without co-resident children.

Table 3.3 provides a similar analysis, this time focusing on ethnic groups. Adults who identify themselves as white have the highest original incomes, on average 2.3 times higher than the ethnic group with the lowest original incomes – the Pakistani and Bangladeshi group. The gap narrows, to 1.9, when we move to gross incomes (including social security benefits) and

***Table 3.3:** Original, gross and disposable incomes by income quintile group and ethnic group*

Age group and income quintile group	Original £ per week	Gross £ per week	Disposable £ per week	Disposable as proportion of original	Population share (%)
White	516	591	435	0.84	91
Black Caribbean	436	519	389	0.89	1
Indian	482	537	395	0.82	2
Pakistani/Bangladeshi	220	305	244	1.11	2
Others	467	530	400	0.86	4
White					
– bottom	28	230	212	7.57	16
– top	1,173	1,191	812	0.69	22
Black Caribbean					
– bottom	20	214	197	9.85	<1
– top	1,059	1,073	746	0.70	<1
Indian					
– bottom	28	164	149	5.32	<1
– top	1,142	1,160	796	0.70	1
Pakistani/Bangladeshi					
– bottom	34	174	162	4.76	1
– top	1,085	1,110	738	0.68	<1
Others					
– bottom	21	201	186	8.86	1
– top	1,198	1,211	856	0.71	1

Notes: Quintile groups defined on distribution of all individuals' original incomes. This table includes adults (aged 18 or over).

Source: Author's calculations using FRS and HBAI 2004/0

narrows further to 1.8 once direct taxes are taken into account. Overall, the tax and benefit system appears to make the most difference to Pakistani and Bangladeshi people's incomes (because they start off poorest), followed by the Black Caribbean population. Other ethnic groups have a similar differential between original and disposable incomes as each other.

Vertical redistribution appears to vary in its impact across ethnic groups, although these estimates are based on relatively small sample sizes so they need to be treated with caution. For example, comparing people in the bottom income quintile group, the ratio of disposable incomes to original incomes is larger for people from a Black Caribbean background than it is for white people, and larger for white people than it is for Pakistani and Bangladeshi people. This is surprising given the income profile of the respective groups. Pakistani and Bangladeshi people in the bottom income quintile group have marginally higher original incomes than their white counterparts in the same income quintile group, but much lower disposable incomes. It is possible that some of the barriers discussed in the next section of the chapter, on inequality of process, are responsible.

Table 3.4 gives a breakdown of the population by age group. Pensioners appear to do best out of the social security and taxation system, with disposable incomes 1.6 times their original incomes (original incomes for pensioners include occupational and private pensions, and any earnings or investment income). Children do marginally better than working-age adults (remembering that the figures are based on household income).

Another way of looking at the effectiveness of the redistribution is to compare down the columns: children's average original income is 73% that of all working-age adults, but their disposable income is 82% that of all working-age adults.

Again, the impact of social security and taxation on original incomes is greatest at the bottom of the distribution for each age group, although the difference between the top and the bottom quintile group for pensioners is less than for younger age groups. In other words, for pensioners, the effects are less strongly redistributive in a vertical sense.

Finally, ***Table 3.5*** gives a breakdown by disability status. The average original income of non-disabled adults is more than twice the average of disabled adults, but the effects of social security and direct taxation reduce this differential.

The impact is concentrated in the lower parts of the original income distribution, where disabled people are significantly over-represented. In the bottom income quintile group, disabled people's disposable incomes are around 10 times their original incomes, compared to six times for non-disabled people in this income group.

None of th figures take into account the higher cost of living faced by disabled people. If this were taken into account, inequality between disabled

Table 3.4: *Original, gross and disposable incomes by income quintile group and age group*

Age group and income quintile group	Original £ per week	Gross £ per week	Disposable £ per week	Disposable as proportion of original	Population share (%)
Children – all	404	483	362	0.90	34
Working age – all	553	606	440	0.80	56
Pensioners – all	214	406	344	1.61	10
Children					
– bottom	25	205	193	7.72	8
– top	1,172	1,196	812	0.69	5
Working age					
– bottom	24	205	189	7.88	8
– top	1,167	1,181	803	0.69	15
Pensioners					
– bottom	34	257	235	6.91	5
– top	1,194	1,351	1,043	0.87	<1

Notes: Quintile groups defined on distribution of all individuals' original incomes. This table includes children (aged 0-17), adults of working age (aged 18-64) and pensioners (aged 65 or over).

Source: Author's calculations using FRS and HBAI 2004/05

Table 3.5: *Original, gross and disposable incomes by income quintile group and disability status*

Disability and income quintile group	Original £ per week	Gross £ per week	Disposable £ per week	Disposable as proportion of original	Population share (%)
Non-disabled – all	555	612	446	0.80	83
Disabled – all	255	411	334	1.31	17
Non-disabled					
– bottom	30	203	185	6.17	11
– top	1171	1,188	810	0.69	21
Disabled					
– bottom	24	253	235	9.79	8
– top	1,119	1,159	812	0.73	1

Notes: Quintile groups defined on distribution of all individuals' original incomes. This table includes adults (aged 18 or over).

Source: Author's calculations using FRS and HBAI 2004/05

and non-disabled people would be greater, but the effectiveness of social security and taxation in reducing the gap in final standards of living would also appear greater.

Equalising but still unequal

This section has demonstrated the strongly equalising effect of social security on incomes and, by implication, on standards of living. It is by far the most significant tool of redistribution in the current policy context. Direct taxation is weakly equalising; with only two rates of Income Tax now in force and NI contributions capped at the upper earnings limit, its potential to contribute to reducing vertical inequality is not being fully realised. Moreover, the calculations by the Office for National Statistics (ONS) indicate that the incidence of indirect taxation cancels out the progressive effect of direct taxation.

Social security also makes a significant contribution to horizontal equality, by redistributing, in effect, from non-disabled to disabled people, from the working-age population to both children and pensioners, and, to a limited extent, from men to women – although this last effect is mainly associated with age and responsibility for children rather than gender itself. Interestingly, many of these functions can be seen as redistribution from one part of a person's lifecourse to another (see Falkingham and Hills, 1995; also Chapter Eight, Rowlingson, this volume). We all begin life as children and many of us will become pensioners; some of us may become disabled. Indeed, a large majority of disabled people in the population at any one time became disabled during working or later life, rather than being born with an impairment. These periods, of childhood, old age and disability, are periods when one is likely to be less able to earn an income and potentially to have higher costs as well. Thus, social security can be seen in large part as a collective insurance policy – not dissimilar to Beveridge's initial intention, although now achieved by a wider range of different types of social security benefits and tax credits (see Piachaud, 2007; Chapter One, Millar, this volume).

Inequalities of process and of autonomy

The measurement framework illustrated in ***Box 3.1*** indicates that we need to think about how outcomes come about in addition to considering outcomes themselves. What is the process by which social security and taxation mitigate inequality in standards of living? To what extent are people treated with dignity and respect? Is autonomy promoted or hindered? In this section of the chapter we look at these issues of process and autonomy at the general level. Other chapters of this book discuss these issues further in relation to specific groups of claimants.

Process

With regard to how the social security system treats people, the general climate of public debate is not encouraging. Government rhetoric and tabloid newspaper coverage frequently depict claimants as potentially or actually fraudulent, and/or work-shy. For example, in a three-month period from November 2007 there were eight headlines in the *Daily Mail* including the term 'benefit[s] cheat' (based on a search of the online version). One of these reported a government initiative to introduce lie detectors for calls to benefit claim phone lines, contributing to a climate of suspicion that is difficult to reconcile with treating people with dignity and respect.

More systematic evidence can be drawn from qualitative studies of the experiences of benefit claimants and frontline staff. An ethnographic study of a Jobcentre in the late 1990s revealed that staff commonly used their own moral judgement to categorise claimants (Wright, 2003). 'Good' clients were those who were keen, smart and well presented, and who were deemed by staff to be unemployed through no fault of their own. 'Bad' clients fell into a number of different categories – 'wasters' (lazy), 'unemployables' (also referred to as 'riff-raff'), 'nutters' (including actually or potentially violent claimants), 'numpties' (causing a nuisance), the 'hoity-toity' (professionals) and those who were 'at it' (fiddling the system). Importantly, these informal labels affected the service that was provided to benefit claimants, in terms of both the nature and the quality of support they received.

In addition to the mode of delivery, structural aspects of the benefits system can also lead to indignities. Means testing itself is often stigmatising. In a study of welfare recipients in Columbia in the US, Stuber and Schlesinger (2006) found multiple sources of stigma: self-blame (for example, the individual feels they have let their family down), social disapproval (the individual feels society blames them for their situation), previous experience of being treated with disrespect when claiming, and the anticipation of being treated badly. Claimants with identities that were already stigmatised – for example, being African American or having a mental illness – were at greater risk of experiencing the stigma associated with claiming welfare benefits.

In the UK, the way in which the discretionary Social Fund is administered has been a focus of criticism. The Fund provides grants and short-term loans for essential items and to cope with emergencies, in cases where the assessing officer deems that the expenditure could not reasonably be met from regular benefit income. Applicants have described the process of applying to the Social Fund as humiliating and unpleasant (Smith, 1990; Huby and Dix, 1992). Many have felt that they were implicitly assumed to be 'trying to pull a fast one', when from their own perspective they were in dire need and had applied to the Social Fund as a last resort (House of Commons, 2001). Some categories of Social Fund applicant, including asylum seekers and applicants with drug and alcohol dependency, experienced the double disadvantage of being subject to the suspicion of their fellow-applicants as well as of the administrators (Legge et al, 2006).

Means testing has an adverse effect on take-up of entitlements and, despite a number of campaigns and rebranding of benefits especially for pensioners, take-up of tax credits and Income Support has not increased. For example, only 62-74% of pensioners estimated to be entitled to Pension Credit were receiving it in 2003/04 and only an estimated 50-61% of potential claimants of income-related Jobseeker's Allowance (JSA) were in receipt of the benefit (Piachaud, 2007).

Even in the absence of means testing, the process of claiming benefits can be fraught. The medical assessments that can form part of the application procedure for Incapacity Benefit (IB) have been sharply and repeatedly criticised for insensitivity and lack of professionalism (for example, House of Commons, 2000; Committee of Public Accounts, 2004; Citizens Advice, 2006). Complaints have included claimants being asked to perform uncomfortable or even painful tests; doctors making assumptions about claimants' conditions based on racial or other prejudices; rudeness; and intimidation. Unfortunately, these medical assessments are set to become a more significant part of the process of application for the Employment and Support Allowance, which is replacing IB from October 2008 (see Chapter Twelve, Sainsbury, this volume). There has also been criticism of the tax credits system for failures to provide timely and accurate information, making it difficult for people to know whether or not they have received the right amounts (see Chapter Thirteen, Millar, this volume).

Members of society fortunate enough not to have to rely on benefits to secure their standard of living are not subject to this degree of intrusion, scrutiny and suspicion. Although taxpayers complete a tax return, it is for the most part a paper-based process based on trust. Being at the sharp end of economic disadvantage, often contributed to, if not caused, by macroeconomic policy and institutional failures of various kinds, should not disqualify you from being treated with dignity and respect (Wolff, 1998).

How then should social security be reorganised to promote the dignity and respect of claimants? Chapter Four (Silburn and Becker, this volume) discusses these issues in more detail. Lister (2008) advocates involving the poor themselves in the design and evaluation of social security, ensuring that their concerns are heard and acted on. This is the starting point for achieving recognition and respect. Consultation with service users – in this case benefit claimants – and especially those at risk of disadvantage, is a central component of the public sector equality duties on 'race', gender and disability, which require public sector employers and service providers to take active steps to tackle discrimination and promote equality (EHRC, 2008).

Autonomy

The measurement framework set out in ***Box 3.1*** indicates that we should also consider the degree to which independence, choice and control are promoted or hindered by the social security system. Here again, we can identify some structural features that are relevant to questions of autonomy, and we can draw on qualitative evidence from the perspective of claimants themselves.

In so far as social security provides a safety net, and a degree of financial security once a claim has been established, it makes a crucial contribution to promoting autonomy and independence. There is no 'choice and control' in a state of destitution. This is particularly valuable where the person has no separate source of income and no immediate means to secure one. Parents (mostly mothers) who are looking after children and not working have emphasised the importance of Child Benefit (CB) being paid directly to the primary carer, as an independent and guaranteed source of income (Goode et al, 1998). Knowing that she is entitled to benefits in her own right may be a crucial guarantee for a victim of domestic violence in deciding to escape her partner. Disability Living Allowance (DLA) paid to a young disabled person can give them a degree of autonomy and financial independence, especially if combined with direct payments from social services (Burchardt, 2005).

However, for the unemployed, lone parents and people on IB, these advantages are attenuated by the conditions attached to receipt of benefits and the manner in which they are administered. Government rhetoric has emphasised choice and flexibility (DWP, 2007b), and in principle the individually tailored welfare-to-work packages envisaged in jobseeker's agreements give claimants a more active role in decisions about their return to work. In reality, however, the power relationships between advisors and claimants, the relatively limited menu of options offered, and the objective constraints of the labour market are not such as to promote meaningful control for the claimant. Claimants are not in a position to decline a job offer; as Standing (2002, p 277) observes, 'Dignified work can only evolve if ordinary people have the capacity to say "no"'.

New jobseeking conditions are being introduced for lone parents in the UK over the period 2008-10, starting with those whose youngest child is aged 12 or over and expanding to include those whose youngest child is aged seven or over. This is a striking example of a targeted reduction in autonomy. The state does not directly interfere in the decision married or cohabiting parents make about how to balance their responsibilities towards their children and paid work, but the new conditionality for lone parents removes that decision from unpartnered mothers on a low income. Choice and control over a matter of intense significance for parents and children alike is being removed from the individual and placed in the hands of the Secretary of State – but only for the poor.

Many of the ways in which social security seems to contribute to inequality of autonomy relate to the current construction of welfare to work and the conditions associated with it. Dean et al (2005) argue that welfare to work can and should be transformed from a 'work-first' to a 'life-first' approach. Such an approach would start from a right to work rather than an obligation to labour, and would entail recognising the value of unpaid work (for example, caring for children or others), as well as a wider range of human needs (for example, to be cared for, to learn and develop, and to interact with others).

Overview

The performance of the UK tax and benefit system is somewhat paradoxical. On the one hand, it is a powerful and effective tool for reducing inequalities in standards of living, both vertically and horizontally. Moreover, as a system based on legal rights and entitlements, social security provides a crucial guarantee of an independent source of income. On the other hand, by treating claimants with disrespect and suspicion, the way in which social security is delivered threatens to undermine key aspects of equality – in particular, equality of process and equality of autonomy. These negative impacts are felt most acutely by those with multiple sources of discrimination and disadvantage: for example, those who are not only poor, but also are from a minority ethnic group, or are disabled or have children to look after.

In terms of securing greater equality of outcome, social security and taxation face an increasingly uphill struggle. Inequality in original, market, incomes has grown significantly since the 1980s, which means that more redistributive effort is required just to prevent the gaps in disposable incomes getting wider. A chasm persists between the top and bottom of the distribution, and some groups – most notably Pakistani and Bangladeshi minority ethnic groups – face an unacceptably high risk of low income.

Social security itself continues to deliver significant equalisation of disposable incomes but the progressive effect of direct taxes is cancelled out by the regressive impact of indirect taxes. The taxation system is neutral with respect to vertical equality – a significant missed opportunity.

This chapter has offered a number of pointers to the ways in which the design and delivery of social security and taxation could be improved: a re-examination of the combined effects of direct and indirect taxes, with a view to maximising their potential as tools of redistribution; involving poor people themselves in redesigning the process of claiming benefits; and reconceptualising welfare to work, acknowledging the interdependence of all members of society whatever their current economic status, and recognising the value of unpaid as well as paid work.

Questions for discussion

(1) What aspects of inequality are most important in relation to the social security system?
(2) Does social security help to create a more equal society? What about direct and indirect taxes?
(3) How could the operation of social security be improved from an equality perspective?

Acknowledgements

I am grateful to Jane Millar, David Piachaud and Polly Vizard for helpful comments on earlier versions of this chapter. Access to the Family Resources Survey and the Households Below Average Income datasets was provided via the Data Archive at Essex University. Responsibility for the views expressed and any errors of fact or interpretation rest with the author alone.

Notes

[1] We also switch from Office for National Statistics (ONS) data to the Households Below Average Income (HBAI) dataset for the year 2004/05. This dataset is produced by the Department for Work and Pensions (DWP), based on a large representative household survey called the Family Resources Survey (FRS) (DWP, 2007a). It uses the same definition of income as the ONS data.

[2] We do not have reliable information on how income is shared within households, although ongoing projects in the Gender Equality Network programme look set to produce some interesting insights (GeNet, 2008). Previous research suggests that women in couples tend to have less personal income in their own right than men, from earnings and pensions, and that in many households the originator of the

income has more control over its use than other household members (Pahl, 1988; Sutherland, 1997).

[3] The ONS add a further stage, allocating a notional amount for benefits in kind from state education, the National Health Service (NHS), housing subsidy, and rail and bus travel subsidies, to calculate 'final income'. This is a controversial step for technical and conceptual reasons. The technical reason is that the evidence base for allocating these services to households is not very robust; for example, health spending is allocated by the age and sex profile of users of different kinds of services and their unit cost, which ignores other potential sources of variation in usage and costs. The conceptual reason is that while benefiting from cheaper travel can be seen as equivalent to a cash benefit, it is more difficult to see why receiving emergency treatment if you have the misfortune to be the victim of a road accident should be regarded as an addition to your household's 'final income'. Health and education services, in particular, are supplied to people who are in need; meeting that need does not add to their income relative to others.

[4] For this analysis, we return to the HBAI dataset described above. These figures do not match the ONS analysis exactly, but the definitions of original, gross and disposable income are comparable.

Website resources

www.dwp.gov.uk/asd/hbai.asp
Department for Work and Pensions: Households Below Average Income series
http://archive.cabinetoffice.gov.uk/equalitiesreview/
Equalities Review
www.equalityhumanrights.com/en/Pages/default.aspx
Equality and Human Rights Commission
www.statistics.gov.uk/StatBase/Product.asp?vlnk=10336
Office for National Statistics: effects of taxes and benefits on household income
www.equalities.gov.uk/
Government Equalities Office
www.statistics.gov.uk/about/data/measuring-equality/default.asp
Office for National Statistics: measuring equality

References

Atkinson, A. B. (2005) 'Top incomes in the UK over the 20th century', *Journal of the Royal Statistical Society*, vol 168, no 2, pp 325-43.

Berthoud, R. (2002) 'Poverty and prosperity among Britain's ethnic minorities', *Benefits: the Journal of Poverty and Social Justice*, vol 10, no 1, pp 3-8.

Berthoud, R. (2003) *Multiple disadvantage in employment: A quantitative analysis*, York: Joseph Rowntree Foundation, www.jrf.org.uk/bookshop/eBooks/1842631233.pdf

Burchardt, T. (2005) *The education and employment of disabled young people: Frustrated ambition*, Bristol: The Policy Press.

Burchardt, T. and Vizard, P. (2007) *Definition of equality and framework for measurement*, Final Recommendations of the Equalities Review Steering Group on Measurement, Paper 1, CASEpaper 120, London: London School of Economics and Political Science.

Citizens Advice (2006) *What the doctor ordered? CAB evidence on medical assessments for incapacity and disability benefits*, London: NACAB.

Committee of Public Accounts (2004) *Progress on improving the medical assessment of incapacity and disability benefits*, Sixteenth Report of 2003-04, HC 120, London: HMSO.

Dean, H., Bonvin, J.-M., Vielle, P. and Farvaque, N. (2005) 'Developing capabilities and rights in welfare-to-work policies', *European Societies*, vol 7, no 1, pp 3-26.

Dworkin, R. (1981) 'What is equality? Part 2: equality of resources', *Philosophy and Public Affairs*, vol 10, pp 283-345.

DWP (Department for Work and Pensions) (2007a) *Households Below Average Income 1994/95–2005/06*, London: DWP, www.dwp.gov.uk/asd/hbai.asp

DWP (2007b) *In work, better off: Next steps to full employment*, London: DWP, www.dwp.gov.uk/welfarereform/in-work-better-off/

DWP (2008) *Households Below Average Income 1994/95–2006/07*, London: DWP, www.dwp.gov.uk/asd/hbai.asp

EHRC (Equality and Human Rights Commission) (2008) 'Public authorities', pages describing the public sector equality duties, www.equalityhumanrights.com/en/Pages/default.aspx

Equalities Review (2007) *Fairness and freedom: The final report of the Equalities Review*, London: Equalities Review, http://archive.cabinetoffice.gov.uk/equalitiesreview/

Falkingham, J. and Hills, J. (1995) *The dynamic of welfare: The welfare state and the life cycle*, Hemel Hempstead: Prentice Hall.

Figari, F., Immervoll, H., Levy, H. and Sutherland, H. (2007) *Inequalities within couples: Market incomes and the role of taxes and benefits in Europe*, GeNet Working Paper No 29, www.genet.ac.uk/workpapers/GeNet2007p29.pdf

GeNet (ESRC Gender Equality Network) (2008) *Project index*, www.genet.ac.uk/projects/index.html

Goode, J., Callender, C. and Lister, R. (1998) *Purse or wallet? Gender inequalities and income distribution within families on benefits*, London: Policy Studies Institute.

Hills, J. (2004) *Inequality and the state*, Oxford: Oxford University Press.

House of Commons (2000) *Medical services*, Social Security Select Committee, 1999/2000 session, 3rd report, London: HMSO.

House of Commons (2001) *The Social Fund*, Social Security Select Committee, 3rd report, HC 232, London: The Stationery Office.

Huby, M. and Dix, G. (1992) *Evaluating the Social Fund*, DSS Research Report No 9, London: HMSO.

Legge, K., Hartfree, Y., Stafford, B., Magadi, M., Beckhelling, J., Predelli, L. and Middleton, S. (2006) *The Social Fund: Current role and future* direction, York: Joseph Rowntree Foundation.

Lister, R. (2008) 'Recognition and voice: the challenge for social justice', in G. Craig, T. Burchardt and D. Gordon (eds) *Social justice and public policy: Seeking fairness in diverse societies*, Bristol: The Policy Press.

ONS (Office for National Statistics) (2007) 'The effects of taxes and benefits on household income, 2005-06', www.statistics.gov.uk/cci/article.asp?ID=1804&Pos=1&ColRank=1&Rank=144

Pahl, J. (1988) *Money and marriage*, Basingstoke: Macmillan.

Piachaud, D. (2007) 'The restructuring of redistribution', in J. Hills, J. Le Grand and D. Piachaud (eds) *Making social policy work*, Bristol: The Policy Press, pp 199-200.

Sen, A. (1985) *Commodities and capabilities*, Oxford: North Holland.

Smith, R. (1990) *Under the breadline: Claimants, the Social Fund and the voluntary sector: A case study*, London: The Children's Society.

Standing, G. (2002) *Beyond the new paternalism: Basic security as equality*, London: Verso.

Stuber, J. and Schlesinger, M. (2006) 'Sources of stigma for means-tested government programs', *Social Science and Medicine*, vol 63, pp 933-45.

Sutherland, H. (1997) 'Women, men and the redistribution of income', *Fiscal Studies*, vol 18, no 1, pp 1-22.

Vizard, P. and Burchardt, T. (2007) *Developing a capability list*, Final Recommendations of the Equalities Review Steering Group on Measurement, Paper 2, CASEpaper 121, London: London School of Economics and Political Science.

Wolff, J. (1998) 'Fairness, respect, and the egalitarian ethos', *Philosophy and Public Affairs*, vol 27, no 2, pp 97-122.

Wright, S. (2003) 'The street-level implementation of unemployment policy', in J. Millar (ed) *Understanding social security* (first edition), Bristol: The Policy Press.

Life beyond work? Safety nets and 'security for those who cannot' work

Richard Silburn and Saul Becker

Summary

'Work for those who can, security for those who cannot': this has been the basis for Labour's welfare reforms for over a decade. Welfare policies and delivery have to date concentrated heavily on the first half of the equation but have neglected 'security for those who cannot' – there is no official standard or measure as to what 'security' actually means in practice. This chapter:

- examines the nature of the current 'safety net' in the social security system and how we got here;
- explores the meaning of 'security';
- assesses whether the benefits system provides 'security' to those who cannot work by examining evidence from a range of living standard proxy indicators, Income Support and the Social Fund;
- considers how the policy focus on 'work for those who can' has undermined the promotion of *real* security for those who cannot.

Work and welfare

The Labour governments under both Tony Blair and Gordon Brown have been committed to the modernising of the welfare state. From the outset, the government set itself ambitious targets for tackling poverty and social exclusion, and for the promotion of opportunity and social inclusion (DSS, 1998a, 1998b, 1999). The core conviction that has driven the government's welfare policy consistently since 1997 is that the most reliable and socially desirable route out of poverty is through paid employment. Essentially, the duty of government is to provide people with the assistance they need to find jobs; the duty of individuals is to seek training (if necessary), find work and thus become independent. It is also clear that the government is convinced that many people who are currently on long-term benefits would prefer to work, and given the right help and support could find and hold down jobs.

During its first and second terms, the New Labour government gradually but determinedly redefined the relationship between benefits ('welfare') and work, as discussed in more detail in various chapters in this volume (Chapter Six, Carmel and Papadopoulos; Chapter Eleven, Wright; Chapter Twelve, Sainsbury). During its third term in government, following the May 2005 General Election, these principles and policies have been reaffirmed, if anything with even greater emphasis. In *The principles of welfare reform* (DWP, 2005, p 2) the first two principles were: '1. Help people to help themselves by offering a ladder to self-reliance and self-determination, not merely a safety-net in time of need. 2. See work as the best route out of welfare'. Two later Green Papers (DWP, 2006, 2007a) set targets and outlined policies to increase employment among lone parents, jobseekers, disabled people and those with health conditions, and other disadvantaged groups. The assertion behind these policies is that 'most people should work: it is good for them, their families and society, and key to tackling child poverty' (DWP, 2007a, p 98).

The 'safety net'

But what of those people who cannot work, either because of old age, illness, disability, mental disorder, frailty or caring/family responsibilities? There is a well-established association between these circumstances and conditions and worklessness – which is itself strongly associated with low income and hardship. Many people in these groups face particular barriers to finding and then keeping jobs. For example, for families with children the biggest constraints on taking paid work are illness, disability and caring responsibilities (Marsh et al, 2001). Many family carers – people who provide unpaid care to other family members – find it hard to access or retain paid employment precisely because of the demands of those caring responsibilities (Becker and Silburn, 1999).

What kind of 'safety net' should there be for these groups, and what standard of living should they be able to afford on benefits – when all around them both policy and discourse are promoting the principles, values, requirements and responsibilities of paid work? The four most important means-tested benefits or payments that comprise the safety net today are presented in ***Box 4.1***.

Box 4.1: The social security 'safety net'

(1) *Jobseeker's Allowance (JSA)*, a benefit for those out of work and seeking work. Unemployed men and women who are fit for work may apply for JSA. So-called income-based JSA can be paid, subject to a means test, to those unemployed people with inadequate National Insurance (NI) contributions, or who have exhausted their entitlement to contribution-based JSA (normally a maximum of 182 days). In May 2007 there were 661,000 claimants of income-based JSA, about two thirds of all JSA claimants. About two thirds of those claiming income-based JSA are single men.

(2) *Pension Credit*, for those who have reached retirement age and no longer need to work. Pension Credit is a means-tested supplement that brings the incomes of retirement pensioners up to a guaranteed minimum level. In May 2007, there were nearly 12 million retirement pensioners of whom 2.7 million were claiming Pension Credit.

(3) *Income Support (IS)*, essentially for those of working age who are unable to work. Income Support is paid (May 2007) to over two million people of working age who for one reason or another are unable to seek work. The three largest categories of IS claimants are: those who cannot work for reasons of poor health; lone parents; and carers. Over half of all IS claimants – 1.2 million people – are disabled or 'incapacitated'. The total number of people claiming Incapacity Benefit (IB) is much larger than this (about 2.5 million), but those whose incomes need topping-up by IS live in the poorest households. The second largest group of IS claimants are lone parents. Rather over 750,000 lone parents (overwhelmingly women) claim IS for themselves and their dependent children. An additional 85,000 IS claimants are carers. In most cases this means that they provide at least 35 hours a week of care for another person, but rely on means-tested benefits for the resources to meet their own needs.

(4) *The Social Fund*, mostly discretionary loans for people who run out of money or need 'extra' cash for specific needs. The Social Fund was introduced in 1988 and provides budgeting and crisis loans, and community care grants, from a discretionary and cash-limited fund for additional expenses that are difficult to meet from regular income, as well as a number of other payments from a 'regulated' Social Fund. In 2005/06 the number of applications for payments from the discretionary fund was 3,796,000, and an award was made in 2,641,000 of them (DWP, 2007b).

How did we get into this situation?

The figures in ***Box 4.1*** suggest that, in the mid-2000s, more than five million people rely entirely on means-tested JSA, Pension Credit or IS, their safety net (see also Chapter One, Millar, this volume). In the rest of this chapter we focus especially on IS and the Social Fund to assess the nature of the safety net and the security and quality of life it provides for those who rely on it. We start by exploring how we got to where we are today, in particular in relation to the reasons for the growth in importance of the means-tested safety net and the attempts to regulate discretion.

The failure of National Insurance

When the British social security system was radically reconstructed at the end of the Second World War, the hope was that most people who were unable to meet their needs from their earnings would be supported by NI benefits, designed to cover all the major contingencies and life hazards. National Insurance benefits would be earned by regular contributions deducted from earnings, and were therefore entitlements to be paid without regard to any other means the claimant may have.

At the same time it was anticipated that there would be a small number of people either who were unable to satisfy the contribution requirements of the NI system, or whose personal circumstances were unusual and whose needs would have to be met by some other means, a social security safety net. This was to be non-contributory and means-tested National Assistance (NA).

The abiding problem with the safety net of means-tested public assistance from the outset in 1948 to the present day is that far too many people have been forced to rely on it. From the very beginning, in July 1948, the number receiving NA was larger than had been anticipated, reaching a million within the first six months. Thereafter the number of claimants rose slowly but steadily until by the time NA was abolished in 1966 the number of weekly allowances in payment was almost two million. The fundamental reason for this unexpected outcome was that the basic rates of NI benefits in 1948 had been set at too low a level, in many cases lower than the levels set for NA. This meant that a very large number of people, especially retirement pensioners, were able to claim NA to supplement their NI payments. Throughout the 18 years of the National Assistance Board (NAB) the majority of NA claimants (usually about 75% of them) were claiming NA to supplement NI payments. It was and still is the failure of NI benefits adequately to meet everyday needs that accounts for the continuing large-scale reliance on the means-tested social security safety net.

The role of discretion

The officers of the NAB inherited from their predecessors in the wartime Assistance Board (and before that the Unemployment Assistance Board) very considerable discretionary powers. The basic scale-rates of benefit were set by Parliament and established a baseline, but beyond that the officers of the Board had the power to make additions to the basic scale-rates where a claimant had a special need. There were two types of discretionary addition. There were *regular additions* to the weekly allowances for claimants with special circumstances and there were *one-off payments* to meet an immediate need. It was for the NAB officer to determine where there was a special circumstance or an immediate need, and how that may best be dealt with by an additional allowance or a single payment. For some years this aroused little concern; but from the late 1950s and gathering force throughout the 1960s and 1970s came the criticism that there were inevitable and serious inconsistencies between officers and between offices in how these powers were interpreted, and that claimants had no clear idea about what they were entitled to. In short, the exercise of officer discretion came increasingly to be seen as arbitrary, and possibly unjust. Around this issue consolidated the welfare rights movement, arguing for much clearer, rights-based, accounts of entitlements.

Meanwhile, there were those who were uneasy at the apparently inexorable rise in claimant numbers and the associated rise in the number and costs of discretionary additional payments. For them the existence of major areas of discretion was an open-ended temptation for claimants and their advisors to push at the soft margins of the system, gradually broadening and deepening the flow of extra payments. If discretion was replaced by regulation, then the situation could be brought under firmer control, in a manner that would reduce or at least control expenditure.

Box 4.2 summarises the ways in which the role of discretion was increasingly regulated and eventually significantly reduced; the first (largely unsuccessful) attempt at regulating discretion by the Supplementary Benefits Commission in 1966; the second (also largely unsuccessful) tightening of regulatory control in 1979, leading to the much more stringent controls introduced in 1988. These reforms, replacing Supplementary Benefit (SB) with IS, were the most far-reaching in their determination to contain costly discretionary additions. Additional Requirements Payments were abolished altogether. Single Payments were replaced by the Social Fund, which only gives grants for maternity and funeral costs and for people leaving residential care. Other claimants have to apply for an interest-free loan, to be repaid by deductions from their ongoing benefit payments. Moreover, and crucially, the Social Fund is cash-limited, so the Social Fund officers work within the constraints of a monthly and annual budget, which cannot normally be exceeded. This, the current safety net, is essentially unchanged, 20 years after it was introduced.

Box 4.2: The erosion of officer discretion

Phase One: National Assistance, 1948–66

Basic scale-rates, supplemented by *discretionary* additions:

- *Special Circumstances Additions*: regular additions to the weekly allowances. Between 1951 and 1965 the proportion of claimants receiving these payments rose from 33% to 58%.
- *Special Needs Payments*: single payments to meet an immediate need. Between 1951 and 1965 the number of these payments increased from 152,000 to 345,000.

Phase Two: Supplementary Benefit, 1966–79

Basic scale-rates, supplemented by *regulated* discretionary additions:

- *Exceptional Circumstances Additions*: regular additions to the weekly allowances. Between 1968 and 1979 the number of these payments increased from 540,000 to 2,252,000.
- *Exceptional Needs Payments*: single payments to meet an immediate need. Between 1968 and 1979 the number of single payments rose from 470,000 to 1,134,000.

Phase Three: Supplementary Benefit, 1979–88

Basic scale-rates, supplemented by *tightly regulated* discretionary additions:

- *Additional Requirements Payments*: regular additions to the weekly allowances. By 1986 nearly two thirds of all SB claimants received these payments, and as many as 98% of all SB pensioner couples (Becker and Silburn, 1990).
- *Single Payments*: single payments to meet an immediate need. Between 1980 and 1986 the number of single payments rose from one million to over four million.

Phase Four: Income Support, 1988–today

Basic scale-rates, supplemented by:

- premiums for defined groups of claimants, replacing Additional Requirements Payments.
- *the Social Fund*: a cash-limited budget giving tightly regulated grants, and discretionary loans.

'Security for those who cannot' work

What does the phrase, 'security for those who cannot' work mean? As a society we have a notion of what 'security' means in principle, even if the concept is more problematic in practice. Security is very much about the *condition* of being secure, having freedom from worry and uncertainty, and of being protected from danger, anxiety or apprehension. It is associated with a feeling of confidence, certainty and safety (***Box 4.3***).

Box 4.3: The meaning of 'security'

I. The condition of being secure. 2. The condition of being protected from or not exposed to danger; safety. 3. Freedom from doubt. Now chiefly, well-founded confidence, certainty. 4. Freedom from care, anxiety or apprehension; a feeling of safety. (*Oxford English Dictionary*, 1973, p 1927)

In 1998 the government confirmed that: 'Those people for whom work is not an option are entitled to an income which allows for *a decent life*' (DSS, 1998a, p 63, emphasis added). The government also identified its responsibility to 'support those unable to work so that they can lead *a life of dignity and security*' (DSS, 1998a, p 80, emphasis added). Here we have further insights into what 'security' might comprise, especially how it can be applied *in practice*. Security is closely linked with 'a decent life' and with 'a life of dignity'. Dignity is defined in the *Oxford English Dictionary* as 'The *quality* of being worthy or honourable; worth, excellence' (*Oxford English Dictionary*, 1973, p 548, emphasis added).

Thus, security is a *type of human condition*, and dignity is a *quality of human worth*. When linked together in policy discourse, security and dignity are concerned with valuing people unconditionally for what they are, and providing them with a standard of living that provides them with protection, safety and certainty in their living arrangements and quality of life. These principles are articulated further, for example, in the government's pledge to give disabled people 'the support they need to lead a *fulfilling life with dignity*' (DSS, 1998a, p 51, emphasis added). More recently, *Ready for work* (DWP, 2007a) affirms that 'the benefit system must also provide a *decent standard of living* for people who are not able to work' (p 98, emphasis added).

We need to note in these phrases not just what is said but also what is not. The references throughout are to security and dignity – not *some* security and *some* dignity – and not for *some* disabled people or *some* of those who cannot work – but presumably 'for all'. The government seems to be saying that there is some *absolute* standard that could be defined as 'a decent life', 'a decent standard of living', 'a life of dignity and security' and 'a fulfilling life with dignity' and that this outcome should be available unconditionally to all those who cannot work. In practice, however, no government has ever revealed or articulated what that standard of security and dignity might be. However, despite the lack of an official measure or standard, it is still possible to assess whether or not those who cannot work are living a life of dignity and security. To do this we need to turn to 'proxy' indicators of 'security', or, more accurately, indicators of a *lack* of security and dignity.

The evidence on 'security' and 'dignity'

There is an abundance of evidence on the circumstances, lifestyles and well-being afforded to people who cannot work and who rely on IS for some or most of their income. Sources include pressure groups, academics, poor people and official government publications. In general terms, most of these sources published over the past 50 years have concluded that benefit levels are inadequate to maintain a *decent* or 'adequate' standard of living.

For example, the Child Poverty Action Group (CPAG) has gathered evidence on the experience of poverty for over 40 years and draws together data from academics, official sources and poor people themselves. For example, *Poverty: The facts* (Flaherty et al, 2004) documents in detail the experiences and living standards of people living on benefits. It shows the long-term effects of living on a low income, how people manage to get by from day to day, and the sacrifices they make in their daily lives. They often go without basic household items and amenities that most of us expect as part of ordinary modern living; they cannot afford a nutritious diet; they do not have enough money for fuel or to meet their clothing needs; many experience considerable or severe hardship and debt: 'Life on a low income means going without, which in turn can lead to longer-term problems such as poor health, debt, poor housing and homelessness' (Flaherty et al, 2004, p 110).

This picture is confirmed by evidence from *academic* sources. Of especial interest is the Budget Standard approach, revived, even reinvented, in the 1970s by the Family Budget Unit at York University. Essentially, Budget Standards are specified baskets of goods and services that (when priced) represent predefined living standards. The methodology can be used to measure the levels below which good health, social integration and satisfactory standards of living are at risk for different groups of people. Early examples of Budget Standard estimates for lone-parent and two-parent families demonstrated that benefit levels were not adequate to provide modest or even basic standards of living. The Family Budget Unit data for families with children showed that when New Labour first came to power, IS was paid at a rate below the level of a 'low cost but acceptable' living standard. Other evidence from that time shows that parents spent far more on their children, including on food, than was allowed in the IS allowances for children (Middleton et al, 1997). And evidence from qualitative, in-depth studies on how people on low incomes actually manage shows how difficult it is to make ends meet (see, for example, Kempson, 1996).

Since then a number of projects have continued to develop detailed budgets to meet the needs of other groups, such as older people (Parker, 2000), children

(Middleton, 2005) and disabled people (Dobson and Middleton, 1998; Smith et al, 2004). Another important study has tried to elaborate a Minimum Income for Healthy Living (MIHL) (Morris and Deeming, 2004). These standards can be used as a yardstick to judge whether or not benefit levels are adequate (see Becker, 1997; Veit-Wilson, 1998).

Other sources of evidence on 'security' include the *voices of poor people themselves* speaking about their experiences. Living on benefits is often experienced in punitive and exclusionary ways (Strelitz and Lister, 2008). Low benefit levels reinforce poverty and social exclusion rather than enabling people to live a life of security and dignity (Legge et al, 2007); they also make it hard if not impossible to gain or maintain independence (Beresford et al, 1999; ATD Fourth World, 2000; Turner, 2000; UK Coalition Against Poverty, 2000). However, it is regrettably rare for the voices and accounts of poor people (with first-hand experience of benefits policy and delivery) to be taken seriously in the policy-making process (Lister, 2002).

Recent *official data* confirm that the poorest in society still experience severe hardship. For example, Marsh et al (2001) show that in the late 1990s many low-income families were unable to sustain a standard of living consistent with good health and family well-being. Substantial numbers reported difficulties affording even the most basic food and clothing items. Few made use of basic financial services such as bank accounts and more than half had accumulated debts. Forty per cent of non-working families were in severe hardship, and this affected lone parents disproportionately. Overall, more than eight in 10 children in all non-working households were living in hardship. It is the presence of illness, disability and caring responsibilities that is most likely to increase the hardship that non-working families experience.

Since Marsh et al's (2001) report was published, changes in levels of benefit and the introduction of tax credits have helped to improve the circumstances of some families and vulnerable groups. There is evidence to show that the circumstances of older people and of families with children have improved although there is still room for further improvement (Hills and Stewart, 2005). Recent evidence from the Families and Children Survey indicates that as the income of poor families rises, there is a drop in hardship (as measured by items such as problems with heating or accommodation, money worries, shortfalls in food, clothing, consumer durables etc). Poor families use their extra finances to improve living conditions for their children (Gregg et al, 2005, p 274; Lyon et al, 2006).

Improving security and dignity?

How far have government policies since 1997 been able to meet their promise of 'security for those who cannot' work? In this section we first consider the organisation of support and services and second the level of support and poverty rates.

There have been significant structural changes intended, at least in part, to provide better support to those who cannot work. The introduction of Jobcentre Plus and the Pension Service in 2001/02 was described by the-then Secretary of State for Work and Pensions as 'the most comprehensive shake-up of welfare delivery for a generation with a clear focus on individual need' (DWP, 2002). In came a new phrase to guide delivery: 'the work you want, the help you need'. Jobcentre Plus personal advisors and those working for the Pensions Service are the first port of call for the 'help you need'. Their concern is not solely to get the right benefits to the right clients at the right time, but to ensure that they also receive any other support that they might need. This recognises that many people who cannot work have multiple needs, and while an adequate income is central to this, so too might be the need for health and social care support (Becker, 1997, 2000). From April 2008 the Pension Service was amalgamated with the Disability and Carers Service to become the Pension, Disability and Carers Service, in recognition that the separate agencies increasingly shared a common customer base.

The government has recognised that 'Services – especially education, health and housing – are at least as important as cash benefits in promoting independence and security; tackling poverty and widening opportunity' (DSS, 1998a, p 4). Significant proportions of the population are frail, have some form of mental illness or disability or are unpaid family carers. Local authority adult social care and children's services exist to keep these and other vulnerable groups – including families with children – safe, and to promote their security, dignity, integration, well-being and independence through the provision, primarily, of care-related *services*. Most users of local authority social care services are also in receipt of social security benefits, especially means-tested payments (Becker and Silburn, 1990; Becker, 1997). Moreover, they are also the most costly clients (in expenditure terms) of social security – older people, sick/disabled people and families (Evandrou and Falkingham, 1998; Evans, 1998). Since 1948, 'cash' and 'care' in the UK have been provided by separate authorities, unlike most other European countries where the functions are often combined in some way (Hill, 2000, p 119). But there are significant overlaps in functions, with local authority services taking on important income maintenance roles, and social security (particularly means-tested benefits) becoming increasingly concerned with 'the whole person'. 'Cash' and 'care' are two sides of the 'security for those who cannot' work coin and will need to work more closely together if 'security' and 'dignity' are to be promoted (Becker, 2003; Glendinning and Kemp, 2006).

Meanwhile, benefit levels have been increased particularly for children and pensioners, and poverty rates for these groups have fallen. The children's rates of IS have been increased substantially in real terms. The number of children in poverty has fallen by 700,000 – a 23% decline since 1998/99 (Harker, 2006; Chapter Nine, Ridge, this volume). Regular annual increases in the retirement pension, but more dramatically the introduction of the Pension Credit, have greatly improved the circumstances of the most disadvantaged retirement pensioners; between the late 1990s and 2004/05 the overall pensioner poverty rate fell from 27% to 17%, with an even greater drop for single pensioners (Palmer et al, 2006; Chapter Ten, McKay, this volume).

Nevertheless, overall levels of poverty and social exclusion remain high. For example, the annual monitoring of poverty and social exclusion conducted by the New Policy Institute and Joseph Rowntree Foundation (Palmer et al, 2006) shows that the number of people living in households with less than 60% of the median income (one of the preferred thresholds of income poverty used by both the European Union [EU] and the UK government) was over 14 million in 1996/97, it then gradually dropped year on year to about 12 million in 2004/05, before rising again to nearly 13 million in 2005/06 (the same level as in 2003/04). This picture, of around one fifth to one quarter of the population living in income poverty, is confirmed by other academic sources. For example, a national Poverty and Social Exclusion Survey, which measured poverty by reference to the enforced lack of socially perceived necessities (Gordon et al, 2000) suggested that at the end of 1999, 14.5 million people (26%) were living in poverty – defined as lacking two or more socially perceived necessities. And this is also confirmed by the government's own statistics – the Households Below Average Income (HBAI) series. The report for the period 2005/06 shows that while there has been significant income growth in real terms at the lower end of the income distribution since 1997, the proportion of the population with less than 60% of the median income after housing costs stands at 22%, just 2% lower than the figure in 1997. The HBAI series also identifies those groups within the population with an above average risk of low income. These include children in families with unemployed parents, and those in families with four or more children, older pensioners, some minority ethnic households, disabled people, households in social housing, and adults without educational qualifications (DWP, 2007c). It is clear from this list that most of the individuals and families identified are likely to have additional and probably multiple needs that must be addressed if the goal of 'security' is to be achieved.

The conclusion is inescapable that while there has been a considerable improvement in the income levels for some families with children, and for retirement pensioners, and some improvement in tackling social exclusion for the population as a whole, there are still millions of people in Britain today living on very low disposable incomes, experiencing considerable hardship and an enforced lack of necessities, and that the groups most likely to be in these situations are largely predictable – those who for one reason or another cannot work or cannot find work.

The Social Fund

In considering 'security for those who cannot' work we must not ignore the role of the discretionary Social Fund in providing a 'safety net' to millions of people on a low income with additional expenses that are difficult to meet from their regular income. There is an extensive literature on the Social Fund, which has been the cause of considerable controversy since it was introduced in 1988, not only because of its discretionary, cash-limited and loan-based nature, but also because of the overwhelming evidence from academic and official reviews, and from many poor people themselves, that it actually contributes to poverty and hardship for many people on a low income, rather than alleviating it (Craig, 1989; Becker and Silburn, 1990; SSRC, 1991; Beresford and Turner, 1997; Legge et al, 2007).

The original justification for the introduction of the Social Fund – to target benefits on those most in need through a process of 'considered decision making', and to control expenditure more carefully (Becker and Silburn, 1989) – has spawned a system where many low-income families are forced to live on levels of benefit well below IS rates because of the need to repay (interest-free) loans. For example, in February 2007, 771,000 claimants on IS (mostly disabled people or single parents) had their weekly benefit reduced by an average of £11.07 by way of loan repayment. In 2006/07, a total of £552 million was recovered. For 2007/08, 'an amount of £610 million has been allocated for loans, of which £523.8 million will be provided through the repayment of loans' (DWP, 2007b, para 6.7).

It is striking to note that in 1988, the last year of the old Single Payments scheme (which the Social Fund replaced), £334 million was distributed as outright grants for exceptional needs (Becker and Silburn, 1989), whereas 20 years later in 2006/07 the total value of grants (the Sure Start maternity grants and funeral payments under the regulated part of the Social Fund, and the discretionary Community Care Grants) was only £307 million.

The Social Fund exacerbates poverty and fuels *in*security for many people. In the absence of clear legal rights, applicants to the Fund experience uncertainty as to whether or not an application will be successful. Waiting for a decision to be made, including the terms of any repayments, adds to their anxiety and apprehension, and many who do get a payment (a loan) have their disposable income reduced below levels that are already insufficient to provide a low cost but acceptable standard of living. These outcomes for applicants are the very antipathy of 'security' (***Box 4.3***).

In 2001, the Social Security Select Committee (now the Committee for Work and Pensions) called for an urgent review of the discretionary Social Fund, and CPAG and others have also called on the government to reform the scheme (Social Security Select Committee, 2001; Howard, 2002). In May 2007, the House of Commons Work and Pensions Committee report concluded that:

> We have been presented with evidence of many of the same problems that existed in 2001: outdated distribution of budgets, inaccurate decisions, lack of consistency and poor management information … there has been no formal consultation process on reform with no timetable for improvements … it is our impression that the Social Fund policy is now in limbo … we recommend that the DWP [Department for Work and Pensions] must now address the performance of the Fund as a matter of urgency, and launch a formal consultation exercise on how it can be improved. (House of Commons Work and Pensions Committee, 2007, p 32)

Assessment and conclusions

In 1999, Bennett and Walker observed that 'the outlines of a complementary New Labour strategy to achieve security and dignity for all those not in paid work are as yet confused, contradictory and incomplete' (Bennett and Walker, 1999, p 35). Ten years on, not much has changed. The overwhelming emphasis on the policy of 'work for those who can' has meant less overt attention paid to the 'security for those who cannot'. Some progress has been made in improving support for some groups, notably children and pensioners. Nevertheless, this is still Labour's 'neglected welfare principle' (Becker, 2003).

Whatever happens to employment rates in future, it will always be the case that there will be a substantial number of people for whom paid work is not a reasonable expectation or possibility, because of the severity of their physical or mental condition, or their heavy childcare responsibilities, or because of the care needs of other family members. We must not be allowed to overlook the fact that 'paid employment is not a viable option for everybody' (Howard, 2001, p 205) and that 'a substantial proportion of the Department's [DWP's] customers are not in the market for work-focused services. Providing security and support for those whom paid employment may never be a realistic goal, and for people in retirement, will be a major service challenge' (Social Security Advisory Committee, 2002, p 3). For these people security is in the first place financial. To sustain 'a decent life' and 'a life of dignity and security' for those in greatest need will require higher disposable income. But there is little evidence that the government has considered in detail what this might mean in practice. The government has no standard or measure by which to judge whether the current benefit levels actually provide security to those who cannot work.

Why is the government so reluctant to engage publicly in a discussion about the adequacy of benefit levels and the redistributive function of social security, or the reform of the Social Fund? This may be partly because it knows that a discussion of this kind will be vindictively distorted by the tabloid press, which is quick to pander to crude anti-claimant prejudice. But it may also be the case that policy makers throughout the postwar period have been influenced by the belief (or the fear) that paying 'adequate' (never mind 'generous') levels of benefits to those who cannot work, and the establishment of a rights-based and grants-dominated safety net for the poorest, will reinforce 'dependency' and act as a magnet to attract people into making claims, thus undermining the guiding principle of 'work for those who can'. The confusion of those who *cannot* work with those who *will not* work has bedevilled both opinion and policy for too long, and has inhibited meaningful debate about the adequacy of benefits and the Social Fund in promoting security and dignity for those in greatest need. Can we hope that when 'work for those who can' has run its course, then the genuine needs of those still in greatest need will be better and more sympathetically understood? If the government truly wants those who cannot work to have an income that allows for 'a decent life' and 'a life of dignity and security' then it must be prepared to grasp the nettle of Minimum Income Standards, and – as the European Commission has suggested – to define a Minimum Income Standard at a level considered 'sufficient to cover essential needs with regard to respect for human dignity' (Becker, 1997, p 166; Veit-Wilson, 1998).

But decency and dignity need more than just money. As important is the 'tone' of the delivery systems. Low take-up of entitlements throughout the postwar period and reluctance to claim them have been partially explained by the enduring stigma that is felt by many. The experience of the Pension Service illustrates what might be possible. Detaching retirement pensioners from IS to a dedicated Pension Service (and, since April 2008, the new Pension, Disability and Carers Service) may gradually lead to a service that is seen as helpful and proactive, rather than grudging and suspicious. Certainly the Pension Service has made a serious effort to increase take-up (which stands at between 60% and 69% of those eligible) by directly contacting potential clients.

The government will also have to engage in a number of other hard debates. It will need to reconsider the relationship between social insurance, private insurance and means-tested benefits and show how each of these relates to issues of personal 'security'. And it will also need to engage in a meaningful debate as to the nature and value of 'work'. The government's equating of work as being synonymous with *paid* employment, and its implicit denigration of other forms of unpaid work in the home and community (such as family care-giving, bringing up children, volunteering and so on), serve to undervalue those people engaged in unpaid work and to downgrade and devalue their contribution to both society and the economy. It is also important that the government remembers that 'security' for those who cannot work is not just a function of social security alone (and adequate levels of benefits in particular), but that security and dignity are best guaranteed through a combination of money and services. Adequate levels of disposable income and reliable, good-quality housing, education, health and social care *services* are the necessary foundations for *real* security for 'those who cannot work', to promote their well-being, independence, dignity and freedom from poverty and exclusion (Becker, 1997). The government will need to think more about how 'cash' and 'care' policy can become more integrated and how money and services can be delivered in a seamless manner, to promote security for those both in and out of work.

Overview

- To promote real security for those who cannot work, the government needs to pay more attention to what 'security' and 'dignity' should mean in practice.
- The government will need to define and measure 'security' and define Minimum Income Standards; it will also need to bring about a closer coordination or integration of the work and functions of social security, housing, health and social care authorities.
- To have a 'life of dignity and security' people who cannot work will require adequate (which means higher) disposable income, and adequate (which means good-quality and reliable) services. Together, 'cash' and 'care' are the foundations for security, dignity, independence and social inclusion.

Questions for discussion

(1) What is the 'safety net' in the current British social security system? Who is it there to help, and why do we need it?
(2) Does the British social security system provide 'security' for those who cannot work?
(3) What type of evidence is available to help us determine whether or not people who cannot work have achieved a 'life of dignity and security'? Which type of evidence do you trust most, and why?
(4) What might real 'security' for those who cannot work comprise in practice?
(5) What are the key agencies that should provide security and help to those who cannot work?

(6) Why do you think successive Labour governments have neglected 'security for those who cannot' work and focused far more on 'work for those who can'?

Website resources

www.cpag.org.uk
Child Poverty Action Group
www.dwp.gov.uk
Department for Work and Pensions
www.jobcentreplus.gov.uk
Jobcentre Plus
www.rightsnet.org.uk
Rights Net

References

ATD Fourth World (2000) *Participation works: Involving people in poverty in policy making*, London: ATD Fourth World.

Becker, S. (1997) *Responding to poverty: The politics of cash and care*, Harlow: Longman.

Becker, S. (2000) 'Carers and indicators of vulnerability to social exclusion', *Benefits*, no 28, pp 1-4.

Becker, S. (2003) '"Security for those who cannot": Labour's neglected welfare principle', in J. Millar (ed) *Understanding social security: Issues for policy and practice* (first edition), Bristol: The Policy Press, pp 103-22.

Becker, S. and Silburn, R. (1989) 'Back to the future: the process of considered decision-making', in G. Craig (ed) *Your flexible friend: Voluntary organisations, claimants and the Social Fund*, London: Social Security Consortium/Association of Metropolitan Authorities, pp 24-40.

Becker, S. and Silburn, R. (1990) *The new poor clients: Social work, poverty and the Social Fund*, Sutton: Community Care/Reed Business Publishing.

Becker, S. and Silburn, R. (1999) *We're in this together: Conversations with families in caring relationships*, London: Carers National Association.

Bennett, F. and Walker, R. (1999) 'Working with work', *Benefits*, no 25, p 35.

Beresford, P. and Turner, M. (1997) *It's our welfare: Report of the Citizen's Commission on the Future of the Welfare State*, London: National Institute for Social Work.

Beresford, P., Green, D., Lister, R. and Woodard, K. (1999) *Poverty first hand: Poor people speak for themselves*, London: CPAG.

Craig, G. (ed) (1989) *Your flexible friend: Voluntary organisations, claimants and the Social Fund*, London: Social Security Consortium/Association of Metropolitan Authorities.

Dobson, B. and Middleton, S. (1998) *Paying to care: The cost of childhood disability*, York: Joseph Rowntree Foundation.

DSS (Department of Social Security) (1998a) *New ambitions for our country: A new contract for welfare*, Cm 3805, London: The Stationery Office.

DSS (1998b) *A new contract for welfare: Principles into practice*, London: The Stationery Office.

DSS (1999) *Opportunity for all: Tackling poverty and social exclusion*, Cm 4445, London: The Stationery Office.

DWP (Department for Work and Pensions) (2002) 'Darling announces radical new jobs target', Press Release EMP1903-Radical, 19 March, London: DWP.

DWP (2005) *The principles of welfare reform: The values and principles which shape the government's vision of the future of the welfare state*, London: DWP.

DWP (2006) *A New Deal for Welfare: Empowering people to work*, Cm 6730, London: The Stationery Office.

DWP (2007a) *Ready for work: Full employment in our generation*, Cm 7290, London: The Stationery Office.

DWP (2007b) *Annual Report on the Social Fund 2006/7*, Cm 7161, London: The Stationery Office.

DWP (2007c) *Households Below Average Income 1994/95–2005/06*, Leeds: Corporate Document Services.

Evandrou, M. and Falkingham, J. (1998) 'The personal social services', in H. Glennerster and J. Hills (eds) *The state of welfare: The economics of social spending*, Oxford: Oxford University Press, pp 189-256.

Evans, M. (1998) 'Social security', in H. Glennerster and J. Hills (eds) *The state of welfare: The economics of social spending*, Oxford: Oxford University Press, pp 257-307.

Flaherty, J., Veit-Wilson, J. and Dornan, P. (2004) *Poverty: The facts*, London: CPAG.

Glendinning, C. and Kemp, P. (eds) (2006) *Cash and care: Policy challenges in the welfare state*, Bristol: The Policy Press.

Gordon, D., Adelman, L., Ashworth, K., Bradshaw, J., Levitas, R., Middleton, S., Pantazis, C., Patsios, D., Payne, S., Townsend, P. and Williams, J. (2000) *Poverty and social exclusion in Britain*, York: Joseph Rowntree Foundation.

Gregg, P., Waldfogel, J. and Washbrook, E. (2005) 'That's the way the money goes: expenditure patterns as real incomes rise for the poorest families with children', in J. Hills and K. Stewart (eds) *A more equal society? New Labour, poverty, inequality and exclusion*, Bristol: The Policy Press, pp 251-75.

Harker, L. (2006) *Delivering on child poverty; what would it take?*, Cm 6951, London: DWP.

Hill, M. (2000) *Local authority social services: An introduction*, Oxford: Blackwell.

Hills, J. and Stewart, K. (eds) (2005) *A more equal society? New Labour, poverty, inequality and exclusion*, Bristol: The Policy Press.

House of Commons Work and Pensions Committee (2007) *The Social Fund*, HC 464, London: The Stationery Office.

Howard, M. (2001) *Paying the price: Carers, poverty and social exclusion*, London: CPAG.

Howard, M. (2002) *Like it or lump it: A role for the Social Fund in ending child poverty*, London: One Parent Families/Child Poverty Action Group/Family Welfare Association.

Kempson, E. (1996) *Life on a low income*, York: York Publishing Services.

Legge, K., Hartfree, Y., Stafford, B., Magadi, M., Beckhelling, J., Predelli, L.N. and Middleton, S. (2007) *The Social Fund: Current role and future direction*, York: Joseph Rowntree Foundation.

Lister, R. (2002) 'A politics of recognition and respect: involving people with experience of poverty in decision-making that affects their lives', *Social Policy and Society*, vol 1, no 1, pp 1-10.

Lyon, N., Barnes, M. and Sweiry, D. (2006) *Families with children in Britain: Findings from the 2004 Families and Children Study*, DWP Research Report 340, Leeds: Corporate Documents Services.

Marsh, A., McKay, S., Smith, A. and Stephenson, A. (2001) *Low-income families in Britain: Work, welfare and social security in 1999*, DSS Research Report 138, Leeds: Corporate Document Services.

Middleton, S. (2005) 'The adequacy of benefits for children', in G. Preston (ed) *At greatest risk*, London: CPAG.

Middleton, S., Ashworth, K. and Braithwaite, I. (1997) *Small fortunes: Spending on children: Childhood poverty and parental sacrifice*, York: Joseph Rowntree Foundation.

Morris, J. N. and Deeming, C. (2004) 'Minimum Incomes for Healthy Living (MIHL): Next thrust in UK social policy?', *Policy & Politics*, vol 32, no 4, pp 441-54.

Palmer, G., MacInnes, T. and Kenway, P. (2006) *Monitoring poverty and social exclusion 2006*, York: Joseph Rowntree Foundation.

Parker. H. (ed) (2000) *Low cost but acceptable incomes for older people: A minimum income standard for households aged 65-74 years in the UK*, Bristol: The Policy Press.

Smith, N., Middleton, S., Ashton-Brooks, K., Cox, L. and Dobson, B. with Reith, L. (2004) *Disabled people's costs of living: 'More than you would think'*, York: Joseph Rowntree Foundation.

Social Security Advisory Committee (2002) 'Promoting social inclusion within the work-focused agenda' (Annex C), in SSAC, *Fifteenth report*, London: SSAC, pp 19-25.

Social Security Select Committee (2001) *A lifeline for the poor – or the fund that likes to say no?*, London: SSC.

SSRC (Social Security Research Consortium) (1991) *Cash limited, limited cash: The impact of the Social Fund on social services and voluntary agencies, and their users*, London: Association of Metropolitan Authorities.

Strelitz, J. and Lister, R. (eds) (2008) *Why money matters*, London: Save the Children.

Turner, M. (2000) *Our choice in our future: Benefits*, London: Shaping our Lives/National Institute for Social Work.

UK Coalition Against Poverty (2000) *Listen hear: The right to be heard: Report of the Commission on Poverty, Participation and Power*, Bristol: The Policy Press.

Veit-Wilson, J. (1998) *Setting adequacy standards: How governments define minimum incomes*, Bristol: The Policy Press.

Racism, ethnicity, migration and social security

Ian Law

Summary

This chapter examines issues of racism, ethnicity and migration and the extent to which social security policy and provision have been structured by and respond to these. The chapter:

- analyses the racism inherent in immigration policy and practice and the consequence of this for the welfare of Britain's minority ethnic groups;
- examines the context of labour market position and poverty for migrants and minority ethnic groups both in the UK and across Europe;
- assesses the extent to which some minority ethnic groups are greater users of social security or certain types of social security than others;
- evaluates the extent to which social security law, rates and regulations impact differentially on different ethnic groups;
- explores the extent to which delivery is differently experienced across ethnic groups.

Introduction

This chapter will introduce the key issues of racism, ethnicity and migration and examine the extent to which social security policy and provision have been structured by and respond to these. The chapter will examine the racism inherent in immigration policy and practice and the consequence of this for the welfare of Britain's minority ethnic groups. It will also examine the context of labour market position and poverty for migrants and minority ethnic groups both in the UK and across Europe. The extent to which some minority ethnic groups are greater users of social security or certain types of social security than others, the extent to which social security law, rates and regulations impact differentially on different ethnic groups, and the extent to which delivery is differently experienced across ethnic groups provide a set of key concerns that are addressed in this chapter.

Racism, welfare and human waste in the UK and Europe

British state policy towards migrants and minority ethnic groups demonstrates a 'long pedigree of racism' (Craig, 2007). Regulation to exclude 'aliens', denizens (permanent settlers without British nationality) and particular racialised categories of British citizens from access to welfare benefits is evident in immigration legislation and wider social policy reforms from the Victorian period onwards. Poor Law rules, pensions law, aliens legislation as well as National Insurance (NI) criteria incorporated such practices (Williams, 1989). The racialisation of the British welfare state drew on eugenic notions of the quality of the race and the nation in order to maintain imperialism, and to manage both the 'burden' of the black, Asian, Irish and Jewish poor and the perceived threat of such groups to the jobs and wages of those in the 'new' mass trades unions. The articulation of race ideas with those of breeding, motherhood, the family, dirt and disease and 'mental deficiency' shows the pervasive nature of racist discourse in policy and practice.

Postwar welfare reforms and immigration legislation have continued to institutionalise racially exclusionary rules that determine eligibility for welfare benefits. These include residence tests, rules on 'recourse to public funds' and sponsorship conditions. Such regulation cannot be explained by reference to the actions of individual gatekeepers to these benefits, or to the functional needs of capitalism or imperialism, or solely to colonial relations and the racialisation of groups outside Europe (as this clearly fails to account for racist discourse internal to Europe whose subject is the Irish, Jewish or gypsies). The normalisation of racism in welfare state policies needs to be understood as an expression of the wider integration of racism, historically, in nationalist discourse and in gendered ruling-class conceptions of subordinate classes.

The complex formation of nation states, class relations, gender relations and colonial relations and their articulation with race ideas provide the discursive context within which rules for access and eligibility for social security have been elaborated.

Immigration policy and social security in the UK

The targeting of racial groups has been a constant feature of immigration policy in the UK, whether Jews, black people, Asians or asylum seekers. More recently policy has been 're-racialised' as new European Union (EU) citizens are substituted for workers from the developing world (Benyon, 2006; Sales, 2007, p 158). New Labour has continued and amplified previous Conservative policy in relation to welfare, immigration and asylum (Morris, 2007; Somerville, 2007), reducing the benefit rights of asylum seekers, tightening job search requirements and availability tests and tightening migration controls except for particular groups of skills migrants. Immigration policy is being shaped by both concerns over the protection of welfare resources and labour market needs, and international conventions and transnational rights. The resulting tensions lead to the deployment of ideological and organisational dimensions of welfare in the management of migration (Daly, 2003; Morris, 2007). Increasing differentiation and conditionality in access to welfare rights has been accompanied by both demonisation and hostility towards asylum seekers and concern that no one should be left destitute. There is fierce debate over the extent to which the government's view, which is that asylum seekers are 'pulled' to the UK by welfare benefits, is correct. This is contested by a group of researchers including Bloch and Schuster (2002), Duvall and Jordan (2002), Robinson and Segrott (2002) and Gilbert and Koser (2003). Other factors including the unregulated labour market and ineffective removal policies are cited as significant in migration decisions. Southern European states with lower levels of welfare have also experienced increasing asylum applications (Sales, 2007).

Immigration law has interacted directly with social security rules that limit access to some benefits for those in a transitional status or seeking family reunification. The two main points of interaction have been the rules around recourse to public funds and the provisions for those seeking refugee status. The 1971 Immigration Act introduced the requirement that those seeking family reunification – that is, applying for dependants from abroad to join them – should have no 'recourse to public funds' at the time of the application and until the dependants are granted residence. Thus, applicants have to demonstrate that they can support their dependants; and should they make a claim following their arrival they risk their dependants' status. Immigration law has also inhibited family reunification through visa requirements, which mean that applications have to be made before departure. The geographical distance of immigration officers making visa decisions from British legal process can limit their accountability (Bevan, 1986). A further obstacle was supplied by the former, notorious, 'primary purpose' rule, which required that a spouse's primary reason for immigration should not be to live in Britain.

Successive immigration rules since 1973 have required people, other than European Economic Area (EEA) nationals, seeking leave to enter or remain in the UK to show that they can adequately maintain and accommodate themselves and any dependants without recourse to public funds. This means they have to show that they have adequate means to support themselves, or be supported, without needing to claim benefits, which are considered to be public funds. The meaning of 'public funds' was first defined in immigration rules in 1995. Since then the list of benefits defined as 'public funds' has grown steadily and in 2005 the immigration rules were further amended to add Child Tax Credit, Pension Credit and Working Tax Credit to the existing definition of 'public funds'. If a person with a public funds restriction claims a benefit, the person's immigration position can be put at risk as the claim may affect their right to remain in the UK or to get an extension of stay. In recent years, benefit rules have been brought into line with immigration rules. Many benefits now have specific immigration conditions attached, which render a person ineligible purely because of their immigration status, for example social security and tax credits law categorises certain people as a 'person subject to immigration control' (PSIC) (Fitzpatrick, 2005).

Labour followed the previous Conservative government in tightening restrictions on welfare for asylum seekers. The 1999 Immigration Act established the National Asylum Support Service (NASS) apart from Department of Social Security provision to arrange accommodation and provide vouchers at 70% of Income Support (IS) rates for adults (although 100% for child dependants). Following a campaign led by Bill Morris, then General Secretary of the Transport and General Workers' Union (TGWU), cash replaced vouchers in 2002 but the provision of funds for basic support remains with NASS and distinct from social security although tied into IS rates. Also for those on Section 4 'Hard Case' support (failed asylum seekers who cannot be returned to their country of origin), vouchers continue to be used (CAB, 2006; Somerville, 2007). A concerted set of measures systematically reducing support for asylum seekers has been implemented including withdrawing support to 'late' applicants, unsuccessful applicants and some families. In addition, increasing exclusion of this group from work and public services including social housing, non-emergency healthcare and secondary healthcare for failed asylum seekers has led to widespread destitution as identified by the UK parliamentary Joint Committee on Human Rights (2007). This has most recently been identified for those processed through the New Asylum Model (Lewis, 2007; Somerville,

2007). As shown in ***Box 5.1***, the new Borders Bill gives immigration officers further powers over those subject to immigration control.

Box 5.1: Immigration and social security since 1997

1999 Immigration and Asylum Act: introduced vouchers for support and devolved the dispersal and accommodation system to NASS.

2002 Secure Borders, Safe Haven White Paper (Home Office, 2002): proposed phasing out of vouchers, but support and accommodation to remain with NASS.

2002 Nationality, Immigration and Asylum Act: introduced new induction/accommodation/removal centres for asylum seekers and withdrawal of support to individual asylum seekers who are 'late' applicants and to unsuccessful applicants.

2004 Asylum and Immigration (Treatment of Claimants, etc) Act: withdrawal of support from families with children under the age of 18 in selected areas; limited rights of appeal.

2006 Immigration, Asylum and Nationality Act: introduced New Asylum Model, giving greater control over asylum seekers with separate procedures for different nationalities.

2007 UK Borders Bill: gives immigration officers further powers, decreasing the rights of those subject to immigration control and creating further duties and penalties for them; anyone subject to immigration control must have a biometric identity card.

Asylum seekers who appeal against a decision about their status can continue to receive support during the appeals process. However, the Refugee Council (2007, p 8) has raised concerns that when claims and appeals have been refused, 'people are not entitled to any housing and financial support and are left totally destitute – unless they fit the tight eligibility criteria for hard case support. Currently the UK is forcing people who have claimed asylum into destitution in the name of immigration control'. A recent report by the Scottish Refugee Council found that 'at least 154 asylum seekers, refugees and their dependants [including 25 children] were destitute in Glasgow between 30 January and 26 February 2006' (quoted in Lister, 2007, p 122).

People from the 'old' EU countries (referred to as the EU15 and which consists of the Eurozone [EUR12] – Austria, Belgium, Finland, France, Germany, Greece, Ireland, Italy, Luxembourg, the Netherlands, Portugal and

Spain – plus Denmark, Sweden and the UK), together with those from some other EEA countries such as Iceland and Norway, may be eligible to claim benefits in the UK. But workers from new EU accession states are allowed entry only on terms that deny access to some benefit rights for the first year, whereas all other workers have no recourse to public funds until they have secured permanent residency. This includes those from the A8 states – the Czech Republic, Estonia, Hungary, Latvia, Lithuania, Poland, Slovakia and Slovenia – which joined the EU on 1 May 2004, and A2 nationals from Bulgaria and Romania. For these groups, means-tested benefits are all subject to the habitual residence test, of which the right to reside test is one part. A2 nationals who are employed in authorised work are able to claim entitled benefits immediately, including Housing Benefit (HB), Council Tax Benefit (CTB), Working Tax Credit (WTC) and Child Benefit (CB). However, if they become unemployed before first completing a year of authorised work they lose their entitlement to benefit. After completing a year of authorised work they are treated in the same way as other EU nationals and have access to any type of work and are able to claim benefits freely (Fitzpatrick, 2007). The experiences of Central and Eastern European migrants include low earnings, long hours, lack of contracts/sick pay and working illegally in breach of immigration status (Anderson et al, 2006; Low Pay Commission, 2007). On arrival in the UK almost half of migrants had no knowledge of the conditions attached to their immigration status or how to access healthcare, with fewer than one in five knowing where to go for advice (Spencer et al, 2007).

Outside the UK, in an examination of the social rights of immigrants in Germany, Sweden and the US, Sainsbury (2006) demonstrates the value of analysis that connects welfare regimes with immigration policy regimes and different forms and categories of immigration. She found that non-citizens received better entitlements in comprehensive welfare states like Germany and Sweden than in the 'incomplete' welfare state of the US, and that differences for female migrants were evident, with lower levels of benefit in Germany than in Sweden. So, different immigration regimes produce differing policy logics of exclusion and inclusion in the provision of welfare. These logics rest on ethical, moral and philosophical principles, which frequently conflict with human rights principles, children's rights and other policy goals such as reducing child poverty and ensuring freedom of movement within the EU.

Migration, settlement and social security

The postwar period saw a sustained level of inward migration to the UK from commonwealth or former commonwealth countries to supply labour. Migration from the Caribbean was followed by that from India and Pakistan and subsequently Bangladesh. Although much primary migration was male, with family reunification (that is, migrants applying for dependants from abroad to join them in the UK) being a subsequent step, this was not the case for Caribbean immigration where there were large numbers of women among primary migrants who came, for example, to take up work in the health service. Expulsion also resulted in settlement by numbers of Vietnamese and East African Asian families around 1970. Since 1970, most primary immigration for employment has been at a standstill, with family reunification and fertility being the routes through which minority ethnic groups have expanded. Refugees have also contributed to a diverse minority ethnic group population, a recent phenomenon being the arrival of asylum seekers from within Europe as well as from further afield.

Reason for arrival and timing of arrival have implications for employment and employment history, with the earlier migrants being concentrated in manufacturing, and in areas and industries, for example the textile industry, which subsequently suffered from processes of deindustrialisation. Later migrants were concentrated less in northern industrial towns and more in the Midlands and, particularly, London. Forced settlement in poorer areas can result in more limited educational opportunities, which continue to restrict the options for future, non-migrant, generations. Employment in vulnerable sectors, alongside discrimination, concentration in poorer areas that offer fewer opportunities and for some groups, notably Pakistanis, Bangladeshis and Black Caribbeans, greater difficulty in obtaining high levels of qualifications, have resulted in both high unemployment for many minority ethnic groups, especially Black Caribbeans, Pakistanis and, particularly, Bangladeshis, and much higher rates of self-employment among certain groups, in particular Indians, Chinese and Pakistanis (Simpson et al, 2006). The role of ethnicity in determining differential labour market outcomes for minority ethnic groups has been described as an ethnic penalty (Heath and McMahon, 1997). Recent research on persistent employment disadvantage (Heath and Cheung, 2006; Tyers et al, 2006; Berthoud and Blekesaune, 2007) confirms the huge employment penalty faced by Pakistani and Bangladeshi women that has not changed much in 30 years. As most of these women are Muslims, it appears that religion is more important than ethnic group as a predictor of employment penalties among women. Among all social groups it is only disabled people who are equally as unlikely to move into employment as Muslim women. Overall, the ethnic employment gap will remain significant for at least another century (Philips, 2007). Minority ethnic groups are disproportionately represented among the Department for Work and Pensions' (DWP's) 'most disadvantaged customer group' facing multiple complex barriers to work including employer attitudes, area-based factors, human capital and 'negotiating identities' in relation to family life, religious and cultural values and work (Hasluck and Green, 2007). In the UK, poor welfare outcomes for migrant and minority ethnic groups have been identified in terms of poverty, housing, education, health, labour market participation and the criminal justice system (Craig et al, 2007; Salway et al, 2007).

All minority ethnic groups show a greater use of means-tested benefits than the white population, and also make relatively lower use of non-income-related benefits, despite the receipt of CB being substantially higher among minority ethnic groups, especially among Pakistanis and Bangladeshis. Greater dependence on means-tested elements is due to:

- *Greater poverty*. A wide-ranging review of ethnicity and poverty in the UK, which draws on research evidence from 350 studies carried out from 1991 onwards, shows that over half of Pakistani, Bangladeshi and Black African children in Britain are growing up in poverty (Platt, 2007). Stark ethnic differences in poverty rates are determined by a variety of factors including persistent discrimination, patterns of educational qualification, labour market outcomes, housing locations, disabilities and ill health (Clark and Drinkwater, 2007; Palmer and Kenway, 2007).
- *Excess unemployment*, which leads to higher claiming of IS and income-based Jobseeker's Allowance (JSA). This is evidenced among all minority ethnic groups, but particularly among Pakistanis and Bangladeshis, and Black Caribbeans (Modood, 1997; ONS, 2000; DSS, 2001).
- *Different patterns of family structure*. For example, Bangladeshis, and to a lesser extent Pakistanis, have large families compared with the national average. Large families are more likely to be in poverty and are harder to support on the relatively low earnings that apply to the sectors in which these families are most likely to be concentrated (Platt and Noble, 1999; Berthoud, 2000; Platt, 2007).
- *Long-term poverty* among pensioners or the unemployed. Some minority ethnic groups are less likely to have accrued assets or savings throughout their lives and are thus more likely to need to claim IS or the Minimum Income Guarantee (MIG). Without such assets or savings they have less of a cushion to protect themselves during any periods of unemployment and this translates into greater hardship in old age. Nearly 60% of Pakistanis and Bangladeshis have no savings compared with 28% of the population as a whole; while over 80% have savings below £1,500 (ONS, 2001b).

On the other hand, minority ethnic groups have a lower reliance on contributory benefits, but a greater use of the categorical benefit CB. The reasons for this include:

- *Different age profiles*. All minority ethnic groups have a younger population profile than the population as a whole, which accounts in part for the higher rates of CB receipt among minority groups. The median age among all minority ethnic groups is 10 years below that of the whole population (26 compared with 36).

- *Differential fertility*. Pakistanis and Bangladeshis also have higher female fertility with families started at a younger age (Peach, 1996).
- *Unemployment* for some minority ethnic groups is both more prevalent and more likely to be long term, particularly for Black Caribbeans (Berthoud, 1999). Thus, entitlement to contribution-based JSA is less likely to be accrued.
- *Insufficient residence to build up contributions records*. For those who migrated in adulthood the opportunity to build up a contributions record, sufficient to claim the basic state pension, may not have been available; while for those who migrated recently, such as refugees, a contributions record may not have been acquired.
- *Interrupted contributions records*. For those with attachments to their country of origin, contributions records may have been interrupted due to extended visits.

Ethnic diversity, racial discrimination and the delivery of benefits

The differentiation in economic position, migration history, political participation and perceptions of social citizenship is significant across minority ethnic groups and is becoming increasingly evident. Recent debate has highlighted the problem of hyper- or super-diversity where professionals and managers face substantial dilemmas in responding to the needs of culturally complex communities (Vertovec, 2006; Mir, 2007). The dangers of simplistic approaches to these questions are exemplified in the discussion of 'ethnic managerialism' in the Benefits Agency (Law, 1997) where failure to adequately identify customer needs leads to poor service. The recent National Evaluation of Sure Start (Craig et al, 2007), a cross-departmental initiative that aimed to enhance the life chances of children less than four years old growing up in disadvantaged neighbourhoods, identified a failure to address ethnicity, which, in the implementation of the programme, was 'fragmented, partial or lacking altogether' (Craig et al, 2007, p ii). Here outcomes for minority ethnic groups could not even be identified because of a failure to carry out detailed ethnic monitoring. This has been a notable failure of DWP activity for decades.

In 1981 the Home Affairs Committee (HAC, 1981) stressed the importance of ensuring that minority ethnic groups were gaining full and equal access to social security because of higher dependency ratios and disproportionate unemployment. Subsequent research in 1993 (Bloch, 1993) investigated the information needs of claimants. This reinforced a strong tendency in the literature – that of stressing the need for linguistic initiatives such as interpreters and translated material (Home Office, 2001; DWP, 2002b). Nevertheless, benefit officers' assumptions about 'foreigners' may continue to impinge on those making use of translation and second language provision as long as the regulations contain within them implicit or explicit distinctions around entitlement and belonging. The exposure of anti-black and anti-Semitic sentiments among staff working in benefit offices has been another persistent theme in the literature (Cooper, 1985). Asians and Jews can be seen as wealthy and exceptionally good at gaining information about and access to benefit – 'they all know where to come and what to ask for', as one Executive Officer put it (Law, 1988, p 12) – and hence their claims may be subject to scrutiny and suspicion, which may constitute unlawful racial discrimination. This links to racially determined demands for additional documentation to establish eligibility, for example, in relation to proof of birth, age, marriage or immigration status. In this context the persistent practice of passport checking is often erratic and unjustifiable. Linked to this process is the range of erroneous assumptions held by staff about family structures or cultural characteristics of minority ethnic families. Treatment of capital held overseas, pooling of household income, family separation and divorce are all areas where misrecognition and misinterpretation has led to exclusion from benefit (CRE, 1985). Patterson (1994) documents discriminatory practices in benefit provision to Irish claimants including exceptional identification requirements, residence rules and neglect of family needs, for example funeral attendance. Also see Hickman and Walter (1997) on the experiences of Irish claimants.

Discriminatory treatment may also be an issue in the way benefit entitlement is established, for example in the use of the habitual residence test or in the extent to which requests for passports or other 'excessive demands for evidence' (Simpson, 1991, p 14) are made when claims are being conducted. Law et al (1994b) found that the Chinese claimants in their study were particularly likely to be asked for passports. The probability of discriminatory treatment may itself be enhanced by, for example, the greater relative dependence on means-tested support among some groups and the higher prevalence of lone parents (already a relatively stigmatised group) among Black Caribbeans (Law et al, 1994a; Law, 1996). Studies have revealed that discriminatory treatment can be an issue in the provision or refusal of benefits: the National Association of Citizens Advice Bureaux (NACAB) highlighted a number of concerns and complaints and examples of benefit wrongly refused, which it summarised in its report on the 'barriers to benefit' in the early 1990s (NACAB, 1991).

Residence requirements, through the 'habitual residence test', can impact on those who have spent or spend substantial periods of time abroad, or who have interests or partners abroad. Where people have geographically distant ties, they may choose, or be obliged, to spend substantial periods away from Britain, a pattern that has been particularly noted for South Asian groups. This may mean that they lose certain social security entitlements. The habitual residence test does not refer to a specific duration of residence prior to claiming, which is required for it to be fulfilled. Partly as a result of its imprecision it has been variously and often restrictively interpreted. Among those operating it there has been a tendency to target particular groups, especially those from minority ethnic groups, as being subject to the test (Bloch, 1997; CPAG, 2000, p 826). It applies only to a certain group of benefits: IS, income-based JSA and CTB. As NACAB (1996, p 20) puts it, the 'habitual residence test has created a space where prejudices and unexamined assumptions concerning race and culture can appear legitimate'.

The existence of discretion in certain areas of social security provision, such as the Social Fund, may increase the likelihood of discriminatory action. The New Deals themselves have aspects of discretion in the form that personal advice can take and in the ways that opportunities and skills are developed. In addition, access to the New Deal for the Unemployed itself can be impeded, as mentioned above, by identifying claimants as eligible for IS rather than JSA.

Under-claiming by different minority ethnic groups has been highlighted in a number of studies (Law, 2002), which have identified the role that stigma and (lack of) information could play in non-take-up of benefits. Law et al (1994a, 1994b), in their Leeds study, found clear evidence of delayed claiming and non-claiming, particularly among Chinese and Bangladeshi respondents; while NACAB (1991) identified the possibility of eligible non-claiming through benefit officer error. A further possibility is that minority ethnic groups are hindered or inhibited from claiming even where there is entitlement. Law et al's (1994a) study identifies that claimant attitudes may themselves inhibit claiming in certain cultural or religious contexts. The study stressed the importance of considering the cultural dimension in the wider context of approaches to claiming (and appealing against decisions); and the ways in which experience and behaviour are both vindicated and resisted, as well as being caused, by attitudes and beliefs. These belief systems based on wider attitudes about rights, entitlement and justice will necessarily interact, in the context of benefit claiming or non-claiming, with the costs of claiming in terms of stigma, information costs, probability (or perceived probability) of rejection and alternatives or perceived alternatives. As the literature on take-up has identified, eligible non-claiming is not necessarily an irrational behaviour (Craig, 1991) and can be expected to persist in an atmosphere that gives it high costs. Research evidence points to some success in the use of outreach and flexible approaches to engage with minority ethnic communities and to increase the take-up of services for which they are eligible (Craig et al, 2007; Hasluck and Green, 2007).

The 'welfare-to-work' policies, which aim to find the means to move people into work, begin to address some of the issues of those who have had limited options of employment. These could be expected to have a greater impact on members of certain minority ethnic groups than others, given higher unemployment rates among Black Caribbean males, and among Pakistanis and Bangladeshis, and, to a lesser extent, among Indians. Black Caribbean lone mothers might also be anticipated to benefit from the options offered through welfare to work given their existing greater propensity to take employment. The New Deals are notable in having been subject to ethnic monitoring of both participation and outcomes. Despite non-comprehensive coverage of ethnicity, indications are, however, that different groups experience different pathways through and out of provision (DfEE, 1999; DWP, 2002a; Hasluck and Green, 2007). Indians, according to figures to the end of 2001, are over-represented in moves into employment and Bangladeshis are most likely to take up the voluntary sector option, with Black Africans more likely to take up further education and training. Thus, as *Jobs for all* (DfEE, 1999) indicates, there may be particular issues in the operation and effectiveness of welfare to work for different ethnic groups. There is additionally evidence that access to the New Deals may be limited by the greater tendency to enable minority ethnic groups to remain on IS rather than on income-based JSA. While this may protect minority ethnic group members to a certain extent from the coercive aspects of welfare to work, it may also reduce their opportunities.

For those in work, the National Minimum Wage (NMW) provides some protection against low wages but minority ethnic group workers are more likely to be unaware of and not receiving it (Low Pay Commission, 2007). Tax credits may improve work incentives for groups such as Bangladeshis and Pakistanis who tend to have larger families and low wages, and higher rates of disability. The current evidence suggests that black and especially Pakistani and Bangladeshi families are over-represented in the Working Families' Tax Credit (WFTC) caseload (PIU, 2002, p 139). On the other hand, increases to IS child payments have improved out-of-work benefit rates for larger families and families with young children in particular. While positive for the overall welfare of those on benefit, these latter changes may also tend to reinforce some of the existing patterns in claiming.

The 2000 Race Relations (Amendment) Act requires public authorities to produce race equality strategies. The DWP's race equality strategy document *Equality, opportunity and independence for all* (DWP, 2002b) committed itself to assessing the possible differential impact of its services and policies and prioritising monitoring and evaluation in relation to the possible scale of the impact. It also committed the DWP to effective ethnic monitoring in all areas of delivery and among its employees, and to evaluations of future policy impact, on which it has failed to deliver. The Commission for Racial Equality, immediately prior to its amalgamation into the new Commission for Equality and Human Rights in 2007, identified poor progress across all Whitehall departments in the implementation of race equality strategies. The bulk of this work is, however, concerned with employment issues rather than service delivery. The continuing failure to demonstrate compliance with race equality requirements in the administration of benefits has recently been confirmed by Aspinall and Mitton (2007) with particular reference to local authority provision of HB and CTB. However, it is not simply the case that individual agencies reforming their practices will transform the delivery of social security to minority ethnic groups; rather it has to be part of a process that also looks more fundamentally at the context of and restrictions on people's lives (as, for example, the Social Exclusion Unit did; SEU, 2000), and considers the way policy regulations themselves are created and maintained.

Overview

- The racialisation of migration and welfare has led to poor welfare outcomes for migrants and minority ethnic groups in the UK. Past immigration policy has structured the settlement patterns and current opportunities of many minority ethnic groups and thus their relative dependence on social security, and there have been explicit links between immigration rules and social security entitlements.
- Although there is significant diversity of circumstances and experiences among and within different minority ethnic groups, there is often a high risk of unemployment, poverty, reliance on means-tested benefits and under-claiming. Persistent disadvantage and complex barriers to both work and benefits are experienced by minority ethnic groups.
- The creation of destitution among some asylum seekers, rising unemployment differentials and failure by the DWP to implement statutory race equality strategies are all signs that indicate poor prospects for the future.

Questions for discussion

(1) What is the relationship between social security policy and immigration policy?
(2) Why do patterns of social security receipt vary between ethnic groups?
(3) What factors need to be taken into account when considering appropriate delivery of social security in a multicultural context?
(4) What are the key ways in which the government has attempted to improve delivery of social security to minority ethnic groups?

Acknowledgement

This chapter includes some edited sections from the longer chapter 'Social security in a multi-ethnic society' by Lucinda Platt from the first edition of this text (2003). Please refer to this earlier version for greater amplification of selected relevant points.

Website resources

www.equalityhumanrights.com
Commission for Equality and Human Rights
www.esrc.ac.uk/ESRCInfoCentre/
ESRC Fact Sheets: Ethnic Minorities & Migration
www.emetaskforce.gov.uk/
Ethnic Minority Employment Task Force
www.fra.europa.eu
European Fundamental Rights Agency
www.homeoffice.gov.uk/
Home Office
www.refugeecouncil.org.uk
Refugee Council
www.runnymedetrust.org
Runnymede Trust
www.cabinetoffice.gov.uk/social_exclusion_task_force
Social Exclusion Task Force

References

Anderson, B., Ruhs, M., Rogaly, B. and Spencer, S. (2006) *Fair enough? Central and East European migrants in low wage employment*, York: Joseph Rowntree Foundation.

Aspinall, P. and Mitton, L. (2007) 'Are English local authorities' practices on Housing and Council Tax Benefit administration meeting race equality requirements?', *Critical Social Policy*, vol 27, pp 381-414.

Benyon, R. (2006) 'Race and immigration: is it the end of the affair?', www.jcwi.org.uk/policy/uklaw/raceandimmigration_spring06.html

Berthoud, R. (1999) *Young Caribbean men and the labour market: A comparison with other ethnic groups*, York: Joseph Rowntree Foundation/York Publishing Services.

Berthoud, R. (2000) *Family formation in multi-cultural Britain: Three patterns of diversity*, Colchester: Institute for Social and Economic Research, University of Essex.

Berthoud, R. and Blekesaune, M. (2007) *Persistent employment disadvantage*, Research Report 416, London: DWP.

Bevan, V. (1986) *The development of British immigration law*, London: Croom Helm.

Bloch, A. (1993) *Access to benefits: The information needs of minority ethnic groups*, London: Policy Studies Institute.

Bloch, A. (1997) 'Ethnic inequality and social security', in A. Walker and C. Walker (ed) *Britain divided: The growth of social exclusion in the 1980s and 1990s*, London: CPAG.

Bloch, A. and Schuster, L. (2002) 'Asylum and welfare: contemporary debates', *Critical Social Policy*, vol 22, pp 393-413.

CAB (Citizens Advice Bureau) (2006) *Shaming destitution: NASS Section 4 support for failed asylum seekers who are temporarily unable to leave the UK*, by Richard Dunstan, London: CAB.

Clark, K. and Drinkwater, S. (2007) *Ethnic minorities in the labour market: Dynamics and diversity*, York: Joseph Rowntree Foundation.

Cooper, S. (1985) *Observations in Supplementary Benefit offices*, Research Paper 85/2, London: Policy Studies Institute.

CPAG (Child Poverty Action Group) (2000) *Welfare benefits handbook, 2000/2001*, London: CPAG.

Craig, G. (2007) '"Cunning, unprincipled, loathsome": the racist tail wags the welfare dog', *Journal of Social Policy*, vol 36, no 4, pp 605-23.

Craig, G. with Adamson, A., Ali, N., Ali, S., Atkins, L., Dadze-Arthur, A., Elliott, C., McNamee, S. and Murtuja, B. (2007) *Sure Start and black and minority ethnic populations*, London: HMSO.

Craig, P. (1991) 'Costs and benefits: a review of research on take-up of income related benefits', *Journal of Social Policy*, vol 10, pp 537-65.

CRE (Commission for Racial Equality) (1985) *Submission in response to the Green Paper on reform of social security*, London: CRE.

Daly, M. (2003) 'Governance and social policy', *Journal of Social Policy*, vol 32, pp 113-28.

DfEE (Department for Education and Employment) (1999) *Jobs for all*, Nottingham: DfEE.

DSS (Department of Social Security) (2001) *Family Resources Survey: Great Britain, 1999-2000*, Leeds: Corporate Document Services.

Duvall, F. and Jordan, B. (2002) 'Immigration, asylum and welfare: the European context', *Critical Social Policy*, vol 22, no 3, pp 498-517.

DWP (Department for Work and Pensions) (2002a) 'New Deal for Young People and Long-Term Unemployed People aged 25+: statistics to December, 2001', *Statistics First Release*, February.

DWP (2002b) *Equality, opportunity and independence for all*, Race Equality Consultation Document, London: DWP.

Fitzpatrick, P. (2005) *Public funds, benefits and tax credits*, Welfare Rights Bulletin, 186, London: CPAG.

Fitzpatrick, P. (2007) *Benefits for Bulgarian and Romanian nationals*, Welfare Rights Bulletin 196, London: CPAG.

Gilbert, A. and Koser, K. (2003) *Information dissemination to potential asylum applicants in countries of origin and transit*, Findings 220, London: Home Office.

Hasluck, C. and Green, A. E. (2007) *What works for whom: A review of evidence and meta-analysis for the Department for Work and Pensions*, Research Report 407, London: DWP.

Heath, A. and Cheung, S. (2006) *Ethnic penalties in the labour market: Employers and discrimination*, Research Summary 341, London: DWP.

Heath, A. and McMahon, D. (1997) 'Education and occupational attainments: the impact of ethnic origins', in V. Karn (ed) *Ethnicity in the 1991 Census. Volume Four: Employment, education and housing among the ethnic minority populations of Britain*, London: The Stationery Office.

Hickman, M.J. and Walter, B. (1997) *Discrimination and the Irish community in Britain*, London: Commission for Racial Equality.

Home Affairs Committee (1981) *First report of the Race Relations and Immigration Sub-Committee*, London: HMSO.

Home Office (2001) *Race equality in public services*, London: Home Office Communications Directorate.

Home Office (2002) *Secure borders, safe haven*, London: HMSO.

Joint Committee on Human Rights (2007) *The treatment of asylum seekers*, Tenth report of session 2006-07, HL Paper 81-I, HC 60-I, London: The Stationery Office.

Law, I. (1988) *Racism and social security in Leeds*, Leeds: Equality Services, Department of Education, Leeds City Council.

Law, I. (1996) *Racism, ethnicity and social policy*, Hemel Hempstead: Prentice Hall.

Law, I. (1997) 'Modernity, anti-racism and ethnic managerialism', *Policy Studies*, vol 18, no 3/4, pp 189-206.

Law, I. (2002) 'Racism, ethnicity and benefits', *Benefits*, vol 10, no 1, pp 30-1.

Law, I., Hylton, C., Karmani, A. and Deacon, A. (1994a) *Racial equality and social security service delivery: A study of the perceptions and experiences of black minority ethnic people eligible for benefit in Leeds*, Leeds: University of Leeds.

Law, I., Hylton, C., Karmani, A. and Deacon, A. (1994b) 'The effect of ethnicity on claiming benefits: evidence from Chinese and Bangladeshi communities', *Benefits*, no 9, January, pp 7-11.

Lewis, H. (2007) *Destitution in Leeds*, York: Joseph Rowntree Charitable Trust.

Lister, R. (2007) 'Social justice: meanings and politics', *Benefits*, vol 15, no 2, pp 113-25.

Low Pay Commission (2007) *National Minimum Wage*, Cm 7056, London: The Stationery Office.

Mir, G. (2007) *Effective communication with service users*, London: Race Equality Foundation.

Modood, T. (1997) 'Qualifications and English language', in T. Modood, R. Berthoud, J. Lakey, J. Nazroo, P. Smith, S. Virdee and S. Beishon (eds) *Ethnic minorities in Britain: Diversity and disadvantage*, London: Policy Studies Institute.

Morris, L. (2007) 'New Labour's community of rights: welfare, immigration and asylum', *Journal of Social Policy*, vol 36, no 1, pp 39-57.

NACAB (National Association of Citizens Advice Bureaux) (1991) *Barriers to benefit: Black claimants and social security*, London: NACAB.

NACAB (1996) 'Failing the test', *Benefits*,no 11, April/May, pp 19-20.

ONS (Office for National Statistics) (2000) *Labour market trends*, March, London: The Stationery Office.

ONS (2001) *Social trends*, 31, London: The Stationery Office.

Palmer, G. and Kenway, P. (2007) *Poverty among ethnic groups: How and why does it differ*, York: JRF.

Patterson, T. (1994) 'Irish lessons: Irish claimants in Britain in context', *Benefits*, no 9, pp 21-7.

Peach, C. (ed) (1996) *Ethnicity in the 1991 Census. Volume Two: The ethnic minority populations of Great Britain*, London: HMSO.

Philips, T. (2007) 'Equality and human rights: siblings or just rivals', *Benefits*, vol 15, no 2, pp 127-38.

PIU (Performance and Innovation Unit) (2002) *Ethnic minorities and the labour market: Interim analytical report*, London: Cabinet Office.

Platt, L. (2002) *Parallel lives? Poverty among ethnic minority groups*, London: Child Poverty Action Group.

Platt, L. (2007) *Poverty and ethnicity in the UK*, Bristol: The Policy Press.

Platt, L. and Noble, M. (1999) *Race, place and poverty*, York: Joseph Rowntree Foundation/York Publishing Services.

Refugee Council (2007) *Parliamentary briefing on the UK Borders Bill*, www.refugeecouncil.org.uk/policy/briefings/2007/borders.htm

Robinson, V. and Segrott, J. (2002) *Understanding the decision making of asylum seekers*, Research Study 243, London: Home Office.

Sainsbury, D. (2006) 'Immigrants' social rights in comparative perspective: welfare regimes, forms of immigration and immigration policy regimes', *Journal of European Social Policy*, vol 16, no 3, pp 229-4.

Sales, R. (2007) *Understanding immigration and refugee policy*, Bristol: The Policy Press.

Salway, S., Platt, L., Chowbey, P., Harriss, K. and Bayliss, E. (2007) *Long-term ill-health, poverty and ethnicity*, Bristol: The Policy Press.

SEU (Social Exclusion Unit) (2000) *Minority ethnic issues in social exclusion and neighbourhood renewal*, London: Cabinet Office.

Simpson, L., Purdam, K., Tajar, A., Fieldhouse, E., Gavalas, V., Tranmer, M., Pritchard, J. and Dorling, D. (2006) *Ethnic minority populations and the labour market: An analysis of the 1991 and 2001 Census*, Research Summary 333, London: DWP.

Simpson, N. (1991) 'Equal treatment? Black claimants and social security', *Benefits*, no 6, September/October, pp 14-17.

Somerville, W. (2007) *Immigration under New Labour*, Bristol: The Policy Press.

Spencer, S., Ruhs, M., Anderson, B. and Rogaly, B. (2007) *Migrants' lives beyond the workplace: The experiences of Central and East Europeans in the UK*, York: Joseph Rowntree Foundation.

Tyers, C., Hurstfield, J., Willison, R. and Page, R. (2006) *Barriers to employment for Pakistanis and Bangladeshis in Britain*, Research Summary 360, London: DWP.

Vertovec, S. (2006) *The emergence of super-diversity in Britain*, Centre for Migration, Policy and Society, Working Paper No 25, Oxford: University of Oxford.

Williams, F. (1989) *Social policy: A critical introduction*, Cambridge: Polity Press.

Governing social security: from protection to markets

Emma Carmel and Theodoros Papadopoulos

Summary

This chapter identifies key developments in two related and interacting dimensions of social security governance: first, policy goals and principles; and, second, policy on the organisation and management of social security. These dimensions are then reviewed through a comparison with developments in European Union (EU) social security governance.

- The first developments include the construction of social security as conditional support rather than necessary protection and the conflation of the right to security with the responsibility to work.
- The second developments include the use of 'quasi-contracts', and recently the creation of a government market for service delivery; the role of operational targets; and performance management.
- The relationship of these two dimensions of governance in Britain with the EU strategies, plans and policies developed over the last decade is reviewed.

Introduction

On the day of Labour's second election victory in 2001, the Department of Social Security (DSS) was transformed into the Department for Work and Pensions (DWP). This chapter takes as its starting point the virtual disappearance of the term 'social security' from the government's policy vocabulary and the major institutional transformations that this symbolises. It offers a general introduction to the ongoing trajectory of reform in social security governance.

We use the term 'governance' to describe a form of political regulation initiated, organised and partially controlled by an actor or actors vested with the political authority to act in an area of public policy. Governance involves the attempt to 'steer' the behaviour of individuals, groups or institutions towards particular social and politico-economic goals via a set of institutions and processes that aim to maintain or change the status quo.

The concept of governance thus enables us to focus on a crucial feature of government policy making: that government is both about legislation and rule creation, and about 'how government is to be done' (Culpitt, 1999, p 44). It thus facilitates an analysis of policy making in two distinct but interrelated domains. The first domain concerns the legislation and regulations that embody policy principles, objectives and intended outputs, which we will refer to as 'formal' policy. The second concerns the organisational arrangements and procedures for policy delivery, referred to here as 'operational' policy. The analytical power of the concept of governance is that it allows enough flexibility to separately analyse both formal and operational policy while simultaneously highlighting their unity. In our governance analysis, the means (operational policy) directly shape the ends (formal policy); the 'how' of doing policy affects the 'what' of 'formal' policy and vice versa.

Both the 'how' and the 'what' of social security policy involve the political regulation of categories of welfare subjects. Thus, the construction of a person through public policy as a citizen or as a consumer, as a 'jobseeker' or as unemployed, depends on the discourse and regulations through which formal policy is expressed and made sense of, and on the social relations experienced and understood in institutions that are created and legitimised through operational policy. Thus, our analysis of social security governance examines the ways in which social subject categories are formed through official discourse and changing institutional arrangements.

Governance in the 'formal' policy domain of social security

This section provides a general overview of the normative contours of social security governance so that the logic of this political regulation can be identified.

Social security as support

Box 6.1 sets out some of the ways in which the nature and purpose of social security has been defined and understood. The term 'social security' as applied to state income maintenance programmes first appeared in the US in 1934 to describe the Roosevelt administration's 'New Deal'. Roosevelt's 1935 Social Security Act was justified as a necessary 'safeguard' against the 'man-made' [sic] contingencies of market failures, evident in the mass unemployment of the Depression years. In this original vision of social security – which after the war found even bolder expression in the constitution of the United Nations' (UN's) International Labour Organisation – society was understood to require protection from socioeconomic forces and circumstances. Thus, underlying this form of social security governance was the principle that the state should provide protection to individuals from socioeconomic situations for which they were not individually to blame and which were perceived to be responsive to state action.

A similar vision also underpinned Beveridge's position. He viewed the contributory principle – benefits paid out in return for previous contributions – as an essential part of a system in which social security was primarily to be provided as of right, rather than according to need. This was a right to protection against the contingencies that affect labour market participation (McKay and Rowlingson, 1999, pp 60-3). Although it was only to provide subsistence-level benefits, this right to protection included the 'full use of powers of the state to maintain employment and to reduce unemployment' (Beveridge, 1941, quoted in Fraser, 1984, p 288).

Box 6.1: Visions of social security

(1) Franklin D. Roosevelt

Message to Congress, June 1934, prior to passing of 1935 Social Security Act (cited in Digby, 1989, p 16):

> Among our objectives I place the security of the men, women and children of the nation first.... People ... want some safeguard against those misfortunes which cannot be wholly eliminated in this man-made world of ours.

(2) William Beveridge

Radio interview, December 1942, on the day his report was published (cited in Fraser, 1984, p 216):

> The Plan for Britain is based on the contributory principle of giving not free allowances to all from the State, but giving benefits as of right in virtue of contributions made by the insured persons themselves.

(3) The Declaration of Philadelphia, 1944 – principles of the International Labour Organisation

> a) Labour is not a commodity; ... d) All human beings, irrespective of race, creed, or sex, have the right to pursue both their material well-being and their spiritual development in conditions of freedom and dignity, of economic security, and of equal opportunity.... peace can be established only if it is based on social justice.

(4) John Moore, Secretary of State for Social Services (Conservative)

Interview in *The Sunday Times*, 28 September 1987:

> Dependency [on the welfare state] can be debilitating.... the best kind of help is that which gives people the will and ability to help themselves.

(5) *New ambitions for our country: A new contract for welfare*

Green Paper on welfare reform (DSS, 1998, p 16):

> The Government is determined to build an active welfare system which helps people to help themselves and ensures a proper level of support in times of need.

(6) *Opportunity, employment and progression: Making skills work*

Green Paper on welfare reform and skills (DWP and DIUS, 2007, p 8):

> A stronger framework of rights and responsibilities means benefit claimants having access to the necessary support, but also a clear responsibility to seize the opportunities that exist, to find a job and gain skills.

(7) *Work for welfare* – Conservative Party Policy Brief, 2008

> Our plans provide a much more comprehensive programme of support for jobseekers. But they also mean that those who refuse to participate in the return to work process will no longer receive out of work benefits. We will ensure that people participate fully by introducing mandatory conditions and time limits [on benefit receipt]. (p 12)

(8) *DWP commissioning strategy: Interim report* (DWP, 2007c)

> We want to change the support we offer and the way we deliver that support, to ensure more people get into and stay in work.... We want the best outcome for every customer and believe that the private, public and third sectors have a key role to play in delivering more specialised support ... We will build a competitive market with larger and longer contracts, rewarding providers for sustained outcomes and significantly reducing costs.

When those original visions for social security are compared with the ones espoused by British political parties at the end of the 20th century, a number of differences emerge. The new consensus is that social security should not provide protection but, rather, support. The crucial difference between these two conceptualisations of security – protection versus support – can be illustrated by considering an example of how the term is used in other contexts. When a private company offers security to a person whose life is threatened, this is clearly meant to be protection from harm, not support once the harm is done. Social-security-as-support is a 'hollowed-out' security; its essence – protection – has been changed. In this vision, social security is not primarily about protection from failures of socioeconomic conditions that state action can alter. Rather, it is a 'helping hand' so that an individual can alter their own behaviour to match the demands arising from these conditions. Indeed, the emphasis on 'help for self-help' implies that benefit recipients are themselves to a large degree responsible for their status; with some (conditional) help, they will be able to end their status as benefit claimants.

There were at least two clear objectives that the first Labour government elected in 1997 had in respect of the social security system. The first was to make (re-)employment the central feature of provision for people of working age. The second was to 'modernise' social security to meet this goal. However, the means to deliver modernisation was the focal point of competing visions and discourses. One vision, expressed by Frank Field, then Minister for Welfare Reform in the DSS, emphasised the need to provide benefits through social insurance, that is, on the basis of the contributory principle. This was necessary in order to overcome the morally debilitating, and economic disincentive, effects of means-tested benefits, which discourage people from taking responsibility for securing their own income, in times of need such as retirement or unemployment. National Insurance (NI) would also, especially for pensioners, maintain the idea that access to social security was a right. The alternative vision, favoured by the Treasury, emphasised outcomes; the form of the benefit was less important than 'whether or not they provide enough help to get people back to work and improve their lives' (Alastair Darling, Secretary of State, DSS, 1998, Ministerial foreword; see also DSS, 2000b, para 6, para 25 and introduction, para 2). This vision was eventually adopted as government policy. However, as a governance perspective highlights, the form of benefit delivery is of considerable significance – it is not just benefit levels that matter but also the conditions attached to benefit receipt.

A new configuration of rights and responsibilities

In a contributory system, the right to protection is the *end* of a process where the claimant 'demonstrates' their responsible behaviour by contributions when employed. The right of the state to 'steer' and monitor the claimant's behaviour after the claim is made is rather weak. Conversely, in a means-tested system the claim for support marks the *beginning* of a process whereby conditions are attached *after* the claim is made. Thus, the right of the state to 'steer' and monitor a claimant's behaviour after the claim is made is strengthened. In this context, the Labour government's social security policy marks a new distribution of rights and responsibilities between the state and the individual where security is seen as support, not a right, whereby the state establishes its right to demand behavioural changes from the claimant in return for providing them with support.

Although the previous Conservative governments introduced some compulsory interviews for unemployed claimants, under the Labour governments this process has gone much further (see Chapter Eleven, Wright, this volume). The New Deal established in Labour's first term, either required or encouraged different groups of 'working-age' claimants to attend interviews, training or take up employment. The separate New Deals for young people, lone parents, the long-term unemployed, older unemployed people, the partners of the long-term unemployed and people with disabilities each had different conditions in respect of benefit entitlement. While this remains the case, the trajectory of reform has been to reduce these differences – to recategorise the working-age population not in terms of their family status or health or age, but much more predominantly in terms of their ever more differentiated labour market status. Differentiation by labour market status provides the organising principles for differential regulation and treatment of social groups according to their 'distance from the labour market' and their 'work-readiness'. The distribution of rights, responsibilities and regulation in social security varies according to this age/labour market status categorisation. Thus, 'work for those who can, security for those who cannot' (see Chapter Four, Silburn and Becker, this volume). Or, to put it another way, work *is* security for the vast majority of people of working age.

Work as security

Following the foundation of the welfare state in the 1940s, individuals and society were seen as needing protection from the risk of being unable to work, which was provided through benefits, and also through state action in the economy to promote high levels of employment of a good standard (for men) (Digby, 1989, p 58). The new consensus that emerged at the end of the 20th century was that for a working-age person there is no clear or explicit right to such protection; employment cannot and should not be deliberately generated by state action, and protection when in employment has reduced rather than increased in the last two decades. Thus, the vision of 'security' for people of working age is the further expansion of individual labour supply in a 'flexible' and insecure labour market. Social security policies have become a means to 'steer' the behaviour of individuals to make them adaptable to what are perceived by the government as the demands of the flexible market economy (Grover and Stewart, 1999, 2002; Wiggan, 2007).

Thus, paid work is associated with the provision of security itself: it is how lifestyles and aspirations are secured, including educational aspirations for one's children, but it is also seen to secure emotional and physical health, good social and educational achievement for children, plus ongoing security into old age, by allowing private savings (for example, HM Government, 2005; DWP, 2007a, p 23; DWP and DIUS, 2007, p 7). However, for many this paid work is itself not secure, and may not provide an income or conditions to permit such security (for example, Evans, 2007). The individual of working age is made responsible for their employment status, and for the provision of their own security, including in old age.

Furthermore, when employment and security are conflated, important welfare-creating activities that are not part of the cash–market nexus are not politically recognised as productive work, such as care work or voluntary work (Levitas, 1998; Lund, 2000, pp 202-3). These normative assumptions underpin the ongoing extension of conditions for those receiving benefits and not engaged in such 'productive' paid employment, notably most recently lone parents and disabled people, and increasingly older age groups, encouraging people to retire later, and to remain in employment during retirement as well. The risk of this approach is that the social differences between non-disabled and disabled people of working age are enhanced, and we produce a rather narrow vision of social life – we do not work to live but rather live to work.

Thus, in the normative vision of Labour's social security governance, security is redefined as support rather than protection, is conditional not on past contribution but on current behaviour, and especially on participation in paid work. At the same time, contractualisation and monitoring of claimants' behaviour enforces a new distribution of rights, responsibilities and risks. This approach is anchored in a productivist logic, in which the main task of government is to create the conditions for economic competitiveness in an internationalised market economy (Grover and Stewart, 1999; Jessop, 1999).

Governance in the operational policy domain

The changes in formal policy have been reflected in the pattern of changes pursued in operational policy. Here too we see a redistribution of rights and responsibilities, but also the messiness of the complicated social world that social security addresses. The renaming of the DSS as the DWP and its restructuring in 2001–06, and the explicit creation of a market in welfare services more recently; the use of quasi-contracts, real contracts, performance indicators and monitoring; and the continuing use of business models and metaphors have all enhanced and sharpened the government's attempt to constitute categories of welfare subject by age and labour market status, highlighting the productivist logic that underpins the changes in the formal policy arena.

New departmental structures

The renaming of the DSS as the DWP and its reorganisation from 2001 to 2006 (the nationwide completion of Jobcentre Plus) was clearly connected to the constitution of welfare subjects in the formal policy domain. Thus, pensioners are now dealt with by the Pension Service; people of working age by the newly combined Employment Service and Benefits Agency outlets of Jobcentre Plus; benefits for the employed are delivered through Her Majesty's Revenue & Customs (HMRC). However, there are many anomalies in this formulation, so that the Pension Credit is also delivered through HMRC, as is Child Benefit (CB). These arrangements can be explained as representing the institutional crystallisation of formal policy: they separate those people who need not be directed towards employment, and are deserving of support because they are unable to work (children and pensioners), from those who are not, and who should be employed (implicitly, everyone else). For the government the cost in organisational complexity – pensions dealt with in places other than the Pension Service, and tax authorities delivering non-tax-related benefits – was accepted as these arrangements so clearly emphasise and support the formal policy goals.[1] Furthermore, a range of benefits are still provided via Jobcentre Plus (Invalid Care Allowance, Carer's Allowance, Maternity Allowance, Social Fund payments) that do not, or do not yet, have work-focused 'responsibilities' attached to them, while the Child Maintenance and Enforcement Commission (that replaced the unloved Child Support Agency (CSA)) continues under the DWP.

The aim in creating Jobcentre Plus was explicitly to 'expand the pool of employable people' (Social Security Select Committee, 2000b). The process of 'building a new culture of work first' (HM Treasury and DWP, 2001, para 1.21) required action to steer the behaviour of DWP staff in order to change the culture of the DSS/DWP itself. The move of the Employment Service into the DWP strikingly reveals the productivist vision in the new social security governance. The Employment Service had two sets of clients – 'jobseekers' and employers. As employers were integrated into the DWP's set of clients, a different emphasis was introduced into the DWP's services for people of working age; the Department must now explicitly meet the needs of employers (DWP, 2002, p 53, also pp 12, 15). Hence, these operational policy changes, and the logics of behaviour that they induce in staff, suggest that even greater emphasis is placed on the creation of employability among claimants than might be assessed from analysing formal policy. The DWP gained a new responsibility in respect of maintaining the economy, and delivering a 'high skill, high productivity economy' (HM Treasury and DWP, 2001, para 4.47, also para 4.40; HM Treasury, 2006; DWP, 2007b).

Contractualism within and beyond government: from Public Service Agreements to the Freud Report

Under the Chancellorship of Gordon Brown, until 2007, the Treasury gained an unprecedented degree of micro-level control over DWP policy.[2] The new regime established Public Service Agreements (PSAs), quasi-contracts negotiated between the Treasury and the spending department regarding policy goals, and performance targets. These were supplemented by Service Delivery Agreements (SDAs), a second set of agreements, in which departments specify how their policy objectives will be met. In these, responsibilities of specific agencies (such as the CSA or Jobcentre Plus) could also be arranged. These were then also supplemented by 'technical notes', which further specified the indicators against which departmental performance would be measured (for example, DSS, 2000a), and on which the department would have to report annually. The new agreements involved a micro-level scrutiny of departmental actions and institutions, and intrusion into departmental autonomy unprecedented in Britain, but one which deliberately cultivated the idea of 'punishing' apparently badly performing departments by further monitoring (Cutler and Waine, 2000; Newman, 2001, pp 91-3). These arrangements were not merely part of an agenda for policy reform, they were also a result of the politics of a government with an exceptionally powerful Chancellor. With Brown now as Prime Minister and the overall weakening of the Labour government, both political and administrative resistance to such a powerful Treasury seem likely to return relations to more historically unexceptional levels.

However, contractualisation has become deeply embedded in the daily practice of social security governance, and extends far beyond that of PSAs and SDAs. Ever since the introduction of the Benefits Agency and the CSA, mechanisms have been required in order to exert control of this process of 'agencification' (Rhodes, 1997). Procedures are required to facilitate government control of policy while engaging a plethora of public, para-public and private institutions in social security policy; what Clarke (2004) has called 'governing at a distance'. With public sector organisations this was done by creating framework agreements with the agencies delivering policy; auditing the services provided; and using performance management techniques imported from the private sector (Rose, 1996b; Clarke and Newman, 1997). If previous governments were concerned with cost, efficiency and value for money (Newman, 2001, p 91), the first decade of this century witnessed a performative managerialism, characterised by a 'developmental approach'. In contrast to the previous governments, this approach is outcome and objective oriented, primarily concerned with achieving particular, measurable, measured and monitored outcomes with the money that is spent (Rouse and Smith, 2002, p 47). Staff promotion is then related to these targets, making individual staff members politically as well as administratively responsible for meeting formal policy goals.

Yet, as Cutler and Waine (2000) point out, the close specification of targets and indicators is likely to stifle innovation and interfere with the development of 'joined-up government'. Staff at all levels can become oriented towards completing, or seeming as if they are completing, such targets; they may focus on complying with procedures at the expense of programme aims (Newman, 2001, p 93). Indeed, meeting these multiple targets can involve contradictory tendencies that are not easily reconcilable for frontline staff, especially when they involve both sets of Jobcentre Plus 'customers' – employers and claimants (Stafford and Kellard, 2007; Chapter Fourteen, Stafford, this volume).

The logic of 'governing at a distance', and of engaging any or all agencies in public service delivery in general has been further extended in recent years. In 2005, as part of a review of third sector involvement in public services, and against the background of a growing but inconsistent engagement of private and third sector organisations in public services, the need to create a government market for service delivery was mooted (HM Treasury, 2005; detailed discussion in Carmel and Harlock, 2008). The intention was to ensure that a range of providers competed for government contracts to deliver services, thus resulting in efficient and effective services.

In the case of social security, this agenda was specified and given some force through the Freud Report (DWP, 2007c), which both emphasised the importance of labour market status as the defining criteria for categorising benefit receipt, and also suggested how operational policy should be structured on the basis of such criteria. Thus, activation services and employment placement should be opened up to tender by both private and third sector contractors, but the latter were expected to be small specialist providers, developing contracted services for clients least 'work-ready', or 'furthest from the labour market' (DWP, 2007c). The logic of political regulation in formal policy, with its emphasis on work as security, and on finely differentiated employment statuses as life-defining, is thus institutionalised in what are claimed to be merely administrative and organisational (efficiency and effectiveness) reforms (for more detail on these reforms, see Chapter Fifteen, Finn, this volume). However, such reforms are highly political, as they partially decouple the citizen from the state and political processes by mediating and dispersing the citizen's experience of policy among a range of organisations that are not politically accountable, and whose contract is with the state, rather than with the client (see van Berkel and Borghi, 2007, p 418). This mediation of citizen–state relations holds in principle, even if both citizens and staff can and often do fashion alternative forms of relationship than that required by formal policy (see Newman, 2005, on different citizen–state relations).

Governing social security: Britain and the EU

The EU famously has no remit in the provision of social policy: it has no independent tax-raising powers and provides no individualised redistribution of resources within its territory. It has no social services, pensions, or employment agencies. However, the EU has a long-standing involvement in social security regulation (for example, establishing minimum standards for maternity and parental leave), and, from the mid-1990s, there was increasing interest in the role of the EU in relation to social security policy. In the examples cited above, the policies mostly arose from the EU's role as a market-creating institution; regulations were introduced that removed barriers to competition and to the free movement of labour, often under health and safety legislation, which had easier voting rules than more substantive changes to EU law.

Interest in the EU's 'social dimension' increased further in the 1990s as some member states, and especially one very active member of the European Commission, Allan Larsson, drove to place employment levels as a legally instituted concern of the EU. Despite opposition from the UK, and resistance or ambivalence from other major EU states (notably France and Germany), promoting employment was made into a legal obligation of the EU in the 1997 Treaty of Amsterdam. The UK had feared that such a move could lead to the imposition of employment and social security policies that looked like those of other EU countries (Johnson, 2005). In the end, the obligations of Amsterdam were met by creating a major new but non-binding 10-year policy programme in 2000: the Lisbon process. This process, which underwent adjustment in 2001, reforms in 2003 and radical reform in 2005, introduced significant shifts in the relationship of the member states to the EU as a whole in both formal and operational dimensions of governance. It also offers some interesting parallels and contrasts with British social security governance.

In terms of formal policy, the Lisbon process was concerned 'to create more and better jobs and greater social cohesion' (Lisbon Extraordinary European Council, 2000, p 1). From the outset, the emphasis on employment was especially strong, and specific outcome targets were established, for employment levels overall (70% employment rate), employment of older workers (60% of 50- to 64-year-olds) and employment of women (50%). These overall targets were supplemented by an expanding number of indicators-cum-targets, against which the performance of each member state was to be assessed – both by the other member states ('peer review') and by the European Commission (which produced reports and recommendations). The mechanism for achieving these goals was through what has become known as the Open Method of Coordination (OMC). For each policy area affected by the Lisbon process, an OMC was developed, with its own targets, measures, peer reviews, schemes to enhance mutual learning about policy lessons between member states and so on.

Significantly for our interest, the UK could sign up to the Lisbon process, both because it assumed the same economic paradigm as the UK government and, as it was without direct sanction (targets were not legally binding, methods of reaching targets were not specified, and no financial or other incentives or sanctions were available to policy makers to encourage member states to make policy changes), it seemed of little threat to UK social security governance. Indeed, the Lisbon agenda on employment and social security has been viewed as the 'uploading' of UK policy perspectives and agendas into the EU – not the usual story about the EU told in the UK media and politics (Büchs, 2008). Thus, the Lisbon process focused on employment, activation and marketisation of employment services. More recently, EU proposals about how to pursue pension reform (extend working life and enhance private saving) would sound remarkably familiar to most British students of social security (see Carmel et al, 2007), and social exclusion policies have remained low profile and of low priority in the Lisbon process and more generally – another 'fit' between EU and British policy agendas. Similarly, the approach to operational policy: using performance measures and policy-by-target approaches to achieve goals seems to place the UK in an unfamiliar position in relation to EU policies on social security: in this case it can claim to be not just a good, but a leading, EU 'citizen', more than meeting employment targets, for example.

The 2005 reform of the Lisbon process was substantial – employment and other targets were simplified; reporting and reviewing procedures were simplified and made less intrusive and intense for member states; and, most importantly, the rationale of promoting employment and education in order to achieve economic growth became explicit, and embedded in institutional arrangements. There are now no separate employment guidelines, but, rather, Broad Economic Policy Guidelines, into which employment concerns must be integrated, while the aim of social cohesion and better jobs appears to have been abandoned, at least in terms of priority (for contrasting assessments of the implications for social inclusion policies, compare Carmel, 2005, and Daly, 2006).

The new Lisbon process, then, resembles UK social security governance ever more closely: it is one where security is to be combined with flexibility. The ambition of the so-called 'flexicurity' model is to 'protect people not jobs'; where security means income and employment security (not job security). The latter is deemed to have been achieved by the state when individuals are employable, and are therefore *able* to take up new employment – irrespective of whether they have done so. Still, the potential for establishing an alternative vision of social security at EU level has not yet run its course. Just as in the case of the UK, we would be foolish to think that alternative visions of the role of the EU in social security – which may include even protecting or enhancing it in an unpredictable global market economy – are not available for political contestation. At the moment, however, there is remarkable congruence in the assumptions, principles and priorities of social security governance in both the EU and the UK. They share an emphasis on the good that markets do, and the social, moral and economic necessity of engaging ever more people in ever more employment, largely irrespective of the terms of that employment.

Conclusion: the governance of social security

This chapter has explored the policy principles, objectives and intended outputs of the Labour government, and the organisational arrangements and procedures for policy delivery. In both domains we can observe a 'contractualisation' of social security: between the DWP's policy makers and the Treasury, between service providers and the DWP and, last but by no means least, between the individual benefit recipient and the state.

In terms of its formal content, social security policy for all people of working age has been transformed to serve labour market policy objectives. It is only with regard to policies for children that we can see a commitment to socioeconomic security, although this is now primarily delivered through the Treasury. In terms of operational policy, these roles are reflected in the departmental structure and in the justification and organisation of the 'welfare market' of service delivery. Thus, the governance of social security in Britain can be characterised as a form of political regulation in which the DWP constructs and 'steers' social subjects towards socioeconomic goals that are clearly anchored in a productivist vision of the role of social security in an internationalised market economy. The distribution of rights, responsibilities and risks for individuals and institutions follows a logic of ever increasing contractualisation of their relationships and extensive monitoring of their behaviour and performance. As such, contemporary British social security can be described as not very social and even less secure.

The influence of a similarly productivist paradigm can be identified in the EU, but this is partially moderated by alternative traditions of social security from elsewhere in the EU, and by the institutionalised involvement of social partners in social policy governance. While the EU is currently dominated by a strongly flexibilising market agenda, also reflected in the as yet abortive Lisbon Treaty, alternative narratives are available at the EU level. These exhort the need for social security and social protection, although the future of such alternative visions for Europe remains unclear.

Overview

- This chapter analyses social security policy across two dimensions of 'governance'. This governance perspective examines how in both policy goals ('formal' policy) and organisational arrangements ('operational' policy) the behaviour of individuals, institutions and social groups is politically regulated in attempts to meet socioeconomic goals.
- The key principles and goals of social security have changed to be about support based on obligations; a reconstitution of welfare subjects predominantly in relation to their labour market status and age; the conflation of security with (paid) work.
- The reorganisation of the DWP confirmed the productivist logic associated with formal policy changes, exemplified in the explicit institutional commitment to meet the demands of employers; the introduction and extension of performance management; and the extended and expanding use of contracts with non-governmental partners to implement policy.
- The EU has instituted a substantial programme in economic and social policy in the past decade – the Lisbon process. The formal and operational dimensions of social security policy at the EU level – in pensions, employment and social inclusion – bear some strong resemblances to those of the UK, notably in the emphasis on employment, employability and marketisation.

Questions for discussion

(1) Explain the distinction between formal and operational policy; how are they related in the case of social security?

(2) In what ways do conceptualisations of 'social security' differ between the Beveridgean ideal and that expressed by Labour governments since 1997?

(3) Identify and explain the main changes in social security operational policy since 1997. Which of these changes is the most significant, and why?

Notes

[1] The government also arranged for these benefits to be delivered under the direct departmental control of the Treasury, and therefore the then Chancellor of the Exchequer, Gordon Brown, and so some political motives for some of the arrangements cannot be discounted.

[2] While similar administrative arrangements as described here existed for all departments, the DWP was both politically weak, and mostly led by close political allies of the Chancellor.

Website resources

www.dwp.gov.uk/asd/asd5/
Department for Work and Pensions – research and publications
http://ec.europa.eu/employment_social/employment_strategy/index_en.htm
EU – European Employment Strategy
http://ec.europa.eu/social/home.jsp?langId=en
EU – Employment, Social Affairs and Equal Opportunities
http://europa.eu/lisbon_treaty/index_en.htm
EU – Treaty of Lisbon
www.hm-treasury.gov.uk/documents/taxation_work_and_welfare/tax_index.cfm
HM Treasury – taxation, work and welfare

References

Büchs, M. (2008) 'The Open Method of Coordination as a "two-level game"', *Policy & Politics*, vol 36, no 1, pp 21-37.

Carmel, E. (2005) 'Governing the European "social"', in J. Newman (ed) *Remaking governance*, London: Sage Publications, pp 39-58.

Carmel, E. and Harlock, J. (2008) 'Instituting the "third sector" as a governable terrain: partnership, procurement and performance in the UK', *Policy & Politics*, vol 36, no 2, pp 155-71.

Carmel, E., Hamblin, K. and Papadopoulos, T. (2007) 'Governing the activation of older workers in the European Union: the construction of the "activated retiree"', *International Journal of Sociology and Social Policy*, vol 27, no 9/10, pp 387-400.

Clarke, J. (2004) *Changing welfare, changing states*, London: Sage Publications.

Clarke, J. and Newman, J. (1997) *The managerial state: Power, politics and ideology in the re-making of social welfare*, London: Sage Publications.

Culpitt, I. (1999) *Risk and social policy*, London: Sage Publications.

Cutler, T. and Waine, B. (2000) 'Managerialism reformed? New Labour and public sector management', *Social Policy and Administration*, vol 34, no 3, pp 318-32.

Daly, M. (2006) 'EU social policy after Lisbon', *Journal of Common Market Studies*, vol 44, no 3, pp 461-81.

Digby, A. (1989) *British welfare policy: Workhouse to workfare*, London: Faber and Faber.

DSS (Department of Social Security) (1998) *New ambitions for our country: A new contract for welfare*, Cm 3805, London: The Stationery Office.

DSS (2000a) *Public service agreement 2001-4: Technical note*, www.dwp.gov.uk/publications/dss/2000/psa_tech/psatech.pdf

DSS (2000b) *Report on the contributory principle: Reply by the government to the fifth report of the Select Committee on Social Security*, London: DSS.

DWP (Department for Work and Pensions) (2006) *A New Deal for Welfare: Empowering people to work*, Cm 6730, London: The Stationery Office.

DWP (2007a) *Ready for work*, Cm 7920, London: The Stationery Office.

DWP (2007b) *Reducing dependency, increasing opportunity: Options for the future of the welfare state* (Freud Report), Leeds: Corporate Document Services.

DWP (2007c) *DWP commissioning strategy: Interim report*, London: The Stationery Office.

DWP and DIUS (Department for Innovation, Universities and Skills) (2007) *Opportunity, Employment and Progression: Making skills work*, Cm 7288, London: The Stationery Office.

Evans, P.M. (2007) '(Not) taking account of precarious employment: workfare policies and lone mothers in Ontario and the UK', *Social Policy and Administration*, vol 41, no 1, pp 29-49.

Fraser, D. (1984) *The evolution of the British welfare state*, London: Macmillan.

Grover, C. and Stewart, J. (1999) '"Market workfare": social security, social regulation and competitiveness in the 1990s', *Journal of Social Policy*, vol 28, no 1, pp 73-96.

Grover, C. and Stewart, J. (2002) *The work connection: The role of social security in British economic regulation*, Basingstoke: Palgrave.

HM Government (2005) *Opportunity age: Meeting the challenges of ageing in the 21st century*, London: The Stationery Office.

HM Treasury (2005) *Exploring the role of the third sector in public service delivery and reform*, London: The Stationery Office.

HM Treasury (2006) *Prosperity for all in the global economy: World class skills*, London: The Stationery Office, www.hm-treasury.gov.uk/media/6/4/leitch_finalreport051206.pdf

HM Treasury and DWP (2001) *The changing welfare state: Employment opportunity for all*, London: The Stationery Office, www.dwp.gov.uk/publications/dwp/2001/emp-opp/employment.pdf

Jessop, B. (1999) 'Narrating the future of the national economy and the national state? Remarks on remapping regulation and reinventing governance', in G. Steinmetz (ed) *State/culture: State formation after the cultural turn*, Ithaca, NY: Cornell University Press, pp 378-405.

Johnson, A. (2005) *European welfare states and supranational governance of social policy*, Basingstoke: Palgrave.

Levitas, R. (1998) *Social inclusion and New Labour*, London: Macmillan.

Lisbon Extraordinary European Council (2000), *Presidency conclusions*, http://ue.eu.int/ueDocs/cms_Data/docs/pressdata/en/ec/00100-r1.en0.htm

Lund, B. (2000) *Understanding state welfare: Social justice or social exclusion?*, London: Sage Publications.

McKay, S. and Rowlingson, K. (1999) *Social security in Britain*, Basingstoke: Macmillan.

Newman, J. (2001) *Modernising governance: New Labour, policy and society*, London: Sage Publications.

Newman, J. (ed) (2005) *Remaking governance*, Bristol: The Policy Press.

Rhodes, R.A.W. (1997) *Understanding governance: Policy networks, governance, reflexivity and accountability*, Buckingham: Open University Press.

Rose, N. (1996b) 'Governing the advanced "liberal" democracies', in A. Barry, T. Osborne and N. Rose (eds) *Foucault and political reason: Liberalism, neo-liberalism and rationalities of government*, Chicago, IL: Chicago University Press, pp 37-64.

Rouse, J. and Smith, G. (2002) 'Evaluating New Labour's accountability reforms', in M. Powell (ed) *Evaluating New Labour*, Bristol: The Policy Press, pp 39-60.

Social Security Select Committee (2000) *Minutes of evidence*, 3 July, www.parliament.the-stationery-office.co.uk/pa/cm199900/cmselect/cmsocsec/662/0070301.htm

Stafford, B. and Kellard, K. (2007) 'Reforming the public sector: personalised activation services in the UK', in R. van Berkel and B. Valkenburg (eds) *Making it personal: Individualising activation services in the EU*, Bristol: The Policy Press, pp 127-48.

van Berkel, R. and Borghi, V. (2007) 'Individualised service provision in an era of activation and new governance', *International Journal of Sociology and Social Policy*, vol 27, no 9/10, pp 413-24.

Wiggan, J. (2007) 'Administering economic reform: New Labour and the governance of social security', *Policy & Politics*, vol 35, no 4, pp 651-66.

Social security in global context

Nicola Yeates

Summary

Social security policy analysis is traditionally concerned with the organisation, delivery and consumption of welfare services at the national level, but there is growing recognition of the importance of the global context in which social policy is formulated and implemented. This chapter explores the global dimensions of social security policy and administration as it relates to the UK. The discussion is structured in three main sections:

- The first reviews the global applicability of the term 'social security' and reflects on how statutory social security operates within broader welfare systems.
- The second contextualises the UK social security system in relation to the variety of systems worldwide, both in the 'developed' and the 'developing' countries.
- The third examines the scope and nature of international collaboration in social security and reviews international governmental organisations' (IGOs') approaches to the role of social security in achieving social justice and security.

Social security and social protection

In the UK 'social security' predominantly refers to the system of cash benefits administered mainly by central government. This equation of social security with state-administered cash benefits is not, however, the international norm. As the International Labour Office notes, 'in many countries a sharp distinction is commonly drawn between social security on the one hand, and poverty alleviation measures on the other' (ILO, 2000, p 29). Thus, in the US, 'social security' refers only to social insurance retirement and survivors' and disability benefits; social assistance payments are referred to as 'welfare'. In France and many Latin American countries, 'social security' refers to social insurance benefits, including healthcare benefits, and excludes some social assistance benefits delivered at local level.[1] In the Republic of Ireland, the term 'social welfare' is used in preference to 'social security', and while these terms are broadly synonymous, social welfare benefits do not include some disability, sickness and maternity benefits that are referred to as 'health-related' payments and administered by regional Health Boards.

The strict identification of social security with government activity and, more specifically, with a particular Department has, of course, become less applicable to the UK due to the relocation of responsibility for the collection of National Insurance (NI) contributions to Her Majesty's Revenue & Customs (HMRC) and the HMRC's role in tax credit policy and administration (see Chapter Thirteen, Millar, this volume). More generally, however, the focus on public arrangements neglects the importance of market-based arrangements and non-statutory providers, such as employers (occupational pensions and sick and maternity pay) and commercial agencies (personal pensions, private savings, private unemployment and care insurance). An exclusive emphasis on public arrangements also neglects the importance of informal arrangements in income maintenance. These arrangements include culturally determined obligations and practices emanating from family, kin, neighbourhood and community ties, and in many countries family members are expected to support one another financially (Midgley and Kaseke, 1996; Millar and Warman, 1997). Such arrangements also include charitable donations arising from religious norms such as *alms-giving* in Christianity and *zakât* in Islam,[2] and cooperative associations or mutual benefit societies, such as funeral, credit and informal savings societies providing assistance in cash and kind (Midgely, 1997). Informal or 'traditional' systems often operate at local level without any state recognition or support, although in some countries statutory and informal systems have been integrated as a means of supporting informal systems and/or extending statutory coverage (Midgley and Kaseke, 1996). Such arrangements are relevant to both 'developed' and 'developing' countries, although they are particularly significant in countries that do not have comprehensive statutory social security systems.

This recognition that income security derives from market and informal arrangements as well as from public arrangements is captured by the term 'social protection', which refers to non-statutory income maintenance schemes, formal and informal, in addition to statutory schemes. This term draws attention to the broad range of welfare arrangements and institutions to which individuals and households turn in order to satisfy their income needs. In addition to the examples cited above, social protection could also include agricultural schemes aiming to maintain farmers' and peasants' incomes, such as micro-credit and crop insurance schemes, farm subsidies and food security programmes (Gough, 2004). Arguably, the European Union's (EU's) Common Agricultural Policy (CAP) can be regarded as a type of income maintenance system for farmers in so far as it aims to 'ensure a fair standard of living for the agricultural community, in particular by increasing the individual earnings of persons engaged in agriculture' (Treaty of Rome, establishing the European Economic Community, 1957, Article 39(b); Kleinman and Piachaud, 1993).

The provision of cash benefits to individual claimants is only one way in which governments pursue the goal of income maintenance. Other ways of doing so include subsidising the prices of welfare goods and services, such as housing, food and energy. This provides a safety net of substantial indirect wage subsidies, which may complement limited cash benefits systems or substitute for them entirely. Finally, we should not discount the importance of employment as a social security system. Where lifetime employment is guaranteed there is no need for the state to provide unemployment benefits. This has been the case for many public sector workers and civil servants around the world. This point is illustrated by the introduction of employment flexibility pursuant to public sector reforms, which has involved the extension of coverage of unemployment benefits to these groups as the guarantee of lifetime employment has been withdrawn.

Social security around the world

The establishment of global social security principles can be considered one of the foremost achievements of international politics in the 20th century. Access to social security was accepted as a human right under the 1948 Universal Declaration of Human Rights (***Box 7.1***) and was reiterated by the International Covenant on Economic, Social and Cultural Rights (1966), which 'recognises the right of everyone to social security, including social insurance' (Article 9).

Box 7.1: Social security and the 1948 Universal Declaration of Human Rights

'Everyone, as a member of society, has the right to social security and is entitled to realization ... of the economic, social and cultural rights indispensable for his dignity and the free development of his personality.' (Article 22)

'Everyone who works has the right to just and favourable remuneration ensuring for himself and his family an existence worthy of human dignity, and supplemented, if necessary by other means of social protection.' (Article 23.3)

'Everyone has the right to a standard of living adequate for the health and well-being of himself and of his family, including ... the right to security in the event of unemployment, sickness, disability, widowhood, old age or other lack of livelihood in circumstances beyond his control.' (Article 25.1)

'Motherhood and childhood are entitled to special care and assistance. All children, whether born in or out of wedlock, shall enjoy the same social protection.' (Article 25.2)

The recognition of the right to social security is also present at the regional level. In the European context, it is affirmed in Article 12 of the Council of Europe's European Social Charter (1961), the EU's Charter of the Fundamental Social Rights of Workers (1989) and the Treaty of Amsterdam (1997), which confirmed member states' 'attachment to fundamental social rights'. It is also present in regional instruments in Latin America (Article 9 of the Treaty of San Salvador 1995) and Africa (Article 16 of the African Charter on Human and Peoples' Rights 1981) (Kulke, 2007).

The political and social reality, however, is that this international consensus of social security as a fundamental social right and a human right has not provided actual income security for most of the world's population. Indeed, billions of people continue to live in poverty. To be fair, there have been important initiatives to keep this issue on the political agenda. One such initiative is the Copenhagen Declaration on Social Development adopted at the World Summit for Social Development in 1995, which committed signatory countries to 'ensure that all people have adequate economic and social protection during unemployment, ill health, maternity, child-rearing, widowhood, disability and old age' (see www.visionoffice.com/socdev/wssd.htm). A second initiative is the Millennium Development Goals (MDGs). In the first of the MDGs the international community pledges to aim to eradicate extreme poverty and hunger, with the specific target of halving the proportion of people living on less than a dollar a day and those who suffer from hunger by 2015. Social security is clearly central to achieving this goal, but progress towards meeting this goal has to contend with new challenges arising from a number of social, demographic and economic changes that are putting already woefully inadequate social security systems under strain.

Coverage

Social security is now an established feature of the advanced industrialised countries where statutory coverage has reached almost 100%. However, outside of these countries coverage is much more restricted; indeed, from a global perspective, the level of provision in countries like the UK is an exception rather than the rule. In 1999 van Ginneken noted that 'more than half of the world's population (workers and their dependants) are excluded from any type of statutory social security protection' (van Ginneken, 1999, p 1). Social security coverage of the working population varies quite substantially by region, ranging from 5-10% in sub-Saharan Africa and South Asia, 50-80% in Central and Eastern Europe, 10-80% in Latin America and 10-100% in South-East and East Asia (the exact percentage depends on the risk or group in question) (van Ginneken, 1999). The situation has not substantially improved since that time, and between 70% and 80% of the world's population have no access to meaningful cash benefits beyond the limited possibilities of families, kinship groups or communities to secure their standard of living. The vast majority of people therefore live in a state of more or less severe 'social insecurity', of whom 20% live in extreme insecurity: poverty (Cichon and Hagemejer, 2007, pp 174-5).

A principal reason for exclusion from social security is the absence of statutory schemes. The number of countries with such schemes grew from 57 countries in 1940 to 172 countries by 1995, but 49 countries and territories around the world affecting 66 million people still do not have any known statutory social security scheme (Dixon, 1999, p 2). Many of these are low-income countries, but there are notable exceptions. The United Arab Emirates (UAE), among the richest countries in the world, does not have a statutory social security system. Furthermore, where statutory schemes do exist the coverage of social risks or groups is not always comprehensive. Programmes in respect of old age, disability, death, sickness and maternity are most widespread, while programmes in respect of unemployment, family and children are most frequently absent (Dixon, 1999). Fewer than one in ten (8%) of the 172 countries and territories in Dixon's study had programmes for all of the following contingencies: old age, disability, death (including survivors' benefits), sickness, maternity, unemployment, family and children. As the International Labour Organization (ILO) notes, those most likely to be excluded from statutory schemes are workers in cottage and small-scale industries, small shops, urban informal workers, agricultural workers, domestic workers and home workers (see www.ilo.org/public/english/protection/condtrav/unprotected). Even people formally covered by operating schemes may not receive benefits, either because they have not been able to make enough contributions or because they have exhausted their benefit entitlement. In some parts of the world, statutory schemes have collapsed or been made inoperative due to war, natural disasters or severe economic dislocation (Dixon, 1999).

The absence of comprehensive statutory social security for informal sector workers raises broader questions about the design of social security systems. An effective social security system requires widespread and sustained participation in it; thus, social insurance schemes require a large proportion of the workforce with a regular job whose earnings can be monitored and on which mandatory contributions can be collected. Unfortunately, this condition does not apply to hundreds of millions of workers worldwide whose employment and earnings are irregular. As van Ginneken (2007) notes, the majority of non-covered and poor workers in developing countries are employed in the informal economy, and many of them are unable or unwilling to contribute the high percentage of their incomes to financing social security benefits that do not meet their priority needs of immediate survival, healthcare and education. Exclusion from statutory social security schemes is also attributable to factors such as legal restrictions, weaknesses in law enforcement and administrative bottlenecks (van Ginneken, 2007, p 40). More generally, effective statutory schemes require a strong public infrastructure and sophisticated managerial and administrative capacities in order for taxes to be collected, entitlements to be calculated and benefits to be delivered (van Ginneken, 1999, 2007). The absence of such an infrastructure is a key impediment to a comprehensive and adequate social security system:

> [Social assistance schemes] require sophisticated administration to determine who is really deserving and to ensure that the benefits reach the target population effectively. Thus the costs of delivering the benefits are high and, without an efficient and accountable control and monitoring system, leakages or corruption are likely.... [Moreover] many social security administrations in developing countries find it difficult to cope with the volume of administrative tasks associated with the operation of a social insurance scheme, which requires the maintenance of accurate lifetime records for insured persons. (van Ginneken, 1999, pp 9, 13)

Expenditure

There is also great variance in social security systems globally in terms of expenditure and financing. Worldwide, public social security expenditure[3] amounted to on average 9.6% of Gross Domestic Product (GDP) in 1990, but there are sharp regional disparities. Social security expenditure accounted for 18.5% of GDP in Europe, 11.2% of GDP in Oceania (Australia, New Zealand and Fiji) and 9.1% of GDP in North America. Trailing well behind the expenditure 'leaders' are Latin America and the Caribbean at 6.0% of GDP, Asia at 3.7% of GDP and, finally, Africa at 2.6% of GDP (ILO, 2000, Table 14, p 312). There are intraregional differences too. Eurostat figures for 2003 show that the 15 'old' member states spend on average about 10% more of their GDP on social protection systems than the 10 'new' members from Central and Eastern Europe. The differences between the old and new EU member states are even greater when expressed in Purchasing Power Standards (PPS), which take cross-border purchasing-price differences into account (www.euractiv.com/en/socialeurope/eu-social-protection-expenditure-rise/article-159368).

Design features

Of course, social security expenditure in itself tells us little about the effectiveness or efficiency of the social security system in achieving its various goals or the quality of social rights. One way of judging the quality of social security systems is by looking at their design features. For example, Dixon (1999) ranked 172 countries according to how well they met ILO minimum social security standard benchmarks. His methodology articulated a comprehensive set of 860 design features for basic and supplementary social security services design and administration. These features incorporated financing, administration, coverage, eligibility and provision (for example, periodicity of payment; benefit generosity relative to prevailing living standards). It should be emphasised that this evaluation methodology measures statutory intent, rather than actual delivery. Scores were assigned for each feature and countries ranked into four 'league tables' or tiers. In this schema, the UK was ranked 37th (jointly with Brazil) and was thus classed as a second-tier system.

Advanced social security systems are sometimes believed to be associated with a high level of economic development. That is, it is argued that only the richer, more economically 'advanced', countries are able to afford 'better', more comprehensive, social security systems. However, Dixon's ranking shows that the level of economic development alone is insufficient to explain why some countries have better-designed systems than others. In order to understand this we also need to consider national institutional, cultural and historical social security and other traditions and arrangements; and political factors, such as the national balance of forces between the state, labour, capital and civil society (Yeates, 2001).

Welfare regimes

The above cross-national comparisons are based on levels of expenditure and on the design features of social security systems. In addition, there is a substantial literature that explores the similarities and differences in 'welfare regimes', and analyses the ways in which they respond to the challenges of economic, social and demographic change. The concept of the 'welfare state regime' was used by Esping-Andersen (1990, p 2) 'to denote the fact that in the relation between state and economy a complex of legal and organisational features are systematically interwoven'. He used the term to distinguish between two approaches to the study of welfare states. The first (and prevailing) approach is an association of welfare state with social amelioration policies and programmes. The second approach – and the one he favours – also takes into account the construction of social welfare policies but links these to their influence on the employment and general social structure (Esping-Andersen, 1990). Thus, an interest in social security from a welfare regimes perspective would not only be interested in the characteristics of the various benefits or how much was spent on them; it would also attempt to understand how countries arrive at particular public–private sector mixes, the extent to which people are dependent on selling their labour and on market income to maintain an adequate standard of living, the wider impact of provision on employment, and the extent to which different social security systems enhance or diminish status and class differences.

A key feature of the welfare regimes approach is the grouping of countries into clusters or groups. This is done either by using a complex quantitative scoring methodology using a wide range of variables and countries to determine the wider impact of welfare provision, or according to a qualitative approach using a smaller number of variables to reveal debates and assumptions underpinning that provision. Esping-Andersen (1990) is an exemplar of the former approach, while Lewis (1992, 1997) is an exemplar of the latter approach. There is a continuing academic debate as to how many different clusters or regimes exist, and which countries belong to which regime, but for the purposes of this chapter it is relevant to note that Esping-Andersen's methodology and typology have been criticised. Feminists argue that in focusing on the interplay of state and market and on the public realm of employment, Esping-Andersen sidelines gender inequalities since he ignores the informal and familial spheres of unpaid work, which impact on women's access to social security benefits (see Sainsbury, 1994, for an overview of feminist critiques).

Esping-Andersen's work has also been criticised as 'core-centric' in so far as it excludes or misunderstands the welfare regimes of 'peripheral' European countries (Ferrera, 1996; Cousins, 1997). There is a more general point here, however, which is that the majority of such welfare regime analysis focuses on core Western advanced capitalist societies with robust and relatively autonomous states. There have consequently been attempts to 'globalise' welfare regime analysis in recent years, the most important and insightful of which is that by Gough and Wood (2004). This study took the welfare regimes conceptual apparatus to examine the public and private combinations of support for poor people's livelihoods in non-rich countries (p 5). It classified different regions of the world broadly into three different regimes – welfare state regimes, informal security regimes and insecurity regimes. Selected features of each meta-regime are shown in ***Table 7.1***. From this vantage point, the worlds of welfare and the conditions under which the majority of the world's population live are far more diverse than even an expanded version of the welfare regimes literature has been able to contemplate. Once again we can see the global exceptionalism of the kinds of social security systems that exist in the advanced industrialised countries of Northern Europe.

Global social security policy

This concern to 'globalise' the analysis of social security falls within a body of scholarship devoted to the study of the global dimensions of social policy. Global social policy is broadly concerned with the ways in which globalisation

Table 7.1: *Selected features of meta-regimes*

	Welfare state regime	Informal security regime	Insecurity regime
Dominant source of livelihood	Access to formal labour market	A portfolio of livelihoods	A portfolio of livelihoods with extensive conflict
Institutional landscape	Welfare mix of market, state and family	Broader institutional responsibility matrix with powerful external influences and extensive negative permeability	Precarious: extreme negative permeability and fluidity
Welfare outcomes	Varying degrees of decommodification plus health and human investment	Insecurity modified by informal rights and adverse incorporation	Insecurity: intermittently extreme

Source: Adapted from Gough (2004, Figure 1.3, p 32)

processes intersect with social policy and provision – the cross-border flows of people, goods, services, ideas and finance as they relate to the provision, finance and regulation of social welfare, the politics and processes of social policy formation in cross-border spheres of governance and their impacts on national welfare systems (Yeates, 2008). I now turn to examine some key ways in which social security is entangled with such processes. My emphasis lies with the involvement of a range of transnational actors in the making of global social security policy. This section begins by reviewing the principal IGOs involved in social security matters.

An overview of international collaboration in social security

There is a long history of intergovernmental cooperation on social security issues (see Walker, 2005, pp 292-9). The early part of the 20th century saw the foundation of the ILO as an affiliated agency of the ill-fated League of Nations (1919). Building on the work of the ILO, the establishment of the International Social Security Association (ISSA) in 1927 brought together governmental organisations involved in social security and gave further substance to international cooperation in that policy arena by providing a forum for policy dialogue among governmental organisations involved in social security administration throughout the world. While this began as an intergovernmental body, over time it has come to include non-governmental bodies, such as Provident Funds and Trust Funds, operating non-traditional social security schemes (Yeates, 2007a).

The ILO has acquired particular expertise in social security, and is the key United Nations (UN) agency that has led the development of the substance of the right to social security as set out in the UN Universal Declaration of Human Rights (***Box 7.1***). Advocating guaranteed minimum standards worldwide, it has adopted over 30 Conventions and 20 Recommendations that deal exclusively with social security (Otting, 1994). One of the issues the ILO is currently facing is whether its 'flagship' Convention – the Social Security (Minimum Standards) Convention (No 102), which has played an instrumental role in defining the parameters of the right to social security – is still an adequate instrument to guarantee universal social security coverage worldwide or whether it needs to be complemented by a new instrument that is able to address the new challenges faced by developing countries in a globalised world (Kulke, 2007). In particular, Cichon and Hagemejer (2007) point to the need for a new international instrument stipulating universal access to a clearly defined social floor as part of a formal endorsement of basic social security rights. The World Health Organization (WHO), another UN agency, also has a mandate in social security through its involvement in health-related aspects of social security schemes.

Other intergovernmental multilateral agencies involved in this field are international financial institutions, notably the World Bank and the International Monetary Fund (IMF). Both of these organisations' policies bear on social security through their lending policies and packages that have required governments to cut back on social expenditure. We examine the role of one of these independent financial institutions – the World Bank – later in this chapter. Social security matters are also part of the mandate of the Organisation for Economic Co-operation and Development (OECD), a policy forum of the world's 29 richest countries. Although perhaps known for its favouring of 'flexible' labour market and social security systems, it is perhaps most notable in some ways for arguing that, in an era of globalisation and rapid socioeconomic changes, states need to spend more – not less as certain other IGOs sometimes argue – on social security provision.

World-regional formations have also shown an interest in social security issues. Most prominent among these is the EU (see Chapter Six, Carmel and Papadopoulos, this volume) but other regional formations such as the Southern African Development Community (SADC), the Association of South-East Asian Nations (ASEAN) and the Southern Core Common Market (MERCOSUR) have or are considering developing social and labour regulation, although to date only MERCOSUR countries have gone as far as a supranational law on the mutual recognition of social security rights in the region (Yeates and Deacon, 2006). Transregional associations of governments are also becoming involved in these matters: in 2007 the Ibero-American Summit on Social Cohesion pledged international cooperation among governments in Latin America, Spain and Portugal to allow migrant workers to transfer social security benefits between their nations as part of a policy agenda to develop publicly funded universal social protection systems. Alongside these intergovernmental organisations, a range of financial actors are also involved in social security policy debates, in particular, regional development banks such as the Asian Development Bank and the Inter-American Development Bank (Lustig, 2001; Ortiz, 2001).

These institutions are not only a debating forum on social security; some of them have specific powers and responsibilities for policy development, and they also attempt to shape global and domestic policy debates and reforms. They do this in a range of ways, including sponsoring research, reports and conferences, providing information, auditing compliance with international standards, and adding authority to critics when domestic policies are judged to fall short of international standards (Burden, 1998). However, policy implementation and enforcement is a weak area for IGOs because they have no recourse to international law enforcement, and effectively depend on the cooperation of national and local officials and politicians to enact international social law. The ILO, for example, has no powers to enforce national compliance and relies on moral persuasion to achieve its objectives. The World Bank is in the same position, but has been able to exert its policy preferences through its financial lending programmes, which require recipient governments to undertake certain reforms as a condition of the loan (for further details of this, see Yeates, 2007b).

Global debates in social security

The international arena has become a battleground over which political struggles about desirable models of welfare and the appropriate role of each of the public, commercial, voluntary and informal sectors are fought out (Deacon, 2008; Yeates, 2008). Social security issues have been a key part of this struggle. One of the key axes of this debate concerns the goals of social security, namely should social security only aim to alleviate poverty or should it also aim to prevent poverty? This debate ties into policy discussions about the role of public policy more generally in underwriting the social costs of economic and political reform. The policy question now being addressed is not whether but *how* globalisation can be harnessed in support of social standards. It is now accepted that globalisation increasingly exposes people to global economic risks and that this strengthens rather than lessens the need for better social security systems. But what constitutes a 'better' system, and should social (security) policy be confined to playing 'handmaiden' to economic growth, or should it be conceived of as a means of promoting social justice?

As noted above, for much of the 20th century the ILO was the dominant IGO in social security matters. The ILO has emphasised that the primary goals of social security should be to ensure access to a minimum standard of living and raise living standards, and its concerns have been with the gradual extension of statutory social security coverage, particularly to informal sector workers. The social security and labour Conventions and Recommendations developed by the ILO have gained international acceptance and influenced legislation used by developed and developing countries alike (Kay, 2000). The ILO has long advocated the idea of an entitlement to basic social protection as a human right. The concept of 'decent work' (ILO, 1999, 2001) and the associated 'decent work strategy' aim at universal social security coverage that protects living standards rather than just alleviating poverty once it occurs, and at 'opportunities to obtain decent and productive work in conditions of freedom, equity, security and human dignity' (see www.ilo.org/public/english/decent.htm). In this account, in return for participation in the social and economic progress of the country or community, there should be a positive duty to promote equality, inclusion and empowerment and an entitlement to a fair share of resources. However, while the ILO remains sympathetic to universalistic social security, recent years have seen it engaging in a search for alternative forms of universalism given the limitations of work-based systems. In particular, part of the ILO's work has involved a growing interest in categorical (age-based) cash benefits to complement limited coverage in the Global South of work-based contributory schemes (Deacon, 2005).

Other IGOs have also become increasingly influential in this policy domain, especially since the mid-1990s. The World Bank is a prominent advocate of the argument that the aim of social security policy should be to enable poor groups to better manage the financial effects of the various social risks they face. Its 'social risk management' approach regards social security as primarily a safety net for the critically poor, but also a springboard out of poverty in so far as social security systems should at the very least not discourage risk taking among the poor (Holzmann and Jørgensen, 2000, p 3; World Bank, 2001). In this framework, the World Bank regards informal and market-based social protection, or 'risk management', instruments as best suited to what it calls 'idiosyncratic' risks of a health (illness, injury, disability), lifecycle (birth, old age, death), social (crime, domestic violence) and economic (unemployment, harvest failure, business failure) nature. Limited public subsidies and provision for low-income groups are justifiable because the poor cannot secure their livelihoods through informal means or commercial schemes alone, but non-poor groups are expected to make their own private 'risk management' arrangements by, for example, drawing on their own savings and resources or purchasing commercial social security protection. Thus, the primary objective of social risk management is to support the 'critically poor'; commercial provision and the family are social security systems of the 'first resort', bolstered by philanthropic and voluntary efforts to compensate for withdrawn or pared-down 'last-resort' public provision. The 'social risk management' approach does not consider as a legitimate goal the promotion of a more egalitarian income distribution, be it achieved through tax-transfer mechanisms or comprehensive public goods provision (Holzmann and Jørgensen, 2000, p 21). This policy orientation reflects neoliberals' preference for individual responsibility that enhances 'choice', self-interest and enforceable contractual rights over collective responsibility that enhances social cohesion, integration and equity (Dixon and Hyde, 2001).

Global pensions policy

Pensions is a key terrain over which these kinds of debates about the appropriate goals of social security and the respective roles of the public, commercial, voluntary and informal sectors have been waged. Minns (2001) characterises this struggle as a 'new Cold War' between Anglo-American models of pension provision on the one hand and European, Asian-Pacific and Eurasian models on the other. Both the World Bank (World Bank, 1994, 2000; Holzmann and Jørgensen, 2000) and the IMF (1996) are at the forefront of those who would encourage the diffusion of the Anglo-American model, already in place in the US, the UK, the Netherlands, Ireland, Switzerland, Chile, Australia and Canada. This has entailed the dismantling of comprehensive publicly managed and provided pensions and the building up of private pensions systems with a view to promoting better 'social risk management' by encouraging private savings and maximising the role of private financial institutions in income maintenance provisions in old age more generally. Thus, the World Bank regards the legitimate role of the state as essentially limited to the regulation of the (private) pensions industry and the provision of a low-level state pension for the poorest of the population, comprising either a minimum flat-rate or means-tested benefit or a reduced pay-as-you-go (PAYG) pension system. It recommends for people who wish to make additional provision a second funded pillar of privately managed pensions savings accounts and a third pillar of voluntary supplementary schemes such as occupational pensions. The World Bank envisages a greater role for the second and third pillars than for the first pillar in the overall system of pension provision (see Chapter Ten, McKay, this volume).

Such interventions have effectively transformed pension privatisation 'from a radical idea to a mainstream, global policy prescription' (Kay, 2000, p 192) and provided legitimacy and support for what Orenstein (2008) calls the 'new pension reforms' that have been adopted around the world. The World Bank has advised governments in Central and Eastern Europe (Deacon et al, 1997; Deacon, 2005), Latin America (Cruz-Saco and Mesa-Lago, 1998) and China (World Bank, 1997), trying to persuade them to adopt its pension reforms model. This advice has in many cases been backed up by the provision of institutional, human and financial resources to assist governments – many of which are dependent on the World Bank for development finance – to reform their pensions along its preferred lines. The World Bank has also formed alliances with other international organisations, such as the United States Agency for International Development (USAID), and regional development banks, such as the Asian Development Bank and the Inter-American Development Bank, to support the promotion of its pensions model (Orenstein, 2008). Bilateral aid has traditionally been a key form of international development assistance provided by 'rich' to 'poor' countries. Governments regularly send civil servants to provide technical or policy expertise to advise other governments on setting up, expanding or restructuring their social security systems and this has as such been a key means by which social security and pensions policy reforms in recipient countries are leveraged by donor countries.

How successful has the World Bank been in getting governments to adopt its pension model? Some of the evidence about this is covered by Orenstein (2008), who argues that 'starting in the early 1990s, new pension reforms inspired by the Chilean model and the World Bank's multipillar model spread to more than 30 countries around the world' (p 212). Most of these countries have been in Latin America and Central and Eastern Europe, but they are starting to inform policy reforms in Africa (Nigeria became the first adopter in 2004 and South Africa was considering them in 2007) and East Asia, where Taiwan adopted the reforms in 2004 (Orenstein, 2008). The World Bank and its like-minded allies have used a variety of methods to promote the new pension reforms: developing pension policy ideas, problems and solutions that are spread through publications and conferences; providing resources to local partners sympathetic to their ideas; providing funds and technical assistance to government reform teams; and providing long-term assistance with reform implementation (Orenstein, 2008).

Much has been made of the dominance of the World Bank model in this policy arena, but it is clear that its influence has not gone unchecked. Some countries have been able to resist the new pension reforms, and their experience demonstrates how IGO prescriptions depend on the national context for how far and in what form the model is actually implemented. As Cruz-Saco and Mesa-Lago (1998) demonstrate in the Latin American context, only Chile's pension system comes closest to the World Bank paradigm. Similarly, Fultz and Ruck (2001) show that most Central and Eastern European countries are reforming their public schemes without establishing a mandatory private pillar. In Korea, Slovenia and Venezuela – all countries with extensive World Bank intervention – concerted political coalitions have managed to prevent these reforms taking hold (Orenstein, 2008). Many would argue that even though the World Bank's policy prescriptions are not adopted or are not followed to the letter, the influence of this organisation cannot be dismissed. Here, the involvement of the World Bank's active partnership with a range of institutions in individual countries, the ongoing individualisation and marketisation of provision, and governments' retreat from the goals of income redistribution, are often cited as evidence in this regard (Dixon and Hyde, 2001; Cruz-Saco, 2002; Deacon, 2005; Orenstein, 2008).

The dominance of the World Bank's approach to pensions provision can also be seen in its effects on the ILO's policy approach to pensions. Traditionally, the ILO stressed the importance of a compulsory universal flat-rate public pension within a tripartite system (the other pillars being public earnings-related schemes and private voluntary schemes) (Otting, 1994). For developed countries the ILO now recommends a four-pillar model consisting of:

(1) a means-tested tier, financed from general revenue;
(2) a PAYG, defined benefit pension worth 40-50% of lifetime average earnings;
(3) a compulsory, capitalised, defined contribution pension; and

(4) an upper tier of voluntary retirement savings and non-pension sources of income.

For developing countries, it recommends prioritising the expansion of coverage to workers in the informal sector, or a national programme that excludes higher-income workers who would be required to participate in a more expensive (probably private) programme. The basic state programme could be limited to disability and survivors' benefits or provide retirement benefits that start at a relatively high age, such as 65 or 70 (Gillion, 2000, p 20; Gillion et al, 2000). As the ILO (2000, p 20) itself states, this model represents an important shift in its thinking, justified in terms of 'allowing for greater diversification of retirement income risks'. The retreat of the ILO from universal provision and its acceptance of a larger role for private pension provision is for some indicative that 'the social security department of the ILO can no longer be regarded as a bulwark against Bretton Woods policies' (Deacon, 2000, pp 11-12).

Although the UK is not dependent on the World Bank for development finance, many of the tenets of its policy paradigms can be seen in British social security discourse and policy over the last three decades. The marketisation and privatisation agenda has involved both the transfer of responsibility for benefits provision and administration to the private sector and the incorporation of private sector values into public sector provision (Walker, 2001, p 124). Overall, although the state continues to play a major role in social security provision and administration, there are concerns that the UK and other richer countries may end up converging on the weaker role for state social security seen in many parts of the world.

Overview

- Social security is something that UK citizens take for granted but despite the international establishment of a right to social security more than half a century ago this right remains an abstract one for the majority of the world's population.
- Debates about the appropriate balance between statutory, commercial and informal arrangements for social security, and about the goals of prevention versus alleviation of poverty are of global significance.
- A concern with minimum standards and extending statutory social security coverage has been the priority of the ILO and this model has influenced the development of diverse national systems throughout the 20th century.
- The most recent phase of the globalisation of social security has entailed the entry of the World Bank into global social security debates. As a 'carrier' of neoliberal, conservative welfare ideologies, it has been less concerned with issues of redistribution and equity, instead advocating selectivist public social

security systems and marketised, privatised and informalised social security provision.
- Ultimately, any reform proposal must be evaluated in the light of whether it makes the right to adequate income security a meaningful one for everyone rather than just for a privileged minority.

Questions for discussion

(1) What are the issues involved in defining social security from a global perspective?
(2) How important is the statutory benefits system in ensuring an adequate income for individuals and households? What other sources of income may also be available?
(3) How does the UK system compare with other countries in terms of expenditure, design, coverage and outcomes?
(4) Compare the approaches of the World Bank and the ILO to (i) social security and (ii) pensions. What are the distinctive features of these IGO approaches?

Notes

[1] This integration of healthcare within social security is why the ILO includes public spending on healthcare in addition to benefits in cash and in kind in its social security expenditure data.

[2] *Zakât* is an obligatory form of alms-giving for Muslims who are required to give 2.5% of their wealth for the benefit of the poor in the Muslim community. These funds are collected and distributed by *zakât* agencies (www.submission.org/zakat.html; www.zpub.com/aaa/zakat.html).

[3] Social security expenditure here covers expenditure on pensions, employment injury, sickness, family, housing and social assistance benefits in cash and in kind, including administrative expenditure.

Website resources

www.fra.europa.eu
European Fundamental Rights Agency
www.homeoffice.gov.uk/
Home Office

www.ilo.org/public/english/index.htm
International Labour Organization
www.imf.org/external/index.htm
International Monetary Fund
www.issa.int/engl/homef.htm
International Social Security Association

References

Burden, T. (1998) *Social policy and welfare: A clear guide*, London: Pluto.

Cichon, M. and Hagemejer, K. (2007) 'Changing the development policy paradigm: investing in a social security floor for all', *International Social Security Review*, vol 60, pp 2-3, pp 169-96.

Cousins, M. (1997) 'Ireland's place in the worlds of welfare', *Journal of European Social Policy*, vol 7, no 3, pp 223-35.

Cruz-Saco, M.A. (2002) *Labour markets and social security coverage: The Latin American experience*, Extension of Social Security Paper No 2, Social Security Policy and Development Branch, Geneva: ILO.

Cruz-Saco, M.A. and Mesa-Lago, C. (eds) (1998) *The reform of pension and health care systems in Latin America: Do options exist?*, Pittsburgh, PA: University of Pittsburgh.

Deacon, B. (2000) *Globalisation and social policy: The threat to equitable welfare*, Occasional Paper 5, Geneva: UNRISD.

Deacon, B. (2005) 'Global social policy: from neo-liberalism to social democracy?', in B. Cantillon and I. Marx (eds) *International cooperation in social security: How to cope with globalisation?*, Amsterdam: Intersentia, pp 157-81.

Deacon, B. (2008) 'Global and regional social governance', in N. Yeates (ed) *Understanding global social policy*, Bristol: The Policy Press, pp 25-48.

Deacon, B., Hulse, M. and Stubbs, P. (1997) *Global social policy: International organisations and the future of welfare*, London: Sage Publications.

Dixon, J. (1999) *Social security in global perspective*, Westport, CT: Praeger.

Dixon, J. and Hyde, M. (eds) (2001) *The marketization of social security*, Westport, CT: Quorum Books.

Esping-Andersen, G. (1990) *The three worlds of welfare capitalism*, Cambridge: Polity Press.

Ferrera, M. (1996) 'The "southern" model of welfare in Europe', *Journal of European Social Policy*, vol 6, no 1, pp 17-38.

Fultz, E. and Ruck, M. (2001) 'Pension reform in Central and Eastern Europe: emerging issues and patterns', *International Labour Review*, vol 140, no 1, pp 19-43.

Gillion, C. (2000) *The development and reform of social security pensions: The approach of the International Labour Office*, Geneva: ILO, www.ilo.org/public/english/protection/socsec/publ/exec.htm

Gillion, C., Turner, J., Bailey, J. and Latulippe, D. (eds) (2000) *Social security pensions: Development and reform*, Geneva: ILO.

Gough, I. (2004) 'Welfare regimes in development contexts: a global and regional analysis', in I. Gough and G. Wood (eds) *Insecurity and welfare regimes in Asia, Africa and Latin America*, Cambridge: Cambridge University Press, pp 15-48.

Gough, I. and Wood, G. (2004) (eds) *Insecurity and welfare regimes in Asia, Africa and Latin America*, Cambridge: Cambridge University Press.

Holzmann, R. and Jørgensen, S. (2000) *Social risk management: A new conceptual framework for social protection, and beyond*, Social Protection Discussion Paper No 6, Washington, DC: World Bank.

ILO (International Labour Organization) (1999) *Decent work*, Report of the Director-General of the ILO to the 87th Session of the International Labour Conference, Geneva: ILO.

ILO (2000) *World labour report 2000: Income security and social protection in a changing world*, Geneva: ILO.

ILO (2001) *Social security: A new consensus*, Geneva: ILO.

IMF (International Monetary Fund) (1996) *Aging populations and public pension schemes*, Washington, DC: IMF.

Kay, S. (2000) 'Recent changes in Latin American welfare states: is there social dumping?', *Journal of European Social Policy*, vol 10, no 2, pp 185-203.

Kleinman, M. and Piachaud, D. (1993) 'European social policy: conceptions and choices', *Journal of European Social Policy*, vol 3, no 1, pp 1-19.

Kulke, U. (2007) 'The present and future role of ILO standards in realizing the right to social security', *International Social Security Review*, vol 60, no 2-3, pp 119-41.

Lewis, J. (1992) 'Gender and development of welfare regimes', *Journal of European Social Policy*, vol 2, no 3, pp 159-73.

Lewis, J. (1997) 'Gender and welfare regimes: further thoughts', *Social Politics*, vol 4, no 2, pp 160-77.

Lustig, I. (ed) (2001) *Shielding the poor: Social protection in the developing world*, Washington, DC: Inter-American Development Bank.

Midgley, J. (1997) *Social welfare in global context*, London: Sage Publications.

Midgley, J. and Kaseke, E. (1996) 'Challenges to social security in developing countries', in J. Midgley and M. B. Tracy (eds) *Challenges to social security: An international exploration*, Westport, CT: Auburn House.

Millar, J. and Warman, A. (1997) 'Family–state boundaries in Europe', in M. May, E. Brunsdon and G. Craig (eds) *Social policy review 9*, London: Guildhall University/Social Policy Association.

Minns, R. (2001) *The Cold War in welfare: Stock markets versus pensions*, London: Verso.

Orenstein, M. (2008) 'Global pensions policy', in N. Yeates (ed) *Understanding global social policy*, Bristol: The Policy Press, pp 207-27.

Ortiz, I. (ed) (2001) *Social protection in Asia and the Pacific*, Manila: Asian Development Bank.

Otting, A. (1994) 'The International Labour Organization and its standard-setting activity in the area of social security', *Journal of European Social Policy*, vol 4, no 1, pp 51-7.

Sainsbury, D. (ed) (1994) *Gendering welfare states*, London: Sage Publications.

van Ginneken, W. (1999) *Social security for the excluded majority: Case studies of developing countries*, Geneva: ILO.

van Ginneken, W. (2007) 'Extending social security coverage: concepts, global trends and policy issues', *International Social Security Review*, vol 60, nos 2-3, pp 39-57.

Walker, C. (2001) 'The forms of privatization of social security in Britain', in J. Dixon and M. Hyde (eds) *The marketization of social security*, Westport, CT: Quorum Books.

Walker, R. (2005) *Social security and welfare: Concepts and comparisons*, Maidenhead: Open University Press.

World Bank (1994) *Averting the old age crisis: Policies to protect the old and promote growth*, New York: OUP.

World Bank (1997) *Old age security: Pension reform in China*, Washington, DC: World Bank.

World Bank (2000) *World development report 1999/2000: Entering the 21st century*, Oxford: Oxford University Press.

World Bank (2001) *Social protection sector strategy: From safety net to springboard*, Washington, DC: World Bank.

Yeates, N. (2001) *Globalization and social policy*, London: Sage Publications.

Yeates, N. (2007a) 'Globalisation and social policy', in J. Baldock, N. Manning, S. Miller and S. Vickerstaff (eds) *Social policy* (3rd edition), Oxford: Oxford University Press, pp 627-53.

Yeates, N. (2007b) 'The global and supra-national dimensions of the welfare mix', in M. Powell (ed) *Understanding the mixed economy of welfare*, Bristol: The Policy Press, pp 199-219.

Yeates, N. (ed) (2008) *Understanding global social policy*, Bristol: The Policy Press.

Yeates, N. and Deacon, B. (2006) *Globalism, regionalism and social policy: Framing the debate*, United Nations University–Comparative Regional Integration Studies (UNU-CRIS) Working Paper 0-2006/6, April, Bruges, Belgium: UNU-CRIS.

Part Two
Lifecourse and labour markets

'From cradle to grave': social security and the lifecourse

Karen Rowlingson

Summary

The Beveridge plan in the 1940s aimed to provide income security 'from cradle to grave' against economic risks such as unemployment, sickness, bereavement and retirement. Since then, however, the nature of the lifecourse has changed substantially and this has had an impact on the nature of the risks people now need security against. For example, as people live longer, the length of time in retirement is increasing and this has led to major debates about the nature of pension provision. Increased life expectancy also raises the issue of care needs and the appropriate way of paying for care. Changes in family forms, such as the growth of cohabitation, divorce and lone parenthood, introduce new risks for the social security system to deal with. This chapter:

- reviews the changes in the lifecourse (and associated economic risks) over the last half-century;
- reviews how the social security system has adapted to these changes;
- examines whether the social security system is (still) able to support people from cradle to grave;
- explores possible reforms of the system to reflect better the current nature of the lifecourse and economic risk, including Basic Income Schemes and new 'asset-based welfare' approaches.

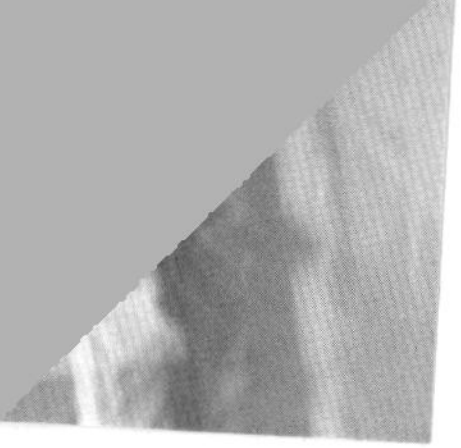

Introduction

William Beveridge set down the main foundations of today's social security system in the 1940s. The Beveridge plan aimed to provide state support from cradle to grave and thereby eliminate the 'five giants' of want, disease, ignorance, squalor and idleness. Within the social security system this was to be achieved by placing insurance (contributory) benefits at the centre of the social security system. National assistance (means-tested) benefits were expected to be a safety net to which few people would have to resort. This system was based on certain assumptions about family and employment patterns. Central to this was the idea of the male breadwinner, working full time throughout the course of his life and married to a housewife who looked after home and family. The 1950s and 1960s were relatively unusual in British history in that this breadwinner/housewife model was the norm, even if it was not entirely universal. But the 1970s saw the beginnings of fundamental change in this model and by the 1980s and 1990s lifecourse patterns had changed considerably. The main aim of this chapter is to consider the relationship between the social security system and these changing lifecourse patterns.

Changes in the lifecourse

The 1950s and 1960s saw relative uniformity in terms of family life. Most children grew up in married couple families; most young adults got married without cohabiting first. Most children were born to married parents. Unmarried motherhood was stigmatised. Divorce was unusual. Most men worked until they retired at the age of 65 and relatively few people lived into their eighties or beyond. Much of this changed from the 1970s onwards.

One of the first changes, starting in the 1960s, was a considerable growth in the number of divorces (see ***Table 8.1***). This increase continued throughout the 1970s before tailing off in the 1980s and actually declining in the 1990s and early 2000s. Nevertheless, there were almost six times as many divorces in 2001 compared with 1961. At the same time, the number of first marriages declined by almost half between 1961 and 2001. These trends might lead us to conclude that marriage became increasingly unpopular over this period but, in fact, there was a considerable increase in the number of remarriages (more than tripling between 1961 and 2001). So the institution of marriage was not being rejected wholesale over this period.

Another potential challenge to the institution of marriage is cohabitation. It has now become the norm for couples to live together before they get married. Haskey (1996) found that, in the mid-1960s, fewer than 5% of never-married women had cohabited prior to marriage; in the early 1990s 70% had done so. Cohabitation is not necessarily an alternative to marriage

***Table 8.1:** Trends in marriage in England and Wales, 1961–2005*

	First marriages for men	Divorces (males)	Remarriages of divorced men
1961	309,000	25,000	19,000
1971	344,000	74,000	42,000
1981	259,000	146,000	79,000
1991	223,000	159,000	75,000
2001	176,000	144,000	68,000
2005	173,000	142,000	69,000

Note: Numbers rounded to the nearest thousand.

Source: ONS (2007a, Table 9.1, p 68)

as it is seen by most cohabitees as a precursor to marriage but it can occur between marriages and it also occurs when a couple have made a conscious decision never to marry. Many cohabiting couples decide to marry before having children but it is increasingly common for couples to have children while still cohabiting and one fifth of all families with dependent children are cohabiting (Haskey, 1996).

Along with conceptions and births within cohabitation there has also been an increase in the number of conceptions and births to single women. Putting these two phenomena together we can estimate the number of extramarital conceptions. In the 1950s and 1960s, the existence of an extramarital conception was a source of shame, perhaps leading to a 'shotgun wedding'. The 1967 Abortion Act provided another route for single women to take if they were pregnant and by the late 1990s about one in five of extramarital conceptions ended in a termination. ***Figure 8.1*** shows that while the number of births *within* marriage fell between 1961 and 2001, the number of births *outside* marriage increased dramatically, particularly during the 1980s. Most extramarital births are registered to two parents living at the same address (63% in 2001).

The 1960s saw a baby boom with the total fertility rate (the number of births per adult female in the population) in the UK at 2.95. This fell to a low of 1.63 in 2001 although it has increased slightly in more recent years, to 1.84 in 2006 (ONS, 2007b). Women today are having children later, if at all. The average age of mothers at first childbirth was 27.3 years in England and Wales in 2005, more than three years older than in 1971 (ONS, 2007c).

As a consequence of declining rates of marriage, increasing rates of extramarital births and rising divorce, there has been a substantial rise in lone parenthood since the 1970s. The percentage of dependent children living in lone-parent families more than tripled between 1972 and 2006 to 24% (ONS, 2007c). Divorced lone mothers were the most common type of lone

Figure 8.1: Births by marital status, 1971–2001

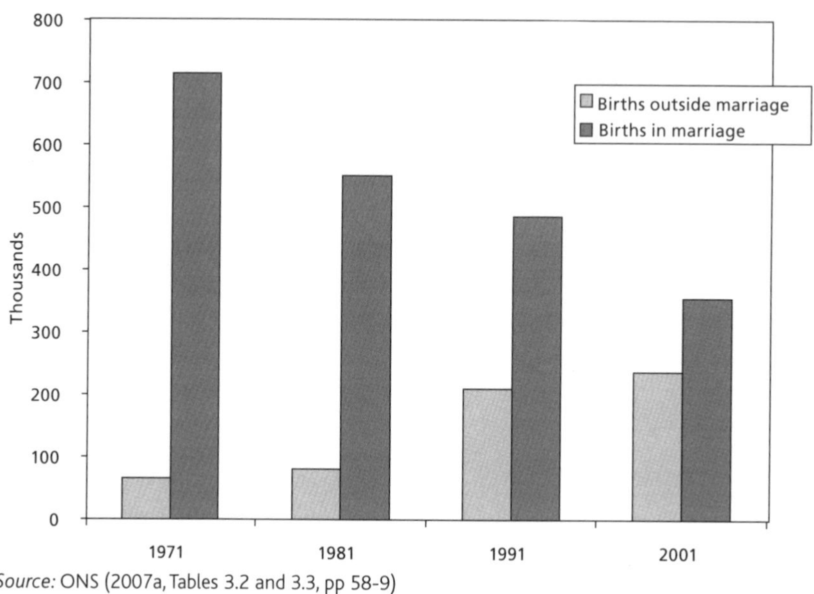

Source: ONS (2007a, Tables 3.2 and 3.3, pp 58-9)

mother in the 1970s and 1980s but in the 1990s never-married lone mothers became increasingly common. This was, in large part, due to the breakdown of cohabiting relationships, but was also due to the growth in the number of births to single women (Rowlingson and McKay, 2002).

One consequence of declining marriage, rising divorce and rising cohabitation has been an increase in the number of stepfamilies. By 2001, 10% of families with children were step-parent families (ONS, 2007d).

Another major change in family forms is the growing number of people living alone. In 1950, fewer than one in 20 people in Britain lived alone. By 1970, 18% of households in Britain were single-person households. By 2001, this figure had risen to 30% (ONS, 2007e). Older age groups, particularly widows and widowers, form about half this group but the largest increase has been among those under retirement age. Younger people are increasingly choosing to set up their own independent households and those in middle age are also doing so, perhaps following partnership breakdown.

The final, major change in lifecourse patterns concerns ageing (see Chapter Ten, McKay, this volume). Over the 1920s and 1930s, male life expectancy at birth increased slowly to a figure of 59.4 in 1940. This was roughly the point at which Beveridge was developing his plan. By 1951 male life expectancy had increased dramatically to 66.2. From then on, life expectancy increased steadily to 73.2 in 1991. The figures for women were 63.9 in 1940, 71.2 in 1951 and 78.9 in 1991 (Laslett, 1996). Life expectancy at age 65 in the UK has also reached its highest level ever for both men and women. Men aged

65 could expect to live a further 16.9 years and women a further 19.7 years if mortality rates remained the same as they were in 2004-06 (ONS, 2007f). Thus, the number of years that people spend in retirement (and receiving state retirement pension) has increased substantially. At the same time, people today often aspire to retire early.

The increase in life expectancy has not been accompanied by a similar increase in healthy life expectancy (ONS, 2004) and so the need for health and social care has grown. Residential care is not common, however, as most care is still provided by family members, and most older people live in the community, including three quarters of people aged 90 or over in 2001 (ONS, 2007g).

Box 8.1 provides a summary of changes in lifecourse patters since the mid-20th century.

Box 8.1: Summary of changes in lifecourse patterns since the mid-20th century

- Divorce rates rose substantially between 1960 and 1990 and then levelled out.
- The number of first marriages has declined dramatically; cohabitation is now commonplace and is no longer regarded as 'living in sin'.
- There has been an increase in births to single women and cohabiting couples.
- From the 1970s onwards, there has been an increase in the number of lone-parent families and stepfamilies.
- More and more people are living alone – both younger people and older people.
- Life expectancies have increased so now people spend much more time in retirement.
- There is greater need for care in later life although most of this is still provided in the community by family and friends.

As we have seen, the lifecourse used to be more predictable in order of events and more stable over longer periods. There is now much more diversity in ways of living and much more movement between different statuses. At the same time, economic risks have also changed, as we shall see in the next section.

Changes in economic risk

The male breadwinner/female housewife model was partly the basis for the welfare state's insurance principle. The main economic risks for men were unemployment, sickness/disability and retirement. Women would gain coverage through their husbands' entitlement to contributory benefits. There have been major changes in economic risk since the Second World War but unemployment is still an economic risk for some. It varies with the economic cycle and rose in the 1970s and 1980s but fell back in the late 1980s. It then rose again in the early 1990s before falling once more. Nevertheless, unemployment in 2007, at 5.3%, was still twice the level experienced in the 1950s and 1960s (ONS, 2007h). And particular groups of men, such as those with no qualifications, have particularly high rates of unemployment – around 15% in the late 1990s (Nickell, 1999). Unemployment is also high among some minority ethnic groups (see Chapter Five, Law, this volume).

While unemployment is still an issue, the 1980s and 1990s witnessed the growth of a new, although related, phenomenon: male economic inactivity. Economic inactivity is a term used to describe people who are not in paid work but are also not unemployed, that is, they are not actively seeking work nor are they available for work. The term can include people looking after the home/family, sick and disabled people who are out of work and those who are 'early retired' but not yet receiving the state pension. This kind of economic risk was envisaged by Beveridge but not on the scale that has been witnessed in the last 30 years. In November 2007, 21% of working-age adults were economically inactive (ONS, 2007g).

Another new area of economic risk concerns the changing nature of the labour market. There has been growth in low-paid insecure employment with Britain coming, in the 1990s at least, near the top of the international low-pay league of the countries in the Organisation for Economic Co-operation and Development (OECD, 1996). Casual workers, those in small firms, those in non-union firms, minority ethnic groups and less-skilled manual workers are all more likely to be low paid (Stewart, 1999). One in every six male workers over the age of 24 was low paid at the end of the 1990s compared with one in 30 in 1968 (Stewart, 1999). And there is strong evidence of a cycle of low pay and no pay, with those on low pay more likely to be out of work in the future and those out of work more likely to get low-paid jobs when they rejoin the labour market. The National Minimum Wage (NMW) has reduced the scale of this risk to some extent, although there is still a considerable problem of in-work poverty in the UK (Cooke and Lawton, 2008).

Increases in unemployment and, in particular, inactivity have largely affected men. Women, by contrast, substantially increased their employment rates in the last half of the 20th century. In 1975, more than 92% of working-age men had a job compared with only 59% of working-age women. By 1998 the figures were 81% and 69% respectively (Desai et al, 1999). The increase in women's employment rates is most pronounced among women with very young children and working partners. However, many women workers, especially those with dependent children, work in part-time jobs, and lone mothers in particular are often located in low-paid, insecure jobs.

Another new economic risk is the growth of lone parenthood. Nine out of ten lone parents are women and these women are less likely to be employed than married or cohabiting mothers (about 55% compared with about 72%; ONS, 2006) and so more likely to be dependent on social security benefits. While the Beveridge system certainly catered for women who were widows, this was expected to be a fairly small part of the system, mainly for older women without children, although the benefits would also cover working-age women with children. But the social security system was not designed for other types of lone mothers such as those divorced or never-married and these families have mainly been supported through the means-tested benefit parts of the benefits system. It is therefore not surprising that there has been some concern that the social security system (and the availability of council housing) may have created incentives for women to become lone parents. There is, however, no strong evidence to support such concern (see Rowlingson and McKay, 2002, for a review).

All of the changes discussed here have implications for people's current incomes. But they also have an impact on the amount people can save for retirement. The 'risk' of retirement has always been recognised in the social security system but, again, the scale of this risk has increased as more people reach retirement and stay retired for longer. The risk of needing health and social care in later life has also increased. ***Box 8.2*** provides a summary of changes in economic risks since the 1970s.

Box 8.2: Summary of changes in economic risks since the 1970s

- The mid-1970s saw a dramatic upsurge in (mostly male) unemployment. It fell back again in the late 1980s before rising again in the early 1990s and then declining once more.
- The 1980s and 1990s witnessed a growth of male economic inactivity on a massive scale.
- The number of low-paid jobs increased in the 1970s and 1980s.
- Women's employment rates have increased but women with dependent children are often employed in part-time jobs.
- Lone parenthood has increased and about 45% of all lone parents are out of work.
- The 'risk' of not being able to save for retirement and health and social care in later life has increased.

To what extent has the social security system adapted to these trends?

One of the first 'economic risks' to challenge the postwar social security system was the growth of unemployment. This was largely caused by changes in the global economy that were heralded by the large increase in oil prices in 1974. Manufacturing and heavy industry declined in Britain as the country moved towards a post-industrial economic base. It is sometimes claimed that high levels of social security encourage people to leave work or discourage those out of work from moving into jobs (see Bryson and McKay, 1994, and Millar and Ridge, 2001, for further discussion). But, over the period we are looking at, social security payments were not significantly increased and so did not pose an increasing disincentive to work. The growth of unemployment was due to fundamental economic change and the social security system acted as a safety net to prevent the most severe hardship that otherwise would have been experienced by many.

A similar story can be told of the growth of economic inactivity as a whole, which also reflected changing economic and social conditions. Once again it is sometimes claimed that the growth in the numbers claiming sickness and disability/incapacity benefits in the 1980s happened at least in part because benefit officers (with the government's implicit approval) encouraged 'unemployed' people to sign on as sick or disabled so that the unemployment figures did not rise too much. In addition, incapacity benefits are more generous than unemployment benefits, which may also have encouraged people to try and claim these. This relative generosity had existed prior to the 1970s but the introduction of new disability benefits in the 1970s probably made economic inactivity a more financially rewarding position to be in compared with unemployment. Berthoud (1998), however, contends that there is no strong evidence to suggest that those on sickness and disability benefits in the 1990s were not actually sick or disabled. So, once again, far from contributing to worklessness, the social security system provided an important safety net for people during difficult times of economic restructuring.

Economic restructuring also led to an increase in the number of low-paid jobs, which create some financial disincentives to work, especially for families with children, as the benefit system takes into account family size whereas wages do not. Family Income Supplement was introduced in 1971 to reduce any disincentives to work and various forms of wage supplementation have continued, since then, to be crucial in supporting families with children, particularly lone-parent families, to combine work with caring responsibilities. However, the most recent version of in-work means-tested support, the Working Tax Credit (WTC) introduced in 2003, has suffered from various problems. These include high levels of administrative complexity and the requirement for claimants to repay money to Her Majesty's Revenue & Customs (HMRC) if they earn more than they had expected to the previous year (see Chapter Thirteen, Millar, this volume).

Another reaction to the problem of low pay was the introduction of the NMW in 1999. This does seem to have reduced wage/income inequality to some extent. In the spring of 1999 when the NMW came into effect, 1.5 million jobs (6.5%) were paid at less than the level of the NMW (£3.60 an hour). One year later, only 300,000 jobs (1.2%) were paid less than the minimum wage and yet the distribution of hourly earnings above the £3.60 mark has been largely unaffected (Stuttard and Jenkins, 2001).

As well as looking at individual reforms that have responded to changes in lifecourse patterns, there is a broader theme in social security policy that has developed over the last 30 years: the importance of paid work. The Conservative governments from 1979 onwards certainly pursued this theme but it was under New Labour that 'activation' became the key policy goal. A host of sound bites soon accumulated, most notably: 'work as the best form of welfare' and 'work for those who can, security for those who cannot'. The key reforms here were the various New Deal policies and work-focused interviews for all benefit claimants, leading to a system denoted by Kemp (2005, p 30) as a 'work-focused benefit regime'.

Attention in recent years has therefore turned to the 'inactive' – lone parents and those receiving Incapacity Benefit (IB). The 2007 Green Paper on welfare reform (DWP, 2007) proposed to extend activation policies to these two groups in particular. (The proposals for disabled claimants are discussed in Chapter Twelve, Sainsbury, this volume.) For lone parents, it proposed that they should face a similar regime to that of the unemployed, being required to be actively seeking and available for work, once their children reach the age of 12. This comes into effect in stages from 2008 and by 2010 it will apply to those with children aged seven and above. This is a substantial change in work requirements for lone parents.

Successive governments have sought to tackle the issue of child support from non-resident parents (mostly fathers) to lone parents (mostly mothers). The initial reforms in this area in the 1980s were primarily motivated by a desire to cut the social security bill for government rather than to increase the amount received by lone parents. The system was flawed from the start. It was perceived to be unfair to non-resident parents in terms of the amounts of money expected, the targeting of 'easy' cases first and the disregard for agreements already made between parents. The system was also complex and lone parents benefited little from it, thus removing incentives to cooperate with the Child Support Agency (CSA). Successive reforms failed to improve the situation and following an independent review (under Henshaw, 2006) in December 2006 a White Paper (DWP, 2006a) set out a new direction. There will be a greater emphasis on people making their own arrangements along with a new enforcement body with even stronger powers. The policy emphasis has also strongly shifted towards child poverty as an objective, and away from the earlier focus on reducing the benefit bill for government.

With people living longer, reform of pensions policy has been on the agenda for all recent governments (see Chapter Ten, McKay, this volume). Fears about the increasing cost of state pensions led the Conservative government in 1980 to remove the link between state pension uprating and earnings. Over time, this reform reduced the role of insurance-based state support in favour of means-tested state support. At the same time, the Conservative government aimed to increase private saving through personal pensions. New Labour initially appeared to follow a similar direction, putting its faith in the market to provide a greater proportion of retirement income for pensioners in the future. But it soon became clear that employers were moving away from generous pension packages. The government therefore needed to rethink its strategy here.

It decided to do so with the help of an independent Pensions Commission (2005), which recommended a rise in the age at which people could first receive state pensions, alongside a renewed role for insurance-based state pensions (through restoring the link between increases in the state retirement pension and earnings) and more support for private saving. The government is now reforming pensions policy in line with the main recommendations of this Commission although it will only restore the link between the state retirement pension and earnings 'subject to affordability' (DWP, 2006b). It is, perhaps, surprising that the age for the receipt of the state pension has been 65 since the birth of Beveridge's insurance-based pensions. It is therefore a major policy change, as is the decision to link rises in the state retirement pension to earnings, a policy change that successive campaigns by pensioner groups and members of the Labour Party (most notably, Barbara Castle) had failed to come close to achieving.

Changes in the risk of poverty from cradle to grave

As a result of many of the trends (social, economic and political) discussed in this chapter, poverty and inequality grew dramatically in the 1980s and early 1990s. In 1979, fewer than one in 10 people were living in poverty but this rate doubled to one in five by 1995/96 (Burgess and Propper, 1999). Economic growth in the 1980s was not shared across households – most of it went to the wealthiest households while poorer ones failed to benefit. Children were one of the main groups to suffer from these trends. In 1979, one in 12 children lived in poor households. By 1995/96, this had increased to about one in three. The causes of growing poverty and inequality are complex but part of the story at least is a lack of commitment from the government during that period to use the social security system to support people who found themselves outside the labour market.

In the last decade or so, the poverty rates for most groups have fallen. For example, child poverty has fallen to 3.8 million children in the UK in 2005/06 after deducting housing costs (using the government's preferred measure of below 60% of median income). This is 0.6 million – or 14% – less than in 1998/99 (New Policy Institute, 2008a). Once again, the causes of this change are complex but the social security system has been used as a policy tool to reduce child poverty through increasing the levels of Income Support (IS) and wage supplements for those in work (Hirsch, 2006). However, the government had hoped to reduce child poverty even more and missed its first target for reducing child poverty by a quarter by 2005/06, leading to claims that the government's strategy is 'largely exhausted' (Palmer et al, 2007, p 9; see Chapter Nine, Ridge, this volume).

Pensioner poverty has had a lower public profile in recent years than child poverty despite the fact that the government has had more success here. The proportion of pensioners living in low-income households (after housing costs) fell throughout the last decade, from 29% of all pensioners in 1996/97 to 17% in 2005/06 (New Policy Institute, 2008b). Pensioners are now less likely to be living in low-income households than non-pensioners (see Chapter Ten, McKay, this volume). The reduction in pensioner poverty has been mostly achieved through changes in the social security system, not least increases in the means-tested benefit, Pension Credit. This has been a controversial strategy in some ways as those pensioners who have made modest amounts of savings or occupational pensions are little, or no, better off than those who have made no such provision. This raises issues of fairness and (dis)incentives to save.

While child poverty and pensioner poverty have clearly been reduced by social security policies in the last decade, poverty among working-age people without children has actually increased (New Policy Institute, 2008c).

Providing 'support' from cradle to grave is not just about relieving or preventing poverty. For example, there is increasing need for long-term care in later life and yet growing concern about the provision of residential care. Both the King's Fund (2006) and Joseph Rowntree Foundation (JRF, 2006) have concluded that the current system is unsustainable. There are also concerns about the care provided by local authorities. The Commission for Social Care Inspection (CSCI, 2008) found that 73% of local authorities planned to refuse care to people whose needs were not considered 'substantial' or 'critical'.

Most statistics look at who is in poverty at a particular point in time but people move in and out of poverty at different points and so the dynamics of poverty are also important to consider. A review by Smith and Middleton (2007) found that poverty is more commonly triggered by changes in income (mainly job loss, then fall in wages) than by a change in household composition.

But gender is an important factor here with employment change being the main poverty trigger for men. For women, both employment and family change are triggers. This reflects the fact that divorce and separation have a more negative economic impact on women than men. Individuals who remain in couples, and who remain childless or do not increase their family size, are most likely to avoid poverty. Retirement can also be a poverty trigger but this depends on an individual's employment history.

Smith and Middleton (2007) also highlighted ways of escaping and/or avoiding poverty. They found that a movement from unemployment to employment was one of the key mechanisms to escape poverty, followed by an increase in wages. But a fifth of poverty exits are associated with household, rather than employment, change. For lone parents, household change – including the formation of a new partnership – is more significant for escaping poverty than for other households. Having said that, most lone parents who move out of poverty do so as a result of employment changes.

The rise in poverty during the 1980s clearly demonstrates that Beveridge's plan for 'cradle to grave' support through a system of universal National Insurance (NI) has not been realised. There were always gaps in coverage among people with less than full employment records, for example young people who had never worked, many disabled people, some women with gaps in their employment or with part-time jobs (Baldwin and Falkingham, 1994). But the rise in poverty was also a direct result of government policy. In the 1970s and particularly 1980s, the commitment of the Conservative government to reduce public expenditure and 'roll back the frontiers of the state' led to a significant reduction in the scope of NI benefits. New time limits were applied to Unemployment Benefit (UB) (now Jobseeker's Allowance – JSA) and Invalidity Benefit (which subsequently bacame Incapacity Benefit – IB). Invalidity Benefit was also made subject to tax. And the level of State Retirement Pension was linked to inflation rather than average earnings. These changes meant that increasing numbers of people both above and below working age had to resort to Income Support to bring their income to a bare minimum.

What kinds of reform could provide support 'from cradle to grave'?

Looking to the future, can the social security system be reformed to adapt to these changing lifecourse patterns? A number of reforms to the system are possible. One approach would be to return to the basic principles of the Beveridge system and increase the role of insurance benefits in the social security system (see Commission on Social Justice, 1994). Another option is to try to target benefits more effectively through means testing. This approach has been popular with both Conservative and Labour governments in the last decade or two. This chapter, however, will focus on more radical options, including a 'basic income' approach based on the principle of universality, and an asset-based welfare approach, which moves away from income-based policies.

So what would a system look like if it were based on the principle of universality? Basic Income Schemes (sometimes called Citizen's Income) are based on the simple idea that every individual should have a basic level of income paid by the state (Fitzpatrick, 1999; McKay and van Every, 2000; van Parijs, 2000). The most universal of these schemes includes paying a basic income to people no matter what their circumstances. Other variations of the scheme link payment of the basic income to some form of 'participation' such as looking after children, actively seeking work and so on. However, the 'purer' form of the scheme has the advantage of requiring no administrative checking on people. Administrative costs are therefore very low. Take-up and stigma would not be problems as everyone would be given the money without any need to apply for it. It is a socially inclusive scheme in which all individuals are treated equally. There would be no direct disincentives to work and/or save, as individuals would keep the basic income even if they earned or saved large sums of money.

However, it is argued that if basic income payments were set at a level to cover people's needs there might be no incentive for people to work at all. This would then lead to a problem of very high tax rates on those in employment to pay for the scheme, and hence declining incentives to work. The purer forms of Basic Income Schemes would be a radical departure from the current social security system and few governments seem keen to propose such a departure, but another way of achieving a similar end might be to increase levels of Child Benefit (CB) as this benefit is universal and so has similar advantages to aspects of a Basic Income Scheme.

Another rather different approach involves 'asset-based welfare'. The main idea behind this is to encourage and enable people to build up a stock of assets that they can then use during times when their income is reduced (for example, if unemployed, sick or disabled, or retired). In theory, this form of welfare could replace existing 'income-based welfare' or become the third 'pillar' of the welfare state – alongside income-based policies and the provision of services (Paxton and White, 2006). One of the problems with this approach is that it is highly individualised and some individuals have greater capacity to build up assets than others. Also, some individuals face greater economic risks than others. Unfortunately, those with greatest capacity to build assets are not necessarily those who face the highest risks and so a system that pools resources is likely to provide the greatest security overall.

To date, asset-based welfare policies have mostly been manifested in two pilot programmes for the Saving Gateway: the full-scale introduction of the Child Trust Fund; and reforms to the treatment of capital and savings within the benefits system (especially Pension Credit and HMRC's tax credits). While these are interesting developments, their impact has been very modest.

Other potential areas for policy development include policies around 'transitional labour markets', which are developed on the basis that the lifecourse has become less predictable, and so requires more flexible social security systems that enable people to move between studying, working part time and caring, working full time, working part time and leisure, volunteering, and so on (Schmid, 2006).

The current direction of government policy appears to suggest that radical reform is not on the agenda. Policy seems to hinge on the primacy of work 'as the best form of welfare' and, linked to this, the idea of moving towards tax credits and away from social security benefits. Such a move reflects the growing interest and power of the Treasury in relation to this field of policy. Many in government see social security benefits as handouts encouraging dependence whereas tax credits are seen as much more closely related to work and therefore independence from the state. 'Activation' and tax credits have been seen as the new panacea for all ills but these do not seem to have provided the much-needed solution and the time seems ripe for some new thinking around welfare reform.

Overview

- There were dramatic changes in lifecourse patterns in the second half of the 20th century. Family life has become more diverse, with increases in cohabitation, divorce, lone parenthood and so on. Life expectancy has also increased dramatically.
- The basis of the Beveridge social security system (namely, full male employment and the breadwinner/housewife model) was fundamentally challenged from the mid-1970s onwards.
- Governments responded to these changes by cutting back on entitlement to NI benefits. The expansion of means-tested benefits, alongside all the other social and economic changes from the 1970s onwards, led to massive increases in poverty, particularly among children.
- More recently, the Labour government has focused on 'work as the best form of welfare', developing 'activation' policies to move people from benefits to employment alongside tax credits to support people financially in work.
- Despite all these reforms, the current social security system does not sit well with contemporary lifecourse patterns and poverty remains widespread. The time is ripe for some new thinking on welfare reform.

- Possible radical reforms could include Basic Income Schemes and/or asset-based welfare policies.

Questions for discussion

(1) What social and economic changes have undermined Beveridge's aspiration to provide 'cradle to grave' support?
(2) What is the relationship between changing levels of poverty and different approaches to social security policy?
(3) What aspects of the current social security system are most at odds with contemporary lifecourse patterns? How could the system be reformed to better meet these needs?

Website resources

www.cabinetoffice.gov.uk/social_exclusion_task_force.aspx
Cabinet Office's Social Exclusion Task Force
http://sticerd.lse.ac.uk/case
Centre for Analysis of Social Exclusion
www.citizensincome.org/
Citizen's Income Trust
www.dwp.gov.uk
Department for Work and Pensions
www.ippr.org.uk
Institute for Public Policy Research
www.jrf.org.uk
Joseph Rowntree Foundation
www.poverty.org.uk/23/index.shtml
New Policy Institute
www.statistics.gov.uk
Office for National Statistics

References

Baldwin, S. and Falkingham, J. (1994) *Social security and social change: New challenges to the Beveridge model*, Hemel Hempstead: Harvester Wheatsheaf.

Berthoud, R. (1998) *Disability benefits: Reviews of the issues and options for reform*, York: Joseph Rowntree Foundation.

Bryson, A. and McKay, S. (1994) 'Is it worth working? An introduction to some of the issues', in A. Bryson and S. McKay (eds) *Is it worth working? Factors affecting labour supply*, London: Policy Studies Institute.

Burgess, S. and Propper, C. (1999) 'Poverty in Britain', in P. Gregg and J. Wadsworth (eds) *The state of working Britain*, Manchester: Manchester University Press, pp 259-75.

Commission on Social Justice (1994) *Social justice: Strategies for national renewal* (chair: Sir Gordon Borrie), London: Vintage.

Cooke, G. and Lawton, K. (2008) *Working out of poverty: A study of the low-paid and the 'working poor'*, London: IPPR.

CSCI (Commission for Social Care Inspection) (2008) *The state of social care in England*, London: CSCI.

Desai, T., Gregg, P., Steer, J. and Wadsworth, J. (1999) 'Gender and the labour market', in P. Gregg and J. Wadsworth (eds) *The state of working Britain*, Manchester: Manchester University Press, pp 168-84.

DWP (Department for Work and Pensions) (2006a) *A new system of child maintenance*, Cm 6979, London: HMSO.

DWP (2006b) *Security in retirement: Towards a new pension system*, Cm 6841, London: The Stationery Office.

DWP (2007) *In work, better off: Next steps to full employment*, Cm 7130, London: HMSO.

Fitzpatrick, T. (1999) *Freedom and security: An introduction to the basic income debate*, London: Macmillan.

Haskey, J. (1996) 'Population review (6): families and households in Great Britain', *Population Trends*, vol 85, pp 7-24.

Henshaw, D. (2006) *Recovering child support: Routes to responsibility*, Cm 6894, London: HMSO.

Hirsch, D. (2006) *What will it take to end child poverty?*, York: Joseph Rowntree Foundation.

JRF (Joseph Rowntree Foundation) (2006) *Paying for long-term care: Moving forward*, York: JRF.

Kemp, P. (2005) 'Social security and welfare reform under New Labour', in M. Powell, L. Bauld and K. Clarke (eds) *Social policy review 17: Analysis and debate in social policy, 2005*, Bristol: The Policy Press, pp 15-32.

King's Fund (2006) *Securing good care for older people*, London: King's Fund.

Laslett, P. (1996) *A fresh map of life* (second edition), Basingstoke: Macmillan.

McKay, A. and van Every, J. (2000) 'Gender, family and income maintenance: a feminist case for Citizens Basic Income', *Social Politics*, vol 7, no 2, pp 266-84.

Millar, J. and Ridge, T. (2001) *Families, poverty, work and care*, DWP Research Report No 153, Leeds: Corporate Document Services.

New Policy Institute (2008a) *Children in low-income households*, London: New Policy Institute, www.poverty.org.uk/08/index.shtml

New Policy Institute (2008b) *Older people in low income*, London: New Policy Institute, www.poverty.org.uk/38/index.shtml?2

New Policy Institute (2008c) *Low-income by work status*, London: New Policy Institute, www.poverty.org.uk/23/index.shtml

Nickell, S. (1999) 'Unemployment in Britain', in P. Gregg and J. Wadsworth (eds) *The state of working Britain*, Manchester: Manchester University Press, pp 7-28.

OECD (Organisation for Economic Co-operation and Development) (1996) 'Earnings inequality, low-paid employment and earnings mobility', *Employment Outlook*, Paris: OECD.

ONS (Office for National Statistics) (2004) *Health expectancy*, National Statistics Online, www.statistics.gov.uk/cci/nugget.asp?id=934

ONS (2006) *Work and family*, National Statistics Online, www.statistics.gov.uk/cci/nugget.asp?id=1655

ONS (2007a) *Population trends, 130, Winter*, Basingstoke: Palgrave Macmillan, www.statistics.gov.uk/downloads/theme_population/Population_Trends_130_web.pdf

ONS (2007b) *Fertility: UK fertility highest since 1980*, National Statistics Online, www.statistics.gov.uk/cci/nugget.asp?id=951

ONS (2007c) *Households and families highlights*, National Statistics Online, www.statistics.gov.uk/cci/nugget.asp?id=1748

ONS (2007d) *Stepfamilies*, National Statistics Online, www.statistics.gov.uk/CCI/nugget.asp?ID=1164

ONS (2007e) *Households: Rise in non-family households*, National Statistics Online, www.statistics.gov.uk/cci/nugget.asp?id=1866

ONS (2007f) *Life expectancy: Life expectancy continues to rise*, National Statistics Online, www.statistics.gov.uk/cci/nugget.asp?id=168

ONS (2007g) *Health and social care: 2.8 m aged 50+ provide unpaid care*, National Statistics Online, www.statistics.gov.uk/cci/nugget.asp?id=1268

ONS (2007h) *Employment: Employment rate increases to 74.7%*, National Statistics Online, www.statistics.gov.uk/cci/nugget.asp?id=694

Palmer, G., MacInnes, T. and Kenway, P. (2007) *Monitoring poverty and social exclusion*, York: Joseph Rowntree Foundation.

Paxton, W. and White, S. (eds) with Maxwell, D. (2006) *The citizen's stake: Exploring the future of universal asset policies*, Bristol: The Policy Press.

Pensions Commission (2005) *A new pension settlement for the twenty-first century: The second report of the Pensions Commission*, London: The Stationery Office.

Rowlingson, K. and McKay, S. (2002) *Lone parent families: Gender, class and state*, Harlow: Pearson Education.

Schmid, G. (2006) 'Social risk management through transitional labour markets', *Socio-Economic Review*, vol 4, no 1, pp 1-33.

Smith, N. and Middleton, S. (2007) *A review of poverty dynamics research in the UK*, York: Joseph Rowntree Foundation.

Stewart, M. (1999) 'Low pay in Britain', in P. Gregg and J. Wadsworth (eds) *The state of working Britain*, Manchester: Manchester University Press, pp 7-28.

Stuttard, N. and Jenkins, J. (2001) 'Measuring low pay using the New Earnings Survey and the LFS', *Labour market trends*, vol 109, no 1, London: The Stationery Office.

van Parijs, P. (2000) 'Basic income and the two dilemmas of the welfare state', in C. Pierson and F. Castles (eds) *The welfare state reader*, Cambridge: Polity Press, pp 355-9.

Benefiting children? The challenge of social security support for children

Tess Ridge

Summary

The Labour government's commitment to eradicate childhood poverty by 2020 has resulted in major welfare reforms, central to which are changes in support for children and their families through the tax and benefit system. This chapter will:

- explore how and why the state provides social security support for children and reflect on the challenge of delivering support to children via their families;
- consider the impact of Labour's welfare reforms on children's lives and well-being in working and workless families;
- examine new ways of delivering welfare to children through measures such as Child Trust Funds (CTFs), which are targeted directly towards children.

Introduction: state support for children

In the early 21st century, the debate about how best to provide state protection and support for children is high on the policy agenda. Labour's pledge in 1999 to eradicate child poverty within 20 years breathed new life into the debate about the type and level of financial support that society and the state should be providing for children and their families. Central to that debate is the issue of where the balance is to be struck between state support for children and state intervention in the private realm of family life. Too much support for children may encourage people to have more children (considered a legitimate use of the social security system in some countries), or might increase the risk of family dissolution; too little support, and children are left to the vagaries of individual family circumstances without any recognition of their social rights and values. Provision of financial support for children and their families is therefore 'linked to deep-rooted moral and ideological questions of freedom, dependency, care and mutual responsibility' (Smith, 1998, p 16).

Social security provisions have an impact on many areas of children's lives, and there is a considerable diversity in the type and level of support that is provided. Benefits for children fall into several different categories, and these may have different rules, aims and intentions, and different treatments and equities. ***Box 9.1*** shows that in the UK, state involvement in the provision of support for children ranges from Child Benefit (CB), the public acknowledgement of society's interest in sharing the costs of raising all children, to Child Support (CS), which is concerned with enforcing financial obligations within the family. Children are also supported through child additions to adult benefits, which therefore involve rules regarding their parents' marital/employment status, income and behaviour. For example, in-work benefits such as Working Tax Credit (WTC) are linked to low-wage parental employment of 16 hours or more per week. Children can also be entitled to welfare-in-kind non-cash benefits – such as free school meals if their parents are on the lowest level of means-tested benefits, for example Income Support (IS).

Box 9.1: State provision for children

- **Child Benefit** (CB) – universal benefit for all children to acknowledge the costs of raising children
- **Child Tax Credit** (CTC) – social support and assistance for children living in low-income families. CTCs are means-tested child payments for children in working and non-working low-income families
- **Child Care Tax Credit** (CCTC) – means-tested payments towards the cost of childcare for low-income working families
- **Support for children with a disability** – this includes Disability Living Allowance (DLA), and disabled and severely disabled elements of CTCs
- **Welfare-in-kind** – means-tested provision of non-cash benefits for some low-income children, for example free school meals linked to receipt of IS
- **Support for low-income working families with children** – WTC is a means-tested in-work support for low-income parents, with the aim of improving overall income within working families for children and parents.

- **Direct payments** – benefits/allowances paid directly to children and young people, for example, CTFs – not accessible to children until the age of 18 – and the Education Maintenance Allowance (EMA) to encourage 16- to 18-year-olds to stay in education
- **Child Support** (CS) – no cash provision but direct involvement of the state in the 'private' realm of family relationships. Intended to ensure that non-resident parents pay CS for their children. Affects children in lone-parent families receiving means-tested benefits

Benefits for children: numbers in receipt and expenditure

Benefit and tax credit expenditure on children involves significant amounts of money, an estimated 2.2% of GDP in 2003/04 (*Hansard*, 2004). Expenditure on children has been rising steadily since 1998 as the government endeavours to further its pledge to halve child poverty by 2010 and eradicate it by 2020. The introduction of CTC in 2003 and improved in-work support for parents through the WTC system has led to significant increases in government expenditure on children. Total expenditure on children in the year 2003/04 including CB and CTC was estimated to be £22.7 billion, a substantial increase on £12.7 billion in 1997/98 (*Hansard*, 2004). The largest part of the government's expenditure on children in 2003/04 came from CB at £9.6 billion, with CTC taking an increasingly large share of expenditure (*Hansard*, 2004).

Responsibility for providing cash-based support for children has largely moved from the social security system administered by the Department for Work and Pensions (DWP) (formerly the Department of Social Security – DSS) to Her Majesty's Revenue & Customs (HMRC). This is a significant administrative change and the impact that such a change will have on the delivery of support for children has yet to be established. However, the initial implementation of the new CTC by HMRC ran into severe administrative failure resulting in problems with over one third of tax credit awards in 2003/04 (HM Treasury, 2006) (see also Chapter Thirteen, Millar, this volume).

Although children's fiscal support is now largely delivered by HMRC, the DWP still plays a significant role in children's lives through disability benefits and social security benefits for adults – their parents. Children cannot be divorced from the financial circumstances of their parents so they are still affected by the adequacy and accessibility of social security payments provided for parents – for example the Social Fund, Jobseeker's Allowance (JSA) and IS.

Why does the state provide support for children?

Children are beneficiaries of social security benefits that are mainly targeted at their parents and so the nature and level of support is mainly determined by issues that apply to the adults, including labour market concerns (for example maintaining work incentives and keeping down wage demands) and family and gender issues (such as providing incomes for mothers, or reinforcing parental responsibility). Fiscal, moral and political concerns of the state can also dominate the issue of benefits and support for children. For example, means-tested benefits for families without a wage earner have traditionally been set at a low level to ensure the maintenance of work incentives. This principle of 'less eligibility'[1] has had severe implications for children living in unemployed families who are traditionally some of the poorest (Ridge and Wright, 2008).

In general, children themselves are rarely the main focus of social security provision. Furthermore, when children are the main focus of social security the underpinning aims of that provision may be quite diverse, and informed by very different notions of children and childhood. ***Box 9.2*** shows the possible aims and intentions of social security policies that are directed towards children.

Box 9.2: Possible aims of social security support for children

- The relief of poverty
- Investment in children
- Recognition of the costs of children
- Redistribution of resources
- Replacing or enforcing parental support
- Incentive payments for parents
- Incentive payments for children
- Citizenship and children's rights

The relief of poverty

The development of benefits for children began in the early 20th century when the extent and severity of child poverty began to emerge as a serious cause for concern, and the welfare of children became an important policy issue. Social security can play a vital role in supporting children when they and their families are at risk of experiencing poverty through low wages, unemployment, sickness, disability and bereavement. Various social, economic and demographic factors affect the likelihood of children experiencing poverty. These include:

- living in a lone-parent family;
- living in a minority ethnic household;
- living in a large family;
- living in a family where there is an adult or a child with long-term sickness and/or disability;
- living in either a workless household or one dependent on low pay (Gordon et al, 2000; Howard et al, 2001; Millar and Ridge, 2001).

These are not discrete factors but elements of disadvantage that can intersect and reinforce each other (Ridge, 2002). However, although these characteristics are important, the extent of child poverty is also dependent on economic context – on each country's employment participation rate and distribution of earnings, and the tax and benefit packages that countries provide to support parents with the costs of raising children (Bradshaw, 1999). All economically developed countries provide support for children through the tax and benefit system and, as Bradshaw argues, 'child poverty is not inevitable – countries make more or less explicit choices about how far they employ social and fiscal policies to mitigate the impact of pre-transfer forces' (Bradshaw, 1999, p 396). For example, Sweden, Norway and Denmark have high levels of state support for children and low child poverty rates. (In the UK, since 1998, the social security system and tax credits have been used extensively as key policy instruments to address child poverty by the Labour government [see further discussion below].)

Investment in children

Another reason for which the state might provide fiscal support for children is as a form of investment in the future. The importance of investing in children was highlighted by Gordon Brown when he was Chancellor of the Exchequer. He argued that the complexity of the modern economy required a future workforce with enhanced knowledge and skills, therefore investment in the children of today would ensure a sound economy in the future. In this instance children are not a private good, relegated to the private realm of the family, but a common interest essential for the future well-being of society (Brown, 2000).

The notion of children as 'social investments' is a common and pervasive theme in UK social policy, which has its origins in times of national renewal and concerns about the future (Daniel and Ivatts, 1998). The appeal of 'investing' in children lies not so much in providing for the best interests of children but in addressing the overriding interests of future economic prosperity and social stability. Lister (2003) argues that it is the child as 'citizen-worker' of the future rather than 'citizen-child' of the present who is targeted by future-oriented discourse and the policies of social investment. However, focusing on children as the adult-to-be can lead to policies taking particular forms, which focus more on the outcomes of childhood than on addressing the needs and experiences of children during childhood (Ridge, 2002).

Recognition of the costs of children

Social security can also be provided to families in recognition of the costs of having children and the value that society places on them. However, providing benefits that recognise the costs of raising children poses questions about the adequacy of benefits and the appropriate balance between parental support and state support. The costs of raising children are considerable: research carried out in 1997 found that a child reaching their 17th birthday may have already cost £50,000 (Middleton et al, 1997). The costs of raising a child with a disability can be three times as much (Dobson and Middleton, 1998). Although state expenditure on children is increasing, the main bulk of the direct costs of children is met by their parents (Smith, 1998). An assessment of children's needs can be obtained from a list of socially perceived necessities (see Middleton et al, 1997; Gordon et al, 2000), or a 'Budget standards' approach that estimates what it costs different types of families to support their children at a low-cost but acceptable standard of living (Parker, 1998). The national Poverty and Social Exclusion Survey (Gordon et al, 2000) lists a diverse range of needs from adequate food and clothing to social participation, developmental stimulation and environmental well-being. Historically, the level of social security support provided for children falls well below the estimated costs of raising children (see Middleton et al, 1997; Dobson and Middleton, 1998; Parker, 1998; Adam and Brewer, 2004).

Redistribution of resources

Social security can also be used to redistribute resources between different groups in society. 'Vertical redistribution' between high-income groups and low-income groups plays an important role in supporting children in low-income families. However, children's interests are also served by 'horizontal redistribution', the distribution of resources from those without children to those with them (see Sainsbury, 1999). It is crucial to find the right mix between vertical and horizontal redistribution as well as the redistribution of resources on other dimensions to ensure that the interests of children are met.

Replacing or enforcing parental support

There is also an important role for social security to play in family welfare through the provision of support for children when their parents are separated. As the number of lone-parent families has increased this has become a significant and sometimes controversial role for social security. To improve incomes in lone-parent families and enforce non-resident parental obligations to support children the Child Support Act was passed in 1991. This introduced a new system whereby levels of child maintenance were determined according to a standard formula administered by a new Child Support Agency (CSA) within the then DSS (now DWP). Lone parents claiming benefits were required to cooperate with the Agency or face a sanction (benefit reduction) (see Garnham and Knights, 1994, and Barnes et al, 1998, for an overview of the Child Support Act). The introduction of this policy was couched in terms of a moral debate about the responsibility of non-resident fathers to pay maintenance for their children (Garnham and Knights, 1994). However, underpinning these concerns were also fiscal interests about the high rate of social security expenditure for lone-parent families (Garnham and Knights, 1994).

The Child Support Act proved to be very controversial and unsuccessful both in increasing compliance with CS obligations and in improving the incomes of children in lone-parent families. Families in receipt of IS had no financial gain in terms of increased incomes, as the state withdrew any CS payments directly from their families' IS payments. In addition to this there was also the potential threat of 'benefit penalties' being applied to mothers who did not cooperate fully with the CSA, and this could potentially result in children living in families on a reduced benefit income for a period of time. Therefore, although the moral framework for the formulation of the Child Support Act appeared to be the welfare and interests of children in lone-parent families, ultimately the needs and rights of children came very low on the policy agenda.

Since its inception, CS has been subject to many attempts to reform the system, including the use of a much simpler formula to calculate liabilities, and the provision of higher disregards for lone parents on IS to enable them to keep more of their CS payments (DWP, 2006).

There are other ways of organising CS payments and this can make a difference in whether or not payments for the poorest children are deducted from state social security payments. The best interests of the child may be better served by a guaranteed payment by the state, which is then claimed back from the non-resident parent as in Denmark, France and Norway, for example. In these countries the child has guaranteed support, although schemes like these can be expensive to administer and suffer from poor rates of income recovery from non-resident parents (Skinner et al, 2007). Overall, a common criticism of many CS regimes is that they do not take enough account of the needs of children (Skinner et al, 2007).

Incentive payments – for parents

Social security benefits are also used as incentives to encourage or reward particular types of behaviour (see Ridge and Wright, 2008). Provision for children can be used as part of an overall package of support that is directed towards unemployed parents to encourage them to take up employment. The relatively new tax credit system has been particularly important in the government's plans to make work pay for low-income parents, especially lone parents. The CTC in conjunction with the CCTC and the WTC have considerably increased the level of support that low-income parents can expect to receive if they take employment and leave social security benefits.

Incentive payments – for children

As we have seen, using fiscal support to incentivise parents and other adult claimants is not uncommon; however, the use of benefit incentives for children and young people is a relatively new policy development. Policies such as EMAs and CTFs (HM Treasury, 2003) are intended to encourage and reward children and young people for particular behaviours.

Education Maintenance Allowances were introduced in 2004 and are intended to encourage children from low-income families to stay on in further full-time education to improve their skills, qualifications and future employability – a 'social investment approach'. Education Maintenance Allowances are paid directly to children and provide a weekly allowance of up to £30 per week; they therefore represent a radical departure from other support for children, which is paid via their parents. The allowance is paid to young people aged 16-19 from low-income households who attend 'appropriate' full-time courses at school or college. Underpinning the measure is a series of carrots and sticks, bonuses for meeting learning targets and doing well and sanctions to encourage compliance. The EMA gives some indication of the potential for benefits and allowances to be used to encourage and control behaviour in a selected group.

The CTF, introduced in 2005, is also a relatively new system involving endowment payments given to children at birth. A lump sum payment of £250 is made for each child born after September 2002, with an additional £250 for children in low-income families. A further government endowment is planned when the child reaches the age of seven, and again low-income families will receive an additional amount. The payments are to be deposited into long-term savings or investment accounts opened by parents but owned by children. The investment can be added to but not withdrawn until the child reaches the age of 18 (HM Treasury, 2003). Child Trust Funds are linked to financial education in the National Curriculum and used to encourage financial competence and the development of regular savings habits in children and their parents. The CTF is an example of asset-based welfare, which is a new direction for government, which seeks to support and encourage savings and the generation of assets especially for those who are experiencing poverty and disadvantage (see Paxton and White, 2006, for a discussion about asset-based welfare; and Chapter Eight, Rowlingson, this volume).

The debate about asset-based welfare has a particular resonance for children. Although touted by the government as a child anti-poverty measure, the full benefit of the CTF will not be felt until the child reaches the age of 18, it is a 'social investment' measure, and child poverty groups such as the Child Poverty Action Group have expressed concern that the needs of children experiencing poverty in childhood should be addressed first if there are additional funds to spare. A universal endowment such as this will ultimately benefit those children whose families are able to add to the savings pot, rather than disadvantaged children whose families will find it very difficult to do so. However, while there are no apparent benefits from the CTF for children experiencing poverty during childhood, research with young people has indicated that the CTF may well present a valuable opportunity for disadvantaged young people to take some control of their lives when they are aged 18 (Gregory and Drakeford, 2006).

Citizenship and children's rights

Finally, more radical agendas propose that support for children should be based on the principle of equity, the notion of citizenship and children's rights. Fiscal support is given as recognition that society has an obligation towards sharing the costs of children and supporting children as individuals in their own right. To approach social security benefits from a children's rights perspective would again raise the issue of adequacy as children and young people would have a right to social protection and an adequate standard of living regardless of the income and circumstances of their parents (Daniel and Ivatts, 1998).

Lister (1990, p 59) has argued that CB should be seen as the child's 'badge of citizenship'. Yet, CB has rarely been viewed as a benefit for children; it has been bound up with gender and employment issues, the debate about motherhood, and 'purse and wallet' debates about how resources are distributed within the household (Daniel and Ivatts, 1998). Where it has been seen as a benefit for children it has invariably been concerned with children as future investments, rather than as a significant element of children's rights and citizenship during childhood (Daniel and Ivatts, 1998).

The role of social security and tax credits in reducing child poverty

When Labour came to power in 1997 it inherited one of the worst rates of child poverty in the developed world with about 4.2 million children (over one third of all children) in 1998/99 living below 60% of median household income after housing costs (DSS, 2000a). This followed a 20-year period of Conservative free market economic policies, when child poverty rates had increased threefold as children had disproportionately suffered from changes in economic conditions and demographic structures (Oppenheim and Harker, 1996).

In 1999, in recognition of spiralling child poverty rates, Blair announced that his government would eradicate child poverty within the next 20 years (Blair, 1999). This was followed by a Public Service Agreement (PSA) to reduce child poverty by at least a quarter by 2004 and by half by 2010 (DSS, 2000b). To monitor the outcomes of its anti-poverty policies, Labour committed itself to an annual poverty audit, *Opportunity for all*, which sets out specific and measurable indicators relating to the well-being of children (see *Opportunity for all* website for current progress: www.dwp.gov.uk/ofa/).

Labour's commitment to eradicate child poverty placed children and their families at the centre of the policy process and resulted in a major reconstruction of the welfare system. ***Box 9.3*** outlines the main changes to social security and fiscal support for children since 1997.[2]

At the heart of the government's reforming agenda were policy measures to promote paid work (for example the National Minimum Wage [NMW] and New Deal programmes), coupled with a radical overhaul of the tax and benefits system to ensure that paid work was rewarded and extra resources were targeted at those who were in the most need (HM Treasury, 1999, 2000). These reforms have fundamentally changed the way in which children are supported by the state.

Total spending on child-contingent support has been rising since 1975 and by 2003 there had been an overall rise since 1975 from £10 billion to £22 billion per year (Adam and Brewer, 2004). However, the largest increase occurred between 1999 and 2003 when expenditure by Labour on children rose by over 50%. Financial expenditure on children is now delivered mainly through the tax credit system and means-tested benefits rather than through universal benefits like CB (Adam and Brewer, 2004).

Box 9.3: Changes to social security and fiscal support for children since 1997

- **Removal of one-parent premium** for lone parents receiving IS and of **One-Parent Benefit** for working lone parents.
- **Increased Child Benefit** (CB) (the universal payment for all children). Was worth £11.05 for the first child in 1997, and £9.00 for any subsequent children. In 2008/09 was worth £18.80 for the first child and £12.55 for each subsequent child. Administered by HMRC.
- **Income Support** (IS) – rates for children were significantly increased and differences between the under 11s and the under 16s were removed. Replaced by CTC in 2006 and now administered by HMRC.
- **Increases in the Maternity Grant** – from £100 to £500. Now called the Sure Start Maternity Grant, this is means tested and in order to receive it the mother, or her partner, must have received information about child healthcare from their doctor, midwife or health visitor. Administered by DWP.
- **Child Tax Credit** (CTC) – a single CTC to replace Children's Tax Credit, and children's rates of IS, JSA, Disabled Persons' Tax Credit and Working Families' Tax Credit (WFTC). Paid for children in low-income families regardless of work status. Administered by HMRC.
- **Working Tax Credit** (WTC) – replaced Working Families' Tax Credit (previously Family Credit), paid at a higher rate, means-tested in-work support for low-income parents working 16 hours or more. Administered by HMRC.
- **Child Care Tax Credit** (CCTC) – linked to WTC, paid to the main carer for childcare costs. Must be working over 16 hours and have one or more children in registered childcare. 80% of childcare costs up to a weekly limit in 2008/09.
- **Child Trust Fund** (CTF) – lump sum endowment at birth with extra payment for low-income children to encourage savings habit in children and parents. Further payments at age seven.
- **Education Maintenance Allowance** (EMA) – means-tested support paid directly to children aged 16 to 18 years who attend full-time courses at school or college. Administered by local education authorities.
- **Child Support** (CS) – several reforms including the introduction of a simpler formula and giving a disregard of CS payments for IS recipients. Administered by the CSA.

Labour's welfare-to-work policies and children

Central to Labour's policy agenda has been the promotion of paid work to lift children in 'workless' families out of poverty (DSS, 1999). To support parents, especially lone mothers, in employment the National Childcare Strategy was launched providing a record investment in childcare provision for children aged

0 to 14 (DfEE, 1998). However, the delivery of quality, affordable childcare has proved problematic for Labour, and although provision has increased overall, there is still a considerable shortfall and costs are rising significantly (Daycare Trust, 2008). The CCTC for families receiving WTC is intended to help with the costs of childcare. But it is restricted to formal childcare provision and many parents use more informal systems of childcare (see Millar and Ridge, 2001). This means that even with CCTC meeting some of the costs, childcare is proving too expensive for many families.

The dominance of paid work within Labour's anti-poverty agenda and the overall lack of support for full-time parental care is not without its critics (Hirsch, 2000; Ridge and Wright, 2008). Furthermore, employment does not guarantee that children and their families are lifted out of poverty: in 2004/05, 33% of children living in households with one or more workers were below the 60% of median income poverty line (after housing costs) (DWP, 2007a). High levels of parental employment may also not necessarily meet the needs of children: research shows that while maternal employment in lone-mother households may bring positive outcomes for some children in terms of increased incomes, quality and stability in employment is a critical factor in family well-being and sustainability of employment (Millar, 2006; Ridge, 2007). The benefits of employment can also come at a cost for some children who may experience a range of changes in their lives including increased household responsibilities and sibling care, loss of family time, or poor-quality childcare (Ridge, 2007).

Initially there was no strong element of compulsion in the New Deal for Lone Parents. However, following Labour's welfare reform Green Paper in 2007 (*Ready for work: Full employment in our generation*: DWP, 2007a), from 2010 lone parents will only be able to receive IS as carers without compulsion to work up to their youngest child's seventh birthday, compared with up to the child's sixteenth birthday prior to 2008 (DWP, 2007b).

Child Tax Credit

A key element in Labour's anti-poverty policies has been the introduction of a new CTC. This represents a new commitment to the welfare of children, and is a radical departure from previous social security support for children. It has a significant role to play in the reduction of child poverty and is set at more generous levels than the benefits it replaced. The method of payment (tax credit) is intended to reduce stigma and improve overall take-up. The intention is to ease the transition into work for low-income parents and potentially improve social inclusion by treating all families alike (Millar, 2001). Payment is made to the main carer and this addresses 'purse and wallet' concerns that money paid directly to the main carer (usually women) is more likely to be spent on children. It also acknowledges society's obligations towards children and proposes secure support for children regardless of their parental employment status.

However, CTC is not a 'universal' benefit for all children as it is income tested. This is intended to be a 'lighter touch' than means testing and introduces a new approach that Labour calls 'progressive universalism'[3] (HM Treasury, 2002). This draws in a larger cohort of children than means-tested benefits but does not provide support for all children as a universal citizenship right. Early days in the administration, assessment and delivery of CTC have proved problematic and uncertainty about assessments and poor delivery by HMRC could lead to greater complexity in the social security system rather than the intended transparency and simplicity (see Chapter Thirteen, Millar, this volume).

Support for children in 'workless' families

Many parents, especially lone parents and families where there are disabilities, experience considerable barriers to entering paid employment (Millar and Ridge, 2001). Therefore, the well-being of children in families without paid employment must also be addressed through improved security and support for children. Children living in 'workless' families have received considerable increases in financial support with an 80% rise in real terms between 1997 and 2001 (Lister, 2001). Changes in the tax and benefits system since 1997 have clearly resulted in the redistribution of income towards families with children (Millar, 2001).

Despite the increase in resources towards children there are concerns about the adequacy of adult rates of IS/JSA (Land, 1999; Ridge and Wright, 2008). Income Support rates for adults have not been increased and remain substantially below the 60% of median income poverty line used by the government (Ridge and Wright, 2008). This dilutes the impact of increases in child premiums, as income provided for children cannot be separated out from overall family income. Furthermore, many low-income families are heavily burdened by debt and have deductions for utilities and Social Fund loans taken from their benefits resulting in a reduced income coming into the household; this means that they will not be able to benefit fully from these changes (Ridge and Wright, 2008).

Trends in child poverty

When Labour came to power in 1997 there were high rates of child poverty. In 1998/99 there were 4.2 million children (over one third of all children) living below 60% of mean household income after housing costs (DSS, 2000a). Following Labour's pledge to eradicate child poverty and halve it by 2010 there has been a significant increase in expenditure on children. However, despite increased expenditure on children the numbers of children living in poverty have proved hard for Labour to reduce. ***Table 9.1*** shows that there were 4.4 million children living below the poverty line in 1998/99 when Labour made its pledge and since then child poverty numbers have reduced substantially, dropping by over 500,000 in 2004/05 when numbers reached a low of 3.6 million. However, in 2005/06 the numbers of children living in households below 60% of median income after housing costs had begun to rise again.

Table 9.1: *Number and % of children living in poverty since Labour came to power in 1997*

Year	Millions	% all children
1997/98	4.2	33
1998/99	4.4	34
1999/00	4.3	33
2000/01	4.1	31
2001/02	4.0	31
2002/03	3.9	30
2003/04	3.7	29
2004/05	3.6	28
2005/06	3.8	30

Note: Poverty measure is below 60% of median income after housing costs.

Source: DWP (2007a)

Labour is committed to halving child poverty by 2010 and this remains a formidable task (House of Commons Work and Pensions Committee, 2008). Several key areas of policy that need to change if child poverty targets are to be reached have been identified:

- First, nearly half of children living in poverty have a parent in employment, so parental employment will, by itself, not necessarily reduce child poverty. Inequalities in employment also need to be addressed, including better pay, improved working hours and secure employment (Harker, 2006; Hirsch, 2006).
- Second, support for out-of-work families needs to be increased (Harker, 2006; Hirsch, 2006). At present, increases in support for children have not been matched by increased IS for their parents, thus diluting extra money for children within the family budget and creating financial instability for families that 'cycle' between employment and benefits.
- Third, CS reforms must deliver an improved system of assessing and enforcing CS payments to children and their families (Harker, 2006).

Benefiting children? The challenge of social security support for children

The concern of the present Labour government to develop support for families and their children has meant that the interests of children have become more central to the policy process (Millar and Ridge, 2002). Labour's focus on child poverty has resulted in increases in tax and benefit provision and greater redistribution of resources to children and their families.

Labour's most ambitious project for the support of children – CTC – represents a new commitment to the welfare of children, and seeks to address concerns about take-up, and stigma, in the current system. However, the complexities of assessment and delivery may well determine how successful it is in delivering the promised benefits.

There are continuing concerns about the dominance of a work-focused policy agenda and the overall adequacy of benefits for children and their parents, particularly those in 'workless' families. Increases in premiums for children have not been matched by increases in premiums for parents. Furthermore, elements of compulsion to work are now appearing in the social security system for lone parents. While employment remains a key route out of poverty for children, and the government has greatly increased support for children living in working families, several key issues remain problematic, including the stability of the labour market and the unacceptable levels of poverty among working families with children.

The challenge for the government of childhood social security provision is how to secure the rights of children as individuals and citizens to an adequate standard of living suitable for their physical, social and developmental needs. To ensure that social security truly does benefit children, the government has to address the less popular issue of support for parents. The needs of children cannot be assumed to be the same as those of their parents, but equally they cannot be separated out from the overall well-being and security of their families.

Overview

- Social security for children can be informed by very different and sometimes competing discourses of family and childhood, and benefits for children can be underpinned by different aims and intentions.
- There is an ongoing tension between parental responsibility for children and the interests and obligations of society and the state towards ensuring the well-being of children.
- Labour's commitment to eradicating child poverty has resulted in a fundamental change in the way in which children are supported by the state and a redistribution of resources towards children and their families.

- Increased support for children has been provided through the tax credits system, increased CB and increases in means-tested child allowances. However, benefit adequacy for parents has not been addressed, thereby diluting the impact of these measures.
- The CTC and the CTF represent new ways of delivering benefits to children and young people.

Questions for discussion

(1) Why and how does the state provide social security for children?
(2) Does society have an obligation to provide for the well-being of children?
(3) How does Child Tax Credit differ from previous support for children?
(4) Does the Child Trust Fund work as a means of delivering fiscal support for low-income children?

Notes

[1] The principle of 'less eligibility' stemmed from the Poor Law reforms of 1834, which aimed to ensure that those people receiving poor relief are always worse off than the lowest-paid labourers (Hill, 1994).

[2] There have also been considerable changes in other areas of support for children that are not our focus here. They include, among others, the Sure Start Programme, Education Action Zones, Health Action Zones, the National Childcare Strategy and the National Family and Parenting Institute (DSS, 1999; Millar and Ridge, 2002).

[3] 'This means supporting all families with children, but offering the greatest help to those who need it most through a light touch income test' (HM Treasury, 2002, p 4).

Website resources

www.cpag.org.uk/
Child Poverty Action Group
www.dwp.gov.uk/asd/asd5/
Department for Work and Pensions
www.ifs.org.uk/
Institute for Fiscal Studies

www.dwp.gov.uk/ofa/
Opportunity for all

References

Adam, S. and Brewer, M. (2004) *Supporting families: The financial costs and benefits of children since 1975*, Bristol/York: The Policy Press/Joseph Rowntree Foundation.

Barnes, H., Day, P. and Cronin, N. (1998) *Trial and error: A review of UK child support policy*, London: Family Policy Studies Centre.

Blair, T. (1999) 'Beveridge revisited: a welfare state for the 21st century', reproduced in R. Walker (ed) *Ending child poverty*, Bristol: The Policy Press.

Bradshaw, J. (1999) 'Child poverty in comparative perspective', *European Journal of Social Security*, vol 1, no 4, pp 383-406.

Brown, G. (2000) *Our children are our future*, Speech by the Chancellor of the Exchequer, Gordon Brown MP, to the Child Poverty Action Group (CPAG) Conference, London: HM Treasury.

Daniel, P. and Ivatts, J. (1998) *Children and social policy*, Basingstoke: Macmillan.

DayCare Trust (2008) *DayCare Trust childcare costs survey 2008*, London: The DayCare Trust.

DfEE (Department for Education and Employment) (1998) *Meeting the childcare challenge: A framework and consultation document*, Green Paper, Cm 3959, Sudbury: DfEE Publications.

Dobson, B. and Middleton, S. (1998) *The costs of childhood disability*, York: Joseph Rowntree Foundation.

DSS (Department for Social Security) (1999) *Opportunity for all: Tackling poverty and social exclusion*, Cm 4445, London: The Stationery Office.

DSS (2000a) *Households Below Average Income: A statistical analysis 1979-1994/5*, London: The Stationery Office.

DSS (2000b) *Public Service Agreements*, London: The Stationery Office.

DWP (Department for Work and Pensions) (2006) *A new system of child maintenance*, Cm 6979, London: The Stationery Office.

DWP (2007a) *Households Below Average Income: A statistical analysis 1994/95-2005/06*, Leeds: Corporate Document Services.

DWP (2007b) *Ready for work: Full employment in our generation*, Cm 7290, London: The Stationery Office.

Garnham, A. and Knight, E. (1994) *Putting the Treasury first: The truth about child support*, London: Child Poverty Action Group.

Gordon, D., Adelman, L., Ashworth, K., Bradshaw, J., Levitas, J., Middleton, S., Pantazis, C., Patsios, D., Payne, S., Townsend, P. and Williams, J. (2000) *Poverty and social exclusion in Britain*, York: Joseph Rowntree Foundation.

Gregory, L. and Drakeford, M. (2006) 'Social Work, asset-based welfare and the Child Trust Fund', *British Journal of Social Work*, vol 36, no 1, pp 149-57.

Hansard (2004) 'Written answers', Monday 11 October, www.theyworkforyou.com/wrans/?id=2004-10-11.187122.h

Harker, L. (2006) *Delivery on child poverty: What would it take?*, DWP, Cm 6951, Leeds: Corporate Document Services.

Hill, M. (1994) *Social security policy in Britain*, London: Edward Elgar.

Hirsch, D. (2000) *A credit to children: The UK's radical reform of the children's benefits in an international perspective*, York: Joseph Rowntree Foundation.

Hirsch, D. (2006) *What will it take to end child poverty?*, York: Joseph Rowntree Foundation.

HM Treasury (1999) *Supporting families through the tax and benefit system*, London: HM Treasury.

HM Treasury (2000) *Budget, March 2000*, London: Public Enquiry Unit, HM Treasury.

HM Treasury (2002) *The modernisation of Britain's tax and benefit system: The Child and Working Tax Credits*, London: Public Enquiry Unit, HM Treasury.

HM Treasury (2003) *The detailed proposals for the Child Trust Fund*, Norwich: HMSO.

HM Treasury (2006) *The administration of tax credits: Sixth report of session 2005-06: Vol 1 Report, House of Commons papers 811-I 2005-06*, London: The Stationery Office.

House of Commons Work and Pensions Committee (2008) *The best start in life? Alleviating deprivation, improving social mobility and eradicating child poverty*, Second report of Session 2007–08, HC 42-I, London: The Stationery Office.

Howard, M., Garnham, A., Finnister, G. and Veit-Wilson, J. (2001) *Poverty: The facts*, London: Child Poverty Action Group.

Land, H. (1999) 'New Labour, new families?', in D. Hartley and R. Woods (eds) *Social policy review 11*, Luton: Social Policy Association.

Lister, R. (1990) *The exclusive society: Citizenship and the poor*, London: Child Poverty Action Group.

Lister, R. (2001) '"Doing good by stealth": the politics of poverty and inequality under New Labour', *New Economy*, vol 8, no 2, pp 65-70.

Lister, R. (2003) 'Investing in the citizen-workers of the future: transformations in citizenship and the state under New Labour', *Social Policy and Administration*, vol 37, no 5, pp 427-43.

Middleton, S., Ashworth, K. and Braithwaite, I. (1997) *Small fortunes: Spending on children, childhood poverty and parental sacrifice*, York: Joseph Rowntree Foundation.

Millar, J. (2001) 'Benefits for children in the UK', in K. Battle and M. Mendelson (eds) *Benefits for children: A four country study*, Ottawa, Canada: The Caledon Institute, pp 187-25.

Millar, J. (2006) 'Better off in work? Work, security and welfare for lone mothers', in C. Glendinning and P. Kemp (eds) *Cash and care: Policy challenges in the welfare state*, Bristol: The Policy Press, pp 171-86.

Millar, J. and Ridge, T. (2001) *Families, poverty, work and care: A review of the literature on lone parents and low-income couple families with children*, DWP Research Report No 153, Leeds: Corporate Document Services.

Millar, J. and Ridge, T. (2002) 'Parents, children, families and New Labour: developing family policy?', in M. Powell (ed) *Evaluating New Labour's welfare reforms*, Bristol: The Policy Press, pp 85-106.

Oppenheim, C. and Harker, L. (1996) *Poverty: The facts*, London: Child Poverty Action Group.

Parker, H. (ed) (1998) *Low cost but acceptable: A minimum income standard for the UK: Families with young children*, Bristol: The Policy Press.

Paxton, W. and White, S. (eds) with Maxwell, D. (2006) *The citizen's stake: Exploring the future of universal asset policies*, Bristol: The Policy Press

Ridge, T. (2002) *Childhood poverty and social exclusion: From a child's perspective*, Bristol: The Policy Press.

Ridge, T. (2007) 'It's a family affair: low-income children's perspectives on parental work', *Journal of Social Policy*, vol 36, no 3, pp 399-416.

Ridge, T. and Wright, S. (2008) *Understanding inequality, poverty and wealth: Policies and prospects*, Bristol: The Policy Press.

Sainsbury, R. (1999) 'The aims of social security', in J. Ditch (ed) *Introduction to social security: Policies, benefits and poverty*, London: Routledge, pp 34-47.

Skinner, C., Bradshaw, J. and Davidson, J. (2007) *Child support policy: An international perspective*, DWP Research Report No 405, Leeds: Corporate Document Services.

Smith, R. (1998) 'Who pays for children?', *Benefits*, no 21, January, pp 16-19.

Reforming pensions: investing in the future

Stephen McKay

Summary

This chapter describes recent changes to pensions policy and debates about the future direction of reform. The chapter investigates:

- the broad outline of different kinds of pensions, and their main features;
- the incomes of today's pensioners;
- future changes in population age structure that are relevant for pensions policy (the 'ageing society');
- changes in labour market behaviour affecting pensions, and the ability of people to save towards their retirement;
- the policy approach of the Labour government since 1997, and the main features of its strategy following the influential reports of the Pensions Commission from 2004 onwards.

Introduction

Many people in Britain want and expect to spend a proportion of their life in 'retirement'. That is, having spent some years working they expect to have a period not in paid work. This feature of the working lifetime is, however, a fairly recent historical development and until the 20th century would have seemed strange. Instead, people worked throughout their lives until forced to stop through death or incapacity. Those unable to work then had to rely on support from their families, or possibly from limited local social support arrangements. The notion that people may actually be retired for a substantial number of years – reflecting increases in life expectancy for older people – is an even more recent phenomenon.

Expressed in such a way, retirement is about the withdrawal from the labour market and as such can be viewed as quite a male concept. You retire from *paid* work, whereas the unpaid work that takes place within the home is presumably expected to continue (Walker, 1992). Retirement therefore affects men and women differently, although this is changing given higher female employment rates among younger population cohorts.

Moreover, retirement can also be viewed less positively as a means of actively excluding older people from the labour market. Between 1931 and 1971 the proportion of men aged 65+ who were retired increased from under one half to more than three quarters. Older people thus may be used as a reserve army of labour, which is tapped into when labour is in short supply, and shed when the demand for labour falls (Walker, 1986).

Taking this as a starting point, the provision of security in retirement must depend on having some access to financial resources other than earnings from paid work. This package of income will comprise any benefits available from the state (safety-net benefits, contributory benefits), and private resources that individuals have managed to save – as cash, as assets of various kinds, or in the form of specific pension products.

For various reasons, the state has a major role in determining the level of people's incomes in retirement across a wide range of countries. This is not just through what the state itself actually provides, but also through how the state regulates the private sector pension market – and indeed often provides financial incentives towards private provision (in the form of 'tax breaks').

In the next section we present an overview of the various sources of income that may be available to pensioners. This is followed by a discussion of the key factors affecting demand for pensions. In the final section we look specifically at current government policy in this area.

Sources of income in older age: an overview

In mid-2006 there were around 4.2 million men aged 65+ and 7.2 million women aged 60+ (the current state pension ages[1]) in the UK. That represents around 14% of men in the UK and 23% of women (ONS, 2007).

Figures from the Department for Work and Pensions (DWP) suggest that almost everyone above state pension age currently receives a key social security benefit or they live in a family where benefit is being received that includes them as dependent. Of the 10.7 million people above state pension age receiving a key benefit, some 2.7 million received a disability-related benefit (DWP, 2004), while close to 1.2 million received Pension Credit (and no disability-related benefits). A total of 6.8 million were covered by the retirement pension, without disability-related provision or Pension Credit.

The total cost of pensions includes various forms of tax relief and rebates to those of working age who contribute to pensions, as well as direct spending on those in retirement. It is generally easier to find regular figures for spending, rather than for indirect government support in the form of tax incentives. However, in 1998 the government produced the following figures representing spending on pensions and pensioners (DSS, 1998a, p 21). We update these, where possible, using information for 2006/07 but since the latter figures are drawn from disparate sources they may be less consistent than the earlier figures:

- £12.2 billion in tax relief on pension contributions in 1998 for those of working age, rising to £21 billion in 2006/07 including employers and employees;
- £7 billion on National Insurance (NI) rebates to people contracted out of the State Earnings Related Pension Scheme (SERPS) (for those of working age), or around £10 billion in 2006/07;
- £30 billion on the Basic State Pension (for current pensioners), now £47 billion;
- £17 billion in other social security spending – SERPS, income-related and disability benefits (for current pensioners) – some £35 billion in 2006/07 including housing-related assistance;
- There was also about £30 billion paid out in private pensions to those of state pension age.

Pension 'pillars'

There are various sources of income people may receive once they are not working. These may be divided into several different kinds, called 'pillars' or 'tiers'. An influential report by the World Bank (1994) sought to encourage an approach to state pension reform based on three tiers or pillars (see ***Box 10.1***). These three pillars represent different types of public and private forms of pension provision (compulsory publicly managed, compulsory privately managed and voluntary private), which also relate, at least in part, to the different objectives that the World Bank identify for pensions systems – to redistribute incomes towards poor pensioners (who should be provided with a 'safety net'), to provide a savings function for most people to acquire sufficient resources to live off in retirement and to provide a form of insurance against the different risks to income and health that old people may face (see also Chapter Seven, Yeates, this volume).

Box 10.1: Multi-pillar pension arrangements

The World Bank (1994) has recommended that all countries adopt a 'multi-pillar arrangement' for pensioners' income:

(1) *a compulsory publicly managed pillar* – which it proposes is funded from general taxation, the aim being to provide a flat-rate benefit (designed to prevent or reduce poverty);
(2) *a compulsory privately managed pillar* – funded from people's contributions to either occupational or personal pension plans, and regulated by government (earnings-related pensions, enabling individuals to smooth income over their lifetimes and maintain living standards in retirement comparable or at least proportional to their standard of living while of working age);
(3) *a voluntary private pillar* – of additional savings vehicles of various kinds – such as personal savings or top-ups to private pensions.

It may be argued that earnings, for those working past 'normal' state pension or retirement age, constitute a fourth pillar of retirement income.

The pensions system in the UK may be described in an analogous manner to the multi-pillar system proposed by the World Bank (1994), although the 'fit' with the World Bank model is far from perfect.

The first pillar comprises the basic pensions provided by government, including:

- the 'Basic State Pension',[2] which is a contributory benefit for individuals who have made sufficient NI contributions over their working lifetime – mostly assuming that people have worked for the majority of their working-age years;
- a range of income-related benefits that are available for those families whose income falls below a level set by their needs. This includes specific support for pensioners (Pension Credit) as well as more general benefits (for example, Housing Benefit [HB] or Council Tax Benefit [CTB] may be paid to those on a low income, to meet the costs of rent or of local taxation). Older people may also qualify for Attendance Allowance if they have significant care needs, and can also receive sizeable winter fuel payments.

The second pillar consists of earnings-related compulsory pensions, to which all employees earning more than a low fixed level are required to contribute. This includes:

- state provision related to past earnings. SERPS provides an income in retirement based on previous contributions made. Over time SERPS is being replaced by the State Second Pension (S2P), which is moving towards a flat rate of payment (see further discussion below);
- occupational pensions. People can choose to opt out of the state earnings-related provision and into an approved occupational or private scheme. Occupational pensions are provided by many companies, although a declining proportion, and are of two main kinds. First, 'defined benefit' schemes are based on providing a target proportion of final or average earnings when people retire (say, half or two thirds of earnings). Second, 'defined contribution' schemes provide pension incomes based on the value of a specified level of contributions while working – say 5% of earnings, often enhanced by an employer contribution of similar or greater size – and will depend on the performance of the investments made with those contributions. There are also hybrid arrangements drawing on both principles;
- private pensions. Individuals may instead opt for one of a range of personal pensions sold by banks and insurance companies – these are very popular with the self-employed for whom occupational pensions are not available, by definition. 'Stakeholder pensions' have been introduced with many characteristics of personal pensions, but having to meet particular standards to qualify. They are aimed at 'moderate' earners who do not have access to occupational pensions, and for whom existing personal pension products may provide poor value (see further discussion below).

The third pillar is voluntary provision and can include a number of different financial products that individuals can buy. These include private pension schemes and also other forms of savings, such as in tax-privileged accounts like Individual Savings Accounts (ISAs). Many occupational pensions also allow people to make top-up contributions in the form of Additional Voluntary Contributions (AVCs), or these may be free-standing if provided by a different company. In the UK, the potential of using housing equity to help fund retirement is recognised.

Finally, there is, arguably, a fourth pillar consisting of earnings. It used to be common for those of state pension age to continue working, although until 1988 they could not both receive their state pension and continue to work. The trend is, however, towards people ceasing employment at earlier rather than later ages; Smeaton and McKay (2003) found that only 9% of women aged 60+ were in paid work and only 8% of men aged 65+.

There are various issues and problems (or, at least, 'features') with all these forms of pension provision. The low level of the Basic State Pension means that many pensioners with little or no other sources of income are eligible for means-tested support, in the form of Pension Credit. Benefits based on means testing are subject to the criticism that take-up rates are often low. In the year 2005/06, there were around 1.2-1.7 million pensioners who were entitled to receive Pension Credit but were not receiving it (DWP, 2007). This represents a take-up rate of between 60% and 69%. However, since those eligible but not receiving Pension Credit were entitled to lower than average amounts, overall between 70% and 78% of the available monetary benefit was being received.

Another criticism of the income-related approach is that means-tested benefits also seem to 'reward' those who have *not* saved for retirement, compared with those who have small private incomes that disqualify them from eligibility. An important question is whether the kinds of criticisms made of means tests are inherent to this method of delivery or instead may be overcome by better design and/or publicity and information.

Earnings-related pensions, public and private, can be criticised on the grounds that they perpetuate inequalities in the labour market into retirement: those with higher earnings will enjoy higher living standards in retirement. Those excluded from the labour market, for long or short periods, will face lower incomes. This has generally not been sufficiently dealt with by 'crediting in' certain groups, such as mothers with young children (who also benefit from 'home responsibilities protection', introduced in 1978). Recent state pension reform goes further, and should ensure that credits are available for such periods out of the labour market.

Occupational pensions may be offering a less secure and lower level of pension. In the past few years there has been a marked shift towards defined contribution, rather than defined benefit, schemes (Pensions Commission, 2004; see page 175 above for discussion of how these work). Traditionally, companies have tended to introduce defined benefit schemes. These are seen as providing a high degree of certainty to employees about the size of their final pension, but they require companies (or their agents) to be aware of how long people are going to live, what level of earnings they will have, and so on, in order to calculate an appropriate level of contributions from worker and employer. By contrast, defined contribution schemes involve the company in no such risk, but the level of pension for the employee is rather uncertain. Balanced against this, defined contribution schemes are more portable when people move jobs. Defined contribution schemes have become more common in recent years and most private sector employers no longer allow new recruits to join existing defined benefit schemes; in extreme cases they are even closing down such schemes.

Various governments have sought to increase the use of private pensions. In the late 1980s, it became possible for people to contract out of SERPS (and subsequently S2P) into a personal pension. At the same time, the right of employers to make membership of occupational schemes compulsory was abolished, in favour of giving people a freer choice of pension product. However, aggressive sales tactics created a rush towards personal pensions, which provide a worse deal for many people. Government intervention forced the payment of compensation in what became a large mis-selling scandal.

In fact the issue of trust, or rather lack of trust, in pension provisions is a major overarching issue for both state and private sectors. It seems that the level of trust and faith in pensions of all kinds is at a low ebb. A number of controversies have afflicted both the state and non-state sectors, as briefly outlined in ***Box 10.2***. The need to find a secure and stable system of support is thus very central to current policy objectives (discussed in more detail below).

Box 10.2: Failure of trust in pensions?

I. State pensions

SERPS is paid to widow(er)s on the death of their spouse. The 1986 Social Security Act halved the amount that could be inherited, from all to 50%. The Department of Social Security (DSS) did not update the information available to the public, and staff gave wrong information were they asked about SERPS – despite the 14-year lead time for the legislation to take effect. A redress package has been put in place. Two official reports, published in 2000, investigated what had happened:

> The Parliamentary Ombudsman finds the Department guilty of maladministration ... I strongly criticise DSS for failing to make their leaflets on retirement pensions and surviving spouses' benefits sufficiently comprehensive and up to date in this important respect following the enactment of the 1986 Act, and for their repeated failure to do so until spring 1996. (Parliamentary Ombudsman, 2000, para 34)

> The full cost of resolving this problem will be at least £2.5 billion and probably considerably more. (NAO, 2000, p 6)

II. Private pensions

Occupational: the Maxwell scandal (1991)

20,000 people lost £480 million in pension funds that were used by Robert Maxwell to (temporarily) prop up ailing companies in his group (the missing money was mostly made good by £100 million from government and a settlement for £276 million from financial institutions).

We might also add problems occurring at the Equitable Life company (issues about guaranteed levels of pension income given to some, but not all, policyholders).

Personal: the mis-selling of pension products
During 1988-94, many people who would have been better off in employer pension schemes were wrongly sold personal pensions. A total exceeding £13 billion is expected to be paid out in recompense by the financial services industry (FSA, 2000).

Pension shortfalls when firms cease trading
Allied Steel and Wire (ASW) went bust in 2002 and left non-retired members with substantially reduced pension pots – some claiming losses of over 80%. This was a risk whenever the parent company of an underfunded defined benefit pension scheme ceased trading, and rules protected existing pensioners rather than workers. In late 2007, it was announced that the Financial Assistance Scheme would be backdated to allow up to 90% of such losses to be made good.

III. Other financial matters
Among recent issues damaging trust in the financial system, although not strictly about pensions, have been:

- the collapse of the Northern Rock bank:
- highly publicised cases where banks have levied high charges for customers going overdrawn on their accounts.

The distribution of pensioner incomes

There are thus a range of different sources of pension income, but which are more important? In the overall composition of pensioner gross income in 2005/06 (DWP, 2007):

- 45% was benefit income;
- 25% was from occupational pensions;
- 12% was from investment income (from savings or a personal pension);
- 16% was from earnings;
- 1% was from other sources.

However, this income was very unequally distributed between pensioners. As ***Figure 10.1*** shows, for pensioner couples, in 1999/2000 state benefits provided most pensioner income among the poorest two fifths of couples. Among the richest fifth, private sources of income were about six times the size of income from state sources. For pensioner couples, the richest fifth had incomes over five times as large as the poorest fifth. In recent times the clear trend has been towards growing inequality, as state benefits have struggled to keep pace with the increases found among private sources of income, including labour market earnings.

Figure 10.1: *Income distribution of couple pensioners, 1999/2000*

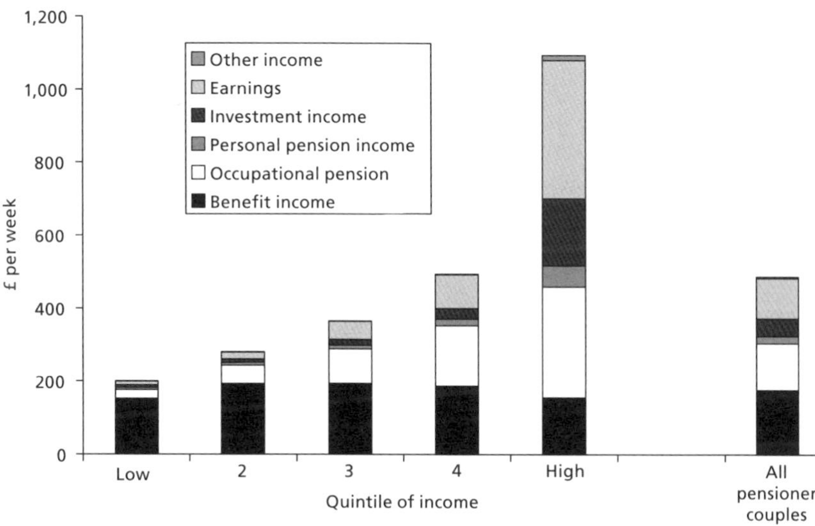

Source: DWP (2000)

First-tier pensions (the Basic State Pension, Pension Credit and other income-related benefits) are relatively redistributive towards groups experiencing lower earnings during their working-age life, and also 'credit in' those out of the labour market for reasons of unemployment, or raising children. However, second-tier pensions (both privately provided and through S2P/SERPS) are linked to the size of contributions made from earnings while in work. By definition these additional pensions tend to be higher among those who had higher earnings during their working lifetimes. Those more likely to be out of the labour market, or on lower earnings, will generally have accumulated smaller additional pensions – or none at all. Those most likely to be in this situation are women, some minority ethnic groups, older pensioners and those living in rented housing (Ginn, 2003; DWP, 2005).

The risk of having a low income in older age is also related to work history – men are least likely to be poor if they worked in professional and clerical occupations; for women, those who worked in professional, clerical and managerial occupations are most likely to avoid low incomes post-60 years of age (Bardasi and Jenkins, 2002).

The self-employed are not included in the S2P, and so have entitlement only to the Basic State Pension unless they make separate private provision of their own.

The demand for pensions

Much of the debate about the future of pensions takes place somewhat under a cloud of demographic developments. It is well known that the population of the UK, like that of most of the richer countries, is 'ageing'. A greater proportion of people are in older years, associated with retirement, and a lower proportion are of working age, or are young. This trend may best be depicted in the form of 'population pyramids'. These graphs show the number of men and women at different ages in the population, at a given date. The estimated population of the UK in 2008 is shown in ***Figure 10.2***.

In 2008, there is a sizeable 'bulge' in the age range of 40–44 (and those a little older or younger). Much of this represents people born in the 1960s' 'baby boom'. The smaller bulge for those in their early sixties represents the children

Figure 10.2: *Population of the UK, 2008 (thousand people per five-year age group)*

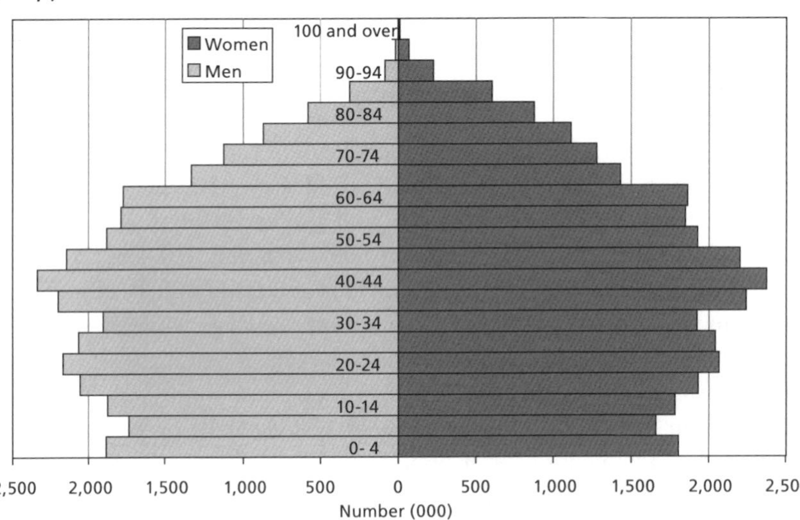

Source: These are the 2006-based principal variant population projections from the Office for National Statistics (ONS)

of a postwar boom in birth rates. Above 65, each age group is successively smaller as a result of mortality. From age 80+, women strongly outnumber men, reflecting their higher life expectancy. The number of children (in each five-year age group) is less than the number of those aged 35-39, or 40-44. This represents a relatively small family size among today's people of family-bearing age: rather than having two children per mother in order to 'replace' each generation, average family sizes are more in the region of 1.7 children per mother. This leads to population ageing, and in time (other things being equal) to population decline (see Chapter Eight, Rowlingson, this volume).

By 2031 in the UK, the bulge of the baby boom people will be reaching retirement and pensionable ages and so the age groups 60-64 and 65-69 are among the fastest growing. Birth rates are projected to remain relatively low – although higher than in most of the rest of Europe – and so the numbers of children will fall gradually behind the numbers of those at slightly older ages. In this way, the population as a whole may be said to be ageing.

Table 10.1 shows the number of people of working age compared with those who are expected (generally) not to be working. This ratio of workers to pensioners is sometimes known as the 'dependency ratio' (or 'support ratio'). In 1971 there were around 4.6 people of working age for every person aged 65+, falling below 4.0 by 2011 and down to 2.4 by 2041. A slightly different picture emerges if we include children as well as older people in the dependent population. This shows an apparent 'improvement' in the dependency ratio until around 2011, and only then a decline after 2021.

It should be remembered, of course, that those figures going far into the future are projections, based on current assumptions about life expectancy, migration and birth rates. Each element is controversial and subject to significant errors

***Table 10.1:** The 'dependency ratio', 1971–2061*

	Year	Aged under 16 (million)	Aged 16–64 (million)	Aged 65+ (million)	Workers per pensioner	Workers per pensioner plus child
Estimates	1971	14.256	34.263	7.408	4.6	1.6
	1981	12.543	35.334	8.709	4.1	1.7
	1991	11.685	36.695	9.059	4.1	1.8
	2001	11.863	37.878	9.373	4.0	1.8
Projections	2011	11.231	40.173	10.489	3.8	1.8
	2021	11.399	40.588	12.740	3.2	1.7
	2031	11.483	40.190	15.340	2.6	1.5
Longer term	2041	11.246	40.214	16.894	2.4	1.4
	2051	11.271	40.377	17.605	2.3	1.4
	2061	11.307	39.869	18.682	2.1	1.3

Source: ONS interactive population pyramids

in measurement. We can have a reasonably good idea of how many of today's 60-year-olds there will be in 20 years' time – as many 40-year-olds as there are now, less an allowance for deaths. Making an allowance for expected net in-migration is rather more difficult. Moreover, to know how many children under the age of five there will be in 20 years introduces a range of assumptions about family formation patterns in the future – including the family formation patterns of migrants. Some of the parents who might have children in 20 years' time are not yet born themselves. Even so, despite the range of uncertainty about future population, a good deal of 'momentum' is built into population trend figures by the characteristics of today's population – future fertility and mortality can alter the extent of ageing, but rapid population ageing over the next few decades will occur under any plausible scenario (Shaw, 2001).

These trends in population ageing are repeated across many countries. The cost to public pensions in terms of extra payments does, however, vary depending on the degree of ageing expected, and the relative generosity of state pensions. As shown in ***Table 10.2***, the proportion of national income going to public pensions is relatively low in the UK at present. This is partly because many elements of pension benefits are uprated only by prices and not by total growth in the economy (such as in line with earnings) – although policy may change in due course. However, when expressed as amounts of money (tens of billions of pounds), even this kind of trend can be made to appear as a quite alarming increase.

The effect of population ageing on constraining policy choices has sometimes been dubbed the 'demographic time bomb'. The analogy is far from perfect, since clearly the consequences of demographic change are likely to be felt gradually (rather than abruptly as with a 'bomb' analogy), plus many of the effects are exaggerated. In particular, there is scope for policies that change the real factors – numbers in work, numbers supported by them. For instance, as people live longer the retirement age could be altered – a policy that has attracted much recent attention (O'Connell, 2002). This has already been announced for women, whose state pension age is rising from 60 to 65

Table 10.2: *Comparative picture of public pension costs: projected spending on public pensions as a percentage of GDP*

	2004	2030
UK	6.6	7.9
Spain	8.6	11.8
Germany	11.4	12.3
France	12.8	14.3
Italy	14.2	15.0
EU25	10.6	11.9

Source: European Commission (2006, p 71)

between 2010 and 2020. The trend for early retirement could also be addressed by policy intervention.

One of the main reasons expressed for concern about population ageing is that state pensions are mostly based on a 'pay-as-you-go' (PAYG) basis. This means that the pensions of today are paid for by taxing the workers of today. In the future, there will be fewer workers to tax for each pensioner, and hence potentially concerns about affordability. This is then said to contrast with private sector pensions, which are based on paying pensions out of contributions that people make during their working lifetime. However, this kind of argument is somewhat flawed. The needs and wants of older groups must be met from what the workforce is able to produce. In a PAYG system, this is operationalised by levying taxes on workers. In a funded system, assets are mostly invested in companies, meaning that pensions are met from company profits – which might otherwise have gone to workers. Barr (2000) also refutes similar myths about pension funding choices: what might appear sensible for an individual acting alone might not be feasible for a whole society. There is no 'planet pension fund' where resources may be discretely stored and then retrieved when people retire. There are, however, important choices to be made about how production may be allocated between workers and non-workers, and the ages at which people cease working. Other things being equal, higher incomes for pensioners mean lower incomes for workers (or vice versa), unless the numbers of workers or pensioners may be altered through labour market policies.

The relatively low cost of the state pension system, at least compared with other countries, and the relatively limited additional ageing anticipated in the UK, mean that there is no reason for the UK to be unduly concerned by the affordability of its state pensions. At least, not in the near future. This breathing space provides some opportunities to make changes, and this has been recognised in policy changes suggested by the Pensions Commission and backed by the government. This is discussed in the next section.

Government policy since 1997

In 1998, a Green Paper set out the main proposed direction of government reforms to pensions (DSS, 1998a). This suggested that there were two main objectives of pensions policy. The first, aimed at lower-income groups, was to ensure that everyone enjoyed a decent income in retirement. The second, addressing a wider group, was to rebuild trust in the overall pensions system, which the government believed had been eroded, perhaps particularly in non-state pensions. The government identified a number of key problems with the system it had inherited (see also DWP, 2001):

- growing inequality of incomes among pensioners;
- large numbers of pensioners living in poverty;
- too many people of working age failing to make sufficient provision for retirement;
- inadequate provision through SERPS for people with low earnings or interrupted employment histories;
- lack of confidence in the pensions system.

For current pensioners, the main aim of the proposed reforms was therefore to tackle pensioner poverty. For future pensioners, there were a number of key aims: to help people to save for retirement; to offer better support to those who cannot save; to regulate the pension system effectively; and to enable the private sector to provide affordable and secure second pensions (DSS, 1998a).

Box 10.3 summarises some of the key reforms that have taken place since 1997.

Box 10.3: Major pension reforms since 1997

(1) *The first pillar: state pensions*

- The Basic State Pension was increased in 2001 and 2002 by more than inflation – but in 2000 by only 75 pence (which was in line with inflation). Has matched or exceeded price changes.
- Introduction of Minimum Income Guarantee (MIG), replacing/renaming Income Support (IS) for pensioners, and then Pension Credit (2003).
- Easing contribution conditions for state pensions (to become around 30 years).
- Restoring, in the next Parliament (from 2009/10), the link between state pensions and earnings growth.

(2) *The second pillar: earnings-related provision*

- SERPS replaced by the S2P, benefiting lower earners (from 2002).
- Changes to the regulation of occupational pensions, their investment strategies and governance.
- Introduction of Pension Protection Fund to protect those whose company goes bust with an underfunded defined benefit pension scheme.

(3) *The third pillar: private (personal) pensions*

- Introduction of stakeholder pensions for moderate earners (starting April 2001).
- Formation of the Financial Services Authority (FSA), becoming the single regulator for financial services in the UK (from 2001).

- Introduction of 'personal accounts' with automatic enrolment – planned from 2012.

(4) *Other*

- Introduction of Winter Fuel Payments (now at £200), and free TV licences for households with someone aged 75+.
- Introduction of 'pension sharing' for divorced couples.
- Introduction of the 'Pension Service' as a separate agency dealing with people of pensionable age (from 2002).

In the first pillar, the role of the basic pension had been becoming less important. In 1977, the state retirement pension was worth 20% of average male earnings, but 20 years later was worth nearer to 15%. In the longer term, the value compared with earnings will continue to decline to well below 10%. During the next Parliament (from 2009 or 2010) the link will be restored, subject to issues of affordability.

The most significant change to basic state provision, to date, has been the replacement of IS for pensions with Pension Credit. This is a means-tested (or income-related) system that provides an income top-up to pensioners whose income falls below the level of guarantee. The government has argued that this represents the best means of channelling additional funds to poorer groups. Some poorer pensioners do not receive the full basic pension or, if they do, they receive income-related benefits on top (such as MIG or HB), which are reduced when pensions rise. So, they argue, increases in the basic pension are not well targeted towards the poorest pensioners. The response from critics has been twofold, in replies that emphasise the disadvantages long associated with a means-tested approach (McKay and Rowlingson, 1999). The first is that many people do not claim the benefits to which they are entitled. The second set of criticisms is based on the incentive effects of means testing. The presence of Pension Credit means that those who have saved towards retirement may be no better off than those who did not. This undermines the incentive to make such self-provision, and may be regarded as itself somewhat unjust.

In the second pillar, the most important reform has been the introduction of a new S2P, replacing SERPS. The plan is that over time S2P will become a flat-rate benefit, rather like the Basic State Pension, rather than being related proportionately to previous contributions (like SERPS, and non-state pensions in general). This means that it will become more redistributional, since those on lower earnings will receive the same S2P, when the scheme matures, as those on higher earnings (non-contracted-out). Moreover, those with earnings less than £10,800 will be treated as if they earned £10,800 a year in calculating benefits, again, advantaging lower earners. Critics allege that S2P is 'best seen as a measure to compensate for the low level of the basic pension rather than as a replacement for SERPS' (Blackburn, 2002, p 305).

In the third pillar, the key reform has been the introduction of stakeholder pensions in 2001, following the 1999 Welfare Reform and Pensions Act. They are designed to be low-cost personal pensions for people who cannot join an occupational pension scheme and who earn over £10,000 a year. Employees with earnings less than this may be better off remaining in SERPS/S2P. Stakeholder pensions schemes cannot make charges of more than 1% per year on the value of each member's funds and members must be able to transfer in and out of the scheme without any extra charges. Schemes should accept small levels of contributions (at least £20). Employers with more than five staff must designate a stakeholder scheme, unless they have approved alternative provision in place.

Stakeholder pensions remain voluntary, and dependent on the marketing activity of providers. Their low charges imply that advice is unlikely to be part of the deal, and it remains unclear how portable they will prove among those changing employers. There must also be an open question about how far lower-income earners will genuinely benefit from them, while means-tested provision remains an important part of pensioner income. And, whether they are able to afford even the modest contributions they are permitted to make. For those with varying incomes, in particular, the choice between remaining in the S2P or instead taking out a stakeholder pension must be finely balanced.

Finally, among other changes there have been some extra resources provided to help the poorest pensioners pay for winter fuel costs and television licences. The 1999 Welfare Reform and Pensions Act introduced 'pension sharing' for divorcing couples from December 2000 (see DSS, 1998b; Joshi and Davies, 1998). This permits (although does not compel) the division of occupational pension rights between husbands and wives, in a way that treats pension rights as another asset to be taken into account. It allows the option for couples to completely separate their financial affairs at that point rather than later. Previously it was only possible to 'offset' the value of pension rights, or (since 1995) 'earmark' the final pension benefits for the partner when the pension matures. There has also been a significant administrative change with the introduction of the 'Pension Service' within the DWP. The Pension Service is responsible for the delivery of state pensions and for providing information and advice on pensions in general (see Chapter Fourteen, Stafford, this volume).

The Pensions Commission and subsequent White Papers

In 2003, continuing issues around pensions led to the creation by the DWP of the independent Pensions Commission. In the first of three reports it concluded that the UK had 'the most complex pension system in the world' (Pensions

Commission, 2004, p 210). It later made recommendations in a range of areas, with the clearest elements of reform comprising reforms to bolster the system of state pensions and the proposed introduction of a new savings programme into which individuals would automatically be entered on starting work.

In response, in 2006 the DWP published two White Papers on pension reform: *Security in retirement: Towards a new pensions system* (DWP, 2006a) gave the structure for the overall reform agenda while *Personal accounts: A new way to save* (DWP, 2006b) set out details of the new savings plan forming the central plank of the new strategy. There was a subsequent Pensions Bill.

The ambitious centrepiece of the reforms are the 'personal accounts', as suggested by the Pensions Commission. These are a new low-cost savings scheme, which in time could cover up to 10 million people who are without access to occupational pensions. These accounts will have a number of features. Employees will be automatically entered into the savings scheme, unless they choose to opt out. Employees will contribute at least 4%, matched by a minimum 3% employer contribution and around 1% in the form of normal tax relief from the state.

Personal accounts have probably received the most attention, but we should not overlook other reforms affecting state pensions and discussed in the earlier of the two White Papers. Among the major elements of reform are:

- future increases in the state pension linked to earnings growth, rather than price inflation as at present – linked to the fiscal situation and affordability;
- a gradual increase in the state pension age, reaching 66 by 2026, 67 by 2036 and 68 by 2046;
- a number of amendments and simplifications to contributory conditions, in particular requiring 30 years of contributions rather than 44 (for those retiring at age 65);
- enhancements to the value of deferred state pensions so that it is more worthwhile for people to continue to work after state pension age and take their pension some months (or years) later. Those who defer may receive either a higher pension or a lump sum.

It is clearly too early to be evaluating reforms that will not have their full impact for several decades. However, the response from the independent Pensions Policy Institute (2006, p 3) has been distinctly unenthusiastic: 'The White Paper proposals change the overall income distribution of older people very little, but if anything give more to higher income people than lower income.'

Remaining issues, gaps and problems

Hitherto there have been two main planks to government reform. First, there has been a renewed emphasis on means testing within the state sector – which may alternatively be described as targeting those in greatest need. Second, there has been encouragement to greater private sector provision, through the new stakeholder pensions. The main reforms to come, following the reports of the Pensions Commission, include measures to enhance state pensions and the introduction of personal savings accounts.

Perhaps the key issue that has not been adequately addressed is that of inequality. Most pensions are based on contributions made during the working lifetime. As a result, the kinds of incomes people have in retirement are roughly proportional to the kinds of *earnings* they had during their pre-retirement lifetime. Those excluded from the labour market, or on low earnings, will have low pensions. This includes, most notably, women, minority ethnic groups and the self-employed – although of course there is considerable diversity within each of these groupings. While there has been some flattening of the link between state pensions and earnings, inequalities of these kinds will remain.

Overview

- State pensions are among the oldest features of social security systems, and account for a high proportion of total spending. In the UK, there is also an active private sector for pensions.
- Over the next 30 years, UK governments face the prospect of rapid population ageing. They also face the challenge of retaining people for longer in the labour market, prior to state pension age. The relatively low levels of state support for pensioners (compared with other countries) means there is room for policy manoeuvre.
- Recent policy has focused attention (and additional spending) on the poorest pensioners, while encouraging employees on moderate earnings to save more towards their retirement.
- The Pensions Commission's recommendations have mostly been adopted by the government, and involve bolstering state pensions and introducing a new system of saving into personal accounts.

Questions for discussion

(1) Is the role of the private sector in pension provision now too great, or still too small?

(2) What should the role of the state be in respect of pensions, both in making provision and in regulation? Should the state do more than alleviate poverty?
(3) How far will demographic changes force the government to reduce pension levels in the future?
(4) Will the new personal accounts increase the amounts that people save towards their retirement?

Notes

[1] In, 1993, the decision was made to equalise state pensions for men and women at 65 (for a discussion see Hutton et al, 1995). This satisfies the needs of formal sex equality, and also helps to keep expenditure lower than alternative equalisation options below the age of 65.

[2] In fact there are a number of 'categories' of state retirement pension, depending on the precise circumstances surrounding entitlement. However, for simplicity these may be collectively referred to as the Basic State Pension.

Website resources

www.dwp.gov.uk
Department for Work and Pensions
www.ifs.org.uk
Institute for Fiscal Studies
www.pensionspolicyinstitute.org.uk
Pensions Policy Institute

References

Bardasi, E. and Jenkins, S. (2002) *Income in later life: Work history matters*, Bristol: The Policy Press.

Barr, N. (2000) *Reforming pensions: Myths, truths and policy choices*, IMF Working Paper WP/00/139, Washington, DC: IMF.

Blackburn, R. (2002) *Banking on death*, London: Verso.

DSS (Department for Social Security) (1998a) *A new contract for welfare: Partnership in pensions*, London: The Stationery Office.

DSS (1998b) *Pensions sharing on divorce: Reforming pensions for a fairer future*, Consultation Paper (part 1 consultation, part 2 draft legislation), London: DSS.

DWP (Department for Work and Pensions) (2000) *The pensioners' incomes series 1999/00*, London: DWP Analytical Services Division.

DWP (2001) *The pensions credit: The government proposals*, London: DWP.

DWP (2004) *Client group analysis of the population over state pension age: November 2004*, London: DWP, available at www.dwp.gov.uk/asd/asd1/state_pension/cga/bulletin_cga_over_sp_age_nov_2004.pdf

DWP (2005) *Women and pensions: The evidence*, London: The Stationery Office.

DWP (2006a) *Security in retirement: Towards a new pensions system*, Cm 6841, London: The Stationery Office.

DWP (2006b) *Personal accounts: A new way to save*, Cm 6975, London: The Stationery Office.

DWP (2007) *Income related benefits: Estimates of take-up in 2005–06*, London: DWP.

European Commission (2006) *The impact of ageing on public expenditure: Projections for the EU25 member states on pensions, health care, longterm care, education and unemployment transfers (2004-2050)*, Brussels: European Commission.

FSA (Financial Services Authority) (2000) 'FSA announces progress and updated redress costs of the pensions review', Press Release FSA/PN/147/2000, 1 December.

Ginn, J. (2003) 'Parenthood, partnership status and pensions: cohort differences among women', *Sociology*, vol 37, no 3, pp 495-512.

Hutton, S., Kennedy, S. and Whiteford, P. (1995) *Equalisation of state pension ages: The gender impact*, Manchester: Equal Opportunities Commission.

Joshi, H. and Davies, H. (1998) *Pension sharing on divorce: Comments on consultation document and draft Bill*, Discussion Paper PI-9812, London: The Pensions Institute (Birkbeck College).

McKay, S. and Rowlingson, K. (1999) *Social security in Britain*, Basingstoke: Macmillan.

NAO (National Audit Office) (2000) *State Earnings-Related Pension Scheme: The failure to inform the public of reduced pension rights for widows and widowers*, London: The Stationery Office.

O'Connell, A. (2002) *Raising state pension age: Are we ready?*, London: Pensions Policy Institute.

ONS (Office for National Statistics) (2007) *Census 2001, National Report for England and Wales*, Data series T01, available from www.statistics.gov.uk

Parliamentary Ombudsman (2000) *State Earnings-Related Pension Scheme (SERPS) inheritance provisions* (3rd report for session, 1999-2000), London: The Stationery Office.

Pensions Commission (2004) *Pensions: Challenges and choices: The first report of the Pensions Commission*, London: The Stationery Office.

Pensions Policy Institute (2006) *An evaluation of the White Paper state pension reform proposals*, London: Pensions Policy Institute.

Shaw, C. (2001) 'United Kingdom population trends in the 21st century', *Population trends, 103*, London: The Stationery Office, pp 37-46.
Smeaton, D. and McKay, S. (2003) *Working after state pension age*, DWP Research Report 182, London: DWP.
Walker, A. (1986) 'Pensions and the production of poverty in old age', in C. Philipson and A. Walker (eds) *Ageing and social policy*, Aldershot: Gower.
Walker, A. (1992) 'The poor relation: poverty among older women', in C. Glendinning and J. Millar (eds) *Women and poverty in Britain in the 1990s*, London: Harvester Wheatsheaf.
World Bank (1994) *Averting the old age crisis*, Washington, DC: World Bank.

Welfare to work

Sharon Wright

Summary

This chapter:

- describes welfare-to-work policies and charts their development in the UK;
- examines their application to different groups such as unemployed people, lone parents and sick and disabled people;
- identifies and examines the main underlying principles and rationales for welfare-to-work policies, and the discourses surrounding them, in relation to the rights and responsibilities of social citizenship;
- considers the ways in which welfare-to-work policies draw on individual behavioural explanations for why people claim benefits, which raises issues of desert, judgements about 'dependence' and 'independence', the value of paid work over unpaid care, conditionality and compulsion.

Introduction

There is no doubt that paid employment is a fundamentally significant part of everyday life in capitalist countries. For many people, having a job is a financial necessity that is also central to their personal identity and intrinsic to their social roles and status. Because the UK government has never provided comprehensive social security benefits at an adequate level (Brown, 1990;

Atkinson, 1995; Tomlinson, 1998; Timmins, 2001; Ridge and Wright, 2008; Chapter Four, Silburn and Becker, this volume), paid employment is the main route out of poverty and, when compared with receiving benefits, is generally associated with better health and well-being (Waddell and Burton, 2006).

Since the late 1990s, the symbolic importance, economic necessity and perceived advantages of paid work for well-being have been used to justify an extensive programme of welfare reform. The UK government now believes that substantial savings can be made by promoting work as 'the best form of welfare' (DWP, 2008a). The goal is to reduce the number of people claiming benefits and to reinforce paid employment as a citizen's primary contribution to society. These welfare-to-work policies are controversial and highly significant as one of the core ways in which rights and responsibilities between citizens and the state are being redefined.

This chapter begins by establishing the context within which welfare-to-work policies were introduced. It then describes the development of a raft of policies since 1997 and considers their interpretation as a 'work first' strategy and their potential to eradicate poverty. This is followed by an examination of the discourse surrounding the implementation of welfare-to-work policies, highlighting the social construction of 'benefit dependency' as a problem and paid employment as the solution. Two key interconnected persistent tensions are then identified and explored: the responsibility to work versus the obligation to care; and employers' preferences versus jobseekers' and workers' needs.

Understanding the context of welfare-to-work policies

Although welfare-to-work policies were not developed substantially in the UK until the late 1990s, a paradigmatic change occurred during the preceding two decades, which laid the groundwork for the acceptance of this approach for dealing with unemployed citizens (Wright et al, 2004). Following the election of the Conservative government in 1979, a rapid and far-reaching shift took place in the dominant ideology, the management of the economy (with a move from Keynesian demand management to monetarism), the primary goals of the labour market and the aims of social security policy. A series of deep-cutting reforms underlined a new acceptance of market values, an affinity for the accumulation of personal wealth and an unsympathetic approach to understanding social problems like unemployment and poverty. Adverse economic conditions resulted in extraordinarily high levels of unemployment during the 1980s, peaking in 1986 with just over three million people claiming unemployment benefits, which was more than 10% of the working-age population (Hicks and Allen, 1999).

As consecutive Conservative governments (1979-97) repeatedly insisted that individuals were responsible for their own misfortune, they simultaneously oversaw the dismantling of the struggling British industries that had provided the traditional cornerstone for working-class male employment in several regions. At the same time, they weakened the powers of trades unions, deregulated the labour market and eroded social security for the unemployed (Gregg and Wadsworth, 1999). This created conditions for the expansion of low-paid, low-quality jobs (Gregg and Manning, 1997). Although unemployment was dropping in the mid-to late 1990s, many workers were left in precarious employment situations, with less collective power to protect themselves from employers' demands and greater pressure to remain in employment.

During this period, access to benefits for unemployment was tightened and made more conditional on availability for work and proof of 'actively seeking work'. Financial savings were made by enforcing penalties for non-compliance, which became much harsher (Blackmore, 2001), and the role of employment advisors became to 'reinforce and police the jobseeking activities of the unemployed and to encourage and increasingly require them to take the low paid jobs being generated in a deregulated labour market' (Finn, 1998, p 109).

These trends were further reinforced by the introduction of Jobseeker's Allowance (JSA) in 1996. Benefits also became worth less because they were made taxable and as a result of the change to linking annual uprating to prices rather than earnings. The consequence of this was a legacy of year-on-year devaluation of benefits in relation to standards of living (Clasen, 1994; Hills, 1997, p 45), which contributed to rising income inequality and the worst record of child poverty in Europe. This was the situation that the Labour government inherited when it took power in 1997.

The development of welfare-to-work policies in the UK

Blair's incoming government had the good fortune that its electoral success coincided with a period of economic growth and low unemployment (Dickens et al, 2003). Blair immediately proclaimed 'this will be the welfare-to-work government' (Blair, 1997) and set the tone of reforms by cutting benefit payments for lone parents (by abolishing the Lone Parent Premium of Income Support [IS] and the One Parent Benefit). Lone parents were instead encouraged to find a job through the voluntary New Deal for Lone Parents (NDLP). Next, Labour announced 'a new welfare contract', meaning: 'We will rebuild the welfare state around the work ethic: work for those who can; security for those who cannot' (DSS, 1998, p 1).

This marked a watershed for social security policy with a 'new consensus' (Theodore and Peck, 1999, p 504; also see Bryson, 2003) among the major political parties on viewing the causes of unemployment and labour market inactivity as largely individual (that is, a lack of motivation to work) rather than structural (such as a lack of employment opportunities, or labour market inequalities). Saving money was a primary motivating factor for the design of the raft of welfare-to-work policies that followed over the next decade (see ***Table 11.1*** for details of the policies). The priority was to stop people claiming benefits by encouraging, supporting or compelling them to find work (see DWP, 2006, 2007b).

***Table 11.1:** Welfare to work in Britain: main measures since 1997*

Year	Development
1997	• New Deal for Lone Parents (NDLP) introduced as a voluntary programme offering advice on jobs, benefits, training and childcare through a personal advisor. Target group is lone parents with children of school age.
1998	• New Deal for Young People (NDYP) introduced as a compulsory programme for those aged under 25 after six months' unemployment – flagship for New Deal programmes: initial intensive job search assistance followed by one of four options: subsidised employment, Environment Task Force, work in voluntary sector or full-time education/training. • New Deal for Long-Term Unemployed (NDLTU) introduced as a compulsory programme for those aged 25+ who have been unemployed for 12 or 18 or 24 months (depending on the area). • New Deal for Disabled People (NDDP) introduced as a voluntary programme offering advice and information. • Prototype Employment Zones set up providing more intensive support for the most disadvantaged jobseekers in high unemployment areas. • Work-Based Training for Young People available to 16- to 18-year-olds not in full-time education or a job. • National Childcare Strategy introduced – aims to provide quality and affordable care for all children aged 0-14.
1999	• Introduction of the statutory National Minimum Wage (NMW). • Replacement of Family Credit and Disability Working Allowance with Working Families' Tax Credit (WFTC) and Disabled Person's Tax Credit (DPTC) respectively; more generous and usually paid direct from employer. • New Deal for Partners of the Unemployed introduced – extends job search assistance and training opportunities to partners of unemployed people, on a voluntary basis. • New Deal 50 Plus for the over fifties introduced on a voluntary basis – offers information and advice, and in-work tax credits and training grants to those aged 50+ on benefits. • Work-Based Learning for Adults provides vocational and pre-vocational training to adults after six months' unemployment

***Table 11.1:** Welfare to work in Britain: main measures since 1997 (continued)*

Year	Development
2000	• 1999 Welfare Reform and Pensions Act comes into force, requiring work-focused interviews; full family benefit sanction. • The ONE pilot integrates benefit claiming and institutes work-focused caseloading for all claimants of working age. • Target set that 70% of lone parents should be in employment by end of the decade. • Employment Zones introduced in 15 specific geographical areas of the UK with high long-term unemployment. • Action Teams for Jobs introduced in 64 specific geographical areas of the UK with high unemployment levels.
2001	• Introduction of joint claims for childless couples requiring that both satisfy benefit receipt conditions. • Job Brokers network introduced for NDDP to provide assistance to disabled people and those with long-term health problems in finding work.
2002	• Jobcentre Plus created as a 'one-stop shop' for claiming benefits and finding a job. • Compulsory work-focused interviews required for new claimants of IS. • New Deal 25+ replaces NDLTU, conforming more to the NDYP model. • Extension of joint claims to childless couples aged under 45.
2003	• Child Tax Credit (CTC) introduced. • Working Tax Credit (WTC) replaced WFTC and DPTC (see above). • Pathways to Work pilots begin for Incapacity Benefit (IB) reform in a number of specific geographical areas, using Personal Capability Assessments, making monthly work-focused interviews compulsory, giving access to the Condition Management Programme (delivered jointly by Jobcentre Plus and the NHS) and the Return to Work Credit. • Job Retention and Rehabilitation pilots introduced in six areas to test out different ways of supporting people to retain their jobs when they have a health condition or impairment and to reduce time spent away from work because of ill health. • Employment Retention and Advancement demonstration project introduced in five pilot areas to support lone parents and long-term unemployed people who have found work after claiming benefits, in order to help them retain their jobs and advance to more secure and better-paid work. • Work Works set up by a National Employment Panel directed to find out how best to persuade lone parents to view paid employment as a viable option in the six cities with the highest rates of lone parenthood.

Table 11.1: Welfare to work in Britain: main measures since 1997 (continued)

Year	Development
2004	• Working Neighbourhood pilots introduced in specific local districts (sometimes jointly with Employment Zones) to offer intensive help to a range of people looking for work (including people claiming benefits as unemployed or claiming lone parent or sickness and disability benefits; partners of benefit recipients; and non-claimants). • 10-Year Strategy for Childcare launched. • New Deal for Skills launched to improve the skills of 16- to 19-year-olds (mainly applying to England, rather than the whole of the UK).
2005	• Children's Workforce Strategy launched, intended to develop skills and capacity in the workforce to improve services for children.
2006	• Pathways to Work provision extended to more districts. • City Strategy Pathfinders established in 15 UK cities to 'tackle worklessness in our most disadvantaged communities' (DWP, 2008b, p 1).
2007	• 2007 Welfare Reform Act passed. • Proposals for steps towards attaining 80% employment rate set out in: – welfare reform Green Paper *In work, better off: Next steps to full employment* (DWP, 2007b); – *World class skills: Implementing the Leitch review of skills in England* (DIUS, 2007); and – *Ready for work: Full employment in our generation* (DWP, 2007a). • Proposals for contracting out employment information and advice and job search assistance to private companies and voluntary agencies, set out in an independent review commissioned by the DWP and conducted by merchant banker David Freud (2007): *Reducing dependency, increasing opportunity: Options for the future of welfare to work*. • Pathways to Work provision extended to more districts.
2008	• Employment and Support Allowance introduced to replace IB and IS disability premiums, making benefits for sick and disabled people more work focused. • Pathways to Work rolled out nationally to all areas. • From October lone parents with a child aged 12 and over are no longer entitled to IS as lone parents.

These reforms began with a range of New Deal programmes offering a series of meetings with a personal advisor to give job-related advice and job search assistance, which was voluntary for some groups (for example, disabled people, lone parents) and compulsory for others (for example, young people and the long-term unemployed). The New Deal programmes offer a 'work first' approach, focusing on getting people into jobs as quickly as possible (see ***Box 11.1***). The impact of these programmes has been mixed (see Dickens et al, 2003). The New Deal for Lone Parents (NDLP) was judged to be successful at moving lone parents into work, but the low take-up of this voluntary programme meant that the overall impact was small (Millar, 2003). The compulsory New Deal for Young People (NDYP) made it nearly impossible for young people (participants are mainly low-skilled young men) to remain long-term unemployed (Blundell et al, 2003). A series of evaluations has shown that although there was an aggregate rise in employment for 18- to 24-year-olds between 1997 and 2001 (of around 17,000 per year), there has not been any dramatic overall change in the youth labour market in the UK (Blundell et al, 2003). In fact, UK youth unemployment began to rise rapidly again in 2006 (OECD, 2007).

Box 11.1: Work first versus human capital development

Although many countries have adopted some sort of 'active' labour market policy, the UK was one of the forerunners in developing the 'work first' type of approach (Lødemel and Trickey, 2000; Peck, 2001; Handler, 2003). This approach relies on moving people directly into jobs, often at the lower end of the labour market. An alternative approach would be to invest in long-term human capital development, which would involve improving training, education, skills, health and personal development.

There has been much debate in the literature as to which is the most effective strategy. Reviewing evidence from Germany and the Netherlands, Bruttel and Sol (2006, p 72) conclude that 'Work First strategies result in a majority of recipients repeating previous experiences of below-poverty, temporary employment without career mobility'. From the US evidence, Walker and Greenberg (2005) conclude that work first strategies are effective in reducing welfare receipt but that this also depends on local circumstances. They also point out that it is a combination of factors that is important.

Lindsay et al (2007, p 558) also argue that:

> Policy makers must accept that Work First works for some but not all jobseekers, and so promote the development of more intensive, longer-term HCD [human

capital development]-orientated provision. If UK policy makers are to reconcile Work First and HCD approaches to employability, compulsory work-focused activity must be balanced by both a strengthening of holistic 'coping and enabling' services, and a commitment to credible, high quality training that can deliver sustainable transitions to work and career progression.

The next stage of the welfare-to-work strategy was twofold: making work possible and making work pay (Millar, 2002). The first part of the strategy, making work possible, involved steps, primarily through the National Childcare Strategy, to increase the availability of affordable childcare in order to reduce the barriers to engage in paid work for those with major childcare responsibilities, which was of particular benefit to lone parents. The second element of making work pay was tackled in 1999 when the National Minimum Wage (NMW) was introduced, which, for the first time in UK history, established a minimum level to prevent exceptionally low wages. In addition to this, tax credits were introduced to top up inadequate wages and, for working parents, to help with the costs of childcare (initially, in 1999, Working Families' Tax Credit [WFTC] and Disabled Person's Tax Credit [DPTC] – later replaced by the Working Tax Credit [WTC] in 2003; see Chapter Thirteen, Millar, this volume). However, the aim of making work pay was undermined by neither the NMW nor the tax credits being set at a level calculated to cover the cost of basic necessities. This means that although these measures have raised the incomes of some of the poorest households, they still do not guarantee an escape from poverty.

Since the first Employment Zones were introduced in 2000, there has also been an increased focus on area-based initiatives. Employment Zones offered a greater role for private companies to give job search assistance and rewarded their efforts by making financial payments to them based on the number of long-term unemployed benefit recipients they got into jobs. Both the emphasis on small localities and the role of non-state organisations in providing employment advice have been developed in major ways since then through the introduction of new schemes (for example, Working Neighbourhood pilots and City Strategies) and the large-scale contracting out of employment advice (see Chapter Fifteen, Finn, this volume).

A key development of welfare-to-work policies in recent years has been the shift towards making access to all social security benefits more conditional on work-related criteria. In the early days of UK welfare-to-work policies, only unemployed people were expected to take part in compulsory employment advice and job search assistance interviews. Since then, however, there has been an intensification of the idea that other types of benefit recipients should also be routinely expected to look for work. In the ONE pilot areas from 2000, work-focused interviews were compulsory for all benefit claimants (including those unable to work because of sickness or disability or having no income while having sole responsibility for raising young children). When Jobcentre Plus was created in 2002 (through a merger of the old Jobcentres with the old Benefits Agency), a 'one-stop shop' for claiming benefits was created (see Chapter Six, Carmel and Papadopoulos, this volume). This involved applying work-focused interviews to all new benefit claimants.

This focus on inactivity, not just unemployment, is reflected in the employment targets that the government has set. Overall, the aspiration is to increase the employment rate to 80%, to increase the lone-parent employment rate to 70% by 2010, and to move one million disabled adults into employment. Older workers are also expected to find jobs (DWP, 2006). These targets have been set in the context of what are already very low unemployment and high employment rates, in historical and international comparison. Since 1997, the unemployment rate (of around 5%) has remained relatively low and stable (Dickens et al, 2003; National Statistics, 2008). Unemployment in the UK has only been consistently below this 5% level at one time in history, that is, the immediate postwar era (Nickell, 1999). Perhaps even more significantly, employment levels have remained above 70% during the period of welfare-to-work reforms detailed here (1997-2008), with the rate of 74.9% in 2008 being the highest level since comparable records began in 1971 (National Statistics, 2008). The UK has one of the highest employment rates in Europe (one of only five countries of the EU27 to maintain a rate of above 70%) and the Organisation for Economic Co-operation and Development (OECD) countries (OECD, 2007; Eurostat, 2008).

However, the focus of government policy is neither the unemployment rate nor the employment rate but the labour market inactivity rate, currently around 20% (National Statistics, 2008). The justification for this is largely based on the fact that, while unemployment has fallen, there are still significant numbers of claimants of incapacity and lone-parent benefits. Policy makers have been especially concerned with the numbers of people claiming Incapacity Benefit (IB), whose numbers have exceeded those claiming benefits for unemployment since 1995. This, along with the desire to encourage lone parents back to work, has led to the complex and varied situations of people who are labelled as 'inactive' (particularly lone parents and ill and disabled people) being bunched together and treated as a functional equivalent of 'unemployed'. Thus, over time, the principles and practices of policies that were developed for one problem – unemployment – have been increasingly applied to another – inactivity. The Labour government's approach has simplified 'the problem' that social security policies are designed to tackle (worklessness) and generalised 'the solution' (getting people into work).

This analysis of the problem has led to a highly significant change in the way financial support is offered to sick and disabled people in the UK (see

Chapter Twelve, Sainsbury, this volume). In October 2008 the Employment and Support Allowance (ESA), replaced existing benefits (IB and IS disability premiums). The main difference is that while previous sickness and disability benefits accepted people to be incapable of paid employment if they were judged as such by stringent independent medical and capability assessments, the new ESA treats all applicants as potentially capable of work, at least for the initial assessment phase (of up to 12 weeks). During this assessment phase, many claimants will receive benefits at a substantially lower rate than they would have been entitled to under the old system. This reform has met with mixed responses. Some campaigners and commentators (House of Commons, 2006) have welcomed the positive assistance to enable people to identify their potential to work, which could be an empowering experience that may lead to a fulfilling outcome. On the other hand, there has been heavy criticism of the inadequacy of the benefit levels (which do not guarantee an escape from poverty, even for people who are judged to be in need of support rather than employment). Similarly, forcing people to attend work-focused interviews and to agree individual employment action plans (on penalty of losing their only source of income) have been criticised as unsuitable for people in vulnerable situations (for example, terminal conditions).

There are also significant changes in entitlements to benefits for lone parents. Since the postwar period, lone parents have been able to claim IS without being required to be available for work, as long as they had a child aged under 16. From October 2008 onwards lone parents will be progressively moved from IS to JSA. This will apply first to those lone parents with a youngest child aged 12 and above. In 2009 it will apply to those with a youngest child aged 10 and above, and in 2010 to those with a youngest child of seven and above. Thus, by 2010 all lone parents with children aged seven and above will have to be available for work as a condition of receiving social security benefits (DWP, 2007b). These measures are also controversial; see further discussion below of support for care obligations.

Discourse and desert: the social construction of 'benefit dependency'

As we have seen, the content of UK welfare-to-work policies has redefined the rights and responsibilities between citizens and the state. However, it is equally important to recognise the implications of the language that has been used to present and justify these changes. For several decades, UK governments have tended towards constructing 'the problem' of unemployment, poverty and, increasingly, inactivity in terms of individual 'benefit dependency' (see ***Box 11.2***). The solution is presented as 'independence' through paid employment. This language of 'dependency' has both contributed to and been influenced by an almost incontrovertible supranational discourse on activation, including that emanating from influential organisations such as the European Union (EU), the OECD and the World Bank (Chapter Six, Carmel and Papadopoulos, this volume).

Box 11.2: Constructing 'dependency' as the problem and paid work as the solution

Over the last decade, Labour politicians have presented work as the main route to 'independence' and have described those claiming benefits as 'passive' and 'dependent'. The following quotes are from a series of key Labour Members of Parliament (MPs). Consider how these politicians transmit messages about:

- the value of paid work over other activities;
- the 'type' of person who is likely to claim benefits and their motivation for doing so;
- the relationship between claiming benefits and 'bad behaviour'.

> *Work* is the *only route to* sustained financial *independence*. But it is also much more. Work is not just about earning a living. It is a way of life.... Work helps to fulfil our aspirations – it is the key to independence, self-respect and opportunities for advancement.... Work brings a sense of order that is missing from the lives of many unemployed young men.... [The socially excluded] and their families are *trapped in dependency. They inhabit a parallel word* where: income is derived from benefits, not work; where school is an option not a key to opportunity; and where the dominant influence on young people is the culture of the street, not the values that bind families and communities together. There are some estates in my constituency where: the common currency is the giro; where the black economy involves much more than moonlighting – it involves the twilight world of drugs; and where relentless anti-social behaviour grinds people down. (Harriet Harman, Minister for Social Security, 1997, cited in Young, 2007, p 1, emphasis added)

> *Work* is the *best road* out of poverty and *dependence*.... The welfare system should ... be geared to assisting people of working age out of the necessity to rely on continuing support, as well as being geared to provide security and decency for those who we would all accept require substantial ongoing personal care. The challenge is how the provision of financial benefits can be turned from a safety net or crutch into a ladder or escalator, assisting people through rapid change and insecurity, and geared to their *return to independence*. What we need is to reinforce the glue of self help underpinned by mutual help. If individuals or

families *sink into long-term hopelessness and dependency*, we all experience the consequences: not just picking up the pieces but in the *behaviour* of society and the *disintegration of communities*. (David Blunkett, Secretary of State for Work and Pensions, 2005, emphasis added)

And my priority is to give everyone the chance to be self reliant in old age, to make the right to work a reality, but also for everybody who can work, to make sure that *they all know* that *they have a responsibility to work*. (James Purnell, Secretary of State for Work and Pensions, 2008, quoted by the BBC, 2008, emphasis added)

The message I want to send is clear – if you can work, you should work and that will be a condition of getting benefits. But there are a small number of people who are determined not to work. *Avoiding work is not an option*. (James Purnell, Secretary of State for Work and Pensions, 2008, quoted in *The Telegraph*, 2008, emphasis added)

The language used by politicians is an important way in which messages are given to us about how we can and should behave, what is valued and what is disapproved of. It is noticeable that in these extracts, the MPs present people who claim benefits as different or separate from the majority of society. This is what Lister (2004) calls 'othering' and is a significant form of stigmatisation. Note also the unproblematic positive presentation of paid work, detracting from a view of work as a source of exploitation or discrimination – the experience of in-work poverty, for example, is not highlighted (see Mooney, 2004, for further discussion).

Each time the story of policy development is told and retold, there is a reinforcement of a familiar false distinction between the old, supposedly ineffective, 'passive' forms of social security and the new, self-evidently better, 'active' policies (Sinfield, 2001). Crespo Suárez and Serrano Pascual (2007) argue that this activation discourse contains two conflicting models of the behaviour of benefit recipients, who are, on the one hand, distrusted and seen as being in need of coercive intervention to change their behaviour, while, on the other hand, considered capable of 'designing their own biography' (Johansson, 2007). The power of this discourse is that it 'deprives us of the tools to conceive of things in any other way' (Crespo Suárez and Serrano Pascual, 2007, p 108). The enduring version of events is one that depoliticises relationships between citizens, the state and employers:

> What is happening, to some extent, is that this paradoxical discourse is unilaterally setting itself up to present as a matter

> of indisputable fact something that is in reality the outcome of a political process that entailed confrontation between differing positions. The paradox is constituted as the monological, unilateral and authoritarian manifestation of a reality which, insofar as it is a political reality, should be understood as dialogical, plural and conflict-ridden. (Crespo Suárez and Serrano Pascual, 2007, p 108)

In short, the language that is used to present welfare reforms allows for a large-scale stigmatisation of people who claim benefits to continue unchecked. Not having a job is becoming increasingly viewed as illegitimate at a time when the labour market is offering decreasing security, with a rise in temporary and flexible employment (Noon and Blyton, 2007).

Persistent tensions

At a superficial level, welfare-to-work policies are presented as neutral and beneficial. However, on closer inspection, we can see that they have deeper implications for UK society as a whole and that they may in fact impact upon particular groups in very different ways. This section considers two persistent and interconnected tensions presented by welfare-to-work policies: the responsibility to work versus the obligation to care; and the preferences of employers versus the needs of jobseekers and workers.

The responsibility to work versus the obligation to care

There is a fundamental tension at the heart of welfare-to-work policies, which centres around the gendered division of labour and definitions of paid and unpaid work. Basing policy on the goal of 'work for all' 'does not address the need that all societies have for unpaid work in the form of caring for the young and the old; work that is performed mostly by women, lone mothers included. Indeed, it effectively devalues this form of work' (Lewis, 1998, p 4). So, although capitalist societies do need people to contribute economically through paid employment, this is not the *only* need that we have. Welfare-to-work policies in the UK are justified, in part, on the grounds that an ageing population, combined with low and declining fertility rates, will eventually create a situation where there are not enough taxpayers to support the needs of older people. This economic interpretation of the demographic situation diminishes interpersonal needs and obligations, particularly in relation to care. This redefinition of citizenship rights and responsibilities associated with welfare-to-work policies represents a major departure from the roles that were set out in the postwar welfare state, where men were expected to be the main breadwinners and it was anticipated that women would contribute to society mainly through bearing and raising children (Lewis, 1992; McLaughlin, 1999; Chapter Eight, Rowlingson, this volume). Thus, the 'male breadwinner model' has been replaced by an 'adult earner model' (Lewis, 2002), within which both men and women are expected to be employed and paid work is seen as a much more valuable contribution to society than unpaid care.

This raises issues that are fundamental to the organisation of society and the values and principles on which welfare arrangements are based (Williams, 2001). Analysts have argued that care is 'a central concern of human life' (Tronto, 1993, p 180), an activity that 'binds us all' together and is a civic responsibility (Williams, 2001, pp 486-7). From this perspective, welfare-to-work policies clash with caring obligations because they view citizenship responsibilities as individual, rather than interdependent. The pursuit of paid employment undermines the value of a range of unpaid activities (for example, bringing up children, caring for relatives, voluntary work, community activities or creative endeavours like music, art or writing) and limits the time and energy available for active participation in these non-economic parts of life. There have therefore been calls to redress the balance by replacing the work ethic as the fundamental principle underlying welfare arrangements with a new 'ethics of care' (Williams, 2001). Welfare-to-work policies pre-empt the outcome of any debate about the reorganisation and recognition of paid work versus unpaid care by shutting off alternative sources of income for many people, which could otherwise be used to sustain unpaid activities, most importantly, caring obligations.

The preferences of employers versus the needs of jobseekers and workers

It is important to recognise that the people who are subject to welfare-to-work policies are already disadvantaged in the labour market and that is at least partly why they have come to rely on social security benefits. The labour market is deeply divided and certain groups face very considerable barriers to recruitment, retention and advancement because they cannot compete on an equal footing with others. Despite recent attempts to promote job retention and advancement for lone parents and ill and disabled people (see ***Table 11.1***) there is still strong evidence that the labour market operates in ways that disadvantage and discriminate against relatively powerless groups such as women (particularly mothers); ill and disabled people (including people with mental health difficulties); and black and minority ethnic groups (Noon and Blyton, 2007). One concern is that rather than creating new employment opportunities for everyone who needs them, welfare-to-work policies may just result in the substitution of one group of disadvantaged workers for another in low-paid and unsustainable jobs, cycling between temporary work and claiming benefits.

In addition, the particular redefinition of citizenship rights and responsibilities that has occurred through the development of welfare-to-work policies allows the consequences of the individual and collective actions of powerful social actors, such as policy makers and employers, to go unnoticed. Attention has thereby been drawn away from the government's own culpability in contributing to the causes of unemployment as an economic manager (which has a key role in interpreting the function of unemployment for the economy) and as a large-scale employer. The government has moved some distance from its traditional role as the employer of last resort and has implemented changes to the civil service that have increased job insecurity and worsened terms and conditions for its own employees (Horton and Jones, 1996; Foster and Hoggett, 1999). For example, the DWP itself issued 30,000 compulsory redundancies between 2004 and 2008. Further major job cuts are expected following the planned radical restructuring of employment services, which will reduce the role of Jobcentre Plus in providing job matching and employment advice and create new insecure forms of employment in private companies and voluntary organisations (see Chapter Fifteen, Finn, this volume).

Conclusion

Over the past 30 years, the UK labour market has changed dramatically. A series of political and economic decisions has resulted in the growth of low-paid, low-quality jobs. The past three decades have also seen a reduction in social protection for people in vulnerable labour market positions and an individualisation of the responsibility to seek paid employment, which has rewritten citizenship rights and responsibilities. Since 1997, a range of predominantly 'work first' policies has been developed to reduce the number of people claiming benefits and increase the employment rate, which was already very high in historical and international comparison. These policies are backed by compulsion, mainly for unemployed people, but increasingly for 'inactive' groups like lone parents and ill and disabled people. Furthermore, the discourse that surrounds their implementation holds implicit and explicit messages about the value of paid work over unpaid activities and obligations such as care. Persistent tensions remain evident in this policy approach because it does not deal adequately with the need that UK society has for unpaid care or with the deeply divided labour market that disadvantages and discriminates against the very groups who are most likely to be encouraged or compelled to find work.

Overview

This chapter has:

- outlined the political, economic and labour market context in which welfare-to-work policies were established in the UK, emphasising the influence of Conservative governments (1979-97) in promoting low-paid and low-quality jobs and eroding labour market protection;
- described the development of welfare-to-work policies in the UK, which began with cutting benefits for lone parents; developed through a range of New Deal programmes giving advice and job search assistance to different groups; pursued strategies of making work possible and making work pay; involved focusing on specific localities, a greater role for non-state organisations in delivering employment services and the establishment of work-focused interviews for all benefit recipients; and culminated in new steps to move people off 'inactive' benefits and into work;
- explored the construction of discourses of dependency and desert implicit and explicit in these policies;
- identified key interconnected persistent tensions between the responsibility to work versus the obligation to care; and between the needs of employers and the needs of jobseekers and workers.

Questions for discussion

(1) In which circumstances might encouraging or compelling people to look for work be an inadequate solution to their welfare needs?
(2) What are the key elements of the discourses surrounding welfare-to-work policies?
(3) What underlying assumptions do welfare-to-work policies make about the causes of unemployment and inactivity?
(4) How effective are welfare-to-work policies in reducing public spending and how might adverse economic conditions impact on this?

Website resources

www.dwp.gov.uk/welfarereform/
Department for Work and Pensions
www.cesi.org.uk/
Centre for Economic and Social Inclusion

www.disabilityalliance.org
Disability Alliance
www.oneparentfamilies.org.uk/
One Parent Families
www.cpag.org.uk
Child Poverty Action Group

References

Atkinson, A.B. (1995) *Incomes and the welfare state: Essays on Britain and Europe*, Cambridge: Cambridge University Press.

BBC (2008) 'Purnell heads reshuffle changes', 21 April, http://news.bbc.co.uk/1/hi/uk_politics/7207497.stm

Blackmore, M. (2001) 'Mind the gap: Exploring the implementation deficit in the administration of the stricter benefits regime', *Social Policy and Administration*, vol 35, no 2, pp 145-62.

Blair, T. (1997) 'The will to win', Speech as Prime Minister, Aylesbury Estate, Southwark, 2 June.

Blundell, R., Reed, H., van Reenen, J. and Shephard, A. (2003) 'The impact of the New Deal for Young People on the labour market: a four year assessment', in R. Dickens, P. Gregg and J. Wadsworth (eds) *The labour market under New Labour: The state of working Britain*, Basingstoke: Palgrave.

Blunkett, D. (2005) 'Work and the welfare state', Speech to the Brookings Institution, 12 September, www.dwp.gov.uk/aboutus/2005/12_09_05.asp

Brown, J. C. (1990) *Victims or villains – social security benefits in unemployment*, York: Joseph Rowntree Memorial Trust.

Bruttel, O. and Sol, E. (2006) 'Work first as a European model? Evidence from Germany and the Netherlands', *Policy & Politics*, vol 34, no 1, pp 69-89.

Bryson, A. (2003) 'Permanent revolution: the case of Britain's welfare-to-work regime', *Benefits*, vol 11, no 1, pp 11-17.

Clasen, J. (1994) *Paying the jobless: A comparison of unemployment benefit policies in Great Britain and Germany*, Aldershot: Avebury.

Crespo Suárez, E. and Serrano Pascual, A. (2007) 'Political production of individualised subjects in the paradoxical discourse of the EU institutions', in R. van Berkel and B. Valkenburg (ed) *Making it personal: Individualising activation services in the EU*, Bristol: The Policy Press.

Dickens, R., Gregg, P. and Wadsworth, J. (eds) (2003) *The labour market under New Labour: The state of working Britain*, Basingstoke: Palgrave.

DIUS (Department for Innovation, Universities and Skills) (2007) *World class skills: Implementing the Leitch Review of Skills in England*, London: The Stationery Office.

DSS (Department for Social Security) (1998) *New ambitions for our country*, London: The Stationery Office.

DWP (Department for Work and Pensions) (2006) *A New Deal for Welfare: Empowering people to work*, London: The Stationery Office.

DWP (2007a) *Ready for work: Full employment in our generation*, London: The Stationery Office.

DWP (2007b) *In work, better off: Next steps to full employment*, London: The Stationery Office.

DWP (2008a) 'Public Service Agreement for 2005-2008', London: DWP, www.dwp.gov.uk/publications/dwp/2004/psa/tech_note_2005_2008.pdf

DWP (2008b) *City strategy*, London: DWP, www.dwp.gov.uk/welfarereform/cities_strategy.asp

Eurostat (2008) *Employment*, Paris: Eurostat, http://epp.eurostat.ec.europa.eu/portal/page?_pageid=1996,45323734and_dad=portaland_schema=PORTALandscreen=welcomerefandopen=/andproduct=STRIND_EMPLOIanddepth=2

Finn, D. (1998) 'Labour's new deal for the unemployed and the stricter benefit regime', in E. Brunsdon, H. Dean and R. Woods (eds) *Social policy review 10*, London: Social Policy Association.

Foster, D. and Hoggett, P. (1999) 'Change in the Benefits Agency: empowering the exhausted worker', *Work, Employment and Society*, vol 13, no 1, pp 25-47.

Freud, D. (2007) *Reducing dependency, increasing opportunity: Options for the future of welfare to work: An independent report to the Department for Work and Pensions*, Leeds: Corporate Document Services.

Gregg, P. and Manning, A. (1997) 'Labour market regulation and unemployment', in D. Snower and G. de la Dehesa (eds) *Unemployment policy: Government options for the labour market*, Cambridge: Cambridge University Press.

Gregg, P. and Wadsworth, J. (eds) (1999) *The state of working Britain*, Manchester: Manchester University Press.

Handler, J. (2003) 'Social citizenship and workfare in the US and Western Europe: from status to contract', *Journal of European Social Policy*, vol 13, no 3, pp 229-43.

Hicks, J. and Allen, G. (1999) *A century of change: Trends in UK statistics since 1900*, Research Report 99/111, London: House of Commons.

Hills, J. with Gardiner, K. (1997) *The future of welfare: A guide to the debate* (revised edition), York: Joseph Rowntree Foundation.

Horton, S. and Jones, J. (1996) 'Who are the new public managers? An initial analysis of "Next Steps" chief executives and their management role', *Public Policy and Administration*, vol 11, no 4, pp 18-44.

House of Commons (2006) *Select Committee on Work and Pensions, third report, session 2005–06*, London: House of Commons, www.publications.parliament.uk/pa/cm200506/cmselect/cmworpen/616/61602.htm

Johansson, H. (2007) 'Placing the individual "at the forefront": Beck and individual approaches in activation', in R. van Berkel and B. Valkenburg (ed) *Making it personal: Individualising activation services in the EU*, Bristol: The Policy Press.

Lewis, J. (1992) *Women in Britain since 1945*, Oxford: Blackwell.

Lewis, J. (1998) '"Work", "Welfare" and Lone Mothers', *Political Quarterly*, vol 69, no 1, pp 4-13.

Lewis, J. (2002) 'Gender and welfare state change', *European Societies*, vol 4, no 4, pp 331-57.

Lindsay, C., McQuaid, R.W. and Dutton, M. (2007) 'New approaches to employability in the UK: Combining "human capital development" and "Work first" strategies?', *Journal of Social Policy*, vol 36, no 4, pp 539-60.

Lister, R. (2004) *Poverty*, Cambridge: Polity Press.

Lødemel, I. and Trickey, H. (eds) (2000) *An offer you can't refuse: Workfare in international perspective*, Bristol: The Policy Press.

McLaughlin, E. (1999) 'Social security and poverty: women's business', in J. Ditch (ed) *Introduction to social security: Policies, benefits and poverty*, London: Routledge.

Millar, J. (2002) 'Adjusting welfare policies to stimulate job entry: the example of the United Kingdom', in H. Sarfati and G. Bonoli (eds) *Labour market and social protection reforms in international perspective: Parallel or converging tracks?*, Aldershot: Ashgate.

Millar, J. (2003) 'The art of persuasion: the New Deal for Lone Parents', in R. Walker and M. Wiseman (eds) *The welfare we want*, Bristol: The Policy Press, pp 115-42.

Mooney, G. (ed) (2004) *Work: Personal lives and social policy*, Bristol: The Policy Press/The Open University.

National Statistics (2008) *Employment*, www.statistics.gov.uk/CCI/nugget.asp?ID=12

Nickell, S. (1999) 'Unemployment in Britain', in P. Gregg and J. Wadsworth (eds) *The state of working Britain*, Manchester: Manchester University Press.

Noon, M. and Blyton, P. (2007) *The realities of work* (third edition), Basingstoke: Palgrave.

OECD (Organisation for Economic Co-operation and Development) (2007) *The OECD employment outlook*, Paris: OECD.

Peck, J. (2001) *Workfare states*, New York: Guilford Press.

Ridge, T. and Wright, S. (2008) *Understanding inequality, poverty and wealth: Policies and prospects*, Bristol: The Policy Press.

Sinfield, A. (2001) 'Benefits and research in the labour market', *European Journal of Social Security*, vol 3, no 3, pp 209-35.

Telegraph, The (2008) 'James Purnell: work or lose benefits', 26 February, www.telegraph.co.uk/news/main.jhtml?xml=/news/2008/02/20/nbenefit120.xml

Theodore, N. and Peck, J. (1999) 'Welfare-to-work: national problems, local solutions?', *Critical Social Policy*, vol 19, no 4, pp 485-510.

Timmins, N. (2001) *The five giants: A biography of the welfare state* (second edition), London: HarperCollins.

Tomlinson, J. (1998) 'Why so austere? The British welfare state of the 1940s', *Journal of Social Policy*, vol 27, no 1, pp 63-77.

Tronto, J. C. (1993) *Moral boundaries: A political argument for an ethic of care*, London: Routledge.

Waddell, G. and Burton, K. A. (2006) *Is work good for your health and well-being?*, London: The Stationery Office.

Walker, R. and Greenberg, D. (2005) 'Determining what works and for how long', in A. Cebulla, K. Ashworth, D. Greenberg and R. Walker (eds) *Welfare to work: New Labour and the US experience*, Aldershot: Ashgate, pp 85-115.

Williams, F. (2001) 'In and beyond New Labour: towards a new political ethic of care', *Critical Social Policy*, vol 21, no 4, pp 467-93.

Wright, S., Kopac, A. and Slater, G. (2004) 'Continuities within paradigmatic change: activation, social policies and citizenship in the context of welfare reform in Slovenia and the UK', *European Societies*, vol 6, no 4, pp 511-34.

Young, J. (2007) *The vertigo of modernity*, London: Sage Publications.

Sickness, incapacity and disability

Roy Sainsbury

Summary

The social security system has evolved over the course of nearly 100 years from a single benefit that provided an income replacement for workers in time of sickness to what has been described as a 'patchwork' of provision that extends to people in and out of work, and provides not only income replacement but also money for the extra needs created by disability.

This chapter:

- explores how sickness and disability benefits have developed (over the last century, but particularly in the last 20 years);
- describes the current range of benefits, and how these have been transformed from being 'passive' to 'active' benefits that support the government's employment policies;
- discusses a number of tensions and challenges still facing the system of sickness and disability benefits;
- presents comparative data on trends in disability benefits in other countries;
- concludes by looking to the future and exploring how sickness and disability benefits might develop.

Introduction: social security for sickness and disability

'The disability income system today is one of the most fragmented sectors of public and private income security.' So begins the first chapter, called 'A muddle from the beginning', of a book written nearly 25 years ago (Brown, 1984, p 1). This current chapter could easily have started with exactly the same words and might have been called 'Disability benefits – the continuing muddle?'. The question mark is deliberate – other authors have used less critical terminology. Burchardt (2003, p 127), for example, prefers 'patchwork' to describe the diverse range of benefits for sickness and disability. Brown (1984) needed over 400 pages to describe and analyse a 'disability income system' within which she included not only social security benefits but also private (tort-based and employment-based) schemes. My aim in this chapter is more modest, but daunting nonetheless. I want to give the reader an understanding of the landscape of sickness and disability benefits in 2008, an account of how we have reached this position, a review of the issues that are still facing the current system, and a look into the future at possible policy developments in the next 10 years or so.

The landscape of sickness and disability benefits

In this section I will attempt to untangle the 'muddle' or 'patchwork' of sickness and disability benefits. What is described below is the result of over a century of change from a social security system that originally comprised essentially only insurance-based, earnings-related benefits for the contingencies of unemployment, sickness or old age. Of relevance for this chapter we have seen the emergence (in the interwar years) of benefits that compensate workers for accident or injury, benefits that recognise the additional costs of disability (from the 1970s onwards) and in-work benefits designed to boost low wages (also from the 1970s).[1] (The scale and scope of changes in family, unemployment, carers and retirement benefits will be apparent from the other chapters in this volume.)

Table 12.1 contains a brief description of the main sickness and disability benefits current at the beginning of 2008. ***Table 12.1*** has been constructed to be as simple as possible but it hides some of the considerable complexity of the full range of benefits for people who are sick or disabled. For example, some people who were awarded the predecessor benefit to Incapacity Benefit (IB) – Invalidity Benefit – still receive the latter under transitional protection arrangements that date back to 1995. Similarly, some people also have transitional protection to Severe Disablement Allowance, a benefit that was subsumed within IB in 2001.

Table 12.1: *Sickness and disability benefits*

Social security benefits	Brief description
Statutory Sick Pay	Statutory Sick Pay is a short-term benefit paid to people by their employer when they are off work for health reasons. Some people not entitled to Statutory Sick Pay may be eligible for short-term Incapacity Benefit (IB) instead.
Incapacity Benefit	IB is either a short-term benefit for people with no access to Statutory Sick Pay or a long-term benefit paid to people out of work for longer than six months (either temporarily or permanently) due to health reasons. Entitlement is based on National Insurance (NI) contributions. IB will be replaced in October 2008 by a new benefit, Employment and Support Allowance (ESA).
Employment and Support Allowance (from October 2008)	ESA is the name for a reformed IB and introduces more stringent eligibility conditions for people out of the labour market because of a health or disabling condition. It also replaces the disability premiums within Income Support (IS) (see below).
Income Support	People eligible for IS can receive additional 'premiums' if they have a health or disabling condition. Entitlement is means tested, not based on NI contributions. Employment and Support Allowance replaces these premiums in 2008.
Disability Living Allowance	Disability Living Allowance (DLA) is an 'extra costs' benefit for people under retirement age. Eligibility is based on a test of physical and mental capacity. It is a 'universal benefit', that is, not based on either means testing or NI contributions.
Attendance Allowance	Attendance Allowance is similar to DLA, paid to people over retirement age.
Industrial Injuries Disablement Benefit	Industrial Injuries Disablement Benefit (IIDB) is paid to people who have an accident at work or contract a prescribed disease and whose functional capacity is reduced as a result. IIDB is a universal benefit.
War Pension	War Pension is paid on a similar basis to IIDB but only to people injured while serving in the armed forces.
Working Tax Credit	Working Tax Credit (WTC) is an earnings top-up paid to people on low incomes. People who are disabled may be eligible for a higher rate of tax credit. WTC is means tested.

Working Tax Credit (WTC) is included in ***Table 12.1*** although there is an argument that this is not strictly a social security benefit but a redistributive element of the tax system. However, in this volume, tax credits are treated as part of the benefit system because they share characteristics of social security benefits (such as a common means test) and because they developed out of previous, now defunct, benefits (Disability Working Allowance and Family Working Allowance). Tax credits are the subject of Chapter Thirteen, Millar, this volume.

Table 12.2 classifies the benefits in ***Table 12.1*** according to two criteria – their main purpose and their main eligibility conditions.

Table 12.2: *Classification of sickness and disability benefits based on purpose and eligibility conditions*

Main purpose	Basis of eligibility		
	NI contributions	Means test	Universal
Earnings replacement	Incapacity Benefit (Employment and Support Allowance from 2008); Statutory Sick Pay	Income Support	
Extra costs		Income Support premiums	Disability Living Allowance; Attendance Allowance
Compensation			Industrial Injuries Disablement Benefit; War Pension
Earnings top-up		Working Tax Credit	

Tables 12.1 and ***12.2*** provide as much clarity as possible about a system of sickness and disability benefits that is only one complicated part of a wider complicated social security system. The distribution of benefits (even the number and type of benefits) in ***Table 12.2*** is not in any way preordained. The pattern observed is the result of policy pressures and choices. In the following sections we will explain why we have this current configuration, why it has its critics, and finally what might be options for the future.

Sickness and disability benefits have become big business over the course of the last 20 years or so. For example, in 2007, 2.6 million people were receiving IB, and 2.9 million were receiving Disability Living Allowance (DLA) compared with only 837,000 recipients of Jobseeker's Allowance (JSA) (DWP, 2007b). In 2003/04 expenditure on IB was £6.7 billion (although this had fallen from a figure of nearly £7.7 billion in 1997) and expenditure on DLA was £7.6 billion (up considerably from the 1997 figure of £4.5 billion) (*Hansard*, 24 April 2006, col 907W).

The numbers of people on sickness and disability benefits and the resultant cost to the public purse have prompted intensive policy interest in the last 20 years and have been framed as a policy 'problem'. Before we explore the intricate nature of the problem, however, the next section takes a brief excursion into history to address the question of how we have ended up where we are in 2008. The answers will provide the context for thinking about the future.

From 'passive' to 'active' welfare

So, how can we understand the current landscape of sickness and disability benefits and the changes that have taken place in the last 100 years? As befitting a complex landscape, unravelling the policy threads that have led to our current arrangements is itself complicated.

If we return to what are often considered to be the origins of the modern social security system in 1911 we see that the first three benefits had the primary aim of alleviating poverty caused by a lack of income from work. In 2008 the benefit system encompasses probably over 30 benefits and some have argued possibly over 40 (see, for example, Work and Pensions Select Committee, 2007). The growth in the benefit system in general and in disability benefits in particular has resulted from the interplay of a number of societal, political and economic influences. For example, groups and organisations in society have consistently argued for greater social security provision for their particular constituencies, evidence about poverty and disability has accumulated, the importance of social security to public finances has increased, and governments have used social security policy to address wider social policy objectives, for example to increase employment rates.

The evolution of sickness and disability benefits has included almost innumerable incremental changes interspersed with the occasional more major reform, all of which contributed to the 'muddle' that Brown identified in 1984 and which have continued to complicate the picture further since then. Examples of incremental changes include:

- age-related additions to basic levels of benefit;
- earnings-related additions;
- introduction of long-term rates;
- consolidation of age-related and earnings-related additions into basic rates;
- changes to the eligibility criteria (for example to Invalidity Benefit, the predecessor of IB) in order to restrict the flow of new claimants.

More major changes have included:

- the introduction of a specific long-term sickness benefit (the current most recent manifestation being IB in 1995);
- new benefits to reflect the extra costs of disability (now incorporated into DLA and Attendance Allowance);
- a new benefit, Severe Disablement Allowance, for people whose onset of disability was at birth or in childhood (subsumed within IB since 2001).

These examples of incremental and more major changes are intended to be illustrative only to show the many ways in which the system of sickness and disability benefits has been shaped over time. Another change that has taken place over the last 10 or so years, which can be considered as part incremental but also somewhat fundamental, is the drive to transform social security in general and sickness and disability benefits in particular from a 'passive' to an 'active' form of financial support.

What do these two terms mean? The *passive* form of sickness and disability benefits is characterised by eligibility criteria that impose no conditions or requirements on recipients to look for or take any steps towards work. The popular notion of the postwar social security system being a 'safety net' that caught and protected people succinctly captures the essence of 'passive'. In today's less graphic policy language, there was no 'conditionality' imposed on recipients of sickness and disability benefits and no link with employment policy. Indeed, until very recently responsibility for the development of policy on social security and employment has been divided between two separate government departments, although these have been merged into the Department for Work and Pensions (DWP) since 2001 (see Chapter Six, Carmel and Papadopoulos, and Chapter Fifteen, Finn, this volume).

Since the General Election in 1997 successive Labour governments have pursued a continuous project of welfare reform under the banner of 'work for those who can, security for those who cannot' that has been characterised by the 'joining up' of employment, social security and tax policy (DSS, 1998). Labour has pursued an explicit 'welfare-to-work' strategy based on the fundamental argument that 'work is the best route out of poverty'. This strategy has two principal components: the development of existing and new employment programmes and a process of benefit reform. In Chapter Eleven, this volume, Wright provides a comprehensive analysis of the former that need not be repeated here. Instead I will concentrate on what has happened to the benefit system since 1997.

The rhetoric of post-1997 welfare reform has been the transformation of sickness and disability benefits from being *passive* to *active*. In practice this has meant essentially two things – introducing new eligibility conditions that make receipt of out-of-work benefits dependent on taking active steps towards looking for work, and introducing new incentives within the tax and benefit systems that 'make work pay'. Universal benefits such as DLA that recognise the extra costs of disability have not been reformed during this time (although at the time of writing a major internal review of DLA is under way within the DWP).

It is worth setting out the main features of the new benefit, Employment and Support Allowance (ESA), which will replace IB (and Income Support [IS] disability premiums) in October 2008, in order to set out the current stage of development of out-of-work disability benefits and to serve as a reference point for the discussion in the next section of the tensions and challenges facing future policy development.

Eligibility for ESA will depend on the outcome of a 'work capability assessment' that will comprise a self-assessment of capabilities and, for some claimants, a medical examination by a designated doctor. The self-assessment will be carried out by completing a questionnaire that asks separate sets of questions about physical and mental capabilities that carry a 'points score'. There will be three possible outcomes of the work capability assessment according to the overall score achieved:

- the claimant qualifies for the 'support group' of ESA recipients;
- the claimant qualifies for the 'work-related activity group';
- the claimant does not qualify for ESA.

People in the 'support group' will receive a higher rate of ESA than other recipients and will not have any work-related conditions imposed on them. They may, if they wish, however, voluntarily take up work-related help. People in the 'work-related activity group' will be required to take part in a series of work-focused interviews with a personal advisor as a condition of receiving benefit. Non-compliance with the work-focused interview requirement will result in the imposition of a sanction.[2] The level of payment for the 'work-related activity group' will be lower than for the 'support group' but higher than JSA. People who do not qualify for ESA will be eligible to claim JSA instead, which has more stringent eligibility conditions.

The incentives within the benefit system designed to encourage people to move towards work will be continued from the current IB scheme. These are:

- the 'permitted work' regulations – these allow people to work part time for up to a year and remain on ESA;

- a 'return to work credit' – this is a tax-free payment (currently £40 a week) payable for up to a year to anyone who takes employment of over 16 hours a week (and who therefore will come off ESA altogether).
- WTC – this is a top-up of low wages paid through the tax system for people coming off ESA into work of over 16 hours a week (see Chapter Thirteen, Millar, this volume).

In this section I have tried to convey a sense of the range of pressures that have shaped our current system of sickness and disability benefits and how the incremental and more major changes that have been made by governments have contributed to a transition from a passive to a more active system. In the next section I set out some of the tensions and challenges that remain.

Tensions and challenges

In this section I will discuss a number of tensions and challenges (some of which I will couch as 'problems') that still beset the system of sickness and disability benefits despite the reforms that will be implemented later in 2008. I have divided these into *boundary* problems (that is, how to define being *in* and *out* of work, and being *capable* or *incapable* of work) and *balancing* problems (between the rights and responsibilities of benefit recipients; and between income replacement and the 'extra costs' of disability).

Boundary problems #1 – in or out of work?

If we return once more to the origins of our system we can identify a coherent philosophy behind the first benefits that was an entirely understandable response to the social and economic conditions of the time. Put simply, people needed an income when out of the labour market. Being *in* the labour market in 1911 meant being a man in a full-time job. Therefore if a man became unemployed he needed an income replacement until such time as he returned to full-time employment. This basic philosophy also prevailed in the Beveridge reforms – the full-time male breadwinner was the stereotype on which the reforms to social insurance were based.

One of the greatest challenges to the social security system has therefore been how to respond to the massive changes to society and the labour market in the last 60 years, such as the increased employment of women, different types of household formation, the growth in part-time employment and the casualisation of the labour market (see Chapter Eight, Rowlingson, this volume). The response, it can be argued, has been typically piecemeal and incremental. We have seen, for example, the introduction of 'earnings disregards' into means-tested benefits allowing people to retain a small amount of earnings from part-time work while still receiving an 'out-of-work' benefit. In sickness and disability benefits there is the much more generous permitted work provision. (At the time of writing, the earnings disregard for IS recipients ranged between £5 and £20 a week. In contrast, IB recipients could earn up to £87.) Fragmented work histories have led to the introduction of a plethora of 'linking rules' for different benefits, which determine the level of benefit people can receive after a limited period off benefits.

In our current benefit system part-time work and full-time work are defined as being under 16 hours per week and 16 hours and above, respectively. This '16-hour rule', as it is known, is essentially an arbitrary threshold – it could equally be 12, 15, 20 hours, for example. But working for 16 hours or more will disqualify a person from means-tested benefits such as IS and sickness benefits such as IB. If you work for 16 hours you leave at least part of the benefit system behind and enter the world of tax credits and the domain of Her Majesty's Revenue & Customs (HMRC).

The confusion and uncertainty that can be caused for people who may move in and out of the labour market or who have unpredictable work patterns (from day to day or week to week) can inhibit movements off benefits and into work. The legacy of making a sharp distinction between out-of-work and in-work benefits is that the employment aspirations of individuals and the policy goals of government may be hindered or thwarted.

Boundary problems #2 – capable or incapable of work?

In the development of policy on sickness and disability benefits one of the key choices to make is where to draw the line between people being capable of work and people being incapable of work. The relevance of this distinction has changed over the years. Until the last 20 years or so, to be defined as 'incapable of work' entitled a person to an income replacement benefit with no work-related requirements attached. Furthermore, the test of whether a person was 'incapable' related to their usual occupation, rather than incapable of any form of work. In the early 1990s when the numbers of claimants of Invalidity Benefit (the predecessor of IB) were climbing dramatically there was a realisation that defining people as 'incapable' had had unintended consequences. At the level of policy they had effectively been left alone – they were not required to look for work and there were no employment programmes for them. Furthermore, there seemed to be a general public understanding that being assessed as incapable of work, which involved the input from medical practitioners, meant that a person *could not* undertake any type of employment. The meaning of 'incapable' seemed to be taken entirely literally.

Reforms to Invalidity Benefit (and its replacement IB in 1995) were attempts to alter this public perception. A new test – the 'all work test' – was introduced, which assessed someone's fitness for work more widely than their own occupation. Being found fit for work under this new test denied eligibility to a sickness-related benefit. The basis of long-term sickness benefits was effectively redefined: a health or disabling condition, even a long-term condition, did not equate to being 'incapable' of work.

Notwithstanding these perceptions, the social security system does to some extent recognise the fact that disability does not mean completely 'incapable' of work and *partial* incapacity has been recognised in the UK and in many other countries for a number of years (Thornton et al, 1997). Examples within our current system include earnings disregards, permitted work provisions and tax credits. Following the 'social model of disability' (see, for example, Barnes et al, 1999) it is widely accepted that ability to work in paid employment is not directly related to a health or disabling condition but to society's response (or lack of response) to disability. However, the persistent public perception that it is the many, not the few, who are literally incapable of work may be hard to alter. Perhaps inadvertently the New Labour banner of 'work for those who can, security for those who cannot', mentioned earlier, serves only to reinforce that perception.

One of the tangible outcomes of the distinction between ability and inability to work is that some people move between IB and JSA as their health status changes over time. Incapacity Benefit recipients are subject to periodic reviews when their eligibility is reassessed. If they 'fail' the review they cease to be eligible for IB and will have to claim JSA. They will then receive a lower rate of benefit and be subject to the more stringent work-related conditions associated with JSA. This creates a perverse incentive not to attempt to improve one's health in order to claim, and remain on, IB.

Balancing problems #1 – rights and responsibilities

Although the language of 'rights and responsibilities' had yet to be established in mainstream political discourse (this was a New Labour introduction) the reforms to Invalidity Benefit in the early 1990s were effectively rewriting the contract between the citizen and the state. The new message can be summarised thus: 'for people with sufficiently serious and long-term health or disabling conditions the state accepts that it is not reasonable for them to be expected to look for work in return for benefit'. The dividing line between these people and those required to look for work was initially the 'all work test' mentioned above, which became the 'personal capability assessment' under the-then new IB in 1995.

What has happened since 1995 has been further shifts in the boundary between the rights and responsibilities of people on IB. When the first new employment programme for IB recipients – the New Deal for Disabled People

(NDDP) – was introduced as a pilot in 1998 it was voluntary. Despite efforts to entice people to take advantage of the new help available, take-up remained stubbornly and disappointingly low (Stafford et al, 2004). The successor to NDDP – the Pathways to Work programme (see Chapter Eleven, Wright, this volume) – adopted a new, and controversial, approach by imposing compulsory work-focused interviews on new IB claimants as a condition of receiving benefit. It should be noted that participation in any subsequent work-related activity was voluntary – the only requirement was attendance at a series of interviews with a Jobcentre Plus personal advisor.

For the present the shift in the balance between rights and responsibilities for claimants of sickness and disability benefits appears to have halted. As noted above, the original conception of ESA (DWP, 2006) was for increased responsibilities (or more 'conditionality') on claimants to undertake work-related activity as well as attend work-focused interviews, but only the latter is now proposed.

Balancing problems #2 – income replacement and 'extra needs'

It has long been recognised that having a health or disabling condition can create extra costs for individuals and families (see also Chapter Four, Silburn and Becker, this volume). An indicative, although not comprehensive, list might include costs of special foods, heating, laundry, domestic assistance, transport, clothing, special equipment and home adaptations.

It is not the intention here to chronicle the long struggle for these costs to be recognised within the social security system. As we have mentioned in another context already, the history of extra costs and social security has been one of incremental change and the occasional more fundamental shift. Perhaps the biggest advance was the creation in the 1970s of two extra costs benefits that, importantly, were universal, that is, not dependent on National Insurance (NI) contributions nor a test of means. These were the Attendance Allowance and the Mobility Allowance, the former intended to make a contribution to the costs of care and the second to the costs of mobility. In 1994 these benefits were amalgamated into DLA, the single benefit for people under retirement age (although it has retained separate care and mobility components) while Attendance Allowance was reformed (that is, excluding any help with mobility costs) for people over retirement age.

Elsewhere in the benefit system we see the costs of disability recognised in additional premiums paid with means-tested benefits and more generally in the higher levels of benefit paid in IB compared with JSA or IS, and in the higher rate of IB paid after 12 months on the benefit. This latter provision compounds the perverse incentive mentioned earlier created by IB being paid at a higher rate than JSA. A higher long-term rate in effect 'rewards' people who stay incapable of work for longer.

The respone to the extra costs of disability is fragmented and, due to incremental policy change, probably warrants the label of a 'muddle'. Disability Living Allowance itself has consistently been criticised for failing to reflect adequately the real costs of disability (most recently by the Work and Pensions Select Committee, 2008). As we shall discuss in the final section of this chapter a review of DLA could constructively form part of a wider review of social security that will better serve the interests of people with health or disabling conditions.

We are not alone – disability benefits in other countries

The challenges and tensions that face sickness and disability benefits policy in the UK are not unique. Many countries in the developed world have witnessed increases in the numbers of people receiving such benefits and have been engaged in reforms to benefits and employment policies in response but with what Kemp describes as 'modest' success (Kemp et al, 2006).

Although based on slightly outdated data the Organisation for Economic Co-operation and Development (OECD) has conducted an analysis that has looked at how a range of countries have approached their overall disability policies, which it separates into what it calls 'compensation' and 'integration' dimensions (OECD, 2003). 'Compensation' essentially refers to social security systems that support sick and disabled people who are out of work. In contrast, 'integration' covers policies and programmes aimed at supporting employment and rehabilitation (see Chapter Eleven, Wright, this volume). The OECD report uses a number of 'sub-dimensions' as the basis for scoring each country on the compensation and integration dimensions, described in ***Box 12.1***.

Box 12.1: Comparing disability policies (OECD, 2003)

The *compensation dimension* refers to the main disability benefit scheme in each country, and has 10 sub-dimensions: coverage, minimum disability level, disability level for a full benefit, maximum benefit level, permanence of benefits, medical assessment, vocational assessment, sickness benefit level, sickness benefit duration, unemployment benefit level and unemployment benefit duration. A higher score means easier access, higher benefit levels, longer duration and so on.

The *integration dimension* refers to employment and rehabilitation measures, and also has 10 sub-dimensions: coverage consistency, assessment structure, employer responsibility, supported employment, subsidised employment, sheltered employment, vocational rehabilitation, timing of rehabilitation, benefit suspension and additional work incentives. A higher score indicates a more active approach.

***Figure 12.1:** A typology of disability policies in OECD countries, c. year 2000*

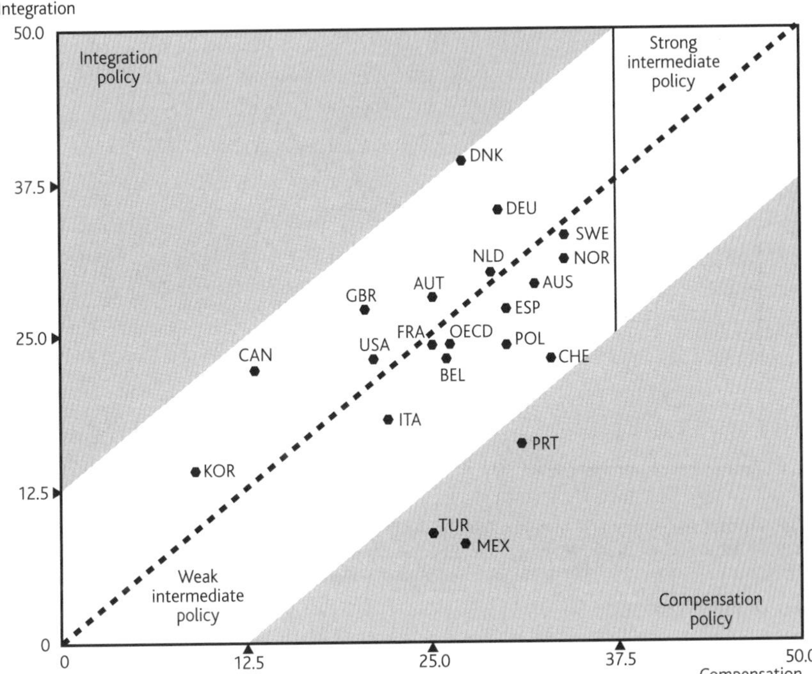

Key: AUS – Australia; AUT – Austria; BEL – Belgium; CAN – Canada; CHE – Switzerland; DEU – Germany; DNK – Denmark; ESP – Spain; NLD – Netherlands; FRA – France; GBR – Great Britain; ITA – Italy; KOR – Korea; MEX – Mexico; NOR – Norway; OECD – all OECD countries; POL – Poland; PRT – Portugal; SWE – Sweden; TUR – Turkey; USA – United States.

Source: OECD (2003)

The effect of plotting the two dimensions of compensation and integration against each other produces some interesting findings, as ***Figure 12.1*** shows. ***Figure 12.1*** shows that in 2000 most countries were pursuing what the OECD report calls 'intermediate' policies that favoured neither an integration focus nor a compensation focus. However, further analysis, in which the countries are grouped into six 'clusters' that share several common features, reveals how the direction of policy between 1985 and 2000 is remarkably consistent across the OECD. ***Figure 12.2*** shows the results of this analysis.

What is noticeable about ***Figure 12.2*** is that it demonstrates how the different clusters of countries have moved upwards on the integration dimension, reflecting a concentration of policy development on employment and related programmes in contrast to the small amount of movement along the compensation dimension. Indeed, what the figure shows is that countries scored less highly in 2000 than

***Figure 12.2:** Changes in OECD countries' disability policies, 1985–2000*

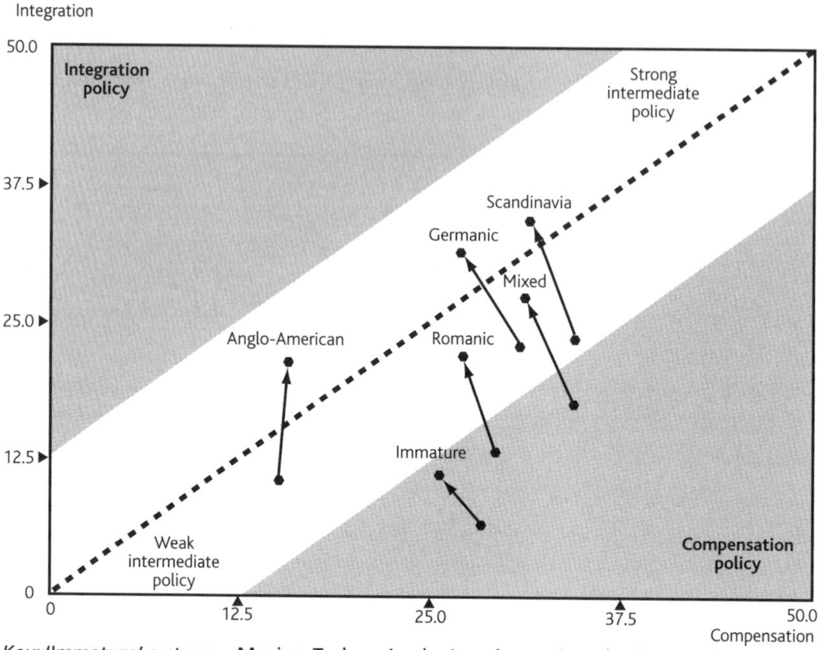

Key: 'Immature' systems – Mexico, Turkey; Anglo-American – Canada, Korea, UK, US; Scandinavian – Denmark, Norway, Sweden; Germanic – Austria, Germany; Romanic – Belgium, France, Italy, Portugal, Spain; 'Mixed' – Australia, Netherlands, Switzerland.

Source: OECD (2003).

they did in 1985, indicating that benefit systems tended to become less generous and more exclusive over the period, in contrast with expanding employment and rehabilitation policies. This picture certainly appears to hold true for the UK, where a number of important policy initiatives have been aimed at getting sick and disabled people into work, and, particularly since 1997, sustaining work once they are there. However, until the introduction of ESA in October 2008 the last major changes to long-term sickness benefits were in 1995, when IB was introduced and the eligibility criteria were tightened considerably.

Future directions

In this chapter I have tried to present an overview in a very restricted space of the system of sickness and disability benefits in the UK and how we reached our current arrangements. Are we then still in a new incarnation of Brown's mid-1990s' 'muddle' or is our current system more coherent and rational than that? It certainly still warrants Burchardt's mid-2000s' description as 'patchwork'. There are compelling reasons why this is the case.

At the risk of oversimplification we can view social security as one of the many instruments of social policy with which governments attempt to create their own particular vision of the good society (Sainsbury, 1999). Decisions about policy are therefore based as much on values and ideologies as on political and economic judgements. Social security policy has been used (and continues to be used) to protect and support vulnerable people, to promote and prevent types of behaviour, to reward and punish, to incentivise and discourage, and to tax and redistribute (between groups in society and between generations). These are aims and purposes that wrestle for supremacy and currently we can see that the aim of an 'active' social security system that promotes work has held sway for the last decade.

Labour governments since 1997, perhaps more than any other postwar governments, have resolutely pursued a social policy based on increasing the labour market participation of all groups in society, including sick and disabled people. The type of employment that people with health or disabling conditions can take is often part time, variable (in hours) and insecure. In an ideal world we could argue that, to use the terminology of the OECD, 'compensation' and 'integration' policies would be developed in a coordinated manner such that they jointly promoted and supported the social policy objectives of increasing employment rates and tackling poverty. However, what the OECD analysis presented earlier suggests is that social security provision across countries had changed less than integration policies between 1985 and 2000. Certainly in the UK we have seen how our current system of sickness and disability benefits has evolved in small steps with the occasional bigger leap forwards, each of which can be understood to be a resolution of competing social, political and economic forces. However, what does *not* appear to have happened, at least since Beveridge, is a fundamental rethink of the whole social security system. Of course, fundamental rethinks are not the sort of exercise that needs undertaking very often. But perhaps the changes in society and in the role of social security in the last 20 years in particular provide an argument for considering one now.

There are two complementary reasons for suggesting that the time is right. The first is that the current system (particularly of sickness and disability benefits) does not support the types of employment programmes aimed at benefit recipients that have been transformed radically since 1997. The social security system can itself act as a barrier to people entering the labour market (NAO, 2005a). The second argument is that the complexity of social security has reached such a degree that measures are required to reduce it (and not just marginally). The case for tackling the complexity of the social security system has been made most forcefully by the National Audit Office (NAO, 2005b) and the Work and Pensions Select Committee (2007). To summarise the arguments in these documents, complexity in social security is not in itself a problem, but it becomes a problem when it becomes dysfunctional, for example by generating errors in benefit payments, by depressing take-up of benefits, by providing opportunities for fraud, by generating avoidable administrative costs (such as in administering appeals), by creating uncertainty and hardship for claimants experiencing processing delays, and, of particular relevance for this chapter, by creating negative impacts on work incentives.

There have been tantalising hints that maybe a fundamental review of the social security system could take place. A government Green Paper of 2006 offered a fairly dim view of the current arrangements: 'The present benefits system for people of working age is too complex. The many different rules make sense in isolation, but together they make for a confusing and incoherent picture' (DWP, 2006, p 92). The Green Paper went on to suggest that a possible response to this assessment might be to move 'in the longer term towards a single system of benefits for all people of working age, with appropriate additions for those who have caring responsibilities and those with a long-term illness or disability' (p 92). An independent review of welfare-to-work policy (Freud, 2007) supported a radical review of benefits as did the Work and Pensions Select Committee (2007), after a strange absence of further comment in another Green Paper in the summer of 2007 (DWP, 2007a).

The latest indication of the government's thinking is in yet another Green Paper in the long line of welfare reform documents (DWP, 2007c). It is not a model of clarity but does suggest, without creating any great expectations, that the current social security system is not the last word in reform: 'We are committed to transforming the benefits system to make it active, not passive, and to ensure social justice. Reform will happen incrementally in line with clear principles and guided by the concept of a single system for working age benefits' (DWP, 2007c, p 96).

Sainsbury and Stanley (2007) make a case for what could be described as a radical proposal to reform benefits, although it could be approached incrementally, which attempts to make the social security system complement employment policy rather than hinder it, and to remove some of the dysfunctions of complexity. A 'single working-age benefit' would replace the current range of different out-of-work benefits for working-age people with a single benefit. Hence, the reason for a person being out of the labour market (straightforward unemployment, sickness or disability, lone parenthood) would cease to be relevant. The single benefit would be for income replacement only; additional needs created by disability or caring responsibilities could be met by a separate benefit (which might, for example, integrate DLA and various premiums paid with current benefits). The benefit could be paid at one rate, and not change over time.

A firm link with employment policy could be established by asking claimants two 'gateway' questions as part of the claiming procedure:

- Do you think you will be able to work at any time in the future?
- Do you want to work at some point in the future?

We know from a number of sources that the majority of people asked these questions, including many people with long-term health and disabling conditions, would answer 'yes' and 'yes'. If they did then the single working-age benefit could be put into immediate payment, and the claimant would begin to work with a personal advisor to plan how the goal of paid employment could be achieved. Answering 'no' to the first question would of course be an entirely legitimate response for people in a range of circumstances, particularly with some types of disability or long-term health conditions. The social security system has always recognised that for some people it is right that they should not be obliged to undertake work-related activity as a condition of receiving benefit. The personal capability assessment has been used to identify people for whom this is appropriate and the work capability assessment under ESA will do this in future.

The *potential* of the single working-age benefit idea, combined with the 'gateway' questions, can be summarised thus:

- People would not have to move between benefits.
- There would be no 'perverse incentive' to claim sickness benefits.
- There would be no financial gain of claiming one benefit over another or of remaining on benefit for a long period.
- For people answering 'yes' to the two gateway questions there would be no need to undergo a 'work capability' or any other medical assessment. Health, disability, caring responsibilities would remain relevant to a discussion about how to get back to work, but they would not be relevant to deciding eligibility for the benefit. The benefit process could be effectively *de-medicalised* for large numbers of claimants.
- The need for sanctions would be reduced.
- A single rate of benefit that does not change over time would remove uncertainties about the effect on benefit levels of trying to work. There would be no need for 'linking rules'.
- The stigma, and possibility of subsequent discrimination, that has been a problem associated with the notion of disability benefits would be reduced. Social security 'labels' would cease to exist.
- Complexity would be reduced. The single benefit is simpler. Understanding would be increased and mistakes and overpayments would go down.

The final and important advantage that might flow from a single benefit would be as a contribution to a more 'inclusive' society for disabled people as envisioned by some disability analysts (for example, Barnes and Mercer, 2003) who argue that policies and societal attitudes to disability have moved from *segregation* to *integration* into mainstream society but have failed to achieve *inclusion*. Integration refers to attempts to assimilate disabled people into society rather than change society to include disabled people (for example, special classes and units within mainstream schools). An inclusive society would treat *all* people as individuals and respond to individual needs. The single working-age benefit could contribute to this aspiration.

We have seen how the system of sickness and disability benefits has changed almost out of recognition compared with its origins in 1911. It is still in a state of flux and probably in need of fundamental reform if it is going to cease to be a 'muddle' and fulfil the complex roles of income replacement and meeting extra needs while being an 'active' system that supports people into work.

Overview

- The system of sickness and disability benefits in this country has grown in size and complexity. Its functions of income replacement and meeting extra needs have become fragmented.
- Eligibility for sickness and disability benefits has become increasingly conditional on participating in work-related activities. There has been a marked shift towards greater 'responsibilities' placed on claimants compared with their rights to financial support.
- The policy challenges of the growing number of recipients of, and increasing expenditure on, sickness and disability benefits are common throughout the developed world.
- There is a case for fundamental reform of sickness and disability benefits so that they become a more effective 'active' system that supports employment policy while providing adequate financial support for those who need it.

Questions for discussion

(1) What are the aims and objectives of the system of sickness and disability benefits in the UK?
(2) To what extent should sick and disabled people be required to work?
(3) Is the balance of rights and responsibilities now skewed towards responsibilities rather than rights?
(4) Is the new Employment and Support Allowance likely to overcome some of the dysfunctions of the current system or will it create new ones?
(5) What can we learn from other countries' experiences of sickness and disability benefits?
(6) Is it possible to design a system of benefits that better supports employment policies? What would it look like?

Notes

[1] The evolution of sickness and disability benefits over the past century is beyond the scope of this chapter, but readers interested in, for example, Housewives Non-contributory Invalidity Pension or Mobility Allowance, are directed towards the succinct historical notes in Ogus, Barendt and Wikeley's series *The law of social security*, now in its fifth edition (2005).

[2] In the original plans for ESA, claimants were also meant to take part in work-related activities (such as training or job searching) as a condition of receiving the benefit but these requirements were dropped in the process of drafting the Social Security Bill that introduced the new legislation.

Website resources

www.dwp.gov.uk
Department for Work and Pensions
www.equalityhumanrights.com/en/Pages/default.aspx
Equality and Human Rights Commission
www.disabilityalliance.org/
Disability Alliance
www.radar.org.uk/radarwebsite/
RADAR: The Disability Network

References

Barnes, C. and Mercer, G. (2003) *Disability*, Cambridge: Polity Press.

Barnes, C., Mercer, G. and Shakespeare, T. (1999) *Exploring disability: A sociological introduction*, Cambridge: Polity Press.

Brown, J. (1984) *The disability income system*, London: Policy Studies Institute.

Burchardt, T. (2003) 'Disability, capability and social exclusion', in J. Millar (ed) *Understanding social security*, Bristol: The Policy Press.

DSS (Department of Social Security) (1998) *New ambitions for our country: A new contract for welfare*, Cm 3805, London: DSS.

DWP (Department for Work and Pensions) (2006) *A New Deal For Welfare: Empowering people to work*, Cm 6730, London: The Stationery Office.

DWP (2007a) *In work, better off: Next steps to full employment*, Cm 7130, London: The Stationery Office.

DWP (2007b) *DWP quarterly statistical summary – November 2007*, www.dwpgov.uk/asd/asd1/stats_summary/Stats_Summary_Nov_2007.pdf

DWP (2007c) *Ready for work: Full employment in our generation*, Cm 7290, London: The Stationery Office.

Freud, D. (2007) *Reducing dependency, increasing opportunity: Options for the future of the welfare state*, London: DWP.

Kemp, P., Sunden, A. and Bakker Tauritz, B. (eds) (2006) *Sick societies?*, Geneva: International Social Security Association.

NAO (National Audit Office) (2005a) *Gaining and retaining a job: The Department for Work and Pensions' support for disabled people*, HC 455, London: The Stationery Office.

NAO (2005b) *Dealing with the complexity of the benefits system*, London: The Stationery Office.

OECD (Organisation for Economic Co-operation and Development) (2003) *Transforming disability into ability*, Paris: OECD.

Ogus, A., Barendt, E. and Wikeley, N. (2005) *The law of social security* (fifth edition), London: Butterworths.

Sainsbury, R. (1999) 'The aims of social security', in J. Ditch (ed) *Introduction to social security: Policies, benefits and poverty*, London: Routledge.

Sainsbury, R. and Stanley, K. (2007) 'One for all: active welfare and the single working age benefit', in J. Bennett and G. Cooke (eds) *It's all about you – citizen-centred welfare*, London: IPPR, pp 43-56.

Stafford, B. et al (2004) *New Deal for Disabled People (NDDP): First synthesis report*, DWP Research Management Report W199, Sheffield: DWP Research Management.

Thornton, P., Sainsbury, R. and Barnes, H. (1997) *Helping disabled people to work: A cross-national study of social security and employment provisions*, Social Security Advisory Committee Research Paper 8, London: The Stationery Office.

Work and Pensions Select Committee (2007) *Benefit simplification*, HC463-I, London: The Stationery Office.

Work and Pensions Select Committee (2008) *The best start in life? Alleviating deprivation, improving social mobility, and eradicating child poverty*, HC 42-I, London: The Stationery Office.

Tax credits

Jane Millar

Summary

Until fairly recently, paid employment and social security benefits were usually seen as alternative sources of income. Wages were assumed to meet needs in work, with a small state contribution to the costs of children. Benefits replaced earnings for those periods when people were unable to support themselves through employment. But, as low-paid work has expanded, for some people wages alone may not be sufficient to provide a household with an adequate living standard, or an individual with sufficient financial incentive to take up paid work.

Thus, employed people have been gradually brought into the social security system, at first through an in-work benefit for low-paid families with children, and now through a system of tax credits. This chapter:

- traces the development of in-work benefits and tax credits in the UK since the 1970s;
- outlines the policy goals and describes the main features of the tax credit system introduced in 2003;
- assesses tax credits against policy objectives;
- sets out the problems that have arisen in the administration of tax credits;
- discusses the role of tax credits in welfare reform.

The start of in-work benefits in the UK: Family Income Supplement

Beveridge's plan for social security set out a scheme with three main elements. These were: *National Insurance (NI) benefits* (funded by contributions from workers, employers and the government, intended as a replacement for earnings loss); *National Assistance (NA) benefits* (funded from general taxation, means-tested support for people with low incomes); and *family allowances* (funded from general taxation, paid at the same rate for all families, regardless of income level). Thus, with the partial exception of family allowances, the main function of social security benefits was clearly to replace lost earnings, not to pay benefits to working people.

This wage replacement system operated successfully in the 1950s and into the 1960s, a period characterised by full employment and stable families (see Chapter Eight, Rowlingson, this volume). Poverty studies at the time suggested that working poverty had been largely eliminated. However, by the mid-1960s the 'rediscovery of poverty' challenged this benign view of welfare state success. In their influential study, Abel-Smith and Townsend (1965) found that poverty was much more widespread than had been thought, and also that it was increasingly a problem for working families, with one in five poor families with children being working families.

Thus, by the early 1970s, the gaps and shortfalls of the Beveridge scheme were becoming much more visible and filling some of these gaps became an important part of the policy agenda. The new measures introduced for non-working people in the early to mid-1970s included non-contributory pensions, the extension of widows' benefits and various benefits for disabled people. In relation to poor working families, various alternatives were being debated and considered. One option would have been for stronger measures of wage protection and regulation, including a National Minimum Wage (NMW). But this was not supported either by the governments of the time or by the trades unions, which were committed to free collective bargaining over wages (Brown, 1983; Millar et al, 1997). There was also a proposal for a 'tax credit' scheme, set out by the government (HM Treasury, 1971), which would have replaced personal tax allowances (which exempt a portion of gross income from tax and so reduce payments to the tax system) with a refundable tax credit (which can reduce tax owed to below zero and so lead to a payment from the tax system). This would have meant that people with earnings below the tax threshold would have received additional cash support. This proposal almost reached the legislative stage before being rejected as too costly.

Thus, in the early 1970s, neither wage regulation nor tax reform was seen as able to provide a solution to the problem of poverty among working families. That left the social security system, and the key measure here was the introduction of Family Income Supplement in 1971. This new means-tested benefit was payable to families with dependent children, with an employed parent working at least 30 hours per week, and with wages below a certain level. It was originally introduced as a temporary measure, while the government considered the future of family support more generally (Deacon and Bradshaw, 1983). In the event, although Child Benefit (CB) was introduced in 1975 to replace family allowances and child tax allowances, Family Income Supplement continued alongside it. Initially, as ***Table 13.1*** shows, this was a rather small and insignificant benefit, it did not cost very much and not many families received it. Take-up rates (the proportion of those eligible who actually received it) started at about 35% in 1971 and had only reached about 50% by 1979 (Brown, 1983).

Table 13.1: *Family Income Supplement, selected years 1971–79*

Year	Numbers in receipt	Costs (£ million) in cash	Costs (£ million) in 2008/09 real terms
1971/72	71,000	4	39
1972/73	106,000	10	95
1974/75	67,000	12	89
1976/77	97,000	18	93
1978/79	88,000	24	101

Source: Millar et al (1997, Table1); DWP (2008, Table 3a: nominal terms and Table 4a: real terms, 2008/09 prices, www.dwp.gov.uk/asd/asd4/medium_term.asp)

The 1986 Social Security Act was an important piece of legislation in this story and one that really established wage supplementation through means-tested benefits as a legitimate, and integral, function of the social security system. Income Support (IS) was introduced to replace Supplementary Benefit (SB), and Family Credit was introduced to replace Family Income Supplement. Common means tests were established for both, and for Housing Benefit (HB), so that benefits in and out of work were more closely aligned. Family Credit was very much intended to act as a work incentive, as the key objectives show: 'to provide extra support to these families in accordance with their needs; to ensure that as far as possible they are better off in work; and to see that they can achieve improvements in family income by greater effort without losing all benefit' (DHSS, 1985, p 29).

The structure and eligibility conditions for Family Credit were much the same as for Family Income Supplement, although it was a more generous system. It was available for families with children, with earnings below a certain level according to family size, and there was a weekly hours threshold (a minimum of 24 hours per week). Eligibility was assessed with reference to family income over a five-week (or two-month) period, and once awarded the amount paid was fixed for the next six months. It was paid to the main carer, either by an order book (cashable at post offices) or directly into bank accounts. This was not what the government originally proposed, which was that it should be paid through the wage packet, and therefore to the wage earner rather than to the main carer. This transfer from 'purse to wallet' was strongly resisted, by women's groups (including Conservative women) and by employers, who were not very willing to take on the responsibility of administering this.

Various rule changes increased the scope of the benefit over the next 10 years, including a reduction in the qualifying hours threshold from 24 to 16 in April 1992, and the introduction of disregards for maintenance and childcare costs. Family Credit receipt started relatively slowly but then began to rise rapidly, as ***Table 13.2*** shows. The number of recipients more than doubled between 1989 and 1996, from almost 300,000 to almost 700,000. Family Credit was available to lone parents on the same basis as it was to couples, and many employed lone parents were (and are) in low-paid work, and so lone parents made up a significant proportion of those in receipt. Take-up also improved, with the Department of Social Security (DSS, 1996) estimating take-up rates in the mid-1990s of about 70% by caseload and 82% by expenditure. Research on non-take-up concluded that many of these non-claiming families were probably only eligible for short periods and for relatively small amounts of money (McKay and Marsh, 1995). The Conservative government regarded Family Credit as one of its great successes, and introduced a similar in-work benefit (the Disability Working Allowance) for disabled people in 1992. It also piloted a similar 'Earnings Top-Up' for single people and couples without dependent children (Finlayson et al, 2000).

Table 13.2: *Family Credit, selected years 1988–96*

Year	Total numbers in receipt	Couples	Lone parents	Costs (£ million) in cash	Costs (£ million) in 2008/09 real terms
1988/89	285,000	177,000	108,000	394	754
1989/90	299,000	180,000	119,000	425	759
1991/92	350,000	213,000	136,000	626	977
1993/94	520,000	293,000	228,000	1,208	1,779
1995/96	693,000	388,000	305,000	1,740	2,449

Source: Millar et al (1997); DWP (2008, Tables 3 and 3a: nominal terms and Tables 4 and 4a: real terms, 2008/09 prices, www.dwp.gov.uk/asd/asd4/medium_term.asp)

'Making work pay': Working Families' Tax Credit

By the time the Labour government won the 1997 General Election the principle of supplementing wages through the social security system was thus well established. In the welfare reform Green Paper, *New ambitions for our country: A new contract for welfare* (DSS, 1998, p 1), the government argued that 'paid work is the surest route out of poverty' but that 'people face a series of barriers to paid work, including financial disincentives'. This started the development of a series of reforms to employment services and benefits (see Chapter Eleven, Wright, and Chapter Fifteen, Stafford, this volume). Measures to improve financial incentives to work included the introduction (for the first time in the UK) of a National Minimum Wage, reductions in tax and NI contributions for low-paid workers, and the introduction of Working Families' Tax Credit (WFTC) and Disabled Person's Tax Credit (DPTC).

It was the Treasury in particular that was driving these measures through, and the tax credits story can be traced through a series of Treasury papers entitled *The modernisation of Britain's tax and benefit system* (HM Treasury, 1997, 1998a, 1998b, 1999, 2000, 2002, 2005, 2008). The second of these, the report on 'work incentives' by Martin Taylor, is a key document in this story (HM Treasury, 1998a). Martin Taylor, Chief Executive of Barclays, was asked to chair a task force set up in May 1997 (immediately after the General Election) with a remit to 'examine the interaction of the tax and benefits systems so that they can be streamlined and modernised, so as to fulfil our objectives of promoting work incentives, reducing poverty and welfare dependency, and strengthening community and family life' (HM Treasury, 1998a, p 5).[1] Taylor starts by rejecting a full-scale integration of the tax and benefits systems on the grounds that these have different objectives, do not cover the same people, and have different units of assessment (individual for taxes, family for benefits). He argues that in-work wage supplements are necessary because there are 'a large number of people whose labour is not sufficiently well rewarded to allow them to support their families in an acceptable way. It seems to me far better that these people should be working, and receiving in-work benefits to top up their net pay, than that they should be idle' (p 8) and he argues for a tax credit, as opposed to a benefit because:

> A tax credit will associate the payment in the recipient's mind with the fact of working, a potentially valuable psychological change. I believe that a payment through the tax system, associated with the recipient's work, is likely to prove more acceptable to society at large. And the establishment of a tax credit system is likely to come in useful in future as a broader delivery mechanism, eventually

> allowing closer integration between the benefits system and conventional income tax. (HM Treasury, 1998a, p 8)

These points were repeated in the next Treasury paper (HM Treasury, 1998b), which set out the details of the new tax credits: 'As a tax credit rather than a welfare benefit, it will reduce the stigma associated with claiming in-work support, and encourage higher take-up. Its clear link with employment should demonstrate the rewards of work over welfare and help ensure that people move off welfare into work' (HM Treasury, 1998b, p 3).

The key rationale for a tax credit, as opposed to a benefit, is thus that taxes are positively associated with paid work while benefits are negatively associated with dependency. This, it is argued, makes tax credits more acceptable to recipients and to the public in general. The language here is also notable: it clearly reflects the influence of the US, where 'welfare' is a negative term associated with dependency and failure (Deacon, 2000; Hirsch, 2000; see also Chapter Eleven, Wright, this volume). Indeed, there has been much policy sharing and policy transfer across countries in respect of tax credit provisions, with the US experience, and values, an important element in this. ***Box 13.1*** outlines the system in the US and gives some further examples of tax credits in other countries.

Box 13.1: Tax credits in the US, Australia and Canada

The US

The 'Earned Income Tax Credit' (EITC) has been in operation in the US as a federal scheme since the mid-1970s, but it is only in the past 10 years or so that it has come to play a central role as part of the drive to 'end welfare' and get people into paid work. It is now a very large programme costing about US$34 billion in 2003 and received by about 19 million families. The EITC is mainly targeted at families with children although it is also available, at lower levels of payment, to childless and to single people. It is a refundable credit, which initially rises as earnings rise, then is paid at a maximum rate over a wide range of income, and finally is reduced as earnings increase until it reaches zero. Most families opt to receive their EITC annually, as a lump sum at the end of the year, rather than as an ongoing payment. Holt (2006, p 1) provides an overview of 30 years of the EITC and concludes that it 'has become a robust and largely successful component of American labor and antipoverty policy'.

Australia

There are two main benefits for children delivered through the tax system in Australia: Family Tax Benefit Part A is a means-tested payment similar to the UK's Child Tax Credit. Family Tax Benefit Part B provides extra assistance to single-income families including lone parents, with higher rates for families with children under five years of age. Around 2.2 million families with 4.3 million children receive Family Tax Benefits, covering about 80% of families. As in the UK, there is an assessment based on annual income with an end-of-year reconciliation. And, also as in the UK, the issue of overpayments has given cause for concern and various reforms from 2006 have sought to reduce these. See the Australian National Audit Office (2006).

Canada

In Canada the Child Tax Credit is available to lower-income families with children, paid monthly, on the basis of annual earnings but with no annual reconciliation. It is therefore very simple in design but set at a relatively low level. There is ongoing debate about the merits of setting up a wider tax credit system to support low-paid workers; see Battle and Mendelson (2005).

See Whiteford et al (2003) for a comparison of how Australia, Canada and the UK have designed their tax credits systems.

However, despite the presentation of these tax credits as something new and different, their structure was in fact very similar to that of Family Credit. As with Family Credit, WFTC was available only for families with children, it was paid to those with earnings below a certain level according to family size, and there was still a weekly hours threshold of 16 hours per week. Once awarded, WFTC remained in payment for six months, regardless of changes in income or circumstances. All this mirrored the Family Credit rules, albeit more generously. Working Families' Tax Credit also included a Childcare Tax Credit (CCTC), which covered up to 70% of eligible costs for registered care, subject to a maximum limit. This was available to lone parents and couples if both parents were in paid work.

Table 13.3 shows the numbers in receipt of WFTC from 1999 to 2002 (it was replaced in 2003). In November 1999 there were about 966,000 families in receipt. Lone parents outnumbered couples (as they had done since about November 1998 for Family Credit) and the average payment was about £66 per week. The numbers in receipt rose steadily every year, reaching 1.3 million families in May 2002 with an average weekly payment of about £84. About 162,000 families were receiving help with childcare costs.

The Treasury was, perhaps not surprisingly, very upbeat in its assessment of WFTC (HM Treasury, 2000, pp 9-10). It had, it argued, tackled the unemployment trap by ensuring that families were 'generally' better off in work and tackled the poverty trap by reducing by two thirds the number of families with marginal tax rates of over 70%. Alongside other measures it had

Table 13.3: Working Families' Tax Credit, 1999–2002

Year	Number in receipt (000s)	Couples (000s)	Lone parents (000s)	Average weekly amount	Childcare Tax Credit (000s)
1999	966	468	498	£66	55
2000	1,061	513	548	£73	108
2001	1,259	617	642	£79	145
2002	1,320	635	706	£84	162

Note: In May of each year, except 1999 November

Source: Inland Revenue (2002)

also helped to increase the number of people seeking to enter work by about 160,000 and it had helped to increase family incomes, especially for the poorest families, and so contributed to reduced levels of child poverty.

Independent research partly confirmed some of this, but also showed a more complex picture (Blundell and Walker, 2001; Brewer and Gregg, 2001; McLaughlin et al, 2001). The financial gains from work were indeed generally higher, but this applied primarily to full-time work and was much less the case for those receiving HB (which is reduced as WFTC is received) and for those with high work costs including childcare costs (which were only partly met by the CCTC). Families in receipt of other means-tested benefits (again particularly HB) still faced high marginal tax rates. The labour supply effect was estimated to be positive for lone parents and for the first earner in a couple. But the incentive for a second earner in a couple to take up work was much reduced.[2]

Tax credits from 2003: Child Tax Credit and Working Tax Credit

The WFTC and DPTC were replaced in 2003 by the 'next generation' of tax credits. Child Tax Credit (CTC) is available to families with dependent children and consists of three elements: the family element, which is the basic payment per family; the child element, which is the amount per child; and a disabled child element for families caring for a disabled child. It has a wide coverage, with about nine in ten families eligible for the family element (see further discussion below).

Working Tax Credit (WTC) is targeted on low-paid workers, including families with children or disabled people if they work at least 16 hours per week, and single people and couples without children if they are aged 25+ and work for at least 30 hours per week. It includes a 30-hour element for those with children (that is, an extra payment for hours of work of 30 and above) and elements for disabled workers and people aged 50+. The WTC also includes a Childcare Tax Credit for lone parents and couples where both are employed for at least 16 hours per week. This pays up to 80% of childcare costs up to a maximum of £175 for one child and £300 for two children or more (rates in 2008). The Childcare Tax Credit is only payable to families using registered childcare.

Aims: supporting work, reducing poverty and modernising systems

Tax credits are a key element in the government's reform programme aimed at increasing employment participation rates and reducing poverty. The key aims for tax credits were set out by HM Treasury (2002, p 3) as follows:

- supporting families with children, recognising the responsibilities that come with parenthood;
- tackling child poverty, by offering the greatest help to those most in need, such as low-income families;
- helping to make sure that work pays more than welfare and that people have incentives to move up the earnings ladder.

In addition, the tax credits were presented by the Treasury as an opportunity to 'modernise' delivery, and in particular to create a simpler and more effective form of means testing, with administration rationalised into one government department, the Inland Revenue (now HMRC), and assessment based on a simpler annual income test. The tax credits were designed to be simpler to administer and understand but also well targeted to people's needs: 'the income tax system provides a light touch and non-stigmatising way of measuring income' (HM Treasury, 2002, para 2.10), which will 'provide continuity of support for those who are not experiencing significant changes in circumstances or income, with the ability to adjust quickly for those who are facing major changes' (HM Treasury, 2002, para 4.1). In order to assess whether tax credits are meeting these aims, we start with an overview of the numbers in receipt since 2003.

Receipt of tax credits

Table 13.4 shows the numbers in receipt of tax credits since 2003. Overall, the number of recipients has remained similar at about six million individuals or families. The six million includes about 1.4 million unemployed families (again the number has remained much the same over time) who are receiving the equivalent of CTC while claiming an out-of-work benefit such as IS or JSA. The number of working people receiving support has also remained steady at about 4.6 million. This represents about one in eight of the UK's working-age population.

Table 13.4: *Working Tax Credit and Child Tax Credit, provisional awards, 2003–08*

	Total	Out of work	In work	In work (000s)			
				No children – WTC only	With children – WTC and CTC	With children – CTC more than family element	With children – CTC family element or less
2003	5.5m	1.4m	4.1m	121	1,465	647	1,851
2004	6.0m	1.4m	4.5m	235	1,589	704	2,013
2005	6.0m	1.4m	4.6m	282	1,531	711	2,115
2006	6.0m	1.4m	4.6m	319	1,565	684	2,033
2007	6.0m	1.4m	4.6m	343	1,645	665	1,966
2008	6.0m	1.4m	4.7m	376	1,715	671	1,898

Note: April each year, except July 2003.

Source: HMRC (2008a, Table 1.1)

In 2003 there were about 121,000 working people without children receiving tax credits, rising to 376,000 by 2008. This is a sharp rise, but nevertheless these are a small minority, and the bulk (over four million) of those in work receiving tax credits are families with children. These families can be divided into three main groups: those getting both CTC and WTC (about 1.7 million families), those getting CTC only but receiving more than just the basic family element (about 671,000) and those receiving only the family element or less (about 1.9 million).

Table 13.5 looks in more detail at the families with children, in order to compare couples and lone parents, using the most recent data for 2008. There are a number of points to note here. Couples make up about 73% of working families in receipt of tax credits and lone parents about 27%. This is not dissimilar to the overall population proportion (lone parents make up about 25% of all families with children).[3] However, lone parents and couples receive different types of support from tax credits. The majority (75%) of couples are receiving CTC only and just 5% are receiving the maximum amount of WTC. By contrast, the majority (81%) of lone parents are receiving both CTC and WTC. This of course reflects the lower earnings of lone parents – mainly lone mothers – and the fact that many of them work in part-time jobs. They are also sole earners (among couples about half of tax credit recipients are sole earners). In addition, almost half a million families are receiving help with childcare costs (a substantial increase since 2002; see ***Table 13.2***), but lone parents are more likely to receive this support than are couples (about 25% compared with about 5%).

Table 13.5: *Tax credits: in-work families with children, provisional awards, 2008*

	Total	Couples	Lone parents
Tax credits	%	%	%
CTC and WTC: maximum	12	5	29
CTC and WTC: tapered	28	20	52
CTC only: more than family element	16	18	9
CTC only: family element	41	53	9
CTC only: less than family element	3	4	*
	(100%)	(100%)	(100%)
Number of families (000s)	4,284.4	3,146.6	1,137.8
Number of children (000s)	7,435.1	5,693.2	1,741.9
Childcare element (000s)	448.8	161.7	287.1

Note: * less than 1%

Source: HMRC (2008a, Tables 2.1, 3.2, 4.4)

Poverty and work incentives

Tax credits are an increasingly significant part of government expenditure. In 2006/07 about £20 billion was paid to tax credit recipients, including about £5.7 billion to families not in work and receiving tax credits for children and about £14.6 billion to working people (HMRC, 2008d). The average payment for a family with two children receiving just the family element of CTC was about £600 per year, rising to over £7,000 for those receiving both CTC and WTC (HMRC, 2008a). Tax credits have increased the financial returns from work, especially for lone parents. In 1999 a one-child family with one adult working part time would have had an income in work of about £136 per week; by 2008 this had risen to £226 per week (TUC, 2008).

Overall employment rates have been rising and poverty rates falling in recent years (see various chapters in this volume, including Chapters Four, Eight, Nine and Ten). However, estimating the direct impact of tax credits on employment rates and poverty is complex because of the range of other factors and policies involved. Brewer and Browne (2006) summarise evidence from five studies looking at WFTC (that is, before the 2003 changes) and conclude that WFTC increased the proportion of lone mothers who work (probably by about five percentage points) but had little overall effect on couples with children. HM Treasury (2008) concludes that WTC has increased employment among childless people.

The child poverty rate for children in working families is much lower than that in non-working families and much of the fall in child poverty rates since 2001 has been attributed to the impact of tax credits. Hirsch (2006, p 42) concludes that initially 'rising employment was the biggest factor behind falls in child poverty, more recently it appears that jobs played a smaller role, and rises in tax credits a relatively large one'. However, he also concludes that the current levels of tax credits will not be sufficient to meet the government's targets for eliminating child poverty, although increasing spending on CTC by £4.2 billion would meet the 2010 target of reducing child poverty by half. Furthermore, receipt of tax credits does not guarantee avoiding poverty. Barnes et al (2008), analysing data from the 2005 Families with Children Survey, show that among those receiving tax credits, about 29% of couples with one earner are in poverty (defined as income below 60% of the median), as are 8% of two-earner couples and 13% of lone parents. To avoid poverty, one-earner couples at the NMW and receiving tax credits would have to work considerably more hours per week than lone parents (House of Commons Work and Pensions Select Committee, 2008).

Tax credits have thus contributed to rising employment and falling poverty. But at the same time there has been significant criticism of both the design and the delivery of tax credits and some concern that failures in administration have undermined the capacity to meet policy objectives.

Modernising design and delivery

As Millar (2008, p 26) points out, there are several features of the administration that are new to the UK, including:

- the use of the tax system to assess and make payments;
- an income test based on an annual assessment of entitlement;
- a simple definition of gross income, not taking into account capital assets;
- limited responsiveness to changes in income and other circumstances during the period of the award;
- separate tax credits for children and adults;
- an integrated system of support for all children, regardless of the employment status of their parents (not yet fully achieved in practice);
- the inclusion of childless and single people.

Delivering such a system has proved very challenging for the government, and especially for HMRC, the department in charge of assessment and payment. As noted above, one of the aims of tax credits was to achieve a light-touch means test that would balance security of support with responsiveness to changes in income and circumstances. This was to be achieved by not seeking to fine-tune the credits to reflect changes as they happen (as is the case for IS, for example). The assessment for tax credits is initially made on the basis of gross family income in the previous tax year. This forms the basis for the provisional award for the following 12 months. During the period of that award recipients are required to report certain changes in circumstances (such as splitting up with a partner) and awards are recalculated during the year. However, not all changes have to be reported and so there may be a difference between the provisional award (based on income in the previous tax year) and the finalised award (based on income in the current tax year). This is dealt with by means of an end-of-year reconciliation. At that point any underpayments are covered by a lump-sum payment at the end of the year and any overpayments are recovered either by adjusting subsequent tax credit awards or by adjusting the main tax codes if tax credits are no longer due.

Under- and overpayments are thus an inherent element of the design of tax credits. But the government was clearly taken by surprise by the extent of these. Over the first few years, overpayments affected about 1.9 million awards per year, costing about £1.6 billion to £1.8 billion annually. Underpayments affected about 0.8 million awards, at about £0.5 billion annually (Millar, 2008). Families receiving both CTC and WTC were the most likely to have under- or overpayments, and these are the lowest-income families, most likely to have volatile income and circumstances and most likely to rely on tax credits for a substantial part of their incomes. The repayment of overpayments has been a source of significant concern and hardship for families, as has the lack of transparency and poor communication. Qualitative research with lone-parent families receiving tax credits has shown how important these are to family income in work but has also highlighted the problems caused by delays, incorrect payments, changes to awards, and a general lack of information and clarity about awards (Millar, 2008; Ridge and Millar, 2009: forthcoming). ***Box 13.2*** summarises some of the key points of criticism of the administration of tax credits.

Box 13.2: The administration of tax credits – issues and problems

Godwin and Lawson (2009: forthcoming) identify the following issues in the delivery of tax credits:

- *Under- and overpayments* – the scale of these, the impact on families and the difficulties in recovering overpayments, leading to the write-off of significant debts.

- *Fraud and error* – estimated at about £1.04 to £1.30 billion in 2004/05. Fraud has included organised fraud on the online claiming system, and there are high levels of customer error due to lack of understanding of the system.
- *Take-up* – the figures for 2005/06 (HMRC, 2008b) show an 82% take-up of CTC and a 61% take-up of WTC. About 1.1 million people are estimated to be eligible non-claimants of WTC, with about £2.2 billion unclaimed.
- *Compliance costs to employers* – these were higher under WFTC, which was paid through the pay packet, which is not the case for CTC and WTC. Godwin and Lawson suggest that the main cost to employers is in providing information to assist people with claims.
- *Compliance costs to claimants* – these include the lengthy claim form, the obligations to report some changes, problems with estimating income and childcare costs, difficulties in accessing helpline services, delays and errors.

Various reports have criticised the administration of tax credits including: NAO (2005); Parliamentary and Health Service Ombudsman (2005); House of Commons Treasury Committee (2006); House of Commons Committee of Public Accounts (2007).

A series of reforms to the system brought in from 2005 onwards was intended to improve the administration of tax credits and specifically to reduce over- and underpayments (Brewer, 2006). The measures included a very large increase in the level of disregarded earnings from £2,500 to £25,000. This means that if income rises by up to £25,000 in one year, the tax credit award for that year will not be adjusted. This provides a significant cushion against overpayments occurring due to income rises. Other measures included changes to the reporting requirements and to the way awards are adjusted in the year. These changes have led to a fall in overpayments of about £0.7 billion, such that in 2006/07 overpayments fell to about £950 million, affecting about 1.3 million awards. Underpayments are still at about £0.5 billion, affecting about 0.8 million people (HMRC, 2008c).

Various wider reforms have been suggested (Brewer, 2006; House of Commons Treasury Committee, 2006; Smithies, 2007) including a return to a fixed period of award, with no requirement to respond to changes in income or circumstances during that time (as in the old Family Income Supplement and Family Credit systems). HM Treasury (2008) argues against this on the grounds of the need for flexibility and effective targeting, and instead proposes further reforms to the administration, including more disregards, lump-sum payments, use of banded income measures, and changes to the delivery of childcare support.

Tax credits and welfare reform

Tax credits are central to the Labour government's welfare reform agenda. Adler (2004) argues that tax credits and the New Deal programmes together represent a 'new and distinctive' approach to social security policy, addressing the new social risks of insecurity in employment and family structure. Tax credits provide income support to people in potentially adverse labour market situations, including low pay, self-employment, part-time work and temporary or irregular work. They are also intended to enable families with just one earner, especially lone-parent families, to sustain employment. Tax credits can therefore be seen as part of a shift towards a 'social investment' welfare state, which promotes self-support through employment, and includes policies intended to improve skills for employment, to invest in children and to enable people to build up assets (Dobrowolsky and Jenson, 2005). Grover and Stewart (2002) interpret these policy developments in a different way, arguing that tax credits and other measures to 'make work pay' are about ensuring that unemployed people are driven into low-paid jobs while the costs of labour to employers are kept low.

The importance of tax credits shows how UK 'social security' has become increasingly focused on wage supplementation rather than on wage replacement, which was the rationale for the system of social insurance designed by Beveridge in the 1940s. Tax credits are also a break with Beveridge in another sense, in that they take the UK even further down the means-testing road and away from universal or categorical ways of targeting support. Compared with any previous measures, tax credits cover more groups of the population and extend higher up the income scale. The attempt to do this by means of a 'light-touch and non-stigmatising' means test has proved to be very difficult to achieve in practice and arguably the changes since 2003 have pushed the system further back into the more traditional form of means-tested support. Balancing simplicity and responsiveness, while still targeting effectively, is an elusive goal.

Overview

- Support for low-paid workers dates back over 30 years in the UK, but has become increasingly important in recent years.
- Tax credits are now a key part of the UK income transfer system, providing financial support to six million people, including 4.3 million working families with children.
- Tax credits are innovative in design, extensive in coverage and generous in level compared with the UK's traditional means-tested social security support.

- There has been significant criticism of the design and delivery of tax credits, in particular the extent of over- and underpayments and how these have been dealt with.
- Tax credits have contributed to rising employment and falling poverty, providing a substantial boost to the incomes of many low-paid people. They are central to the government's welfare reform agenda.

Questions for discussion

(1) Why have tax credits become such an important part of government policy?
(2) Has the government found the right balance between simplicity, targeting and responsiveness in the design of the Child Tax and Working Tax Credits?
(3) How could the administration of tax credits be improved?

Notes

[1] The report covered NI contributions and benefits for the partners of unemployed claimants as well as tax credits, but we focus on the latter here.

[2] This disincentive to the second earner also existed under Family Credit, of course, although less strongly because the level of benefit was lower. This problem is inherent in a family-based means test – when the second earner enters work the amount of benefit received starts to reduce. This is one of the arguments used in favour of a more individualised system of benefits (Millar, 2005).

[3] See also Brewer and Shaw (2006) for a discussion of the estimates of the numbers of lone parents receiving tax credits.

Website resources

http://www.hm-treasury.gov.uk/documents/taxation_work_and_welfare/work_and_welfare/tax_workwel_index.cfm
HM Treasury: taxation, work and welfare
http://www.hmrc.gov.uk/stats/personal-tax-credits/cwtc-quarterly-stats.htm
HM Revenue & Customs – tax credit statistics

References

Abel-Smith, B. and Townsend, P. (1965) *The poor and the poorest*, London: Bell and Sons.

Adler, M. (2004) 'Combining welfare-to-work measures with tax credits: a hybrid approach to social security in the UK', *International Social Security Review*, vol 57, no 2, pp 87-106.

Australian National Audit Office (2006) *The Auditor-General audit report no. 12: Management of family tax benefit overpayments*, Canberra: Commonwealth of Australia, www.anao.gov.au/uploads/documents/2006-07_Audit_Report_12.pdf

Barnes, M., Lyon, N. and Millar, J. (2008) *Employment transitions and the changes in economic circumstances of families with children: Evidence from the Families and Children Study (FACS)*, DWP Research Report No 506, Leeds: Corporate Document Services.

Battle, K. and Mendelson, M. (2005) *A working income tax benefit that works*, Ottawa: The Caledon Institute, www.caledoninst.org/Publications/PDF/563ENG%

Blundell, R. and Walker, I. (2001) *Working Families' Tax Credit: A review of the evidence, issues and prospects for further research*, London: Inland Revenue.

Brewer, M. (2006) *Tax credits: Fixed or beyond repair?*, IFS Green Budget, London: Institute for Fiscal Studies.

Brewer, M. and Browne, J. (2006) *The effect of the Working Families' Tax Credit on labour market participation*, Briefing Note No 69, London: Institute for Fiscal Studies.

Brewer, M. and Gregg, P. (2001) 'Lone parents, the Working Families' Tax Credit and employment in households with children', in R. Dickens, J. Wadsworth and P. Gregg (eds) *The state of working Britain: Update 2001*, London: Centre for Economic Policy.

Brewer, M. and Shaw, J. (2006) *How many lone parents are receiving tax credits?*, London: Institute for Fiscal Studies.

Brown, J. C. (1983) *Family Income Supplement: Family Income Support*, London: Policy Studies Institute.

Deacon, A. (2000) 'Learning from the USA? The influence of American ideas on New Labour thinking on welfare reform', *Policy & Politics*, vol 28, no 1, pp 5-18.

Deacon, A. and Bradshaw, J. (1983) *Reserved for the poor: The means-test in British social policy*, Oxford: Martin Robertson.

DHSS (Department of Health and Social Security) (1985) *The reform of social security*, London: HMSO.

Dobrowolsky, A. and Jenson, J. (2005) 'Social investment perspectives and practices: a decade in British politics', in M. Powell, L. Bauld and K. Clarke (eds) *Social policy review 17*, Bristol: The Policy Press, pp 203-30.

DSS (Department of Social Security) (1996) *Income-related benefits: Estimates of take-up in 1994/95*, London: HMSO.

DSS (1998) *New ambitions for our country: A new contract for welfare*, Cm 3805, London: DSS.

DWP (Department for Work and Pensions) (2007) *Households Below Average Income 1994/5 to 2005/6*, London: DWP, www.dwp.gov.uk/asd/hbai/hbai2006/contents.asp

DWP (2008) *Benefit expenditure tables*, London: DWP, http://www.dwp.gov.uk/asd/asd4/medium_term.asp

Finlayson, L., Ford, R., Marsh, A., Smith, A. and White, M. (2000) *The first effects of earnings top-up*, DSS Research Report No 112, Leeds: Corporate Document Services.

Godwin, M. and Lawson, C. (2009: forthcoming) 'Hidden costs of the welfare state: employers' compliance costs and the working tax credit', *Social Policy and Society*, vol 8, no 2.

Grover, C. and Stewart, J. (2002) *The work connection: The role of social security in British economic regulation*, Basingstoke: Palgrave.

Hirsch, D. (2000) *A credit to children: The UK's radical reform of children's benefits in international perspective*, York: York Publishing Services for the Joseph Rowntree Foundation.

Hirsch, D. (2006) *What will it take to end child poverty? Firing on all cylinders*, York: Joseph Rowntree Foundation.

HM Treasury (1971) *Reform of personal direct taxation*,Cmnd 4653, London: HMSO.

HM Treasury (1997) *The modernisation of Britain's tax and benefit system number 1: Employment opportunity in a changing labour market*, London: HM Treasury.

HM Treasury (1998a) *The modernisation of Britain's tax and benefit system number 2: Work incentives: A report by Martin Taylor*, London: HM Treasury.

HM Treasury (1998b) *The modernisation of Britain's tax and benefit system number 3: The Working Families Tax Credit and work incentives*, London: HM Treasury.

HM Treasury (1999) *The modernisation of Britain's tax and benefit system number 5: Supporting children through the tax and benefit system*, London: HM Treasury.

HM Treasury (2000) *The modernisation of Britain's tax and benefit system number 6: Tackling poverty and making work pay: Tax credits for the 21st century*, London: HM Treasury.

HM Treasury (2002) *The modernisation of Britain's tax and benefit system number 10: The Child and Working Tax Credits*, London: HM Treasury.

HM Treasury (2005) *The modernisation of Britain's tax and benefit system number 11: Tax credits: Reforming financial support for families*, London: HM Treasury.

HM Treasury (2008) *The modernisation of Britain's tax and benefit system number 12: Tax credits: Improving delivery and choice – a discussion paper*, London: HM Treasury.

HMRC (HM Revenue & Customs) (2008a) *Child and Working Tax Credits statistics: Provisional awards*, London: HMRC, www.hmrc.gov.uk/stats/personal-tax-credits/cwtc-apr08.pdf

HMRC (2008b) *Child Tax Credit and Working Tax Credit: Take-up rates 2005/6*, London: National Statistics.

HMRC (2008c) *Child and Working Tax Credits statistics: Finalised annual awards 2006/7: Supplements on payments*, London: National Statistics.

HMRC (2008d) *Child and Working Tax Credits statistics: Finalised annual awards 2006/7*, London: National Statistics.

Holt, S. (2006) *The Earned Income Tax Credit at age 30: What we know*, Research Brief, Washington, DC: Brookings Institution, www.brookings.edu/~/media/Files/rc/reports/2006/02childrenfamilies_holt/20060209_Holt.pdf

House of Commons Committee of Public Accounts (2007) *Tax credits*, Twenty Second Report of Session 2006-07, HC 487, London: The Stationery Office.

House of Commons Treasury Committee (2006) *The administration of tax credits*, Sixth Report of Session 2005-06, HC 811-1, London: The Stationery Office.

House of Commons Work and Pensions Committee (2008) *The best start in life?: Alleviating deprivation, improving social mobility and eradicating child poverty*, Second Report of Session 2007-08, HC 42-I, London: The Stationery Office.

Inland Revenue (2002) *Working Families' Tax Credit statistics quarterly enquiry*, London: Inland Revenue.

McKay, S. and Marsh, A. (1995) *Why didn't they claim? A follow-up study of eligible non-claimants of Family Credit*, London: Policy Studies Institute.

McLaughlin, E., Trewsdale, J. and McCay, N. (2001) 'The rise and fall of the UK's first tax credit', *Social Policy and Administration*, vol 35, no 2, pp 163-80.

Millar J. (2005) 'Simplification, modernisation and social security', *Benefits*, vol 13, no 1, pp 10-15.

Millar, J. (2008) 'Making work pay, making tax credits work: an assessment with specific reference to lone-parent employment', *International Social Security Review*, vol 61, no 2, pp 21-38.

Millar, J., Webb, S. and Kemp, M. (1997) *Combining work and welfare*, York: Joseph Rowntree Foundation.

NAO (National Audit Office) (2005) *Inland revenue: Standard report 2003-2004: Child and Working Tax Credits and Stamp Duty Land Tax*, London: NAO.

Parliamentary and Health Service Ombudsman (2005) *Tax credits: Putting things right*, 3rd Report of Session 2005-2006, HC 124, London: The Stationery Office.

Smithies, R. (2007) 'Making a case for flat tax credits: income fluctuations among low-income families', *Benefits*, vol 15, no 1, pp 3-16.

TUC (Trades Union Congress) (2008) *The tax credit success story*, London: TUC.

Whiteford, P., Mendelson, M. and Millar, J. (2003) *Timing it right? Tax credits and how to respond to income changes*, York: York Publishing Services for the Joseph Rowntree Foundation.

Part Three
Users and providers

Service delivery and the user

Bruce Stafford

Summary

This chapter focuses on users' experiences of social security and how it is delivered. Users' perspectives are important because it is their experiences that help define the reality of the social security system. Specifically, the chapter covers:

- the main characteristics of the user base;
- criticisms of service delivery and the key themes that characterise recent policy initiatives;
- the administration of Housing Benefit and Council Tax Benefit by local authorities;
- a discussion of customer and user perspectives on social security.

Introduction

Delivery is at the heart of the Labour government's reform of social security, because it recognises that the effectiveness of policies is influenced by how they are implemented and delivered. Under Labour there has been a period of piloting, experimentation and restructuring of the organisations responsible for delivering benefits and support services. Initiatives of particular significance are the use of personal advisors (or caseworkers) and the increased use of telephony. As in other areas of social policy, Labour refers to users of social security as consumers, even as citizen-consumers, implying that they have an individualised and market-like nexus with service provision. However, social security users do not exercise the sort of 'consumer sovereignty' characteristic of competitive markets. Admittedly, some people purchase pension and other insurance policies in the marketplace, but users of state-funded social security are not consumers in a conventional competitive market sense. The dissatisfied disabled person, for instance, is unlikely to be in a position to return their Disability Living Allowance (DLA) to the Department for Work and Pensions (DWP) and to 'shop' for financial support elsewhere.

The delivery of social security is organisationally disparate in the UK. Many users deal with the DWP and its agencies:

- Jobcentre Plus delivers benefit and employment services at local level to people of working age.
- the Pension, Disability and Carers Service is a new agency created on 1 April 2008 from the Pension Service and the Disability and Carers Service. It deals with current and future pensions (mainly by a telephone-based service) and delivers disability and carers benefits.
- The Child Support Agency (CSA) administers child support services.

There is also the centralised delivery of Child Benefit (CB) and tax credits and the collection of National Insurance (NI) contributions by Her Majesty's Revenue & Customs (HMRC), while local authorities have responsibility for the administration of Housing Benefit (HB) and Council Tax Benefit (CTB). In addition, the Social Security and Child Support Appeals Tribunal administers appeals for benefit, tax credit and child support services; and the Home Office and the Ministry of Defence have responsibility for benefits for asylum seekers and war pensions respectively. Largely as a consequence of this structure there are client 'silos', with services accessed on the basis of a person's categorisation as a lone parent, jobseeker, pensioner and so on.

In the next section the size of the user 'base' and the key characteristics that affect the delivery of social security are briefly discussed. The key policy themes underpinning recent policy initiatives are then outlined. The administration of HB and CTB is briefly discussed. The final section discusses user involvement and consumerism in social security.

Users

Arguably, in the UK everyone is at some point in their life a user of the social security system. Parents or guardians may receive CB and possibly a Child Tax Credit (CTC) for their children, many people of working age pay NI contributions and claim out-of-work and/or in-work benefits or tax credits, and older people receive benefits and/or the state pension. Two key features follow from this: first, the user base for social security is very large (see ***Box 14.1***), and second, there is a great deal of variation within and between groups of users.

Box 14.1: Size of the user base

The users of the social security system can include at a given point in time:

Children and families

- 10.1 million children living in 5.7 million families benefit from a tax credit (2005/06).
- 12.9 million children in 7.3 million families are receiving CB (August 2007).
- There are 1.2 million Child Support cases with an assessment or calculation for child maintenance (September 2007).

Working-age population

- 5.2 million people of working age (14%) are claiming Bereavement Benefit, Carer's Allowance, Disability Living Allowance, Incapacity Benefit, Income Support, Jobseeker's Allowance, Severe Disablement Allowance and/or Widow's Benefit (May 2007).

Population over state pension age

- There are 12 million people over state pension age and living in Britain claiming Attendance Allowance, Incapacity Benefit, Severe Disablement Allowance, Disability Living Allowance, Pension Credit, Retirement Pension and/or Widow's Benefit (May 2007).

Other key benefits

- 3 million households are receiving Housing Benefit (June 2007).
- 3.8 million households are receiving Council Tax Benefit (June 2007).
- 1.3 million people have been awarded a Social Fund budgeting loan and 1 million a crisis loan (2006/07).

Contributors

- 28.3 million people paid National Insurance contributions in 2004/05 (UK).

Notes: Unless otherwise indicated all figures relate to Britain. The tax credits are Child and Working Tax Credits.
Sources: DWP (2007a, 2007b); HMRC (2007a, 2007b); National Statistics (2007); DWP's Tabulation Tool (www.dwp.gov.uk/asd/tabtool.asp) and Housing Benefit Operational Database (www.dwp.gov.uk/asd/hobod/index.php)

In addition, employers are a major 'user' group. Employers have a key role in collecting NI contributions, providing occupational pensions and sick pay, supplying placements for the New Deals and other employment programmes and offering job vacancies. However, the following sections concentrate on individuals, not firms, as users.

Some people's contacts with the social security system are non-problematic and routine. For others, however, dealings with the social security system occur at a key transitional point in their lives, for example when a partner has left them, or they have lost a job. So many users come into direct contact with the system when they are at their most vulnerable, suffering a loss of self-esteem and unsure of what the future may hold.

Users have a range of requirements of the social security system. Their levels of confidence and competence to deal with the system will vary – some need little or no support, but others require significant advice and help (Bailey and Pryes, 1996). Contacts with the social security system are further complicated when users have problems with literacy and numeracy.

The difficulties that users have encountered

Labour inherited a social security system that was heavily criticised for delivering a poor standard of service. For example, the system was too complex, a 'big hassle' for many claimants; users were often confused about which organisations administered which benefits and services; people often had to deal with more than one organisation and provide the same item of information more than once; and claim forms were lengthy and complicated and contained poorly worded questions (Stafford, 2003; Finn et al, 2008). Labour ministers were also initially highly critical of the way in which benefits were delivered (see, for instance, DSS, 1997).

Notwithstanding changes in the delivery of social security, progress in addressing some of the above issues has been slow and some new issues have emerged:

- Although a degree of complexity in the social security system is inevitable, even desirable to deal with diverse circumstances and varying needs of users, the system's complexity is '*dysfunctional*' (Work and Pensions Committee, 2007, p 5). Users continue to be confused about what is expected of them and about key details with regard to the operation of the system (such as the sanctions regime; see Joyce and Whiting, 2006).
- Users can have to deal with more than one agency. Notwithstanding various initiatives since the 1990s to improve joint working across the system (see Stafford, 2003), for some users services across the DWP's agencies continue to be '*poorly joined-up*' (PMDU, 2007). For example, call centre staff in one

agency are unable to transfer users' telephone calls to another agency (NAO, 2006c). In addition, there is a lack of integrated delivery with HMRC over tax credits, which adds to users' levels of confusion about the system (Work and Pensions Committee, 2007). Yet it is often the most vulnerable people who by the nature of their complex needs have to join up '*islands*' of service provision (Varney, 2006).

- Large numbers of users have '*failed to benefit*' from reforms to the child support system; difficulties include a backlog of applications, and low rates of assessing applications accurately (NAO, 2006a).
- The service provided to tax credit users has been assessed by a parliamentary committee to be '*poor*' (Committee of Public Accounts, 2007, p 15), in particular there have been delays in assessing applications and the recovery of overpayments has caused hardship for some users (Parliamentary and Health Service Ombudsman, 2007).
- Shortcomings in communications with the public persist. For example:
  - Leaflets can be poorly designed, the information they contain can be inaccessible to some users, such as disabled people and those whose first language is not English, and many leaflets are not available at departmental or other relevant sites, and when available they are not always up to date (NAO, 2006b).
  - Staff at Jobcentre Plus call centres, who are required to follow a set script for each call, lack the opportunity and training to give callers a more flexible and informed service about their entitlement to a range of benefits and services (Work and Pensions Committee, 2007).
  - For some people, claim forms continue to be too long and complicated, and evidence requirements can be onerous (NAO, 2005; Hawkins et al, 2007).

This does not mean that all users' experiences of the social security system are negative; for instance, 86% of Jobcentre Plus users (Sanderson et al, 2005) and 81% of Pension Service users (Kelly et al, 2004) say they are satisfied with the service they receive (although minority ethnic users of Jobcentre Plus rated the performance of the agency less highly than did white users; Johnson and Fidler, 2006). Moreover, an official assessment of DWP's capability found that it had 'an excellent understanding of customer satisfaction', had some 'excellent practice' in dealing with high volume day-to-day transactions and staff were 'passionate about their commitment to their customers' (PMDU, 2007, pp 16, 17, 21). Similarly, HMRC has improved users' access to, and the reliability of, the advice and information it provides (Parliamentary and Health Service Ombudsman, 2007). Moreover, the DWP is using information and communication technology and data sharing to improve service delivery (see

Chapter Sixteen, Hudson, this volume). Nonetheless, poor service delivery can lead to hardship and anxiety for users.

Service transformation?

From a user perspective the delivery of social security remains inherently consumerist; the individual is not treated as a citizen but as a customer (Ling, 1994). In Chapter Six, this volume, Carmel and Papadopoulos highlight the emergence of 'new public management' in social security, which has had a customer focus since the mid-1980s (Newman, 2000). Consumerism in social security (and elsewhere in the public sector) aims to make those delivering services more responsive to the needs of their customers, in effect to mimic consumer sovereignty in the competitive market. However, the focus on (quasi-)markets and individual preferences inherent in consumerism serves to undermine a notion of social citizenship where people have acquired rights to welfare services, and draws on a broader neoliberal agenda (Dwyer, 2004; Miller, 2004).

Recently, governmental announcements refer to 'service transformation', which is depicted as a radical reform of public service delivery (Varney, 2006). The aim is that government departments will 'build services around the needs of citizens and business' (HM Treasury, 2007, p 38) and that this will lead to more personalised services and less 'compartmentalisation' of delivery. Proposals include a rationalisation of government websites, accrediting call centres and (yet again) trying to realise the ambition that people have to give information only once about changes of circumstance (HM Government, 2007) (see also Chapter Sixteen, Hudson, this volume). It is too early to tell whether 'service transformation' is little more than a rebranding of 'joined-up' government.

In addition, Labour has made a number of delivery-related initiatives that are, to varying degrees, underpinned by five key themes/changes: choice, personalisation, telephony, the use of compulsion and benefit simplification. We now consider each in turn.

Emergence of choice

Building on the previous Conservative administration's championing of the public service user as a 'consumer' through such initiatives as the 1991 Citizens Charter, Labour has argued that people want more choice in, and control over, their lives (Clarke et al, 2007; PMSU, 2007). Choice of provider is, via competitive pressures, believed to engender efficiency and innovation. This 'choice' discourse has centred on education, social care and health services rather than social security.

Labour maintains that choice 'means giving users the ability to decide where, when, by whom or how a public service is provided to them' (PMSU, 2006, p 62). While there are organisations, such as charities, that will provide financial and other support to vulnerable people, and many people have a degree of choice in the provision of pension and other employment-related benefits, there is, in general, limited user choice in social security. For example, although many services can be accessed by multiple channels, benefit services are increasingly accessed via a call centre (see below). Users often see themselves as exercising little or no choice in the services on offer – especially if they are worried about being sanctioned for non-compliance. However, two employment programmes – Employment Zones and New Deal for Disabled People (NDDP) – have sought to provide some participants with a choice of contracted provider, and the piloted Local Housing Allowance was meant to give private sector tenants an incentive to choose between landlords. Yet users' choices in, for example, NDDP were limited by a lack of information about the different services that providers could offer, and participants tended to contact the organisation that was geographically closest and accessible (Stafford et al, 2007).

Nonetheless, the government is proposing that contracted private and voluntary sector organisations should deliver employment services to those furthest from the labour market (Freud, 2007) (and see Chapter Fifteen, Finn, this volume), and the DWP expects providers to offer users 'informed choices in the opportunities and services they receive' (DWP, 2007d, p 10). The risk is that such a welfare 'mix' will undermine attempts to provide a more integrated service. Indeed, the establishment of a myriad of subcontracted services operating within an area could make the system more complex for users (CPAG, 2007).

The government also sees increased personalisation of services as offering a form of choice (PMSU, 2006).

Personalisation

The 1998 welfare reform Green Paper proposed a '*flexible, professional, personalised service*' (DSS, 1998, p 28, emphasis in original) to help people meet the obligations that accompany benefit receipt and to assist people into work. The notion that service delivery should be flexible and personalised is a central and long-standing theme of Labour's modernisation agenda (see, for example, *Modernising government*, Cabinet Office, 1999; *Reforming our public services*, OPSR, 2002; and the Prime Minister's Strategy Unit's policy review of public services, PMSU, 2007), and was re-emphasised in the recent Green Paper, *In work, better off: Next steps to full employment* (DWP, 2007c). The aim is to provide a personalised service with the tailoring of advice and support to users as opposed to a 'one-size-fits-all' approach to service delivery. A more personalised approach is deemed necessary because of rising public expectations about public services that have accompanied demographic changes, increased globalisation and technological developments (DSS, 1998; HM Treasury, 2007). Current policy proposals seek to make the system more flexible and personalised, in particular to introduce a more flexible New Deal (DWP, 2004, 2007c).

Personalisation does not necessarily equate to face-to-face contacts as it can be provided by multiple channels, including telephony and the Web. The New Deals and associated personal advisors do provide some tailoring of services to the needs of users. Personal advisors conduct work-focused interviews with users to explore work aspirations, and the barriers to and opportunities for employment. The personal advisor model operates in Jobcentre Plus and in contracted provision such as Employment Zones and NDDP (where they were called job brokers) (see Chapter Eleven, Wright, and Chapter Fifteen, Finn, this volume).

Generally, both staff and users have positive views about the personal advisor model (Stafford, 2003; Coleman et al, 2005; Griffiths et al, 2005; NAO, 2006d). Personal advisors are seen as being more effective, friendlier and more relaxed than previous provision. In general, users feel listened to and respected. The personal advisor–client relationship is seen as central to the effectiveness of the government's employment policy, especially for older people and disabled people (NAO, 2006d; Stafford et al, 2007). Nevertheless, there is a degree of ambiguity about the scope and nature of the personal advisor's role and some users have mixed views about the service they receive.

One of the main tasks of personal advisors is to identify clients' needs and any barriers to labour market participation (DSS, 1998; NAO, 2006d). However, the scope of this could range from a narrow focus on work-related issues to a more 'holistic' approach that examines the wider social and economic needs of the individual (Lewis et al, 2000); although personal advisors tend to provide a service more narrowly focused on work outcomes, especially for (non-Jobseeker's Allowance [JSA]) users with complex needs (Kelleher et al, 2002).

Delivering work-focused interviews can be problematic (Kelleher et al, 2002; Osgood et al, 2002). Early meetings with users tend to concentrate on their claim for benefit, and work-related issues are generally neglected. Indeed, for existing (as opposed to new) users they can be used to reassure individuals that there is no pressure on them to return to work (Dixon et al, 2007). The work-focus element tends to be limited to collating basic details and undertaking a job search for users; there is no systematic assessment of users' employability (Kelleher et al, 2002; Osgood et al, 2002). This is because of limited time and, as might be expected, sorting out the claim is the primary focus of users. Nevertheless, some users are disappointed because there is no discussion of training opportunities.

In addition, some users have expressed concerns over the appropriateness of the timing of work-focused interviews for disabled people and carers (Coleman et al, 2004, 2005), and have mixed views on whether they should be mandatory (Dixon et al, 2007).

A personalised service means that users may have to be referred to specialist help and support services. However, in practice, the number of referrals by personal advisors can be relatively low because advisors may (Stafford, 2003; Griffiths et al, 2003b):

- be reluctant to give up exclusive 'ownership' of a client;
- not want their clients to undergo another familiarisation and orientation process with someone else;
- be unaware of the full range of services available locally;
- lack the assessment skills to identify the need for a referral;
- believe that a provider will impose a course of action that does not address the person's needs;
- be confronted by an inadequate supply of the desired provision; and
- know that some providers have a reputation for delivering a poor-quality service.

As a consequence, some users are directed by personal advisors towards Jobcentre Plus in-house provision (Griffiths et al, 2003a).

There is an element of individualisation to work-focused interviews as an assessment of labour market circumstances and needs is conducted with the user and tailormade services are provided (Millar, 2003). Moreover, there is a potential trade-off between staff delivering a personalised, individualised service and a 'collective customer service' (Talbot et al, 2005). The former involves spending time with each user to establish their needs and providing a range of information, advice and support. The latter involves attempting to provide a service to all customers, dealing with their concerns quickly and minimising queues in the office. While the former would, for instance, mean not answering the telephone during the course of an interview, the latter would. Frontline staff can prioritise collective service provision, effectively delivering a quick and efficient service rather than the more tailored, individualised service implied by personalisation.

Personalising employment programmes, by definition, entails decision makers exercising more discretion. Indeed, the DWP has been explicit about giving more discretionary powers to advisors in order to secure a more flexible service (see DWP, 2004). However, where people do not receive services as a (social) right, service provision can be inequitable, the decision-making process can appear to be arbitrary (a postcode lottery), and it can add to the complexity of the benefit system.

There is also the risk that increased flexibility in employment programmes will mainly benefit users who are closer to the labour market because they are easier to help compared with the 'harder to reach' (such as ex-offenders and homeless people) (Griffiths et al, 2003a, 2003b). This risk is greater where advisors have job entry targets and/or contracted providers have performance-related funding regimes where payments are tied to securing (sustainable) job entries. Users further from the labour market may be referred by contracted providers back to Jobcentre Plus or to other services (such as drug counselling services).

Personalisation may also be adversely affected by high advisor caseloads. There is some evidence that high caseloads (say, over 40) adversely affect the quality and effectiveness of service provided by some advisors because they lack the time to spend with users and/or to carry out activities (such as contacting employers) on their behalf (Joyce and Pettigrew, 2002; Stafford et al, 2007).

Telephony

In recent years users have increasingly dealt with social security services by telephone (NAO, 2006c; SSAC, 2007). Call centres and helplines have been established for a wide range of services, notably child support, disability and carers, and Jobcentre Plus and pension services (see Chapter Sixteen, Hudson, this volume). Conducting business with social security agencies by telephone has been associated with users having high assessments of the quality of service and high satisfaction levels compared to other modes of contact (Stafford, 2003; Coleman et al, 2005; NAO, 2006c). Call centres provide easier and more convenient access to some services as well as faster processing of claims (NAO, 2006c). However, there are also disadvantages to telephone contacts: users can have insufficient time to reflect before having to answer questions; getting through can be difficult; and the cost of a call can be high if using a mobile phone (Stafford, 2003; NAO, 2006c; Social Fund Commissioner, 2007; SSAC, 2007). In addition, some people with specific communication barriers, such as hearing impairments or users whose first language is not English, have reported difficulties in contacting Jobcentre Plus by telephone; although some prefer to use it because it reduces communication barriers (Hay and Slater, 2007).

Increased use of compulsion

For the population of working age there has been an increase in the use of compulsion, with claimants required to attend a work-focused interview at the beginning of their claim for out-of-work benefits (see Chapter Eleven, Wright, this volume). This does not mean that non-JSA recipients have to seek work, merely that they are required to discuss work-related matters with a personal advisor. (Recipients of JSA continue to have to be available for work and actively seeking work.) Mandatory work-focused interviews are seen as providing immediate help and support to those who otherwise might become dependent on benefits. However, mandatory interviews may overemphasise attitudinal and motivational barriers to work at the expense of other more 'real' obstacles (Bennett and Walker, 1998). There is also the risk of the interview being counterproductive and demotivating if the personal advisor fails to manage it sensitively and/or the user feels that the advisor lacks sufficient knowledge about relevant issues, such as benefits or the local labour market.

This increase in the use of compulsion for those out of the labour market is an example of 'creeping conditionality' in UK welfare (Dwyer, 2004); arguably, a form of social control by the state. Nevertheless, Labour has continually stressed the rights and responsibilities of users of social security – in particular that the unemployed should find paid work.

Benefit simplification

A complex social security system will give users a poor quality of service and risks stigmatising them. The potentially adverse consequences for users include (CPAG, 2007):

- lower take-up of benefits and tax credits and/or reduced savings for pensions because entitlement rules are not understood (NAO, 2005);
- unintended errors by both users and staff;
- delays in processing claims and so possibly financial hardship for those claiming a benefit or tax credit.

For users, complexity in the social security system arises from a number of factors including the interactions arising from claims for more than one benefit, conflicting and too detailed rules and entitlements, and having circumstances and needs that require regular contact with an agency and/or dealings with more than one agency (NAO, 2005).

However, radical reform of the system, to produce a simpler one, is not necessarily in the best interests of all users. Benefit complexity has partly arisen because governments have wanted a 'rule based system that is equitable and accessible and … [safeguards] the system against abuse' (NAO, 2005, p 8). A degree of complexity is necessary if the system is to be sensitive to people's varying needs and situations (CPAG, 2007). Indeed, the introduction of some regulations (or complexity) can benefit some users (NAO, 2005). Moreover, a simpler system might be more discretionary, and this can lead to arbitrary decision making by officials (CPAG, 2007). Nonetheless, some commentators suggest that there is a case for more simplification of the system (DWP, nd; NAO, 2005; CPAG, 2007; Work and Pensions Committee, 2007).

The DWP has made some progress in simplifying the benefit system, for example, a 26-page HB/CTB claim form for Pension Credit claimants has been reduced to three pages (DWP, nd). While many of the measures taken relate to the alignment of benefits (Work and Pensions Committee, 2007), which may make the administration of benefits easier for staff, it does not follow that the social security system is any easier to comprehend or to access for users, although processing times may be cut and hence benefits paid more quickly. The approach to simplification adopted so far is ad hoc and reactive rather than involving a systematic review across benefits (Work and Pensions Committee, 2007). This incremental approach means that there has been no real attempt to change the underlying structure of the benefit system (for instance, by merging working-age benefits; see Freud, 2007).

Delivery by local authorities

Local authorities administer HB and CTB on behalf of the DWP. Although legislation details national entitlement and benefit rates and there are national performance standards, local authorities have a relatively high degree of discretion in administering the benefits. They can, for instance, procure computer systems from different suppliers. As a consequence, local authorities do differ in the way in which they deliver HB and CTB (Stafford et al, 1999; Boath et al, 2007). For example, while all authorities accept a postal claim for benefit, 10% allow an electronic claim and 2% permit a claim by telephone (Durrant et al, 2007).

Critics have highlighted the wide variation in local authorities' performance in delivering HB and CTB (Audit Commission, 1999). For instance, the speed with which claims are processed varies considerably (Stafford et al, 2000). This means that users receive a different quality of service depending on where they live. But it can be argued that benefit delivery by local authority offers:

- increased democracy and local accountability – although benefit administration is rarely an election issue;

- the opportunity for local politicians and managers to adapt delivery to the local social and economic environment and to the size and composition of the caseload.

Consumers or users?

The DWP emphasises that it is 'relentlessly customer-focused' (DWP, nd, p 25) and wants 'to meet customers' needs in the round' (p 15). These statements reflect wider governmental calls that public services must be more customer focused (see, for instance, OPSR, 2002; HM Treasury, 2007; PMSU, 2007).

However, the DWP seeks to achieve this customer focus largely through '*customer insight*', which is based on evidence and understanding of users' experiences, needs and views obtained from staff and key stakeholders (for instance, suppliers and partner organisations) (DWP, nd; Cabinet Office, 2007) – but, crucially, it does not explicitly involve social security users themselves. This is despite empowering service users being an explicit objective of (wider) public service reform (HM Treasury, 2007; PMSU, 2007). Giving users more of a 'voice' is seen as building upon the introduction of more personalised services and, alongside choice, is designed to help promote the reform of public services.

User involvement implies some form of participation by customers in the provision and delivery of services and a change to the governance of social security: it is a participatory form of democracy; its objectives are to give individuals and the wider community a collective 'voice' and some control over the decisions being made.

Hirschman (1970) points out that individuals dissatisfied with the provision of a good or service can remain loyal to the provider organisation, voice their dissatisfaction, or exit and transfer their custom elsewhere. In social security a voluntary exit and private insurance is possible, but this may entail financial and other hardships, so that for most people there is no real alternative except 'voice' and 'loyalty'. Consumerism as it has developed in the UK public sector is an attempt to redress the imbalance of power between providers and receivers of services through giving customers a voice in service provision and delivery. However, social security managers determine delivery priorities and service standards; there is insufficient engagement with users on defining service quality. In other areas of social policy, for example social housing and social care, users can be more actively involved in decision making.

There are various consultative arrangements between the DWP and users, for example ministers and senior staff meet user representatives and hold regular liaison and consultation meetings with groups such as Age Concern and Citizens Advice. While these links are to be welcomed, they constitute a limited form of user engagement. However, there are some exceptions: Swift et al (1994) and NCC et al (1999) document examples of user involvement and more recently the Pension Service is a leading partner in the LinkAge Plus pilot, which involves older people in the design of services. The Work and Pensions Select Committee has recently called for more user participation (Work and Pensions Committee, 2007, p 30). Such a development is not unproblematic, especially as it implies a shift in power from managers to users (and frontline staff) and a degree of conflict and 'passion' if a tokenistic participation or consultation exercise is to be avoided (Newman, 2000; Stafford, 2003; Miller, 2004; Carr, 2007). It also requires resources and sensitive methods of engagement if those (more articulate) groups with informational (or cultural) capital are not to dominate proceedings and the socially excluded and more vulnerable members of the community are not to be marginalised or ignored (Cowden and Singh, 2007). Some may not be able to articulate their needs, others may not wish to be involved, or may psychologically be unable to do so (Miller, 2004).

Overview

In summary, the individual users of the social security system are a large and very diverse population. Some users are more confident and competent than others when dealing with the system.

There are a number of problems with the delivery of social security that largely arise from its complexity, the diverse nature of the user population and the organisationally disjointed nature of provision.

The key themes that underpin recent policy initiatives to modernise service delivery are:

- the increased emphasis on the personalised delivery of services;
- the expansion of telephony;
- the introduction of the requirement that most people of working age making new or renewed claims for out-of-work benefits must attend a work-focused interview as a condition of benefit entitlement;
- ad hoc attempts to simplify the benefit system.

From one perspective the government's agenda has been radical. However, its approach to reform remains consumerist and there are persuasive arguments for greater user involvement in social security policy making. There are also formidable obstacles, but other public services have successfully addressed these and found ways of ensuring that users participate in decision making on service delivery issues.

Questions for discussion

(1) How far should the government go in tailoring employment services to the needs of individual users? What factors might limit the extent to which services can be personalised?
(2) Should the delivery of social security be primarily concerned with ensuring 'the right amount of benefit, first time, every time', or are there other objectives in the delivery of welfare services?
(3) What factors do policy makers need to consider when designing systems for the delivery of social security?

Website resources

www.cabinetoffice.gov.uk/public_service_reform.aspx
Cabinet Office – public sector reforms (general)
http://archive.cabinetoffice.gov.uk/opsr/public_service_reform/Archive
Cabinet Office – public sector reforms (general – archive)
www.scotland.gov.uk/Topics/Government/PublicServiceReform
Public sector reforms – Scotland
http://wales.gov.uk/about/strategy/makingtheconnections/?lang=en
Public sector reforms – Wales

Delivery organisations

www.dwp.gov.uk/resourcecentre/corporate-publications.asp
Department for Work and Pensions
www.jobcentreplus.gov.uk/JCP/Aboutus/Publications/index.html
Jobcentre Plus
www.thepensionservice.gov.uk/aboutus/home.asp
Pension Service
www.dwp.gov.uk/lifeevent/benefits/dcs/
Disability and Carers Service
www.csa.gov.uk/en/about/index.asp
Child Support Agency
www.hmrc.gov.uk/about/reports.htm
HMRC
www.osscsc.gov
Social Security and Child Support Commissioners

References

Audit Commission (1999) *Fraud and lodging: Progress in tackling fraud and error in Housing Benefit*, London: Audit Commission.

Bailey, L. and Pryes, J. (1996) *Communications with the Benefits Agency*, DSS In-house Report 20, London: DSS.

Bennett, F. and Walker, R. (1998) *Working with Work: An initial assessment of welfare to work*, York: Joseph Rowntree Foundation/York Publishing Services.

Boath, M., Hogg, V. and Wilkinson, H. (2007) *Benefits administration performance*, DWP Research Report No 465, Leeds: CDS.

Cabinet Office (1999) *Modernising government*, Cm 4310, London: The Stationery Office.

Cabinet Office (2007) *Establishing an effective customer insight capability in public sector organizations*, London: Cabinet Office.

Carr, S. (2007) 'Participation, power, conflict and change: theorizing dynamics of service user participation in the social care system of England and Wales', *Critical Social Policy*, vol 27, no 2, pp 266-76.

Clarke, J., Newman, J., Smith, N., Vidler, E. and Westmarland, L. (2007) *Creating citizen-consumers: Changing publics and changing public services*, London: Sage Publications.

Coleman, N., Rousseau, N. and Carpenter, H. (2004) *Jobcentre Plus Service Delivery Survey (Wave 1)*, DWP Research Report No 223, Leeds: CDS.

Coleman, N., Kennedy, E. and Carpenter, H. (2005) *Jobcentre Plus Service Delivery Survey Wave Two: Findings from quantitative research*, DWP Research Report No 284, Leeds: CDS.

Committee of Public Accounts (2007) *Tax credits*, Twenty-Second Report of Session 2006-07, HC 487, London: The Stationery Office.

Cowden, S. and Singh, G. (2007) 'The "user": friend, foe or fetish? A critical exploration of user involvement in health and social care', *Critical Social Policy*, vol 27, no 1, pp 5-23.

CPAG (Child Poverty Action Group) (2007) *Benefit simplification*, London: CPAG.

Dixon, J., Mitchell, M. and Dickens, S. (2007) *Pathways to work: Extension to existing customers (matched case study)*, DWP Research Report No 418, Leeds: CDS.

DSS (Department of Social Security) (1997) 'Harriet Harmon sets out plans to transform delivery of social security', DSS Press Release, 22 July.

DSS (1998) *New ambitions for our country: A new contract for welfare*, Cm 3805, London: The Stationery Office.

Durrant, C., Winter, E. and Yaxley, D. (2007) *Local Authority Omnibus Wave Fourteen*, DWP Research Report No 440, Leeds: CDS.

DWP (Department for Work and Pensions) (nd) *Department for Work and Pensions simplification plan 2007-08*, London: DWP.

DWP (2004) *Building on New Deal: Local solutions meeting individual needs*, London: DWP.

DWP (2007a) *Child Support Agency quarterly summary statistics: September 2007*, www.dwp.gov.uk/asd/asd1/child_support/csa_quarterly_sep07.asp

DWP (2007b) *Annual report by the Secretary of State for Work and Pensions on the Social Fund 2006/2007*, Cm 7161, London: The Stationery Office.

DWP (2007c) *In work, better off: Next steps to full employment*, Cm 7130, London: The Stationery Office.

DWP (2007d) *DWP commissioning strategy: Interim report*, London: DWP.

Dwyer, P. (2004) *Understanding social citizenship*, Bristol: The Policy Press.

Finn, D., Mason, D., Rahim, N. and Casebourne, J. (2008) *Problems in the delivery of benefits, tax credits and employment services*, York: Joseph Rowntree Foundation.

Freud, D. (2007) *Reducing dependency, increasing opportunity: Options for the future of welfare to work*, DWP Report, Leeds: CDS.

Griffiths, R., Irving, P. and McKenna, K. (2003a) *Synthesising the evidence on flexible delivery*, DWP Research Report W171, Sheffield: DWP.

Griffiths, R., Irving, P. and McKenna, K. (2003b) *New Deal for Young People: Introducing a more 'tailored' approach*, DWP Research Report W164, Sheffield: DWP.

Griffiths, R., Stuart Durkin, S. and Mitchell, A. (2005) *Evaluation of the single provider Employment Zone extension*, DWP Research Report No 312, Leeds: CDS.

Hawkins, J., Goldstone, C. and Bhagat, M. (2007) *Knowing and understanding disability and carers service customers*, DWP Research Report No 439, Leeds: CDS.

Hay, C. and Slater, A. (2007) *The use of Jobcentre Plus telephony and face-to-face first contact services by customers with specific communication barriers*, DWP Research Report No 446, Leeds: CDS.

Hirschman, A. (1970) *Exit, voice and loyalty: Responses to decline in firms, organisations and states*, London: Harvard University Press.

HM Government (2007) *Service transformation agreement*, London: HM Treasury.

HM Treasury (2007) *Meeting the aspirations of the British people: 2007 Pre-Budget report and Comprehensive Spending Review*, Cm 7227, London: The Stationery Office.

HMRC (Her Majesty's Revenue & Customs) (2007a) *Child benefit statistics: Quarterly statistics August 2007*, London: HMRC.

HMRC (2007b) *Child and Working Tax Credits statistics: Finalised annual awards 2005–06*, London: HMRC.

Johnson, S. and Fidler, Y. (2006) *Jobcentre Plus customer satisfaction: Ethnic minority booster survey 2005*, DWP Research Report No 338, Leeds: CDS.

Joyce, L. and Pettigrew, N. (2002) *Personal advisers in New Deal 25+ and Employment Zones*, DWP Research Report W139, Sheffield: DWP.

Joyce, L. and Whiting, K. (2006) *Sanctions: Qualitative summary report on lone parent customers*, DWP Working Paper No 27, Leeds: CDS.

Kelleher, J., Youll, P., Nelson, A., Hadjivassiliou, K., Lyons, C. and Hills, J. (2002) *Delivering a work-focused service: Final findings from ONE case studies and staff research*, DWP Research Report No 166, Leeds: CDS.

Kelly, G., Williams, B., Howat, B. and Kay, S. with Scheer, R. (2004) *The Pension Service Customer Survey 2003*, DWP Research Report No 205, Leeds: CDS.

Lewis, J., Mitchell, L., Sanderson, T., O'Connor, W. and Clayden, M. (2000) *Lone parents and personal advisers: Roles and relationships*, DSS Research Report No 122, Leeds: CDS.

Ling, T. (1994) 'Case study: the Benefits Agency – claimants as customers', in H. Tam (ed) *Marketing, competition and the public sector: Key trends and issues*, Harlow: Longmans.

Millar, J. (2003) 'Squaring the circle? Means testing and individualisation in the UK and Australia', *Social Policy and Society*, vol 3, no 1, pp 67-74.

Miller, P. (2004) *Producing welfare: A modern agenda*, Basingstoke: Palgrave Macmillan.

NAO (National Audit Office) (2005) *Dealing with complexity of the benefits system*, HC 592, London: The Stationery Office.

NAO (2006a) *Child Support Agency – Implementation of the child support reforms: Executive Summary*, HC 1174, London: The Stationery Office.

NAO (2006b) *Using leaflets to communicate with the public about services and entitlements*, HC 797, London: The Stationery Office.

NAO (2006c) *Delivering effective services through contact centres*, HC 941, London: The Stationery Office.

NAO (2006d) *Jobcentre Plus: Delivering effective services through personal advisers*, HC 24, London: The Stationery Office.

National Statistics (2007) *Annual abstract of statistics 2007 edition*, Basingstoke: Palgrave Macmillan.

NCC (National Consumer Council), Consumer Congress and Cabinet Office (1999) *Involving users: Improving the delivery of benefits*, London: Cabinet Office.

Newman, J. (2000) 'Beyond the new public management? Modernising public services', in J. Clarke, S. Gewirtz and E. McLaughlin (eds) *New managerialism new welfare?*, London: Sage Publications, pp 45-61.

OPSR (Office of Public Services Reform) (2002) *Reforming our public services: Principles into practice*, London: OPSR.

Osgood, J., Stone, V. and Thomas, A. (2002) *Delivering a work-focused service: Views and experience of clients*, DWP Research Report No 167, Leeds: CDS.

Parliamentary and Health Service Ombudsman (2007) *Tax credits: Getting it wrong?*, HC 1010, London: The Stationery Office.

PMDU (Prime Minister's Delivery Unit) (2007) *Capability review of the Department for Work and Pensions*, London: Cabinet Office.

PMSU (Prime Minister's Strategy Unit) (2006) *The UK government's approach to public service reform: A discussion paper*, London: Cabinet Office.

PMSU (2007) *Building on progress: Public services*, London: Cabinet Office.

Sanderson, I., Fidler, Y. and Wymer, P. (2005) *Jobcentre Plus National Customer Satisfaction Survey 2005*, DWP Research Report No 282, Leeds: CDS.

Social Fund Commissioner (2007) *Social Fund Commissioner's annual report 2006/2007*, Leeds: CDS.

SSAC (Social Security Advisory Committee) (2007) *Telephony in DWP and its agencies: Call costs and equality of access*, Social Security Advisory Committee Occasional Paper No 3, www.ssac.org.uk/pdf/occasional/SSAC_paper_on_call_costs_paper_3.pdf

Stafford, B. (2003) 'Service delivery and the user', in J. Millar (ed) *Understanding social security: Issues for policy and practice*, first edition, Bristol: The Policy Press, pp 213-34.

Stafford, B., Vincent, J., Walker, R. and Beach, J. (1999) *The Beacon Council Scheme: Modern service delivery: Improving Housing Benefit and Council Tax Benefit administration – output 2*, CRSP Working Paper No 373, Loughborough: CRSP.

Stafford, B., Adelman, L., Trickey, H. and Ashworth, K. (2000) *Housing Benefit administration and the speed of claims processing*, DSS In-house Report 69, London: DSS.

Stafford, B. et al (2007) *New Deal for Disabled People: Third synthesis report – key findings from the evaluation*, DWP Research Report No 430, Leeds: CDS.

Swift, P., Grant, G. and McGrath, M. (1994) *Participation in the social security system*, Aldershot: Avebury.

Talbot, C., Wiggan, J., Hendey, N., Rafferty, A., Calcraft, R., Freestone, M. and Wyatt, B. (2005) *Jobcentre Plus customer service performance and delivery: A qualitative review*, DWP Research Report No 276, Leeds: CDS.

Varney, D. (2006) *Service transformation: A better service for citizens and businesses, a better deal for the taxpayer*, London: HM Treasury.

Work and Pensions Committee (2007) *Benefits simplification*, Seventh Report of Session 2006–07, Volume 1, HC 463-1, London: The Stationery Office.

The 'welfare market': private sector delivery of benefits and employment services

Dan Finn

Summary

Since the 1980s successive governments have transformed the traditional public sector bureaucracies that deliver benefits and employment services. This chapter assesses the role that private and third sector providers now play in the delivery of the government's welfare-to-work strategy.

- It discusses the creation of a new 'welfare market' where a core of 'prime contractors' will deliver services directly or through other providers and be paid largely according to the number of people they place in sustained employment.
- It reviews the evolution of the contracting regime that has been used to steer the work of these agencies and considers evidence on the impacts that such market delivery has had on the experience and prospects of participants.
- It also reviews evidence on the quasi-market welfare-to-work delivery systems in Australia and the US, which British reforms are intended to emulate.

Introduction

Successive British governments have reformed both the formal objectives of the welfare state and the ways in which policies are implemented. In addition to its traditional remit of assessing eligibility for and paying income-related benefits, the social security system now is expected to play a far greater role in preparing working-age people for, and connecting them to, the labour market. The objective is to create an active benefit system that connects people with work, reinforces work incentives and reduces costs and 'welfare dependency' (see Chapter Eleven, Wright, this volume).

There are three core components of the welfare-to-work strategy. The first element involves extending job search and work preparation requirements to lone parents and people with health problems and disabilities. The second is to 'make work pay' through tax credits, a National Minimum Wage (NMW) and a variety of other services to assist with childcare and the transition into work. The final element is the development and implementation of a wide range of employment programmes and their delivery through contracts with for-profit private companies and through the non-profit and voluntary organisations now frequently characterised as being part of the 'third sector'.

The strategy has been developed by ministers and senior civil servants in the Treasury and Department for Work and Pensions (DWP). It is implemented through a redesigned delivery system that has integrated the previously separate Employment Service (ES) and Benefits Agency (BA) into 'Jobcentre Plus'. Benefit claims and payments are administered by a network of contact centres and benefit delivery offices. Employment services and the monitoring and enforcement of activity requirements are handled through a network of over 800 frontline Jobcentres. These offices have been modernised and designed to reinforce the principle that everyone has an obligation to support themselves, in particular through paid employment (NAO, 2008). More intensive employment programmes, including most components of the New Deals for the unemployed, are delivered under contract through an extensive network of non-profit and for-profit providers.

The contracted-out employment services system has the characteristics of a 'quasi-market' where the state has separated out its roles as both purchaser and provider of public services (Le Grand, 2002). These arrangements resemble markets because they induce competition between different service providers which may be for-profit, non-profit or independent entities within the public sector. They are 'quasi-markets' because, unlike ordinary markets, purchasing power comes not directly from consumers but from the state. Advocates of such market-based provision suggest that it allows the public sector to focus on those things it does well, for example policy management and ensuring continuity and stability of services, while drawing on the strengths of the for-profit and third sectors. Private providers are thought to be better at 'innovating, replicating successful experiments, adapting to rapid change, abandoning unsuccessful or obsolete activities and performing complex or technical tasks' (Osborne and Gaebler, 1993, p 46). The diverse, mainly non-profit, organisations that comprise the third sector are characterised by value-driven 'social missions' and have a capacity to build social capital and better meet and reflect the needs of disadvantaged individuals and groups.

British policy makers now anticipate that competition in the delivery of employment programmes in a 'welfare market' will lead to service innovation, improved accountability, better job outcomes, greater value for money and better 'customer service' (DWP, 2008a). The next section of the chapter traces the increased role of the private sector, in particular since the 1980s.

Public sector reform and the role of the private sector

The welfare state in its broadest sense has always delivered services through a 'mixed economy of welfare', consisting of public, voluntary and private sector organisations (Powell, 2007). After 1945, however, the role of the private and voluntary sector diminished. Service delivery and administration were entrusted to hierarchical public sector bureaucracies. By the 1980s these institutions were under attack. Critics argued that state bureaucracies were provider dominated and interested primarily in promoting the growth of their own budgets, responsibilities, status and job security. As large monopoly providers they offered poor value for money and gave insufficient attention to the needs and experience of service users. There was also a lack of clear accountability for expenditure and performance (Butcher, 1995).

In the 1980s Conservative governments sought to reduce public expenditure, diminish the role of the public sector and introduce market mechanisms into the delivery of public services. Welfare state agencies were required to sell assets, 'contract out' services and apply market principles to their operations. One key feature of reform was a radical change in the role of the Civil Service. From the late 1980s its traditional dual role of providing advice and implementing policies was split. Executive agencies were 'hived off' across central government with the aim of creating a more businesslike culture; other services were contracted out to the private sector. As part of this reform process, emphasis was placed on meeting the needs of users and publicly monitoring service delivery targets.

The chief executives and Boards of these new agencies, such as the ES and the BA, had operational freedom but remained 'steered' by central government departments through performance targets and budgets. The BA was responsible for the assessment and administration of all state benefits and a national network of local offices. The ES was responsible for delivering unemployment benefits and for providing employment-related services through Jobcentres and contracts with private providers. The work of the Civil Service staff employed in both agencies was increasingly reorganised to better meet both financial and performance targets.

From their inception the ES and the BA were under constant pressure to reduce operating costs and obtain better value for money (Butcher, 1995; Fletcher, 1997). Benefit delivery systems were restructured, making greater use of computerisation. The agencies were required to undergo 'market tests' and to contract out services if they could be delivered more cheaply by the private sector. Many components of service delivery were contracted out, ranging from the relatively routine, such as cleaning and security, through to the more complex, such as medical assessments for disability benefits and the information technology systems used to deliver benefits and office processes.

Both the BA and the ES retained direct control and were accountable for frontline user contacts with their services. The ES, for example, retained control of advisory interviews, job-broking and vacancy placement, and outright privatisation was not considered feasible (Price, 2000, p 304). By 1996, however, the ES had withdrawn from most direct employment programme provision for the longer-term unemployed and these services were contracted out via competitive tendering to a diverse range of private providers including for-profit and voluntary sector organisations, colleges, local government and religious groups.

The modernisation process in the BA culminated in the 'Change Programme' in 1996. It included the proposed use of telephone call centres for 'first contacts' with claimants; an appointment-based system for interviews and a market test that involved a 'purchaser–provider' split, which would allow the private and voluntary sector to be involved in benefit delivery (Allbeson, 1997). In 1998 the Department for Social Security (DSS) also transferred ownership of all its offices and property to a private company in a 'Private Finance Initiative' deal known as 'PRIME' (NAO, 2005). This was designed to raise money and give its executive agencies more flexibility through paying rents. By 2008 the successor DWP owned almost no physical assets, with all property, information technology and telephone technology being outsourced and paid for through rent and service charges (DWP, 2008b).

Many of the developments envisaged in the Change Programme were eclipsed by the 1997 election of the Labour government, committed to its own approach to welfare reform and public services. The new Secretary of State for Social Security suggested that the government would adopt a 'non-ideological approach to the best way of delivering public services', in contrast with the 'public bad; private good' mantra of the previous administration (Harman, 1997, col 9).

Subsequent public sector reforms dropped an 'automatic preference for private service delivery' but they have still favoured the injection of market-based values and practices in the management and delivery of public services (Grimshaw et al, 2002, p 480). Another significant change is that such reform has taken place alongside increased public sector investment. The ambition of policy makers has been both to get value for money, by keeping costs down, and to engineer a fundamental change in service design and delivery with a strong emphasis on 'customer service'. This represents 'a significant change in interpretation of the role of the market in public sector delivery' (Entwhistle and Martin, 2005, p 239).

The New Deals and Jobcentre Plus

In 1997 New Deal employment programmes and 'make work pay' policies were implemented swiftly. The core principle of Labour's New Deal for unemployed people in receipt of Jobseeker's Allowance (JSA) is that individuals are guaranteed intensive employment assistance after a particular duration of unemployment. At a certain point all claimants without a job must, as a condition for receiving benefit, participate in a full-time employment activity (this may include work experience or short periods in subsidised employment). Other, less intensive, voluntary New Deal programmes were targeted at lone parents, disabled people and unemployed people aged 50+.

The key service delivery innovation was the introduction of New Deal personal advisors who, like case managers in other countries, provide a more tailored service by assessing employment barriers, developing an individual action plan and providing job search assistance. These advisors also refer participants to support programmes delivered by externally contracted providers.

In addition to developing its New Deal programmes, in 1998 the government announced more radical proposals to develop a 'single work-focused gateway' to the benefit system. A culture change would be induced through the introduction of compulsory 'work-focused interviews' requiring all working-age claimants to engage with the employment assistance available. The aim of the 'gateway' was to bring together the separate work of the ES, the BA and local authorities and to provide personal advisors for all working-age claimants. Three different models of what was then called the 'ONE' service were tested in pilot areas. These were: a 'basic model', a 'call centre' variant and a version delivered by private and voluntary sector organisations.

In 2002 responsibility for delivering what was now characterised as the 'employment first' welfare state was given to the newly created DWP and Jobcentre Plus, an executive agency that integrated the ES and the BA (but not local authorities). The subsequent modernisation of Jobcentre Plus services cost over £2 billion and involved major changes in working practices, including the redesign of local offices and the extensive use of call centres to accept benefit claims and administer payments (NAO, 2008).

Increased investment in the New Deals and frontline service delivery was paralleled by the government's objective of ensuring efficiency by benchmarking public sector performance against that of the private sector. As it developed new services the government contracted out to private and voluntary sector organisations to learn from the innovations and to put competitive pressure on mainstream public agencies. In addition to the ONE private sector variant, external organisations were contracted to deliver a range of employment programmes. Some of these experiments were designed to stimulate innovation in the New Deals. Others tested new ways of delivering services to workless people with significant employment barriers, as with the private sector 'job brokers' who delivered the New Deal for Disabled People (NDDP).

Contracting with employment programme providers: the transition to job outcome payments

In the late 1970s and early 1980s large-scale employment and training programmes were rapidly introduced and expanded in response to significant increases in youth and long-term unemployment. Many of these initiatives were delivered by external contractors, especially in the non-profit sector. When these were found to be relatively ineffective, the focus shifted towards intensive short-term job search and training programmes, designed to complement what was known as the 'stricter benefit regime' for the unemployed. By the late 1980s participation in such programmes had become compulsory for the young and the long-term unemployed.

Initially, external contractors were paid to provide work experience or training places for participants. Funding methodologies were reformed to ensure that providers were paid only for participants who attended. Subsequently, greater emphasis was placed on how many participants providers helped to obtain jobs and/or qualifications. The most radical development happened in 1988 when responsibility for purchasing training programmes for the unemployed was transferred from the public sector to a national network of local Training and Enterprise Councils (TECs). These independent, employer-led companies were funded increasingly on the basis of achieved training or employment outcomes, a funding system they also used with the subcontractors through whom they delivered locally (Jones, 1999). The ES continued to separately purchase job search and work experience programmes but it also placed greater emphasis on the job outcomes secured by providers.

After 1997 the ES was given lead responsibility for the delivery of the New Deals and TECs were replaced by a new national Learning and Skills Council (LSC) responsible for distributing funding for all post-compulsory-school-age education and training (apart from higher education). The ES (subsequently Jobcentre Plus) and the LSC had different employment- or training-related targets but both continued to deliver most of their programmes through contracts with a range of public, private and voluntary sector organisations.

The market evolved further when ministers revised policy objectives to harness what they considered to be the innovative skills, practices and finances of private for-profit organisations. The first indication of a new approach was in 1998 when private sector organisations were invited to run Labour's flagship programme, the New Deal for Young People (NDYP), eventually catering for about 10% of participants. This was followed by other contracted-out initiatives with the most radical of the experiments taking place in 'Employment Zones' (EZs) (see ***Box 15.1***).

Box 15.1: Employment Zones

The EZs were established in 2000 in 15 areas of high unemployment. Providers were paid a fee for completing an action plan with each participant but most of their income depended on getting people into employment that was sustained for at least 13 weeks.

Subsequently, the number of zones was rationalised and by 2007 there were seven 'single provider' zones (where the contractor has a monopoly of provision) and six 'multiple provider' zones (where several contractors compete with each other). There are now seven organisations that deliver EZ contracts, nearly all of which are for-profit businesses.

The EZs were not designed to provide a direct comparison between state and private delivery of employment services, as the New Deal is also in part delivered by contractors. However, the EZs could be used to assess whether contractors could deliver better outcomes when they have more flexibility to design their own interventions rather than following the more prescriptive sequence of employment assistance available in the standard New Deals.

The evidence on outcomes is mixed: see further discussion below.

There were changes too in the contracting regime for the mainstream New Deals. In 2006 new contracts placed greater emphasis on price competition and job outcome payments, and fewer organisations were given contracts. In place of 1,000 individual contracts the New Deals are delivered through 94 'prime contracts', of which 53 are for-profit, 27 are non-profit and 14 are public sector organisations (DWP, 2007a). These 'prime contractors' are expected to manage delivery in their district, working with more specialist subcontractors where necessary.

The prime contractor model was further extended to the delivery of 'Pathways to Work', an employment programme targeted at people receiving Incapacity Benefit (IB). 'Pathways' was initially delivered by Jobcentre Plus in partnership with the National Health Service (NHS) but its extension to the remaining two thirds of the country in 2008 was exclusively contracted out to private and third sector organisations. A small number of prime contractors, most of whom are for-profit, will have greater flexibility in how they deliver the programme and will be paid largely on the basis of getting people into jobs that are sustained for at least 26 weeks. Participation in Pathways will be mandatory for many of those people with disabilities and health problems who claim Employment and Support Allowance (which replaced IB in October 2008). (See also Chapter Twelve, Sainsbury, this volume.)

By 2006/07 it was clear that a different type of performance-funded regime was emerging in a welfare market which in that year included a national network of some 900 for-profit and non-profit providers delivering employment services, with an estimated contract value of about £950 million (DWP, 2007a, p 28). The key developments were the introduction of prime contractors and a growing emphasis on job outcome-related funding (see ***Box 15.2***).

Box 15.2: Job outcome and performance targets

The UK government assesses the performance of its welfare-to-work policies primarily in terms of the number of people in different target groups it gets into employment. Each time that Jobcentre Plus assists someone into a job it earns a designated number of points towards the total in its overall annual job outcome target. The points awarded are weighted to clearly signal the priority attached to different groups with, for example, a greater value of points given for getting a lone parent on benefits into a job.

Contracted providers have an additional interest in getting their service users into employment because some or all of the payment they receive may depend on securing a 'job outcome'. The proportion of funding involved varies significantly. In the initial New Deal contracts for the unemployed, for example, only around 10% of payments were linked directly to movement into a job. In EZs the proportion has been much higher. In deciding on the relative value of such job outcome payments for external providers policy makers are seeking to balance the incentives created. If the payment is marginal there may be little incentive for the provider to get a participant into work. If the value is too high the provider may concentrate their efforts only on those easiest to place and give little service to the hardest to help.

The most significant fee for a job outcome is usually paid only when employment has been sustained for a specified period, often set at 13 weeks in the UK, although in some contracts smaller payments may also be made after 26 weeks. This requirement is designed to ensure that providers do not place participants in very short-term jobs. Paradoxically, Jobcentre Plus has no duration requirement and is awarded points for any job outcome. This difference has been criticised because there is little incentive to ensure that Jobcentre Plus staff place service users into longer-lasting jobs, and external providers view it as preferential treatment.

The value of these job outcome performance measures is that they directly reflect the government's priorities, are relatively simple to check and are easy for those delivering welfare-to-work services to understand and relate to their day-to-day work. The difficulty is that they may create perverse incentives and some may be tempted to manipulate their results.

The welfare market

In 2006 and 2007 the Labour government commissioned a series of major high-level reviews of its welfare-to-work and employment policies. These identified the progress made and outlined the policy and implementation options available to the government if it was to realise its new ambition of an 80% employment rate for working-age people (DWP, 2006).

One report explicitly addressed the future role of private sector delivery. It followed a decision by ministers to move towards a 'managed welfare market' and to centralise procurement of all employment programmes within the DWP (Freud, 2007). David Freud, the author of the report, was asked to undertake a long-term review of the government's welfare-to-work strategy. The report proposed a major restructuring of employment programmes and the benefit system and recommended that job search requirements be extended to lone parents. It suggested little change to Jobcentre Plus-delivered work-first services for the short-term unemployed but radical change for the longer-term unemployed and other groups. It recommended that these 'harder-to-help' groups in future should be serviced by private organisations using a model of performance-based contracting (Freud, 2007).

The Freud report stressed, however, that existing contracting arrangements were inadequate. They too often specified process rather than outcome, limiting the value that private providers could add. The contracts had restrictions on recruitment and expenditure that prevented providers from expanding provision or being rewarded for overachievement. Contracts were small scale, had a multiplicity of requirements and start and finish dates, and were too short, discouraging providers from making the investment necessary to improve performance. The report proposed instead a different performance-based model based in part on the lessons from EZs.

The basic principle of the proposed contracts was that the government and providers would share the savings in benefits over a three-year period that accrues when a participant obtains employment. The provider would be paid outcome fees slightly lower than these average benefit savings once a participant achieves certain milestones. Phased payments would be made for sustained employment after 13 weeks, six months and one, two and three years, with additional payments for pay progression and the achievement of vocational qualifications. Successful providers would be awarded seven-year contracts and act as the single prime contractors in each region of Britain, subcontracting as they wished with smaller providers. These 'multi-billion pound' contracts would encourage larger for-profit and non-profit organisations to borrow and invest in advance in service provision knowing they would have an effective monopoly and an income stream from outcome fees over an extended period. Some of the risks associated with investment in employment assistance then could be shifted from government to the private sector. The proposed sequence of outcome payments would ensure also that providers had an incentive to invest in improving the skills and longer-term employability of participants.

The government welcomed Freud's proposals and subsequently the DWP published an overall 'Commissioning Strategy' outlining how the welfare market will be shaped over the next decade. The DWP envisages that it will do '80% of its business' with a 'stable core of reliable' providers capable of delivering multiple contracts across the country (DWP, 2008a, p 10). Smaller providers will act mainly as subcontractors. Successful prime contractors will be awarded contracts that will usually last for five years, with the possibility of two-year extensions. Most of the funding will reward sustained job outcomes for employment that lasts for six months initially, but with the aim of moving beyond this to reward providers if they keep people in employment for a year or 18 months. This will be developed through future experiments with 'alternative reward mechanisms' that will also give incentives to providers to help 'people progress in terms of skills and earnings' (DWP, 2008a, p 22).

The DWP intends to play an active role in managing the market, and local 'supply chains', through contract reviews, inspection and 'intervention'. It plans also to further develop a 'star rating' system by which regular public performance measurement will be used to identify poor performers, determine business allocation and potentially inform user choice. There also will be a process of reintegrating the contracting processes through which the DWP and a proposed adult Skills Funding Agency (which will replace the LSC in England in 2010) procure their respective provision with significant implications for the further development of the British welfare market (DCSF and DIUS, 2008).

The principles of the DWP Commissioning Strategy will be applied first to the 'Flexible New Deal' that will replace all existing New Deal and EZ provision for the JSA unemployed from 2009 (DWP, 2007b). In this new system all JSA jobseekers will be serviced by Jobcentre Plus in the first year of unemployment. After a year claimants will be required to enrol with a specialist return-to-work private provider of which there will be at least two delivering services in most districts.

When announcing the Commissioning Strategy the Secretary of State for Employment emphasised that the government was 'creating a market for the long term' that would 'free' providers 'from central control and allow them to innovate'. The future delivery of employability services through these performance-based contracts represents 'a major milestone in [the] welfare reform programme' and for successful providers 'the rewards will be high, with longer contracts and a growing market' (Purnell, 2008).

There is broad political consensus on the 'direction of travel' represented by the government's development of a welfare market, with the Liberal Democrats' (2007) and Conservative Party's (2008) respective approaches to welfare reform also including further growth of the market. Opposition to the 'marketisation' of welfare reform has been expressed only by a relatively weak coalition of 'back bench' Labour Members of Parliament (MPs), public sector trades unions and some welfare rights groups (Davies, 2006).

The risks involved in contracting out employment services

The literature on the contracting out of public services suggests that there are important consequences for accountability when the direct control previously exercised over staff and levels of service is replaced by indirect control exercised through contracts. There are two particular risks associated with welfare-to-work performance-based contracts. The first is that of 'creaming', where contractors who are paid by results are likely to concentrate their efforts on those participants who are closest to the labour market and more easily placed in a job. The second criticism is that of 'parking' where other participants will receive a bare minimum of services and are unlikely to make any progress while participating in a programme. Arguably, the most disadvantaged – those with the greatest employment barriers – are the most likely to be 'parked'.

Other risks concern the ability to regulate and ensure the quality of the services delivered by profit-seeking agencies; and the potential for market failure, where government has no choice but to intervene and either 'bail out' a failing provider or quickly find an alternative to continue the delivery of services.

The evidence from evaluations of performance-based contracts in the UK is mixed. Private and voluntary sector providers have introduced new approaches, and appear to work well with some claimants, but evidence of greater efficiency or performance is more limited. The EZs, which were subject to continuous quantitative and qualitative evaluation, were found, for example, to have used their flexibilities to improve the 'quality, intensity and customer orientation' of their services and that participants responded (Griffiths and Durkin, 2007, p 34). Evaluations reported that service users preferred the more informal and friendly atmosphere of EZs (in contrast to Jobcentres) and appreciated the intensive and more individual support received. Participants were more likely to report that EZ advisors had been more supportive and more frequently were thought to have influenced the outcome when a job had been obtained. Zone participants also were more likely to suggest that the programme's content had been organised to suit their individual needs, rather than the programme having a 'menu' of activities to which they were directed (Joyce and Pettigrew, 2002).

Other evidence from the EZs indicated that providers concentrated advisor support on those who were the 'key to making profits', with the hardest to help receiving little assistance (Hirst et al, 2002, p vi). This frontline rationing of employment assistance is, however, found also in public sector systems, where advisors must balance the needs of the long-term unemployed, available job opportunities and restricted public funds. This process may be exacerbated by the commercial pressures to which private providers are subject but evaluations found no evidence that EZs achieved their better performance through 'creaming' or through 'parking' clients who were more disadvantaged than did comparator New Deals (Griffiths and Durkin, 2007, pp 57-60).

Impact studies, which measured the relative performance of EZ and New Deal provision in assisting long-term unemployed people to get and keep jobs, reported that EZs performed somewhat better. One DWP study found, for example, that 8% more 25- to 50-year-old EZ participants started jobs, and 10% more retained those jobs at 13 weeks (Griffiths and Durkin, 2007). The studies found that both EZs and New Deals worked best for those with a better employment record and were least effective for those who had no qualifications, were unemployed longer and had an unstable pattern of employment. One study reported that some 20 months after being eligible to participate, almost half the participants in both programmes had spent no time in paid work (Hales et al, 2003).

There has been no equivalent impact evaluation of the performance of EZs that started to recruit lone parents on a voluntary basis after 2003. Broad outcome data reported to Parliament indicated, however, that by the end of 2006, 38% of lone parents who had contact with an EZ advisor had moved into work (*Hansard*, 8 January 2007, col 209W). The cost of helping each lone parent was estimated at £1,900 compared with a cost of £600 for each person helped through the comparable New Deal. The direct comparison may be misleading because EZs work in more disadvantaged areas and with participants who may have been more difficult to place. There had also been design problems with the incentive structure. After these were changed providers began to make greater efforts with this client group. The important point this demonstrated was that 'providers generally innovate where they are financially incentivised to do so' (Griffiths and Durkin, 2007, p 4).

Evaluations of the parallel private sector-delivered NDDP for those on disability benefits found that of the 260,330 voluntary registrations between July 2001 and November 2006, 110,950 (43%) had found jobs by November 2006 (Stafford et al, 2007). Nearly 60% of those who got jobs sustained employment for 13 weeks or more, albeit most entered routine, unskilled occupations. Detailed assessments of financial costs and employment impacts found that the investment in the programme saved the government money and the net social and employment benefits were larger for longer-term than for more recent claimants. Whether these returns will be sustained in future private sector-delivered provision for those on disability benefits has yet to be assessed.

Employment Zone provision for the unemployed may have been estimated to outperform the New Deals for the unemployed but it proved more costly. It is unlikely that the government will be as generous in the design of its future contracts and this may have implications for the quality of provision. The challenge for policy makers will be to more carefully design incentives and flexibilities to secure value for money while avoiding the type of 'parking' and service reduction strategies that emerged as costs were cut in the privatised Job Network in Australia (Considine, 2001).

One other significant finding was that in both EZ and New Deal areas many of the jobs that were sustained for over 13 weeks did not last in the longer term. This reflects, in part, labour market opportunities for the long-term unemployed. Many jobs were temporary, were with small employers and offered low wages. The personal barriers of the participants, such as ill health and a lack of skills and qualifications, also contributed to the short duration of job tenure. The implication is that simply remaining in work for 13 weeks did little to enhance the longer-term employability or skills of those who found jobs (Griffiths and Durkin, 2007). It remains to be seen if the incentives created by the longer duration outcome payments envisaged in the DWP Commissioning Strategy will result in more sustained employment for those who participate in future contracted-out services.

The evidence on market failure is limited. Performance has been regulated through contract management and inspections. Zone providers have been financially viable but there have been a number of cases where providers of other DWP programmes have gone out of business, causing much disruption to individual service users and requiring speedy intervention by the public sector to shore up the capacity of local delivery systems. The continuing role of Jobcentre Plus, with its national coverage, and the DWP's commitment to actively manage the market and ensure that there are at least two private providers operating in most regions, should minimise although not eliminate the risk of performance or financial failure.

Welfare markets in Australia and the US

The experience of other countries, especially Australia and the US, has helped shape UK policy in this area. For example, the design of the EZ contracts and the 'star rating' system for providers was based on practices developed in Australia after the public Employment Service was wholly privatised and replaced by a 'Job Network' in 1998 (Morrell and Branosky, 2005). The interim DWP Commissioning Strategy was itself influenced by and published alongside a review of lessons from the contracting out of welfare-to-work services in the US, where some states have used a prime contractor delivery model (Finn, 2007).

While it is difficult to disentangle the impacts of market-based delivery systems from the wider work-based welfare reforms that they are designed to implement, there is a wealth of analysis available from both Australia and the US. This body of knowledge gives valuable insight into issues likely to emerge as the British welfare market evolves (Considine, 2001; Bryna Sanger, 2003; Sol and Westerveld, 2005).

Proponents of the new systems argue that private contractors have brought innovation and new capacity to service delivery and that competition and payment for performance has generated efficiencies and cost savings. Officials involved in the delivery of welfare-to-work services stress that contracting out has enabled them to speedily and flexibly expand capacity and restructure delivery systems (including, where required, the ability to renegotiate contracts). Critics dispute the idea that the conditions for effective competition exist, and deem efficiencies and savings claimed as illusory. The transaction costs of designing, awarding and subsequently managing contracts are high, with critics finding that expenditure savings have come from 'reducing services to clients while increasing profits to agencies' (Considine, 2005, p 67; see also Brodkin, 2005). As problems have emerged public purchasers have been forced into frequent redesign of contracts and as regulations have become more prescriptive, providers have less operational flexibility and capacity or ability to innovate.

In both countries there has been much debate about the role of large-scale national providers and controversy about their operation. In the US in particular there has been much criticism of large providers in certain states (similar criticisms have now been made of some of the larger British providers: Davies, 2006). The US critics cite examples of corporate malpractice, including inadequate and poor provision of services, misappropriation of funds and other financial irregularities (Bryna Sanger, 2003; DeParle, 2005). In some US states the organisations involved have lost contracts; in others they have taken remedial action and continue to deliver services. The largest providers themselves point to their successful delivery of many other contracts and continue to stress the strength of the organisational and management capacities they bring to the market.

On a more general level the large providers in both Australia and the US have emerged as a powerful interest group, locally and nationally, lobbying, for example, for further privatisation of services, and for changes in their contractual terms. In the UK such providers are now organised into the 'Employment Related Services Association' and they have played a significant part in the debate on the future direction of the British welfare market. Unsurprisingly, they are in favour of longer and more flexible contracts.

Involvement in welfare markets has had a major impact on voluntary sector organisations in both Australia and the US. A detailed study of larger non-profit organisations in the US found that some struggled with the challenge of delivering major contracts but others had improved their performance and 'developed services consistent with their social mission' (Bryna Sanger, 2003, p 69).

The impact on smaller non-profit organisations has been less transparent, but many have lost contracts or chosen to withdraw from providing services. The experience of New York City, which introduced a prime contracting model, illustrates the impact of a 'shake-out' of community-based and smaller non-profits that followed. For some the loss of these 'less effective' providers increased efficiency, thereby improving services for clients. Others have argued that clients with special needs may be less well served and that while the loss of many of these local organisations 'might not show up on a balance sheet', it undermines the already limited social capital of poor communities (Fischer, 2001, p 1; Bryna Sanger, 2003).

Wider concerns have been expressed about the impact of welfare-to-work contracting on the values and practices of the non-profit sector (Murray, 2006). There has been 'mission drift' induced through the requirements of contracts and by the involvement of non-profits in processes that impose benefit sanctions, often on large numbers of disadvantaged and poor people. Others fear that contractual involvement reduces the autonomy and vitality of the voluntary sector actors and may 'mute their advocacy on behalf of disadvantaged communities' (Brodkin, 2005, p 77).

Overview

This chapter has assessed the role of for-profit and non-profit organisations in the delivery of the social security system. It has described in particular the creation of a welfare market and the key role that private sector providers are now playing in the delivery of welfare-to-work programmes. It has shown also some of the risks involved in making such changes.

Over the next decade it will become clearer whether British policy makers and those entrusted with implementing the welfare market have managed to fashion a contracting regime that has harnessed the resources and the capacities of the private and third sectors to deliver services that assist workless people to get and keep jobs.

It may be that contracting out these services will simply reduce the visibility of government decisions and disguise reductions in the funding and quality of welfare-to-work programmes. We may also find that the new delivery systems become mired in the same delivery problems that undermined the bureaucratic systems they have replaced.

Questions for discussion

(1) How has the role of the private sector changed in the delivery of British welfare-to-work programmes?
(2) What gains and risks are involved in the delivery of welfare-to-work programmes by private providers?
(3) Why is the government using private agencies in the delivery of welfare-to-work programmes?
(4) What does the evidence tell us about the impact of welfare-to-work contracting on service users and third sector organisations?

Website resources

www.dwp.gov.uk/asd/asd5
Department for Work and Pensions – Research
www.ersa.org.uk
Employment Related Services Association
www.cesi.org.uk
Centre for Economic and Social Inclusion

www.workdirections.co.uk
Work Directions
www.workplace.gov.au/workplace
Department of Employment, Education and Workplace Relations (Australia)
www.sprc.unsw.edu.au
Social Policy Research Centre, University of New South Wales
www.bsl.org.au
Brotherhood of St. Laurence
www.ja.com.au
Jobs Australia
www.hhs.gov
US Department of Health and Human Services
www.irp.wisc.edu
Institute for Research on Poverty, University of Wisconsin-Madison
www.mathematica-mpr.com
Mathematica Policy Research, Inc.

References

Allbeson, J. (1997) *Short changed: A briefing on cuts in social security running costs*, London: National Association of Citizens Advice Bureaux.

Brodkin, E.Z. (2005) 'Towards a contractual welfare state? The case of work activation in the United States', in E. Sol and M. Westerveld (eds) *Contractualism in employment services: A new form of welfare state governance*, The Hague: Kluwer Law International.

Bryna Sanger, M. (2003) *The welfare marketplace: Privatization and welfare reform*, Washington, DC: Center for Public Service, Brookings Institution Press.

Butcher, T. (1995) *Delivering welfare: The governance of social services in the 1990s*, Buckingham: Open University Press.

Conservative Party (2008) *Work for welfare: REAL welfare reform to help make British poverty history*, Policy Green Paper No 3, London: Conservative Party.

Considine, M. (2001) *Enterprising states: The public management of welfare-to-work*, Cambridge: Cambridge University Press.

Considine, M. (2005) 'The reform that never ends: quasi-markets and employment services in Australia', in E. Sol and M. Westerveld (eds) *Contractualism in employment services: A new form of welfare state governance*, The Hague: Kluwer Law International.

Davies, S. (2006) *Third sector provision of employment-related services: A report for PCS*, Leeds: Public and Commercial Services Union.

DCSF (Department for Children, Schools and Families) and DIUS (Department for Innovation, Universities and Skills) (2008) *Raising expectations: Enabling the system to deliver*, Cm 7348, London: The Stationery Office.

DeParle, J. (2005) *American dream: Three women, ten kids and a nation's drive to end welfare*, New York: Penguin Books.

DWP (Department for Work and Pensions) (2006) *A new deal for welfare: Empowering people to work*, Cm 6730, DWP Five Year Strategy, London: DWP.

DWP (2007a) *In work, better off: Next steps to full employment: Impact assessment*, London: DWP.

DWP (2007b) *In work, better off: Next steps to full employment*, Cm 7130, London: The Stationery Office.

DWP (2008a) *Department for Work and Pensions Commissioning Strategy*, Cm 7330, London: The Stationery Office.

DWP (2008b) *Three year business plan 2008–2011*, London: DWP.

Entwhistle, T. and Martin, S. (2005) 'From competition to collaboration in public service delivery: a new agenda for research', *Public Administration*, vol 83, no 1, pp 233-42.

Finn, D. (2007) *Contracting out welfare to work in the USA: Delivery lessons*, DWP Research Report No 466, London: DWP.

Fischer, D. J. (2001) *The workforce challenge: To place is to win*, New York City: Center for an Urban Future.

Fletcher, D. (1997) 'Evaluating special measures for the unemployed: some reflections on recent UK experience', *Policy & Politics*, vol 25, no 2, pp 173-84.

Freud D. (2007) *Reducing dependency, increasing opportunity: Options for the future of welfare to work*, An independent report to the DWP, London: Department for Work and Pensions.

Griffiths, R. and Durkin, S. (2007) *Synthesising the evidence on Employment Zones*, DWP Research Report No 449, London: DWP.

Grimshaw, D., Vincent, S. and Willmott, H. (2002) 'Going privately: partnership and outsourcing in UK public services', *Public Administration*, vol 80, no 3, pp 475-502.

Hales, J., Taylor, R., Mandy, W. and Miller, M. (2003) *Evaluation of Employment Zones: Report on a cohort survey of long-term unemployed people in the zones and a matched set of comparison areas*, London: National Centre for Social Research.

Harman, H. (1997) *Oral answers*, Parliamentary Debates, Official Report, Fourth Volume, col 9, 30 June, London: Hansard.

Hirst, A., Tarling, R., Lefaucheux, M., Rowland, B., McGregor, A., Glass, A., Trinh, T., Simm, C., Shaw, H. and Engineer, R. (2002) *Qualitative evaluation of Employment Zones: A study of local delivery agents and area case studies*, WAE 124, Sheffield: DWP.

Jones, M. (1999) *New institutional spaces: Training and Enterprise Councils and the remaking of economic governance*, Regional Policy and Development Series 20, Regional Studies Association, London: Jessica Kingsley Publishers.

Joyce, L. and Pettigrew, N. (2002) *Personal advisers in New Deal 25+ and Employment Zones*, WAE 139, Sheffield: DWP.

Le Grand, J. (2002) 'Models of public service provision: command and control, networks or quasi markets?', in *Public services productivity*, papers presented at a seminar held in HM Treasury, 13 June, London.

Liberal Democrats (2007) *Freedom from poverty, opportunity for all*, Policy Paper 80, London: Liberal Democrats.

Morrell, H. and Branosky, N. (eds) (2005) *The use of contestability and flexibility in the delivery of welfare services in Australia and the Netherlands*, DWP Research Report No 288, Leeds: DWP.

Murray, P. (2006) *A job network for job seekers*, Discussion Paper, Curtin, ACT, Australia: Catholic Social Services Australia.

NAO (National Audit Office) (2005) *Transfer of property to the private sector under the expansion of the PRIME contract*, London: NAO.

NAO (2008) *The roll-out of the Jobcentre Plus office network*, London: NAO.

Osborne, D. and Gaebler, T. (1993) *Reinventing government: How the entrepreneurial spirit is transforming the public sector*, New York: Plume, Penguin Group.

Powell, M. (2007) *Understanding the mixed economy of welfare*, Bristol: The Policy Press.

Price, D. (2000) *Office of hope: A history of the Employment Service*, London: Policy Studies Institute, University of Westminster.

Purnell, J. (2008) *Written ministerial statements*, Official Report, 28 February, col 88WS, London: Hansard.

Sol, E. and Westerveld, M. (eds) (2005) *Contractualism in employment services: A new form of welfare state governance*, The Hague: Kluwer Law International.

Stafford, B. with others (2007) *New Deal for Disabled People: Third synthesis report – key findings from the evaluation*, DWP Research Report No 430, London: DWP.

Social security and information technology

John Hudson

Summary

This chapter examines the implications of information and communication technology (ICT) for social security. It outlines:

- the 'information age government' agenda that has been a central part of recent attempts to 'modernise government';
- the ways in which technology is being used to deliver social security;
- the challenges government faces in utilising complex technologies.

Introduction

This chapter examines the central role information and communication technologies (ICTs) play in the delivery of social security. As a conversation killer, the topic ranks up there with the best of them. The eyes of strangers can glaze over in nanoseconds when the seemingly dry and technical issue of social security is raised in polite conversation. Explain that you want to address not just the supposedly dry and technical questions of social security per se, but also what appear to be even drier and more technical issues about *computing* and social security, and oftentimes you have apparently stumbled across one of the most effective sedatives known to the human race!

Curiously, this sedative often proves effective not just when talking to lay people but also when talking to many of those charged with delivering social security services, creating social security policy or researching it. Despite the fact that it would be absolutely impossible to deliver a modern social security system without considerable reliance on ICTs, few politicians have grasped the key policy issues raised by technology, few university courses on social security include a discussion of the topic and most textbooks either push the issue to the margins on the basis that it is a very new development or just ignore it altogether. Given these general perceptions of the topic in hand, it is worth dispelling some myths before turning to a detailed examination of key issues.

Dry and technical?

Far from being a dry topic, any discussion of social security and ICTs actually requires us to engage with potentially some of the most explosive political issues imaginable. At the time of writing, Gordon Brown's UK government faced huge political difficulties because of a repeated failure to protect the confidential personal information of citizens. Most notably, in 2007 the names, addresses and bank account details of almost every family with children in the UK were put onto two CD-ROM disks and sent through the post from one government agency to another. When it transpired that these disks had gone missing the general reaction was one of complete disbelief that standard operating procedures had failed to prevent this from happening. Indeed, the Information Commissioner described the incident as 'unprecedented … a really shocking example of loss of security' (House of Commons Justice Committee, 2008, para 2). Had policy makers thought more deeply about how computer systems ought to store and transmit such information it would not have happened. This is not a dry technical issue; it is a basic policy issue concerned with how the routine collection of personal information required to process benefit claims can be carried out in a manner that protects our right to privacy.

While such issues obviously have a technical dimension, participation in debates does not demand a detailed knowledge of the technical aspects of ICTs. When it comes to thinking through the implication of ICTs for government services, many politicians seem happy to revel in an ignorance of the key issues. For instance, when Tony Blair was Prime Minister he admitted to a key parliamentary committee that he did not know the web address of his government's main internet site – despite the vast resources ploughed into it – and happily conceded that he was 'a technophobe' (House of Commons Liaison Committee, 2005, Q86-Q91). Some of the Members of Parliament (MPs) supposedly calling him to account at the meeting responded not with outrage but with guffaws of laughter. His explanation that he regarded ICTs as being of vital importance but that he delegated the work to experts who could take care of this kind of thing for him seemed to satisfy most of the committee members, but should it have done? It is difficult to imagine a situation whereby the Prime Minister would say that the ultimate decisions in health or education policy in these fields lie outside of his or her expertise and that MPs would nod in agreement as responsibility is handed over to doctors or teachers. Yet, it is a basic truth that computers are incredibly *less* complex than human bodies or human minds. If experts can take second place to policy makers in questions about the deployment of education and health resources then they can do so in questions about the deployment of computing resources. In other words, while education, healthcare and ICT policy debates all have a significant technical dimension, there are also major social, ethical and political dimensions that policy makers and policy analysts have a fundamental duty to make their business.

A new development?

Given that the words 'information technology' typically invoke images of cutting-edge devices and futuristic possibilities it also would be easy to presume that any discussion of ICTs and social security must necessarily have a short time frame and that the key policy debates are likely to still be in their infancy. However, it would be a mistake to make such presumptions.

First, the history of computing and social security is almost as long as the history of social security itself. More than perhaps any other field of public policy, social security is reliant on the systematic collection and analysis of personal information. Indeed, the very idea of social insurance is reliant on the existence of systematic contribution records for each individual citizen. Consequently, very early debates about modern social security systems had to engage with practical issues concerning the collection and storage of personal information. In the late 19th and early 20th centuries these technologies were primarily based on paper records and manual filing cabinet systems operated by huge numbers of bureaucrats, but the development of machine-readable punchcards in the 1920s and 1930s allowed social security agencies to speed up the retrieval of information and increase their ability to analyse and interrogate that information too. Much of IBM's early business came from the supply of punchcard computers needed to manage the collection of social insurance contribution data (Hally, 2005); indeed, the award of a US government contract to support the data needs of the 1935 Social Security Act increased IBM's revenues sixfold and propelled it into the realm of mega-business (Black, 2002). In the UK, more recognisably modern computers were commissioned for the processing of social security payments in the 1950s (Margetts, 1991) and by the late 1970s and early 1980s the UK government had developed significant plans to use modern network-based computing technologies that would mechanise many key social security processes and place thousands of computer terminals in local social security offices in order to give staff instant access to each of their clients' social security records (see Fallon, 1993).

Second, much of the ICT used today in the delivery of the UK's key social security benefits is far from cutting edge. In fact, some of the main processes in the sector still rely on equipment that is well over a decade old. The reasons for this are varied, but in large part it is a consequence of the enormity of the systems. The UK is unusual in having such a centralised social security system and one outcome of this is that computer systems need to be national in scope, often covering every individual living or working (or, indeed, once living or working) in the country. For example, the National Insurance Record System (NIRS) that was developed in the 1960s and 1970s had almost 80 million individual contribution records and was connected to most of the key social security benefit systems. Managing the transition to a new system (NIRS2) took more than a decade, not least because programmers had to write more than 14 million lines of computer code to make the system operational. As such, NIRS2 was one of the largest computer projects in the world and managing a project of such scale presents considerable technical challenges. More importantly, perhaps, replacing systems of such a scale is complicated, time consuming and very costly. Such an issue is far from insignificant in policy terms, for delays in rolling out new systems have sometimes resulted in delays in implementing new benefit rules or new types of benefit. Consequently, as Collingridge and Margetts (1994) noted, information technology (IT) systems in the sector have a tendency to be in use for some considerable time and rather than being cutting-edge enablers of change can often be historic monsters that hold back change.

Back to the future

Yet, while the history of social security and computing is a long one, the decade or so since New Labour came to power in 1997 has been arguably the most significant period for computing and government services for one simple reason: the internet. When Blair came to power, few people had used the internet. In fact, just 8% of households had an internet connection in 1998. However, it was already apparent that the internet was ripe for a rapid growth in usage and, by 2007, the majority of households had such a connection – some 61% in total with take-up still rising (National Statistics, 2007). Given that Blair's government had ambitious plans to roll out a wide-ranging strategy for 'modernising government' (discussed in Chapter Six, Carmel and Papadopoulos, this volume), making greater use of emerging internet technologies as part of this process seemed an obvious thing to do and an ambitious plan to have 100% of government services available electronically by the end of 2005 was drawn up (Cabinet Office, 1999, 2000; Hudson, 2002).

This commitment to rapidly roll out 'e-government' marked a watershed moment in the history of government and computing in the UK. Prior to this, ICTs had been hugely important to the delivery of public services, but their functions were almost entirely related to the back-office processes, meaning that the public did not see the machinery or use it directly to interact with government departments. The e-government agenda changed this entirely by suggesting that internet-enabled devices should play a central role in the interaction of citizens with the state. Crucially, this information-age government agenda had radical intent. Policy documents spoke of ushering in an era of 'citizen-centric service delivery' in which ICTs would allow automated public services to be:

- available 24 hours a day, seven days a week;
- accessible electronically from any place the citizen finds convenient;
- automatically tailored to individual needs on the basis of personal information provided by each citizen;
- delivered in a seamlessly integrated fashion, with each government agency's services provided through a one-stop internet-based portal (PIU, 2000).

Considerable investment in e-services followed these pronouncements – around £6 billion on new ICT developments over the period 2000-05 (NAO, 2007) – and, by the end of 2005, the government concluded that its target of making all government services available electronically had been effectively met (with a final figure of 96% by the deadline day). Mindful of suggestions in some quarters that many of these new e-government services were often little more than 'brochureware' that advertised services rather than actually delivering them online (see NAO, 1999, 2002; Hudson, 2006), the government shifted its attention towards a second phase of e-government in which deeper change would be delivered.

In some ways, early policy documents had offered a cautious approach to the roll-out of e-government services, online services acting as an addition to existing face-to-face services and an additional spending commitment (Cabinet Office, 2000). The second phase of e-government, however, was based on a more hard-headed approach first flagged in the Treasury-commissioned Gershon Review (Gershon, 2004). It argued that ICTs offered the potential for considerable cost savings: automating the manual process and forcing some customers to migrate to electronic channels would mean some face-to-face services could be closed. A year later, a new strategy for ICTs and public services titled *Transformational government* (Cabinet Office, 2005) took this same thinking forward, stressing the need for a firmer grip on the £14 billion devoted annually to government ICT spending and the need to rationalise public services, with electronic channels playing a larger role and, conversely, face-to-face services playing a smaller one in the future. In short, while the first phase of e-government had focused on giving public services an online presence, the second phase was committed to making the presence of public services more of an online one.

ICTs and social security: the opportunities

What then have been the implications of this information-age government agenda for social security? In terms of regularity of contact with the public, few areas of policy – if any – rank higher than social security. Consequently, those driving the e-government agenda have been keen to deploy new technologies in the delivery of key social security services. Perhaps the potential benefits of greater use of ICTs are best illustrated by some examples of flagship projects that have been implemented during recent years. We will focus here on transactional services rather than simple information provision, although the latter remains a crucial part of e-government (see ***Box 16.1***).

Box 16.1: The advantages of online information

Much of the early phase of e-government focused on placing information about services online rather than providing transactional services. Although sometimes dismissed as 'brochureware' that merely mimics printed leaflets in electronic form, the advantages of providing information online should not be underestimated, particularly in terms of making information more easily accessible for many citizens.

At the forefront of the UK government's web presence is its main citizen portal Directgov (www.direct.gov.uk), which acts as the first-stop shop for citizens by bringing together information about services provided across all of the government's different departments. At the start of 2008, it was registering more than six million hits per month, with 86% of visitors questioned rating it as good or better (Kable, 2008a). From a social security perspective, it is worth noting that the 'money, taxes and benefits' section is the third most popular section of the site with over 800,000 hits per month. To put this provision of information into context, we might usefully compare it with the volume of information provided by the DWP's core printed leaflets: in 2004/05 it printed 451,000 copies of its guide to benefits and services for those of working age ('The work you want, the help you need'), 300,000 copies of its 'Pensioners' guide', 428,000 copies of its 'Bring up children on your own?' and 51,000 copies of 'Access to work: information for disabled people' (NAO, 2006a). As just one source of online information about social security benefits – the DWP's own websites provide information too – Directgov is clearly well on its way to competing with the traditional printed materials used to outline entitlements and services provided by the social security system.

Significantly, Directgov's role in communicating information to citizens is expected to increase considerably in coming years as government departments will gradually migrate information and services from their own websites to Directgov so that by 2012 it will become the main online focal point for e-services provided to citizens (Varney, 2006). Given that the DWP's business gives it regular contact with a substantial number of citizens, social security services are expected to feature even more prominently in the enhanced Directgov; so much so, in fact, that from April 2008 the DWP was given overall control of the Directgov service (Kable, 2008b).

Directgov improves access to information not only by being available at any time and from any place, but by presenting information about government services in a user-friendly fashion: rather than organising information by government agency or government department, it instead organises it around key themes (such as 'home and community', 'environment and greener living' and 'money, taxes and benefits') and life episodes (such as 'Britons living abroad', 'caring for someone' and 'parents'). The significance of such an innovation should not be underestimated; pooling information from multiple agencies under meaningful headings was no mean feat and keeping the information up to date is a not inconsiderable task. It is also a crucial first step in the process of 'joining up' government.

The most popular of all e-services provided in the sector is the Jobcentre Plus website. For the most part, visitors are attracted by the site's job search facility. The site allows users to undertake tailored searches for employment opportunities in which they can restrict search findings by various criteria including employment sector, job location, travel-to-work time, hours of work and so on. Users who register on the site can create their own personal profile, store job searches that can be automatically repeated on future visits and save the details of jobs of interest to them. Vacancy listings provide details of how to apply for posts and carry links to other relevant information about public services (for example information on in-work tax credits). As well as offering a service to potential employees, the site offers a valuable service to employers, who can advertise vacancies free of charge and upload vacancies to the site themselves. For both employers and employees the advantages of utilising e-government in job search are similar: the service is low cost, it can be accessed at any time from any place, it puts the user in control and it is fast, allowing vacancies and candidates to be matched swiftly using straightforward search criteria. Moreover, there are benefits of scale too, for employees can search the entire database of vacancies (usually around 400,000 at any one time according to the Department for Work and Pensions [DWP]) and employers can reach a wide audience too, with more than a million visitors to the site each week according to the DWP (Jobcentre Plus, 2008).

Yet, despite the substantial innovation behind the Jobcentre Plus job search site, in essence it is still an information provision service, albeit considerably enhanced by intelligent search technologies; in order to apply for a job, users almost always have to make a telephone call during working hours to Jobcentre Plus. What the service lacks is *transactional* capability: users cannot initiate and complete their dealings online. Such transactional capability is the key goal for truly electronic services, and the tax credits portal, launched in 2004, was designed as a flagship example of such a service. Two key innovations were at the heart of this service. First, it had an intelligent expert inquiry service that allowed users to input information about their circumstances (for example, family size, household income and hours worked) and then computed whether they were entitled to tax credits and, if so, how much they could expect to receive. Given the complexity of the tax credits system, this service itself was of considerable use, but on top of this the site allowed people who had identified an entitlement to make a claim online. Unlike many other e-services this was a proper online transaction and not simply a procedure centred around printing off an online form, filling it in by hand and posting it. Again, the advantages of this service are clear: available at any time and from any place, expert information on entitlement provided instantly and, best of all, the possibility of making a claim for an entitlement without having to leave the home or workplace. However, the service has faced considerable operational difficulties in practice and, at the time of writing, the online claims service had been shut for more than two years, an issue we will return to below.

These examples of e-services highlight some of the outward-facing developments that have taken place as the internet has become a key tool for government agencies to interact with citizens. However, many important innovations in the use of ICTs in social security have remained internally focused and, again, it is worth offering a few examples. Here the focus is much less on computers themselves and more on how ICTs enable business processes to be enhanced or reconfigured. Arguably the most prominent development has been the increased use of call centres (or contact centres as they are often termed to reflect the fact that they often handle e-mail, fax and postal queries too). The number of DWP contact centres, all of which rely on sophisticated ICT-based customer relationship management systems, has increased considerably in the past decade, from just 10 in 1998 to reach a peak of more than 80 by 2004 (NAO, 2006b). This increase reflects a deliberate shift towards a new model of interaction with service users in which less emphasis is placed on traditional face-to-face meetings in social security offices and much more on telephone-based contact and, where necessary, face-to-face follow-up (see also Chapter Fourteen, Stafford, this volume). Indeed, the Pension Service is in many ways a virtual organisation, for contact is overwhelmingly telephone based and 'local' pension centres can often be hundreds of miles away. The advantages of this approach for the Pension Service are numerous, not least it can make considerable financial savings by basing more staff in areas of the country where costs are lower – because if contact with the customer is electronic the actual location of the staff member is largely irrelevant – and, added to this, by routing the majority of routine queries to centralised contact centres, the Pension Service can free up locally based staff for more intensive home visits for those with more complex needs or queries, thus maintaining a face-to-face service when e-channels are inappropriate.

The importance of contact centres can also be illustrated in a second example of innovative use of ICTs behind the scenes: take-up campaigns. With the social security system in the UK being increasingly based around means-tested benefits and tax credits, (non-)take-up of entitlements is becoming an increasingly important issue with billions of pounds of potential payments remaining unclaimed each year (Dornan and Hudson, 2003). When the Pension Credit was launched in 2003, the Pension Service utilised detailed customer information to implement the most sophisticated take-up campaign ever put in place in the UK social security system. Specifically, it utilised so-called market segmentation techniques, analysing data in its own records about potential claimants alongside detailed geo-demographic data held by marketing companies in order to mail targeted information packs carrying different information to different groups of pensioners. The campaign was successful in so far as it helped the Pension Service exceed its targets for generating claims for Pension Credit (NAO, 2006c). In addition, the increased accuracy of the targeting of information was demonstrated by the fact that 30% fewer people who were in fact *ineligible* for the benefit attempted to make a claim after receiving marketing material when compared with a less sophisticated take-up campaign for the Pension Credit's predecessor, the Minimum Income Guarantee (MIG) (NAO, 2006d, p 64). Contact centres were central to the Pension Credit take-up campaign: mimicking private sector marketing campaign techniques, queries generated by the postal campaign were routed through contact centres, with mailings distributed in pre-planned phases and in carefully managed numbers that varied from place to place so that call volumes to each contact centre could be effectively managed and response times reasonably swift (NAO, 2006c).

While the analysis of customer data has long been used to tackle fraud and error – particularly through data-matching techniques that might, for example, identify individuals fraudulently or erroneously claiming multiple benefits (see Dornan and Hudson, 2003) – the use of similarly sophisticated data analysis to promote the claiming of entitlements is a more recent development. Since 2005, Jobcentre Plus has begun to roll out its own in-house Geographic Information System (GIS) that holds the potential for even more targeted activity in the future. Combining data from customer records along with a wealth of geo-demographic data from government surveys and other administrative sources, the Jobcentre Plus GIS is a powerful tool that allows managers and analysts to spot patterns in benefit claims, employment activity and specific local factors and so devise very localised strategies for, say, combating low employment levels or pinpointing localised barriers to employment (ODPM, 2005).

In short, ICTs have considerable potential for improving the quality, convenience, speed, accuracy, efficiency and take-up of social security entitlements and services (see also ***Box 16.1***). However, while the technology can bring real advantages, it can also – as we have hinted at – bring its own problems and disadvantages too and it is to this that we now turn.

ICTs and social security: the threats

Almost any discussion of government and computing seems incomplete without some reference to 'Big Brother'. While there are undoubted advantages for service delivery that arise from the state having access to large amounts of information about its citizens, it is fair to say that there is considerable unease about the level of personal information being routinely collected, stored, analysed and transmitted by government, much of it within the social security sector. Perri 6 (2001) has usefully observed that what we often term the 'information society' might better be termed the 'personal information society' given that so much of the information being bought, sold, processed and analysed is, in practice, information about people and the Information Commissioner recently warned that the UK is sleepwalking into a surveillance society as a consequence of increased collection of personal data (see Surveillance Studies Network, 2006). While the state has the power to use personal information for positive ends that are unlikely to cause too much concern – such as informing people of benefit entitlements – it can also use this information as part of a campaign of intensive surveillance when it suspects someone *might* be fraudulently claiming benefits. While it is, of course, perfectly reasonable for the state to protect taxpayers' money, there is a line somewhere between the state's right to check the validity of a benefit claim and the individual's rights to privacy or to fair and equal treatment. So, for instance, we might ask whether it is reasonable for a benefit fraud investigation team to collect the number plates of cars parked each night outside the home of someone claiming benefits for lone parents and then run these number plates against the government's driving licence database to see if a suspected undeclared partner is, in fact, resident at that address. Likewise, we might ask if it is fair for an analysis of the characteristics of past fraudsters to be used to create profiles of 'high-risk' claims so that fresh benefit claims by those fitting such profiles can be subjected to more intensive scrutiny than is the norm, even when those claimants themselves have no record of any wrongdoing (see Dornan and Hudson, 2003).

An additional dimension to the privacy debate comes not so much in terms of what the state might do with personal information it holds, but what it might fail to do in terms of guarding it. As we noted in the introduction of this chapter, the Brown government has faced difficult questions about its competency following a number of high-profile instances in which personal information has gone missing. While the loss of disks containing Child Benefit (CB) data for 25 million people was the most high-profile case, it was by no means an isolated incident. Indeed, as Anderson (2008) has argued, when personal data is placed into centralised computer systems that many people have routine access to, the risk of such data leaking out of the system is not one of degree but is a certainty. Absolute privacy and security is impossible to guarantee in practice; while loss on the scale of the CB disks is rare, employees accessing information for unofficial purposes is much less rare.

Significantly, this loss of security is a two-way process. While computer systems have proved hugely effective in tightening the robustness of payment processing mechanisms and helped to tackle benefit fraud, they have also opened up new opportunities for criminals. Undoubtedly the biggest and most damaging incident to date took place over the course of 2005 when the personal information of 1,500 DWP employees was stolen and used to make fraudulent claims for tax credits using the online tax credits portal (McCue, 2005). On discovery of the fraud, Her Majesty's Revenue & Customs (HMRC) shut down its online tax credit application service and, in 2007, the government conceded that it would reopen no sooner than two and half years after its closure and, possibly, would not reopen at all (House of Commons Treasury Select Committee, 2007, Q88-Q91). Given its status as a flagship transactional e-service this was a considerable blow to the e-government agenda and has injected a huge level of caution into the agenda; indeed, truly paperless services are essentially non-existent in the social security system at the time of writing because of such security fears.

We should also note that while e-channels are welcomed by many, there are a great number who feel uncomfortable with e-services or lack the skills or equipment to make use of them. While the context for e-government is rapidly rising internet access, even in 2008 almost two in five households do not have internet access and, moreover, access rates are substantially below average for those in lower-income households and for older people (National

Statistics, 2007). Given that much of the social security sector's work engages with those least likely to have internet access, the so-called 'digital divide' is an issue that its e-services agenda must grapple with and certainly this is one reason why contact centres have thus far played a more prominent role than websites in the sector's shift to electronic services. However, caution needs to be exercised not just in the obvious area of internet use, but in the transition to electronic services more generally. For instance, we might question whether it is right for a high-profile public service such as the Pension Service to have such a small physical presence or whether the drive to automate services in order to save on labour costs is sensible. The Gershon Review (2004) suggested that stronger use of ICTs could eliminate 40,000 Civil Service jobs, the vast bulk of them within the social security sector. Yet, since the government began the process of slimming down its workforce in the sector, morale among employees has fallen and there are suggestions that service quality has been compromised (see BBC News, 2007, for example). Likewise, while the DWP's Payment Modernisation Programme, which replaced old paper-based order books with direct electronic payments into bank or Post Office accounts, has been hailed as a success by the National Audit Office (NAO, 2006e) and has certainly been welcomed by the vast majority of benefit recipients, it would be wrong to overlook the fact that a not insubstantial number of (particularly older) people felt that the old system was better (see Adams et al, 2004).

Finally, it is worth highlighting that while governments have long stressed the efficiency savings that can be generated by computerising public services, in practice such savings have often been very difficult to quantify and the process of delivering ICT-enabled change has often proved to be far from smooth in practice. In fact, parliamentary select committees have regularly had cause to investigate significant overspends in social security computing projects or report on operational deficiencies arising from inadequate computing systems. For example, a damning House of Commons Work and Pensions Select Committee (2005, p 16) report on the Child Support Agency's (CSA's) failings concluded that 'There is no doubt that many of the problems faced by the CSA are caused, or at least affected, by the lack of a fully operational IT system'. In seeking an explanation as to why the systems had fallen short of what was required, the committee pointed its finger at the DWP's failure to understand how far ICT-related change would require deeper change in business processes and a weak control over the main IT contractor, EDS. Crucially, these two issues were interrelated: the DWP's weak understanding of the nature of ICT-enabled change placed it in a weak position with regards to the management of its ICT contractors. Indeed, while it was clear for some time that EDS was underperforming in delivering new systems to support the CSA, the DWP did not exercise its right to cancel its £500 million contract with EDS because 'a lack of in-house technical expertise meant the Department was unable to challenge its supplier' (House of Commons Committee of Public Accounts, 2007a, p 10).

The CSA example is indicative of a broader issue. The widescale contracting out of ICT-related functions began in the 1980s and was designed to save money by drawing on supposedly more efficient private sector services. However, this process also served to reduce the government's capacity to deliver ICT-enabled change by replacing in-house expertise with hired contractors. Relationships with contractors are often extremely unequal as a consequence, with detailed technical knowledge of how the systems work on a day-to-day basis resting largely outside of government. This in turn makes replacing a poorly performing contractor difficult, not least because the government must rely on the outgoing contractor to assist its replacement. So, for instance, when the HRMC launched a 're-competitioning' process (dubbed ASPIRE – Acquiring Strategic Partners for the Inland Revenue) for its ICT services, the cost of replacing EDS/Accenture with Capgemini cost £47.5 million purely in terms of payments to manage the transition from one set of contractors to another (House of Commons Committee of Public Accounts, 2007b, p 9).

As another House of Commons Committee of Public Accounts report (2007c) noted, consistently relying on external consultants to perform central tasks is unlikely to provide value for money in the long run. Certainly, there are large profits to be made in providing ICT services to the social security sector: ASPIRE is likely to generate profits of more than £1 billion for Capgemini over its 10-year term (House of Commons Committee of Public Accounts, 2007b, p 6). Ironically, for all the money spent on hiring experts to assist with the computerisation of social security, the UK has a poor record on delivering successful projects that meet their stated goals on time and on budget. Cynics might argue that such a record of failure suits the major ICT consultancies because a project that runs over time and over budget needs more contractors to be hired for more time and for more money. This would be an unfair characterisation because it overlooks the genuine complexity of the projects on the ground, but it is certainly true that the incentives to keep projects under budget and to time have often been rather weak. Indeed, in an international analysis of e-government, Dunleavy and Margetts (2006) found the UK to have a comparatively very poor record of delivery because three key weaknesses that can hamper projects were so prevalent: a heavy reliance on the five biggest international ICT consultancy firms; limited effective competition for contracts; and little in-house expertise. Each of these factors serves to boost the power of contractors vis-à-vis the government, and Dunleavy and Margetts' work suggests that the high failure rate of government ICT projects in the UK is in large part a consequence of structural factors working against strong governmental control over projects.

In short, because so many of those responsible for making policy in the social security sectors regarded ICT as a 'technical' issue that need not be under their direct control, the UK managed to sow the seeds for some significant future policy failures at precisely the moment ICT was set to become central to the process of modernising government. Rectifying this structural problem is a far from easy task that will require cultural and institutional changes and not merely technological ones.

Overview

Such has been the scale of activity in the past decade that in this chapter it has been possible to offer no more than a very brief review of some of the key issues surrounding social security and ICTs.

Among the key advantages of greater use of ICTs is the potential for faster, more convenient, more personalised, more targeted, more flexible, more efficient services. Yet, the disadvantages can often simply be the other side of the same coin: the potential for more surveilling, more robotic, more minimal, less private services.

That said, there are few inevitabilities in this field and it would be wrong to presume that any of these effects automatically flow from the deployment of ICTs. Instead, policy makers have choices about which technologies they deploy, how they deploy, for whom and in what circumstances, and we should avoid falling for a lazy technological determinism that sees change or the direction of change as being inevitable.

It has been shown in the course of this chapter that it is difficult to understand the development of recent social security policy without an appreciation of how ICTs can and do underpin key delivery processes. Perhaps too it has shown that it is difficult to comprehend why so few look to gain such an appreciation of the role of ICTs when seeking an understanding of social security policy.

Questions for discussion

(1) How might ICTs improve the quality of services?
(2) Should protecting privacy be a greater priority than improving the efficiency of services?
(3) Why has the government found it so difficult to control the private contractors responsible for delivering computing projects in the social security sector?

Web resources

www.direct.gov.uk
UK government's main online presence
www.cio.gov.uk/
UK government's Chief Information Officer
www.kablenet.com/
Independent source of news about government and computing projects
http://whitehallwebby.wordpress.com/
A blog that offers an 'insider's perspective' on e-government
www.oecd.org/topic/0,3373,en_2649_34129_1_1_1_1_37405,00.html
Data about e-government in 30 of the richest nations

References

6, P. with Jupp, B. (2001) *Divided by information?*, London: Demos.

Adams, L., Bunt, K. and Bright, D. (2004) *Customer experience of Direct Payment*, DWP In-house Research Report 150, London: DWP.

Anderson, R. (2008) *Security engineering: A guide to building dependable distributed systems* (second edition), London: Wiley.

BBC News (2007) 'Life inside the beleaguered HMRC', BBC News Online, 21st November, http://news.bbc.co.uk/1/hi/uk/7104395.stm

Black, E. (2002) *IBM and the Holocaust: The strategic alliance between Nazi Germany and America's most powerful corporation*, California, CA: Three Rivers Press.

Cabinet Office (1999) *Modernising government*, London: Cabinet Office.

Cabinet Office (2000) *E-government: A strategic framework for public services in the information age*, London: Cabinet Office.

Cabinet Office (2005) *Transformational government: Enabled by technology*, London: Cabinet Office.

Collingridge, D. and Margetts, H. (1994) 'Can government information systems be inflexible technology? The Operational Strategy revisited', *Public Administration*, vol 72, pp 55-72.

Dornan, P. and Hudson, J. (2003) 'Welfare governance in the surveillance society', *Social Policy & Administration*, vol 37, pp 468-82.

Dunleavy, P. and Margetts, H. (2006) *Digital era governance: IT corporations, the state and e-government*, Oxford: Oxford University Press.

Fallon, I. (1993) *The paper chase: A decade of change at the DSS*, London: HarperCollins.

Gershon, P. (2004) *Releasing resources to the front line: Independent review of public sector efficiency*, London: HM Treasury/HMSO.

Hally, M. (2005) *Electronic brains: Stories from the dawn of the computer age*, Cambridge: Granta.

House of Commons Committee of Public Accounts (2007a) *Child Support Agency: Implementation of the child support reforms: Thirty-seventh report of session 2006-07*, HC-812, London: The Stationery Office.

House of Commons Committee of Public Accounts (2007b) *HM Revenue and Customs: ASPIRE – the re-competition of outsourced IT services: Twenty-eighth report of session 2006–07*, HC-179, London: The Stationery Office.

House of Commons Committee of Public Accounts (2007c) *Central government's use of consultants: Thirty-first report of session 2006-07*, HC-309, London: The Stationery Office.

House of Commons Justice Committee (2008) *Protection of private data: First report of session 2007–08*, HC 154, London: The Stationery Office.

House of Commons Liaison Committee (2005) *Oral and written evidence: Oral evidence given by the Rt Hon Tony Blair MP, 8th February 2005, Session 2004–05*, HC 318-I, London: The Stationery Office.

House of Commons Treasury Select Committee (2007) *The administration of tax credits, minutes of evidence, 14th March 2007, Session 2006–07*, HC 382-i, London: The Stationery Office.

House of Commons Work and Pensions Select Committee (2005) *The performance of the Child Support Agency, Session 2004–05, second report (volume I)*, HC 44-1, London: The Stationery Office.

Hudson, J. (2002) 'Digitising the structures of government: the UK's information age government agenda', *Policy & Politics*, vol 30, pp 515-31.

Hudson, J. (2006) 'e-government in the UK', in A. Anttiroiko and M. Mälkiä (eds) *The encyclopedia of digital government*, Hershey, PA: IGI.

Jobcentre Plus (2008) *The 4 key benefits of Employer Direct Online*, London: Jobcentre Plus.

Kable (2008a) 'Directgov hits third spot', *Kable News*, 30 January, www.kablenet.com/kd.nsf/FrontpageRSS/C65F7788B85E7EE0802573E0003532F8!OpenDocument

Kable (2008b) 'Directgov on the way to DWP', *Kable News*, 25 January, www.kablenet.com/kd.nsf/FrontpageRSS/CE45C46A38228663802573DB004533B9!OpenDocument

Margetts, H. (1991) 'The computerization of social security: the way forward or a step backwards?', *Public Administration*, vol 69, pp 325-43.

McCue, A. (2005) '1,500 civil servants victims of tax credit ID theft', *Silicon.com News*, 2 December, www.silicon.com/publicsector/0,3800010403,39154779,00.htm?r=5

NAO (National Audit Office) (1999) *Government on the Web*, London: NAO.

NAO (2002) *Government on the Web II*, London: NAO.

NAO (2006a) *Department for Work and Pensions: Using leaflets to communicate with the public about services and entitlements*, London: NAO.

NAO (2006b) *Department for Work and Pensions: Delivering effective services through contact centres*, London: NAO.

NAO (2006c) *Progress in tackling pensioner poverty: Encouraging take-up of entitlements*, London: NAO.

NAO (2006d) *Progress in tackling pensioner poverty: Encouraging take-up of entitlements – Technical Report*, London: NAO.

NAO (2006e) *Delivering successful IT-enabled business change: Case studies of success*, London: NAO.

NAO (2007) *Government on the internet: Progress in delivering information and services online*, London: NAO.

National Statistics (2007) *Internet access 2007 – households and individuals: First Release*, London: National Statistics.

ODPM (Office of the Deputy Prime Minister) (2005) *Inclusion through innovation Tackling social exclusion through new technologies, a Social Exclusion Unit fin report*, London: ODPM.

PIU (Performance and Innovation Unit) (2000) *E.gov: Electronic government servic for the 21st century*, London: Cabinet Office.

Surveillance Studies Network (2006) *A report on the surveillance society: For Information Commissioner by the Surveillance Studies Network*, London: Informat Commissioner's Office.

Varney, D. (2006) *Service transformation: A better service for citizens and busine a better deal for the taxpayer*, London: HM Treasury/HMSO.

Index

Page references for notes are followed by n

6, Perri 304

A

Abel-Smith, B. 234
active labour market policies 18, 19, 24, 146, 203, 204, 218-19, 227
Adam Smith Institute 14
Additional Voluntary Contributions (AVCs) 175
Adler, M. 247
adult earner model 206
Africa 114, 125
age
  and income inequality 37, 38
  and income redistribution 44, 45, 46
  minority ethnic groups 82-3
  single-person households 136
all work test 221-2
Allied Steel and Wire (ASW) 178
Anderson, R. 305
area-based initiatives 200
Ashby, P. 14
Asians 84
Aspinall, P. 87
ASPIRE (Acquiring Strategic Partners for the Inland Revenue) 307
asset-based welfare 145-6, 159
asylum seekers 77, 78-9, 81, 256
Atkinson, A. B. 36
Attendance Allowance 174, 215, 218, 223, 257
Australia 124, 238-9, 288-9
autonomy 33, 46-7, 49-50

B

Bangladeshis 80
  child poverty 82
  employment 81, 82
  family structure 82
  fertility 83
  income inequality 37, 38
  income redistribution 43, 44
  New Deals 86
  savings 82
  tax credits 86
  under-claiming 85
Barclay, Sir Peter 17
Barnes, M. 244
Barr, N. 183
Basic Income Schemes 145
Basic State Pension 5, 144, 173, 174, 176, 184, 185, 189n
benefit dependency 13, 68, 194, 202-5, 238
Benefits Agency (BA) 83, 100, 101, 201, 276, 277-8
Bennett, F. 67
Berthoud, R. 140
Beveridge, William 12, 95, 96, 134, 234, 247
Black Africans 82, 86
Black Caribbeans
  discriminatory treatment 84
  employment 81, 82
  income inequality 37, 38
  income redistribution 43, 44
  unemployment 83
  women migrants 81
Blair, Tony 160, 195, 296-7
Blunkett, David 203-4
Borrie, Sir Gordon 17
Bradshaw, J. 155
Brewer, M. 20, 243-4
Brown, Gordon 101, 106n, 155
Brown, J. 214, 217, 226
Browne, J. 243-4
Bruttel, O. 199
Budget Standards 62-3, 156
Burchardt, T. 32, 33, 214, 226

C

call centres 259, 264, 278, 279, 302-3
Canada 124, 239
Capgemini 307
care 22, 205-6, 207
  in later life 137, 139, 143
carers 56, 57
Castle, Barbara 142
categorical benefits 2, 3, 216
Central and Eastern Europe 80, 124, 125
Change Programme 278
Child Benefit (CB) 145, 152, 161, 235
  autonomy 49
  children's rights and citizenship 159
  coverage 4, 257
  data disks 296, 305
  delivery 100, 256
  expenditure 4, 153
  minority ethnic groups 82-3

Child Care Tax Credit (CCTC) 161, 162
Child Maintenance and Enforcement Commission 100
child poverty 20, 37, 38, 151, 160
changes 64-5, 142, 143, 163-4
and ethnicity 82
social security and tax credits 154-5, 160-4, 244
Child Poverty Action Group (CPAG) 62, 67, 159
Child Support (CS) 141-2, 152, 153, 157-8, 161, 257
reforms 164
user difficulties 259
Child Support Act 1991 16, 157
Child Support Agency (CSA) 100, 101, 141, 157, 256, 306-7
Child Tax Credit (CTC) 78, 152, 158, 161, 162-3, 165, 197, 240
expenditure 153
modernising design and delivery 244-6
poverty and work incentives 243-4
receipt 241-3
Child Trust Fund (CTF) 146, 153, 158-9, 161
childcare 161-2, 198, 200
Childcare Tax Credit (CCTC) 158, 239, 240, 241
children
aims of social security support 154-9
benefit and tax credit expenditure 153
challenge of social security support 165
Commission on Social Justice 20
income redistribution 44, 46
state provision 151-3, 198
user base 257
Chile 124, 125
China 124
Chinese 81, 84, 85
choice 33, 49-50, 260-1
Church of England Board for Social Responsibility 14
Cichon, M. 120
Citizen's Income 145
citizenship 159, 165
City Strategy Pathfinders 198, 200
Civil Service 207, 277, 306
claimants *see* users
Clarke, J. 101
cohabitation 134-5
Collingridge, D. 298
Commission for Racial Equality 86-7
Commission on Social Justice (CSJ) 12, 16-20
Committee of Public Accounts 307
Common Agricultural Policy (CAP) 113
compensation dimension 224, 225, 226, 227
complexity 23, 227-8, 229, 258, 265-6
compulsory privately managed pillar 173, 174, 175
compulsory publicly managed pillar 173, 174
conditionality 19, 23-4, 200-1, 265
lone parents 49-50
sickness and disability benefits 219, 223
Conservative Party
child poverty 160
Family Credit 235-6
Fowler reviews 12, 13-16
means testing 145
pensions 142
poverty 144
public sector reform 277-8
rights and responsibilities 98
social security governance 96
social security reform 16-17, 285
users 260
welfare to work 24, 141, 194-5
consumerism 256, 260, 267-8
contracting 280-8
contracturalism 101-3, 105
contributory benefits 2, 3, 97, 112, 116
Beveridge 95, 134, 144, 234
minority ethnic groups 82-3
sickness and disability 216
Council Tax Benefit (CTB) 174, 256, 257, 266-7
coverage 4-5, 257
children's benefits 153
global context 115-17
in-work benefits 235, 236
tax credits 239, 240, 241-2
creaming 285, 286
Crespo Suárez, E. 204-5
Cruz-Saco, M.A. 125
Cutler, T. 102

D

Dahrendorf Commission 17
Darling, Alastair 97
Dean, H. 50
defined benefit pension schemes 175, 176-7
defined contribution pension schemes 175, 176
delivery 255-6, 276
by local authorities 266-7
Child Tax Credit 163
choice 260-1
contracting with employment programme providers 280-3
contracturalism 101-3
ethnic diversity and racial discrimination 83-7

new departmental structures 100-1
pensions 186
personalisation 261-4
public sector reform and role of private sector 277-9
telephony 264
user difficulties 258-60
see also users
Denmark 155, 157
Department of Social Security (DSS) 94, 99, 100, 177, 236, 278
Department for Work and Pensions (DWP) 94, 99, 100-1, 105, 107n, 218
benefit simplification 23, 266
children 153
choice 261
Commissioning Strategy 284-5, 287, 288
contact centres 302-3
contracturalism 105
customer focus 267
delivery 256, 258-60, 279
and Directgov 301
DLA 219
employees' personal information 305
ICTs 306
minority ethnic groups 81, 83
older people 172-3
outsourcing 278
Payment Modernisation Programme 306
pension reform 187
personal advisers 263
printed leaflets 300-1
race equality 86
redundancies 207
social security governance 96
welfare to work 276
dependency 13, 68, 194, 202-5, 238
design features 117-18
digital divide 305-6
dignity 33, 47-9, 61, 62-6, 67-9
Dilnot, A.W. 14
Directgov 300-1
disability 33, 156
income inequality 37, 39
and income redistribution 44, 45, 46
see also New Deal for Disabled People (NDDP)
Disability and Carers Service 64, 256
disability and sickness benefits 140, 201-2, 214-17
children 152
future directions 226-30
older people 173
in other countries 224-6
passive to active welfare 217-20
tensions and challenges 220-4
Disability Living Allowance (DLA) 49, 152, 215, 216, 218, 219, 223, 257
Disabled Person's Tax Credit (DPTC) 196, 197, 200, 237
discourse 203-5
discretion 59-60, 85, 263-4
divorce 134, 135, 137, 144
pension sharing 185, 186
Dixon, J. 115, 117
Dunleavy, P. 307
Durkin, S. 286, 287

E

e-government 299-304
earnings disregard 220-1
earnings-related pensions 173, 174, 175, 176, 184, 185-6
East African Asians 81
economic inactivity 138, 139, 140, 141, 201
economic risk 137-9, 140-2
EDS 306-7
Education Maintenance Allowance (EMA) 153, 158, 161
employers 21, 100, 246, 258
employment 193-4, 201
and child poverty 162, 164, 165
Commission on Social Justice 18-19
and ethnicity 81
Lisbon process 103, 104
older people 175-6
as security 98-9, 113
and sickness and disability benefits 220-2
and tax credits 243-4
women 138
see also unemployment; welfare to work
Employment and Support Allowance (ESA) 48, 198, 202, 215, 219-20, 223, 231n, 282
Employment Related Services Association 289
Employment Service (ES) 100, 276, 277-8, 280-1
Employment Zones 196, 197, 198, 200, 261, 262
lone parents 286-7
performance-based contracts 281, 282, 284, 286, 287, 288
Equality Act 2006 33, 34
equality measurement framework 32-3
Equitable Life 178
Esping-Andersen, G. 118-19
ethnicity 33, 76
and employment 81, 206
and income inequality 37, 38
and income redistribution 43-4
and means-tested benefits 82
and poor welfare outcomes 81-2
and service delivery 83-7

European Union (EU) 114, 121
activation 203
Common Agricultural Policy 113
migration 79-80
social security expenditure 117
social security governance 103-5
Evans, M. 16
expenditure 4-5, 13, 19
on children 153, 160
global context 117, 127n
in-work benefits 235, 236
pensions and pensioners 173, 181
tax credits 243
extramarital conceptions 135, 136, 137

F

families
changes 134-6
income transfers 4
minority ethnic groups 82
size 181
user base 257
workless 163
family allowances 234
Family Credit 15, 235-6, 239, 246, 248n
Family Income Supplement 140, 235, 246
fertility 83, 135
Field, Frank 17, 97
Finn, D. 195
Fleckenstein, T. 24
flexicurity 104
Fowler reviews 12, 13-16
France 112, 157
fraud 13, 47, 246, 303-5
freedom 32
see also substantive freedom
Freud Report 102, 198, 283-4
Fultz, E. 125

G

Gaebler, T. 276
gender 33
and benefits 134
income inequality 36-7
and income redistribution 42-3
and poverty 144
and welfare regimes 118
see also men; women
Germany 80, 199
Gershon Review 299, 306
GIS (Geographic Information System) 304
Glennerster, H. 16
global social security policy 119-26
Godwin, M. 245-6
Gough, I. 119
governance 94, 105
Britain and EU 103-5
formal policy domain 95-9
operational policy domain 99-103
Greenberg, D. 199
Gregg, P. 20
Griffiths, R. 286, 287
Grover, C. 247

H

habitual residence test 80, 84-5
Hagemejer, K. 120
hard case support 78, 79
Harman, Harriet 203, 278
Haskey, J. 134
healthcare 112, 127n
Hills, J. 15-16
Hirsch, D. 244
Hirschmann, A. 267
HM Treasury *see* Treasury
HMRC (Her Majesty's Revenue & Customs) 100, 153, 256
ASPIRE 307
tax credits 112, 163, 241, 244, 259, 305
Home Affairs Committee (HAC) 83
Home Office 256
horizontal redistribution 1, 32, 42-6, 156
Hoskins, Dalmer 21
House of Commons Liaison Committee 296-7
Households Below Average Income (HBAI) 65
Housing Benefit (HB) 174, 235, 240
coverage 5, 257
delivery 256, 266-7
human capital development 199-200

I

IBM 297
immigration policy 76, 77-80
in-work benefits 234-6
see also tax credits
inactivity 138, 139, 140, 141, 201
incapacity 221-2
Incapacity Benefit (IB) 140, 141, 197, 201, 215, 218, 257
coverage 5, 57, 216
eligibility 222
expenditure 216
higher rate 223-4
medical assessments 48
Pathways to Work 282
permitted work provision 221
rights and responsibilities 222-3
see also Employment and Support Allowance
incentive payments 158-9
inclusion 229, 230

income, measuring 35, 39-40, 51n, 52n
income inequality 34
as an outcome 35-9
and earnings-related pensions 176
impact of tax-benefit system 34, 39-46
National Minimum Wage 141
pensioners 178-80, 184, 187, 188
income redistribution 1, 39-46, 156
Income Support (IS) 15, 57, 59, 144, 235, 257
Budget Standards 62
children 86, 143, 157, 161
coverage 5
discretion 60
earnings disregard 221
lone parents 195, 202
minority ethnic groups 82
proposed abolition 23
rates 163
sickness and disability 215
income testing 163, 166n
independence 49, 63, 202, 203
Indians 80
income inequality 37, 38
income redistribution 43
New Deals 86
self-employment 81
Industrial Injuries Disablement Benefit 215
inequality 1, 20
framework for analysing 32-5
of process and of autonomy 46-50
see also income inequality
information and communication technologies (ICTs) 295-7
history 297-8
New Labour 298-300
opportunities 300-4
threats 304-8
information provision 299, 300-1, 302
Inquiry into Income and Wealth 17
insurance benefits *see* contributory benefits
integration 229-30
integration dimension 224-5, 226, 227
international collaboration 120-2
International Covenant on Economic, Social and Cultural Rights 113
International Labour Organisation (ILO) 95, 96, 112, 120, 121-3
exclusion from statutory schemes 115-16
healthcare 127n
pensions 125-6
International Monetary Fund (IMF) 121, 123-4
International Social Security Association (ISSA) 21, 120
internet 298-9, 305-6
Invalidity Benefit 144, 214, 221-2
Ireland 112, 124
Irish 84

J

Jews 84
job brokers 197, 280
job outcome payments 282-3
Job Retention and Rehabilitation 197
Jobcentre Plus 100, 197, 201, 207, 256, 276, 279, 285
Freud report 283
GIS 304
job outcome payments 283
Pathways to Work 282
personal advisers 64, 262
user difficulties 259
website 301-2
Jobcentres 201, 276
Jobseeker's Allowance (JSA) 5, 57, 82, 195, 202, 216, 222, 257
joined-up working 258-9, 301
Joint Committee on Human Rights 78
Joseph Rowntree Foundation 17, 65, 143

K

Kay, S. 124
Kemp, P. 141, 224
King's Fund 143
Korea 125

L

Labour Party
child poverty 151, 160-4, 165
choice 260-1
Commission on Social Justice 12, 16-20
computing and government services 298-300
contracting regime 280-3
contracturalism 101-2
delivery 255-6, 258
immigration policy 77, 78
means testing 145
New Deals 279-80
pensions 142, 183-7
personalisation 261-4
public sector reform 278-9
rights and responsibilities 98, 265
safety net 67
social security governance 94, 97
tax credits 237, 247
welfare market 283-5
welfare to work 23-4, 56, 141, 194, 195-202, 218, 222, 227
Larsson, Allan 103
Latin America 112, 114, 124, 125

Law, I. 84, 85
Lawson, C. 245-6
Learning and Skills Council (LSC) 280-1, 284
less eligibility 154, 166n
Lewis, J. 118
Liberal Democrats 285
life expectancy 21, 34, 136-7, 172
Lilley, Peter 17
Lindsay, C. 199-200
LinkAge Plus 268
Lisbon process 103-5
Lister, R. 13, 16, 48, 155-6, 159, 204
local authorities 256, 266-7
Local Housing Allowance 261
lone parents
  activation policies 141
  autonomy 49-50
  benefit cuts 195
  Black Caribbean 84
  changes to social security 161
  child support 141-2, 157-8
  economic risks 138-9
  Employment Zones 286-7
  Family Credit 236
  Income Support 57
  poverty 144
  rise in numbers 135-6
  tax credits 242-3
  welfare to work 197, 198, 201, 202, 276
  see also New Deal for Lone Parents
low pay 138, 139, 140-1

M

McKay, S. 22, 176
male breadwinner model 134, 137, 205-6, 220
Margetts, H. 298, 307
marriage 134-5, 137
Marsh, A. 63
Maternity Grant 161
Maxwell, Robert 177-8
means-tested benefits 2, 3, 97, 112, 134
  minority ethnic groups 82, 84
  rights and responsibilities 97-8
  sickness and disability 216
means testing 19, 20, 144-5
  equality of process 47, 48
  pensions 176, 185, 188
  and tax credits 247
men
  economic risks 137, 138, 139
  income inequality 36-7
  income redistribution 42-3
  life expectancy 136-7
  marriage 135
  migration 80-1
  poverty 144
  retirement 172
  state pension age 189n
Mesa-Lago, C. 125
Middleton, S. 143, 144
migration 76, 80-3, 121, 181
  see also immigration policy
Miliband, D. 19
Millar, J. 244
Millennium Development Goals (MDGs) 114-15
Minimum Income Guarantee (MIG) 184, 303
Minimum Income for Healthy Living (MIHL) 63
Minimum Income Standards 68
Ministry of Defence 256
Minns, R. 123
minority ethnic groups *see* ethnicity
Mitton, L. 87
Mobility Allowance 223
Moore, John 96
Morris, Bill 78
multi-pillar pension arrangements 173-4
Murray, C. 13
Muslims 81, 112, 127n

N

National Assistance (NA) 58, 60, 234
National Assistance Board (NAB) 19, 58
National Association of Citizens Advice Bureaux (NACAB) 84, 85
National Asylum Support Service (NASS) 78
National Audit Office (NAO) 227, 266, 306
National Childcare Strategy 161-2, 196, 200
National Consumer Council (NCC) 14, 268
National Council for Voluntary Organisations 14
National Insurance 58-60, 97, 144
  collection of contributions 112, 256
  women 4, 16, 18
National Insurance (NI) benefits *see* contributory benefits
National Insurance Record System (NIRS) 298
National Minimum Wage (NMW) 20, 86, 138, 141, 160, 196, 200, 234, 237, 276
Netherlands 124, 199
New Deal 160, 199, 247, 276
  contracting regime 281
  discretion 85
  effectiveness 286
  minority ethnic groups 86

personalisation 262
rights and responsibilities 98
welfare market 279-80
New Deal 25+ 197
New Deal 50 Plus 196
New Deal for Disabled People (NDDP) 196, 197, 206, 222-3, 261, 276, 287
job brokers 262, 280
New Deal for Lone Parents (NDLP) 162, 165, 195, 196, 199
New Deal for Long-Term Unemployed (NDLTU) 196
New Deal for Partners of the Unemployed 196
New Deal for Skills 198
New Deal for Young People (NDYP) 196, 197, 199, 281
New Labour *see* Labour Party
New Policy Institute 65
Nigeria 125
non-profit sector 276-7, 289
Northern Rock 178
Norway 155, 157

O

occupational pensions 175, 176-7, 184
older people 172-80, 201, 257, 268
income redistribution 44, 46
see also pensioner poverty
One Parent Benefit 161, 195
ONE pilot 197, 200-1, 279
Open Method of Coordination (OMC) 103-4
Orenstein, M. 124-5
Organisation for Economic Co-operation and Development (OECD) 121, 203, 224-6, 227
Osborne, D. 276
othering 204

P

Pakistanis 80
child poverty 82
employment 81, 82
family structure 82
fertility 83
income inequality 37, 38
income redistribution 43, 44
savings 82
tax credits 86
'parking' 285, 286
passive labour market policies 24, 204, 218
Pathways to Work 197, 198, 223, 282
Patterson, T. 84
pay-as-you-go (PAYG) pension system 183
Pension Credit 57, 78, 143, 146, 174, 184, 185
coverage 5, 173, 176, 257
delivery 100
simplification 266
take-up campaign 303
Pension, Disability and Carers Service 64, 68, 256
Pension Service 64, 68, 100, 185, 186, 256, 268, 303, 306
pension sharing 185, 186
pensioner poverty 20, 37, 38, 144, 184
changes 143
and ethnicity 82
falling 65
pensions 172-80
changes 144
demand for 180-3
EU proposals 104
Fowler reviews 15
global policy 123-6
government policy 183-7
prime market 4
reform 142
remaining issues, gaps and problems 188
Pensions Commission 142, 183, 186-7, 188
Pensions Policy Institute 187
performance measures 282-3
personal accounts 185, 187, 188
personal advisors 255, 262-4, 279
personal information 296, 304-5
personal pensions 172, 173, 175, 177-8, 184-5, 186
personalisation 261-4
Pirie, Madsen 17
population ageing 180-1
poverty 65, 142-4, 234
Commission on Social Justice 20
and disability 217
and ethnicity 82
global context 114-15
and social security 1, 14-15
and tax credits 243-4
and welfare to work 194
see also child poverty; pensioner poverty
Poverty and Social Exclusion Survey 65, 156
PRIME 278
prime contractors 281-2, 284
private sector 276, 277-80, 283-5
process 33, 46-9
progressive universalism 163
public funds 78
public sector reform 277-9
Public Service Agreements (PSAs) 101, 160
Purnell, James 204, 285

Q

quasi-markets 276

R

Race Relations Amendment Act 2000 86-7
racism 76
immigration policy 77
and service delivery 83-7
welfare and human waste 76-7
refugees 81
religion 33, 34, 81
respect 33, 47-9
Restart programme 25n
rights, children 159, 165
rights and responsibilities 19, 21, 22, 97-8, 105, 194, 207
sickness and disability benefits 222-3
work and care 205-6
Roosevelt, Franklin D. 95
Ruck, M. 125

S

safety net 56-7, 218
assessment and conclusions 67-9
history 58-60
security and dignity 60-6
Social Fund 66-7
Sainsbury, D. 80
Sainsbury, R. 228
savings 22, 82, 146, 158-9, 174, 175
Schlesinger, M. 47
security 60-1
assessment and conclusions 67-9
evidence 62-3
and flexibility 104
improving 63-6
protection or support 97
work as 98-9
Seeleib-Kaiser, M. 24
Sen, Amartya 32
SERPS (State Earnings Related Pension Scheme) 15, 173, 175, 177, 184, 185
Serrano Pascual, A. 204-5
Service Delivery Agreements (SDAs) 101
service delivery *see* delivery
service users *see* users
Severe Disablement Allowance 214, 257
sexual orientation 33, 34
sickness benefits *see* disability and sickness benefits
Sinfield, A. 24
Single Payments 66
single-person households 136, 137
single working-age benefit 228-30
Skills Funding Agency 284
Slovenia 125
Smeaton, D. 176
Smith, John 12, 17
Smith, N. 143, 144
Smith, R. 152
social assistance benefits *see* means-tested benefits
Social Fund 47-8, 57, 59-60, 66-7, 257
social insurance benefits *see* contributory benefits
social investment 155-6, 159, 247
social protection 112-13
social risk management 123, 124
social security 1, 6
around the world 113-18
challenges for the 21st century 20-4
and changes in poverty risk 142-4
and child poverty 160-4
children 151-65
Commission on Social Justice 16-20
and economic risks 140-2
ethnic diversity and racial discrimination 83-7
Fowler reviews 13-16
global 119-26
governance 94-105
and immigration policy 77-80
impact on inequality 32, 33-5, 39-46
and information technology 295-311
and migration 80-3
policy goals 1-2
reform 2, 11-12, 14, 17, 144-6
safety net 56-69
for sickness and disability 214-30
and social protection 112-13
as support 95-7
types of benefits 2, 3
welfare regimes 118-19
Social Security Act 1986 15-16, 25n, 177, 235
Social Security and Child Support Appeals Tribunal 256
Social Security (Minimum Standards) Convention 120
Sol, E. 199
South Africa 125
South Asians 85
stakeholder pensions 175, 184, 186, 188
standard of living 34, 61-3
see also income inequality
Standing, G. 49
Stanley, K. 228
state pensions
age 172, 182-3, 189n
reform 184, 185, 187
trust 177
see also Basic State Pension

State Second Pension (S2P) 175, 184, 185-6
Statutory Sick Pay 215
stepfamilies 136
Stewart, J. 247
Stuber, J. 47
substantive freedom 32-3
Supplementary Benefit (SB) 13, 15, 59, 60, 235
Sure Start 83
Sure Start Maternity Grant 161
Sweden 80, 155
Swift, P. 267-8
Switzerland 124

T

Taiwan 125
take-up campaigns 303-4
tax credits 3, 20, 146, 215-16, 221, 276
  coverage and expenditure 4, 5, 153, 257
  delivery 259
  equality of process 48
  fraud 305
  history 234
  ICTs 302
  and income inequality 40, 63
  minority ethnic groups 86
  as public funds 78
  in US, Australia and Canada 238-9
  user difficulties 259
  and welfare reform 247
  welfare to work 200
  see also Child Care Tax Credit; Child Tax Credit; Working Families' Tax Credit; Working Tax Credit
taxation 2, 3, 4, 39-46
Taylor, Martin 237-8
telephony 256, 259, 264, 278, 279, 302-3
television licences 185, 186
third sector 276-7, 289
Timmins, N. 13, 17
Townsend, P. 234
Training and Enterprise Councils (TECs) 280
Transformational Government 22-3, 299-300
Treasury 101, 105, 106n, 146
  tax credits 237-8, 239-40, 241, 246
  welfare to work 97, 276
Treasury and Civil Service Select Committee 14
Tronto, J.C. 206
trust 177-8, 183

U

unemployment 138, 139, 140, 194-5, 201
  minority ethnic groups 81, 82, 83
Unemployment Benefit (UB) 144
United Arab Emirates (UAE) 115
United States Agency for International Development (USAID) 124
universal benefits 2, 3, 216
Universal Declaration of Human Rights 113, 114, 120
unpaid work 50, 69, 205-6, 207
US
  equality of process 47
  ICTs 297
  New Deal 95
  pensions 124
  social security 112
  tax credits 238
  welfare market 288-9
  work first strategies 199
users 22-3, 256-8
  autonomy 49-50
  compliance costs of tax credits 246
  or consumers 267-8
  difficulties 258-60
  equality of process 47-9
  information needs 83-4
  service transformation 260-6
  see also employers

V

van Ginneken, W. 115, 116
Veit-Wilson, J. 24
Venezuela 125
vertical redistribution 1, 32, 40-2, 46, 156
Vietnamese 81
Vizard, P. 32, 33
voluntary private pillar 173, 174, 175
voluntary sector 276-7, 289

W

wage supplementation *see* in-work benefits
Waine, B. 102
Walker, R. 67, 199
War Pension 215, 256
welfare-in-kind 152
welfare market 276-7, 283-5
  Australia and US 288-9
Welfare Reform Act 2007 198
Welfare Reform and Pensions Act 1999 186, 197
welfare regimes 118-19
welfare to work 56, 141, 193-4, 207, 218, 227, 228, 275-6
  Australia and US 288-9
  autonomy 49-50
  and care 205-6, 207
  and children 161-2
  conditionality 23

context 194-5
contracting with employment programme providers 280-3
development 195-202
discourse and desert 202-5
minority ethnic groups 86
New Deals and Jobcentre Plus 279-80
persistent tensions 205-7
risks of contracting out 285-8
welfare market 283-5
see also New Deal
whites
income inequality 37, 38
income redistribution 43, 44
Widow's Benefit 257
Williams, F. 206
Winter Fuel Payments 174, 185, 186
women
benefits 4, 16, 18, 22
care 205, 206
cohabitation 134
economic risks 137, 138-9
employment 206
extramarital conceptions 135, 136, 137
fertility 135
income inequality 36-7
income redistribution 42-3, 46
life expectancy 136-7
lone parents 135-6
migration 81
pensions 180
personal income 51-2n
poverty 144
state pension age 182-3, 189n
Wood, G. 119
work 68-9
see also employment
Work and Pensions Select Committee 67, 227, 228, 268, 306-7
work capability assessments 219, 229
Work First 194, 199-200, 207
work-focused interviews 200-1, 202, 219, 223, 262-3, 265, 279
Working Families' Tax Credit (WFTC) 86, 196, 197, 200, 237-40, 243-4
Working Neighbourhood 198, 200
Working Tax Credit (WTC) 78, 140-1, 152, 153, 158, 161, 197, 200, 240-1
disability 215, 220
modernising design and delivery 244-6
poverty and work incentives 243-4
receipt 241-3
workless families 163, 164, 165
World Bank 121, 122, 123, 203
pensions 123-5, 126, 173-4
World Health Organization (WHO) 120

Y

young people 199
see also New Deal for Young People